CONTENTS

Sixth Edition

CUSTOMER SERVICE

Emer ... *ategy*

PEARSON

Boston   Columbus   Indianapolis   New York   San Francisco   Upper Saddle River
Amsterdam   Cape Town   Dubai   London   Madrid   Milan   Munich   Paris   Montréal   Toronto
Delhi   Mexico City   São Paulo   Sydney   Hong Kong   Seoul   Singapore   Taipei   Tokyo

Editor in Chief: Stephanie Wall
Acquisitions Editor: Sarah McCabe
Editorial Project Manager: Karin Williams
Editorial Assistant: Kaylee Rotella
Marketing Manager: Erin Gardner
Production Project Manager: Romaine Denis
Art Director: Jayne Conte

Cover Designer: Suzanne Behnke
Cover Art: Fotolia
Full-Service Project Management: Mogana Sundaramurthy, Integra Software Services, Pvt. Ltd.
Printer/Binder: RR Donnelley
Cover Printer: Lehigh-Phoenix Color/Hagerstown
Text Font: Minion Pro, 10/12

Photo Credits: Chapter 1: goodluz/Fotolia; Chapter 2: Andres Rodriguez/Fotolia; Chapter 3: Fedels/Fotolia; Chapter 4: Elenathewise/Fotolia; Chapter 5: pressmaster/Fotolia; Chapter 6: Monkey Business/Fotolia; Chapter 7: mangostock/Fotolia; Chapter 8: Image Source IS2/Fotolia; Chapter 9: WavebreakmediaMicro/ Fotolia; Chapter 10: Monkey Business/Fotolia; Chapter 11: WavebreakmediaMicro/Fotolia; Chapter 12: diego cervo/Fotolia; Chapter 13: lichtmeister/Fotolia

Credits and acknowledgments borrowed from other sources and reproduced, with permission, in this textbook appear on the appropriate page within text.

Many of the designations by manufacturers and sellers to distinguish their products are claimed as trademarks. Where those designations appear in this book, and the publisher was aware of a trademark claim, the designations have been printed in initial caps or all caps.

Library of Congress Cataloging-in-Publication Data
Timm, Paul R.
  Customer service : career success through customer loyalty / Paul R. Timm.—6th edition.
    pages cm
  ISBN-13: 978-0-13-305625-9 (alk. paper)
  ISBN-10: 0-13-305625-2 (alk. paper)
  1. Customer services.   2. Consumer satisfaction.   3. Customer relations.   4. Success in
business. I. Title.
HF5415.5.T513 2014
658.8'12—dc23
                                                                                2012051589

13   16

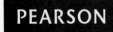

ISBN 10:   0-13-305625-2
ISBN 13: 978-0-13-305625-9

FROM THE AUTHOR

YOU MAY BE ASKING: WHAT'S IN THIS BOOK FOR ME?

Thank you for considering this book. By doing so you are making a potential investment. You may be spending some money for the book or, at least, you will be making an investment of your time to read it. You have the right to ask, "What's in it for me?" That's a fair question.

Here is a direct answer: learning to build your customer service skills will have a powerful impact on your career success as well as success in other areas of your life. Is this an overstatement? I don't really think so. Based on my 30-plus years of organizational experience in many capacities, I feel confident in saying that there is a direct relationship between service skills and career achievement.

My reasoning lies in the fact that a loyal customer is a company's most valuable asset. Without customers, no organization can long exist, and customer loyalty is built one relationship at a time with people just like you.

Sure, every organization talks about giving great service. Likewise, people in all kinds of professions acknowledge the importance of serving their customers, clients, patients, shareholders, passengers, employees, and other stakeholders. Despite these good intentions, everyday experience quickly shows that great service is not commonplace. Far too often, customers receive less-than-great value, are forced to wrestle with ineffective processes, or encounter people who make them want to do business somewhere else.

You can change those negative experiences for people you serve. You can help your organization and your career by translating your good service intentions into a workable plan. This book provides much of what you need to devise such a plan. Build your career success by applying proven principles that create customer satisfaction and loyalty. Your customers can and will become your promoters, fueling positive word of mouth and repeat business.

The true winners in today's economy do more than just talk about great service—they find ways to consistently deliver it. The payoff is enormous.

Other books on customer service often take one of two forms: Either they give an assortment of tips and techniques for boosting service quality or they describe the story of one company's successes—"how we did it at X Corporation." Such books can have value, of course, as long as the reader can effectively apply these ideas to his or her own organization. But such books seldom show a systematic way to build the specific skills needed to succeed with customers.

This book is a response to the need for a different approach to learning the skills needed to be an exceptional service provider. It is skill-based and offers practical, immediately applicable information. In *Customer Service*, I tie together the best information from bookstore trade books and school textbooks—and present it in an easy-to-remember format.

Some of what you'll learn includes ways of developing the following aspects:

- A heightened awareness of the challenges and opportunities in customer service
- The willingness and ability to gather performance-enhancing feedback
- Specific personal and communication behaviors that engage customers
- Telephone techniques for excellent service
- The ability to maximize technology and create friendly Web sites, personable email, and clear written messages that delight customers
- An enhanced level of customer trust—their confidence in your desire to be ethical and fair
- Tools for dealing with and recovering disappointed or unhappy customers
- An understanding of the powerful impact of exceeding expectations and the enhanced likelihood that they will give more back to you in repeat business, positive word of mouth, and the like
- Specific techniques for exceeding expectations in value, information, convenience, and timing, thus creating greater customer loyalty

- The ability to lead, expand, and empower the service process
- Skills for managing others in the pursuit of service excellence
- An understanding of the future directions in customer service

KEY FEATURES OF THIS BOOK

I have worked hard to make this book enjoyable and engaging with features like these:

- **The Way It Is** stories and illustrations start each chapter by showing the current state of customer service in a variety of organizations, large and small.

> **The Way It Is ... What Happened to the "Service Economy"?**
> In the rather distant past, flying commercial airlines was an adventure afforded only the economically upscale and successful people. Passengers dressed in suits and dresses (as shown in the recent television program *Pan Am*). They were served by uniformed flight attendants with white-glove service fit for a king or queen. If you have flown lately, you know that service standard no longer exists, triggering feature articles such as one in *USA Today* titled "Oh, the humiliation of flying."[1] Although airlines face unusual service experience has diminished.

> **SERVICE SNAPSHOT**
> **Steph Remembers Sparky**
>
> Stephanie Burge owns a used-car business specializing in high-quality cars with a lot of life still in them. And Steph herself has a lot of life in her! She works tirelessly to build relationships with her repeat customers. Literally hundreds of people in her city wouldn't even bother shopping elsewhere. When they (or someone they care about) need a good car, they just go over and see Steph. They know she can be trusted to give them a good deal on a good car.
>
> family. Their conversations seem to pick up where they left off last time—even if it's been months or even years.
> The "little thing" that sealed the deal for a continuing business relationship for one customer was when he stopped to look at a spiffy red sports car she had on her lot. Several years earlier he had owned a Mazda Miata which he named Sparky. They had no sooner begun talking about sports cars when Steph asked, "Are you think-

- **Service Snapshots** briefly cite innovative ideas and practices of real people giving real service.

- **Action Tips** show you, the reader, how to apply specific ideas discussed.

> **ACTION TIPS FOR TELEPHONE USE PROFESSIONALISM**
> **Action Tip 1—Check Your Phone Use Attitudes**
>
> People tend to have a love–hate relationship with the telephone. Of course, we all know that the telephone can be a powerful tool for sales, information gathering, and relationship building—by receiving and initiating calls, we can accomplish a lot. Yet some people are phone shy. They are hesitant to call others and sometimes hesitant about answering incoming calls. They perceive the phone call as an intrusion on their other activities. Perhaps this attitude is reinforced by the annoyance of dinnertime telemarketers.
>
> *Some people see the incoming call as an annoyance. That call should be seen as an opportunity.*

> **LOOK INSIDE**
> **Applying the Mrs. Williams Example to Your Company**
>
> Let's take a few moments and go back to the Mrs. Williams example, but instead use your own organization. Suppose that you lose one customer and the other statistics hold true. Take a few moments to calculate the numbers as they apply to your organization. If you work for a nonprofit or
>
> government agency where the dollar sales are not a relevant measure, calculate the number of people who may be aggravated or upset with you and your organization. Think in terms of the psychological price that must be paid as you deal with frustrated, angry, upset patrons on a day-to-day basis.

- **Look Inside** activities are a series of self-evaluations that can help you better understand your own behaviors and attitudes about service.

- **Another Look** segments feature the thinking of people with fresh ideas and, sometimes, contrasting opinion. These can stimulate your thinking about fresh and creative applications of ideas.

> **ANOTHER LOOK**
> **Why Customer Satisfaction Is Not Enough**
>
> World-class organizations unleash their potential for growth by optimizing their customer relationships. Organizations that have optimized engagement have outperformed their competitors by 26 percent in gross margin and 85 percent in sales growth. Their customers buy more, spend more, return more often, and stay longer.
> Several studies by the Gallup polling organization look at the connection between customer satisfaction and
>
> that month. Those who reported being "extremely satisfied" but did not also have a strong emotional connection to the month) and spent less ($144). In this case, extreme satisfaction represented no added value to the store.
>
> **Probes**
> 1. What does this research suggest about companies that simply measure customer satisfaction?

- **Reviewing the Facts** and **Applying the Ideas** sections at the end of each chapter recap and let you test yourself for comprehension of key points.

> **Reviewing the Facts**
>
> 1. What defines a "customer" (using this term in the broad sense)?
> 2. What are some attitudes or orientations that define a customer relationship? What factors account for a strengthening of this relationship?
> 3. In what ways are customer service skills valuable even in nonprofit organizations (or organizations that have no competitors)?
> 4. Why does word-of-mouth "advertising" work so effectively?
> 5. How do ripple effects escalate the problem of the lost customer?
> 6. What three key characteristics define real customer loyalty according to the Gallup organization?
> 7. What do we mean by an "engaged" customer, and how does this relate to customer loyalty?
> 8. What characteristics are often confused with customer loyalty but do not represent real loyalty?
> 9. What are the six core competencies? Give a brief example of each as it applies to your business or job.
>
> **Applying the Ideas: Interview Service Providers**
>
> 1. Interview five people about their customer service attitudes. Specifically, ask them to describe their internal and external customers and ask what they do to best serve.
> 3. Describe three businesses that have won your customer loyalty—places you enjoy doing business and are likely to remain a customer. Make a list of what, specifically, causes you

- **Consider This Case** presents brief application cases at the end of each chapter, followed by a few probing questions designed to stimulate your thinking.

- **Building a Customer Service Strategy: Your Ongoing Case.** This feature is new to this sixth edition. Readers are encouraged to select an ongoing hypothetical case (which they refer back to after each chapter) or to apply chapter ideas to a real-world organization. You will then consider key application questions as you develop **Strategy Planning Activities.**

Overall, I believe these features make for a more enjoyable learning experience and, more importantly, provide an in-depth picture of the many facets of exceptional customer service. I think you'll agree.

New to the Sixth Edition

This sixth edition of *Customer Service* reflects a major revision with extensive new material.

Overall, the structure of the material has been reorganized to build around an easy-to-remember acronym. The acronym is the simple word "LIFE" (so I guess we'll be talking about the meaning of life!). I have found this acronym to be a useful memory aid as I teach, train, and consult with businesses across the United States and in Europe.

LIFE stands for *little things, insight, feedback,* and *expectations*. These terms will become more meaningful to you as you read the book. The last chapter talks about tips for *living LIFE*—applying the principles and helping others (such as employees who may report to you) do so as well.

Chapter 1 presents a compelling case for the importance of providing excellent customer service in today's economy. In the chapter, I refer to Ockham's razor—the notion that often the simplest explanation for an outcome is the best one. Simply put, good service distinguishes successful companies (and people) from the less successful.

I have added material about the importance of good service to *internal customers*—employees. The best companies to work for succeed in large measure by the relationships they build with employees. Good "service" to employees leads to decreased turnover, better recruits, and higher productivity—all of which contribute to the bottom line. Additionally, employees tend to treat their customers the way they are treated by company associates and leaders.

The central challenge of many organizations is to get beyond good intentions and slogans to clear strategies for winning customer and employee loyalty. I include some updated information about changes in the diverse nature of today's customers.

The goal remains the same: attracting and keeping long-term, loyal customers.

Chapters 2 through 5 focus on some of the "little things" that can make or break an organization's service efforts. Chapter 2 describes specific behaviors and communication techniques that create customer engagement through the power of personality. Chapter 3 presents material on the critical importance of listening as we seek to create customer loyalty. The reader will gain specific tactics (action tips) for improving this key communication skill.

Chapter 4 delves into telephone techniques and offers additional specific action tips. Phone responsiveness can be an important first step toward customer loyalty. New material on using better phrasing and on the importance of call centers is added to this edition.

Chapter 5 has been extensively reworked to show how today's organizations can make the most of those increasingly important service delivery options: Web sites, Twitter, texting, blogs, social networking, and other electronic communication. Today's customer demands almost instant responses to requests. Today's "Net generation" holds expectations about service that have not been common in the past, and most of these expectations stem from better technology.

Chapters 6 and 7 address the third letter of our LIFE acronym: Insight. Two kinds of insight are of particular value: insight into the kinds of things that are likely to turn our customers off and insight into emerging trends in our ever-changing economy. Chapter 7 considers possible future changes that can have a dramatic impact on a company's success. The possible changes are widespread, although some service factors will remain the same.

The third letter of our *LIFE* acronym refers to feedback and that is the theme addressed in Chapters 8 and 9. Chapter 8 stresses the importance of being open to customer complaints and to accept such feedback as a form of coaching. Companies improve their service to the degree that they get and use customer feedback. They also build stronger loyalty through such two-way communication. Chapter 9 further explains how we can use feedback to recover potentially lost customers. Studies show that customers who complain and experience some of these simple recovery tactics discussed in this chapter are actually more likely to be loyal to a company than customers who never have a complaint! Service recovery is a critical key to success.

The fourth letter of our LIFE acronym stands for expectations. Chapters 10, 11, and 12 deal with the most powerful ways to create customer loyalty, "exceeding customer expectations." Chapter 10 shows ways we can surprise the customer with an enhanced sense of *value*. Chapter 11 explains how to use enhanced *information* to exceed expectations, and Chapter 12 talks about giving better *convenience* and attention to *timing*. These chapters explain why this works and specifically how you can do it. These updated chapters provide powerful ideas based on the author's years of experience as a consultant and that are not found anywhere else.

Chapters 13 is organized under a part heading called Living LIFE. It describes many things managers can do to hire service-oriented people (those with high "emotional intelligence," for example), effectively direct their actions, and create a culture that reinforces individual efforts to give great service.

Overall, this book reflects substantial enhancements over the already-successful earlier editions. It provides a comprehensive and up-to-date look at customer service and the skills needed in today's economy.

Instructor Resources

All instructor resources can be downloaded from the Pearson Higher Ed instructor resources website at *www.pearsonhighered.com/irc*.

VIDEOS FROM JWA CATALOG   JWA is a producer of professional commercial training films on customer service, workplace communication, and management topics in DVD format. Up to three DVD selections are available free-of-charge upon adoption of this text. Please contact your local representative for details. To see a complete listing of JWA videos, visit *www.jwavideo.com*.

Special Thanks

This book was developed with the help of many people. I want to especially thank my editors for their valuable input. Thanks also to the good people who took the time to review the manuscript as it developed and provide excellent guidance. These reviewers include Susan Moak Nealy, Baton Rouge Community College; Margaret Clark, Cincinnati State Technical and Community College; Cheryl Byrne, Washtenaw Community College; Talula Guntner, North Virginia Community College—Annandale; Deb Pein, Idaho State University—Pocatello; and Yun Chu, Robert Morris University.

Finally, I'd like to dedicate this book to my brilliant and talented wife, Dr. Sherron Bienvenu, and to my good friend (and the guy who got me into the study of customer service) Jack Wilson. I'd also like to thank my many students and seminar participants, especially those at Brigham Young University, Aalto University (formerly the Helsinki School of Economics and Executive Education) in Finland, and numerous client organizations.

I sincerely hope that you, my readers, enjoy using this book. I'd love to hear about your experiences. Feel free to contact me at *DrTimm@gmail.com*.

Paul R. Timm, Ph.D.
February 2013

ABOUT YOUR AUTHOR

I've had the privilege of writing more than 40 books on a variety of topics dealing with challenges managers and career-oriented people deal with every day. My books on customer loyalty, human relations, management communication, and self-management have been translated into dozens of languages and sell worldwide. I have also written and appear in a series of videotape training programs produced by Jack Wilson & Associates (*www.JWAvideo.com*).

My writing is based on more than 30 years' experience as a professor, trainer, consultant, and entrepreneur. I have held positions with large companies (Xerox and Bell South) and have led small organizations (such as Prime Learning, Inc.). I have consulted and trained with many companies and taught at universities in the United States, Finland, Scotland, Singapore, and Poland. In an earlier life, I served in a helicopter company in the U.S. Army in Vietnam.

For fun I run (marathons and triathlons), play golf, read, and enjoy observing the kinds of customer service people give—or, more often, fail to give.

I strongly believe that no arena offers as much opportunity for your professional advancement as does the field of customer service and loyalty. And with the skills taught in this book, you will greatly enhance your ability to build and sustain your greatest asset—your relationships with loyal, committed customers and employees—through exceptional service.

CHAPTER | 1

Know Why Service Matters

Recognizing the Role of Customer Service in Your Career Success

After reading this chapter, you should be able to

1. Explain why attracting and keeping loyal customers—people with whom we exchange value—is critical to business and personal success.

2. Describe examples of how customers are identified by various names and include both external and internal relationships.

3. Explain how customers can become partners through service intimacy and an ongoing relationship.

4. Recognize the impact of positive word of mouth in getting and keeping customers.

5. Calculate the possible impact of lost customers on a business or organization.

6. Explain six core competencies necessary for service success.

7. Understand and describe some of the challenges associated with translating slogans and good intentions into a strategy for better customer service.

8. Articulate how to get customers beyond mere satisfaction and develop ongoing customer loyalty.

The Way It Is ... What Happened to the "Service Economy"?

In the rather distant past, flying commercial airlines was an adventure afforded only the economically upscale and successful people. Passengers dressed in suits and dresses (as shown in the recent television program *Pan Am*). They were served by uniformed flight attendants with white-glove service fit for a king or queen. If you have flown lately, you know that service standard no longer exists, triggering feature articles such as one in *USA Today* titled "Oh, the humiliation of flying."[1] Although airlines face unusual and often uncontrollable challenges, no one would argue that the general level of the airline passenger's service experience has diminished.

Similarly, decades ago a gasoline fill-up at a "service station" was pumped by an attendant and accompanied by window washing and an oil check. That was before self-service, which is often associated with no service. In many stores, helpful retail sales associates have been replaced by do-it-yourself shopping (which has its advantages, but also reflects less service). Banks, once well regarded for sophisticated service, now charge fees for the opportunity to *speak* with an employee.

And then there is the service of repair people who come to your home. Picture this worst case illustration: Two characters show up on your doorstep from the appliance repair service. They have the appearance and demeanor of a pair of street thugs, but they smile and say hello. One of them looks at the worksheet and mispronounces your name.

They wipe their feet on the mat, carefully place their toolbox on your kitchen counter, pull out the refrigerator, and set to work. While disassembling the innards of your fridge, they chat between

1

themselves about an apparently lively weekend party but they seem to work competently. After half hour and some cussing, the older man explains to you that they had to put in a temporary part because the factory-recommended part has to be shipped from a distant city. But it's been ordered, he reassures you. They also say that they will return and install that when it comes in. They clean up their mess, push the fridge back, and leave, promising that the part would arrive shortly.

Weeks pass and you hear nothing from them. The ordered part apparently never arrived and your refrigerator is running okay, but you wonder about possible harm due to the substandard fix. You make several calls to the company and are reassured that the part will be in soon, but after months, you have never heard from them again and keep your fingers crossed that the temporary fix will continue to work. How do you feel about this customer service?

Ah, the "service economy."

GAINING A FOCUS ON SERVICE IMPORTANCE

Some people are wondering, Where is the service in the "service economy"?

Every person reading this book could describe customer service disappointments. We all encounter substandard service regularly, and much of that poor service can be attributed to poor attitudes and inappropriate behaviors of individuals and organizations. Companies make business decisions (change policies, close offices, reduce employee training, install excessively complex pricing systems, fail to follow up on commitments, etc.) with insufficient thought about the impact on customers. Individuals fail to recognize the impact of their behaviors (or lack of behaviors) on customers.

Satisfactory customer service isn't a differentiator; it's an expectation in any successful organization.

Despite this, every company touts its great customer service—often citing this as what differentiates it from their competition. But, when everyone claims good service as their uniqueness, it cannot, by definition, be unique. It's an expected component—a minimum requirement for being in business. Satisfactory service is a commodity, a raw material, not the key differentiator between competing companies. Only consistently *exceptional* service can distinguish one organization from others.

Substandard or inconsistent service, however, continues to damage companies. And, in today's world of high interconnectivity, poor service experiences are quickly shared in cyberspace. Social networks, emails, and blogs turbocharge the opportunities to broadcast sour service experiences. True, we can tell people about good and bad service, but it's the bad experiences that are most likely to trigger a posting online. The impact on businesses and individuals is dramatic. Companies and people that consistently give good service build successful relationships while poor service providers fumble and eventually fail. It's as simple as that.

Today's social networking spreads the word about customer service experiences faster than ever—for better or for worse.

An industry white paper by Oracle Corporation similarly concludes that "Ultimately there are only two things that can provide unique, long-term, sustainable advantage in the marketplace—a company's culture and the *relationships it fosters with its customers*."[2]

A Simpler View

But let's dial back the business terminology like "sustainable advantage" and "company culture" for a moment and look at the importance of customer from another perspective. Usually attributed to William of Ockham, a fourteenth-century English logician and Franciscan friar, proposed what has come to be known as "Ockham's razor." This logical principle asserts that, when trying to understand a situation, the simplest explanation is usually the right one. Put into the context of customer service, Ockham's razor can slice through (pun intended) the many debates about what accounts for a business's success. It's really simple: The fair exchange of value with satisfied, loyal customers makes for successful organizations.

Think about competing retailers like Kmart and Walmart, for example. Since the early 1960s, these pioneering big box stores have competed head-to-head. They are very similar in many ways—sell the same kind of stuff for about the same prices in stores with similar locations and layouts and so on. They are, in essence, the same, save for some small details. Given this, if you ask people which of these two they would choose to shop at (and these were the only two choices) the vast majority of people will say Walmart. (Your author has asked this question to thousands of people in audiences over the past 20+ years and the percentage favoring Walmart is at least 80 versus 20 for Kmart.) Is it any wonder, then, that Kmart (and merger partner Sears) sales are about $50 billion a year while Walmart sells $400 billion.

While many business analysts cite "supply chain management" (how efficiently the company gets products to the customer) and other complex measures as keys to Walmart's success, I argue the Ockham's razor logic—the simplest explanation is the best one: The shopping experience at Walmart is usually perceived as being better than at Kmart. In fairness, there are many excellent Kmart stores and also more than a few substandard Walmarts. But overall, given a choice, customers opt for the service difference provided at Walmart.

Replace Kmart and Walmart with other competing businesses you choose from. Why do you select Burger King over McDonalds, Staples over Office Max, Verizon over AT&T, Allstate over State Farm, your credit union over a bank (or the opposite of any of these)? Often we find Business-X providing virtually the same goods or services as Business Y but we develop a loyalty to one or the other. Occasionally it's because of dramatically better prices or convenience. But, in most cases our repeat business stems from our service experience.

The bottom line: satisfied, loyal customers make for successful organizations.

Rather widespread discontent with the service customers get can be viewed as a positive opportunity. The upside potential for those who give good service is unlimited. By making the process of satisfying customers a part of our daily lives, we can virtually guarantee our professional success.

It's also more fun to work for companies that give great service—to their customers and to their employees. A quick look at *Fortune* magazine's annual "The 100 Best Companies to Work For"[3] shows service leaders like Google, Wegman's Food Markets, REI, Edward Jones, The Container Store, Marriott, Nordstrom, eBay, FexEx, Zappos, and others—all companies that clearly illustrate the linkage between great service and great employee morale. Says consultant Chip Bell, "[These kinds of companies] boast the lowest turnover (a cost saver), the best recruits (an investment), the highest productivity (another positive hit to the balance sheet) and the greatest profits. Companies in the top 20 percent of the highly revered American Customer Satisfaction Index outperformed the Dow Jones industrials average by 90+ percent, the S&P 500 by 200+ percent and the NASDAQ by 350+ percent."[4]

The upside potential for those who learn to give great service is unlimited.

Great businesses or organizations succeed by building customer satisfaction and loyalty. Conversely, no person can make a good living long term without meeting the needs of his or her customers. That is what people *do* in organizations: They serve others. And they succeed through service.

What If You Don't Work with "Customers"?

Most people would agree that a business needs customers—but not everyone works in business. What about other kinds of organizations? Does a government agency need customer satisfaction to succeed? Does a civic organization, church congregation, political party, family, service club, school, or fraternity need satisfied customers to succeed? To answer these questions, we need first to define what we mean by a customer. The common perception is that a customer is someone who buys something from you. Most people assume that to buy involves the exchange of money. In many cases, that is true enough. But an expanded definition of "customer" can be useful. In its broadest sense a customer is *someone with whom we exchange value.* Taking this broader view expands our opportunities to apply customer service skills—to our advantage.

The broad definition of "customer" is anyone with whom we exchange value.

"Customer" Implies an Exchange of Value

As human beings we are constantly exchanging value with each other. We are, by nature, social beings. When we exchange money for a product or service, we are customers. When we provide work in exchange for a wage, our boss and our company are our customers. When we participate in a civic organization or church group, the people to whom we give support, advice, ideas, or information are our customers. When we give of ourselves to contribute to a strong family, our spouse, parents, kids, and others become our customers. When we build and maintain networks of friends and associates, we become each other's customers.

Exchanging such value involves give and take. We give and accept social support to and from friends and family. We give and take ideas and information to and from teachers or work teams. We give and accept buying recommendations to and from trusted associates; we give and take gifts and tokens of appreciation to and from others. In short, much of life involves **exchanges of value**. As such, many of our interactions are with "customers" as we have broadly defined that term. The ideas on improving customer service found in this book can be equally applied to all kinds of relationships, not just commercial transactions.

Principles of good customer service can be applied to all kinds of relationships.

External and Internal Customers

Different names for customers can imply different kinds of transactions.

In our commercial dealings, we have a lot of names for customers, often varying by the nature of our business or organization. Some examples of these names include clients, patients, passengers, patrons, members, associates, insureds, users, buyers, subscribers, readers, viewers, purchasers, end users, guests, or cases. These are **external customers**—people outside of our company with whom we do business.

Internal customers—employees—are an equally important target for customer service efforts.

Internal customers are typically a company's employees. Employee relationships are crucial to organizational success. If a company has high turnover of employees quitting and having to be replaced, it will face serious challenges. Replacement of employees bears a huge cost as the company needs to spend money and effort to attract, recruit, and train replacements.

Virtually everything we will discuss in this book about customer service also applies to employees, our internal customers.

By accepting this broader view of what it means to be and have customers, we will see that applying the principles of customer service results in much more than just business or financial success. Yes, customer service is a key to career success but, more importantly, it is a master key to success in all the relationships in one's life. By applying the customer service principles in this book to every aspect of your life, you can gain exceptional levels of success and life satisfaction.

CUSTOMER RELATIONSHIPS CAN BECOME PARTNERSHIPS

Relationships with customers can evolve into rich and fulfilling partnerships. Such customer partnerships arise from certain attitudes or orientations. True partnerships are anchored in an attitude of generosity and trust so that the people involved enjoy extending the relationship beyond just meeting a need or requirement. Generally partnerships require some joint purpose and are marked by truth, candor, and straight talk mixed with compassion and care. Having a genuine affection for partners is also helpful. People who like people do best at building partner-like relationships. And, as the song goes, people who like people are the happiest people in the world.

Is it possible to have a business that doesn't need to build relationships? Possibly. If you work for a traveling carnival and you sell cotton candy to people you will never see again, perhaps relationship building is not important. If you engage in any such one-time transactions, you might argue that you'll never deal with these people again so customer service isn't important. But such a viewpoint can be shortsighted for two reasons. First, very few businesses are one-time, isolated transactions. The potential for repeat business is always there. Second, even if your business is a transaction business, **word of mouth** to other customers can help or hurt you. If you are an unusually grouchy cotton candy vendor, people will tell others and those others may avoid even that one transaction with you. Or, if you are exceptional in your friendliness, positive word may get around. So, even transactions businesses have the potential for becoming relationship businesses.

The ideal goal in most businesses is to create partnerships with customers.

Not every customer relationship becomes a partnership, but such partnerships represent the highest level of customer–provider affiliation. Exhibit 1.1 represents two dimensions that define levels of customer relationships: the degree of **service intimacy** and the extent of ongoing

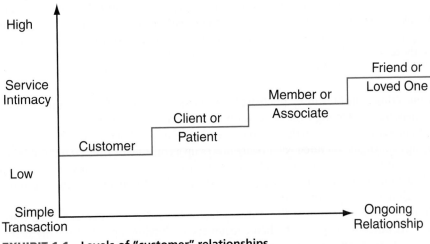

EXHIBIT 1.1 Levels of "customer" relationships.

relationship. When relationships evolve into something personally "intimate"—that is, people get to know each other and strive to meet the needs each has—and continue over a period of time, they can become rich and satisfying.

Notwithstanding the semantic distinctions about customers, it remains useful to agree that we all have customers, or people we interact with who depend on us for information, guidance, services, products, or social support—in short, value. In exchange for value we provide, they will give something back. This exchange system defines, on the most basic level, what it means to be a customer. When this exchange evolves into something more than an isolated transaction, when we move up the stair steps of relationship building through increased service intimacy over time, we will enjoy immense levels of career and personal satisfaction.

POSITIVE WORD OF MOUTH GETS AND KEEPS CUSTOMERS

New customers can be tough to get. An oft-quoted statistic says that it costs five or six times as much to get a new customer as it does to keep an existing one. So logically, it makes sense to focus on satisfying customers you already have, thus encouraging repeat business. Without customer retention, you'll spend a lot of time and effort refilling a leaky bucket as you chase an ever-replenishing supply of new customers. (This is the dilemma faced by companies that offer shoddy products or poor service. People may buy from them one time but will not come back.)

Some people think that advertising generates sales and, undoubtedly, good ads do have an impact. A closer look, however, sees the relationship of ads-to-sales as slightly more complex. The "purchasing funnel" explains what tends to happen. Television and other mass media impact our buying decisions at the broad end of the funnel by creating awareness of products and generating interest in them. The final decision to actually buy, however, occurs at the narrow part of the funnel and this is where personal recommendations of other people have the most impact.[5] A television industry publication concluded thus:

> TV was the most impactful medium as far as awareness, consideration, preference and purchase are concerned. The Internet was second in each case. The study measured responses to ads across 15 categories, including vehicles or auto dealers, financial services, restaurants, insurance, telecommunications, home improvement and health care.
>
> For most product categories, television made the biggest contribution to increased awareness of the product being advertised. But the size of its contribution varied by category.

Getting new customers and replacing those lost is an expensive part of any business.

For example, in the entertainment category, TV contributed 48 percent to awareness and 51 percent to interest and had an impact on purchase among 39 percent of those surveyed. For automotive, TV generated awareness for 44 percent of those surveyed and interest among 40 percent. Just 22 percent said TV impacted their purchase decision.

Consulting firm McKinsey published a discussion of word-of-mouth impact on sales in a recent newsletter.[6] Among their conclusions are that consumers have always valued opinions expressed directly to them. Marketers may spend millions of dollars on elaborately conceived advertising campaigns, yet often what really makes up a consumer's mind is not only simple but also free: a word-of-mouth recommendation from a trusted source. As consumers overwhelmed by product choices tune out the ever-growing barrage of traditional marketing, word of mouth cuts through the noise quickly and effectively.

Indeed, word of mouth is the primary factor behind 20–50 percent of all purchasing decisions. Its influence is greatest when consumers are buying a product for the first time or when products are relatively expensive, factors that tend to make people conduct more research, seek more opinions, and deliberate longer than they otherwise would.

The article goes on to say that the influence of word of mouth will probably grow since the digital revolution has amplified and accelerated its reach to the point where word of mouth is no longer an act of intimate, one-on-one communication. Today, it also operates on a one-to-many basis: Product reviews are posted online and opinions disseminated through social networks.

Exemplary service generates positive word-of-mouth "advertising" and repeat business. People talk to others about a service experience when it is exceptional, out of the ordinary. You can offer the best products available, but if you fail to supplement them with a positive service experience, few customers will notice the difference between you and your competition. Service success is a matter of setting yourself apart from others through unexpected excellence.

The Impact of E-Commerce on Word of Mouth

Use of electronic media in the form of Web pages, email, social networking sites, and blogs are commonplace in today's business world. Such e-commerce capabilities have turbocharged the process of spreading the word about businesses—good and bad. With electronic technology, the problem and opportunity of word of mouth takes on an even greater impact.

Spreading the word about a business is simpler than ever with forwarded emails or by copying in dozens of people in our email address book. Easier yet, posting your experiences on Facebook, MySpace, or LinkedIn (which together with similar sites have millions of users) gets the word out with unimaginable efficiency. Web sites and Web logs (blogs) are popping up all over for the sole purpose of praising or trashing businesses. In the mid-1990s film *Rainman*, Dustin Hoffman's character, an autistic man, repeatedly states that "Kmart sucks" and the phrase caught on, much to the chagrin of Kmart executives. Today, Web users have the opportunity to regularly rate the relative "suckiness" of any company, and they do. Numerous sites (see, for example, *www.WebGripeSites.com*) provide the opportunity for anyone to evaluate a business, politician, product, entertainment, and much more. The Web provides an additional megaphone for personal opinion, thus turbocharging the power (for better or for worse) of what some call "word of mouse."

Companies cannot long get away with mediocre service. In this age of technology and ubiquitous communication, there are few secrets. Customers will get the word out about your company's service. The challenge is to make that the good word.

THE DAMAGING COST OF A LOST CUSTOMER

As the old joke setup goes, I have good news and bad news. The bad news is that the typical company will lose 10–30 percent of its customers per year—mostly because of poor service. When customers have a choice, they'll go to the competition without hesitation. Customer satisfaction is like an election held every day, and the people vote with their feet. If dissatisfied, they walk (sometimes run) to another provider—a competitor. When customers don't have a choice—such as in dealing with public utilities or government agencies—they'll use their feet for something else: They'll kick back. Employees will feel the brunt of customer dissatisfaction, dealing with unhappy customers day after day. The cost to the company comes when frustrated employees get fed up with hearing customer grief and leave. The company then faces the cost and disruption of having to replace employees—their internal customers.

The good news about the relatively poor state of customer service is that organizations that initiate effective customer retention programs may see profits jump 25–100 percent. Nonprofit groups or organizations with no serious competition see reduced turnover, better financial results, and happier staffs.

Calculate the Terrible Cost of the Lost Customer

What happens when poor service causes a customer to quit being a customer? Let's look at a somewhat simplified example from a business we are all familiar with: a grocery supermarket. Let me tell you the story of Mrs. Williams:

Harriet Williams, a 60-something single woman, has been shopping at Happy Jack's Super Market for many years. The store is close to home and its products competitively priced. Last week, Mrs. Williams approached the produce manager and asked, "Sonny, can I get a half head of lettuce?" He looked at her like she was crazy and curtly said, "Sorry, lady. We just sell the whole head." She was a bit embarrassed but accepted his refusal.

Later she had several other small disappointments (she wanted a quart of skim milk and they only had half-gallons), and when she checked out with her groceries she was largely ignored by the clerk who was carrying on a conversation with a fellow employee. The clerk made matters worse by abruptly demanding "two forms of ID" with Harriet's check (What do they think I am, a common criminal?) and failing to say thank you.

Mrs. Williams left the store that day and decided that she was no longer going to do business there. Although she had shopped at Happy Jack's for many years, she realized that she had never felt that her business was appreciated. She got the overall feeling that Happy Jack's employees couldn't care less if she shopped there. She spent about 50 hard-earned dollars there every week, but to the store employees she was just another cash cow to be milked without so much as a sincere "thank you." Nobody seemed to care if she was a satisfied customer. But today is different—no more "nice" Mrs. Williams! Today she decided to buy her groceries elsewhere. Maybe—just maybe—there is a store where they'll appreciate her business.

What do the employees think about Mrs. Williams' actions? They're not worried. Life is like that. You win some; you lose some. Happy Jack's is a pretty big chain and doesn't really need Mrs. Williams. Besides, she can be a bit cranky at times and her special requests are stupid. (Who ever heard of buying a half head of lettuce!) Happy Jack's will survive just fine without her $50 a week. Too bad she's unhappy, but a big company like this can't twist itself into contortions just to save one little old lady from going down the street to the competition. Sure, we believe in treating customers well, but we're businesspeople. Let's look at the bottom line. After all, it can hardly be considered a major financial disaster to lose a customer like Mrs. Williams. Or can it?

Acknowledge the Cost of the Lost

The employees at Happy Jack's need to recognize the "**ripple effects**" of their service, not just the immediate profit from an individual purchase. Just as the ripples swell when a rock is dropped into a pond, the impact of one unhappy customer can move far beyond that one person.

The shortsighted employee sees Mrs. Williams as a small customer dealing with a big company. Let's change that view: Look at the situation from another, broader perspective.

The loss of Mrs. Williams is not, of course, just a $50 loss. It's much, much more. She was a $50-a-week buyer. That's $2,600 a year or $26,000 over a decade. Perhaps she would

Ripple effects happen when upset customers tell other people.

shop at Happy Jack's for a lifetime, but we'll use the more conservative 10-year figure for illustration.

But the ripple effects make it much worse. Studies show that *an upset customer tells on average between 10 and 20 other people about an unhappy experience.* Some people will tell many more (especially with today's communication media), but let's stay conservative and assume that Mrs. Williams told 11. The same studies say that these 11 *may tell an average of 5 others each.* This could be getting serious!

How many people are likely to hear the bad news about Happy Jack's using our very conservative example? Look at the math:

Mrs. Williams	1 person
tells 11 others	+11 people
who tell 5 each	+55 people
Total who heard =	67 people

Are all 67 of these people going to rebel against Happy Jack's? Probably not. Let's assume that of these 67 customers or potential customers, only one-quarter of them decide not to shop at Happy Jack's. Twenty-five percent of 67 (rounded) is 17.

Assume that these 17 people would also be $50-a-week shoppers, and Happy Jack's stands to lose $44,200 a year, or $442,000 in a decade, because Mrs. Williams was upset when she left the store. Somehow, giving her that half head of lettuce doesn't sound so stupid.

Although these numbers are starting to get alarming, they are still very conservative. A typical supermarket customer can easily spend $100 a week or more, so losing a different customer could quickly double these figures.

How Much Will It Cost to Replace These Customers?

Customer service research says that *it costs about five to six times as much to attract a new customer* (mostly advertising and promotion costs) *as it costs to keep an existing one* (where costs may include giving refunds, offering samples, replacing merchandise, or giving a half head of lettuce). One report put these figures at about $19 to keep a customer happy versus $118 to get a new buyer into the store.

Again, some quick math shows the real cost of the lost Mrs. Williams:

Cost of keeping Mrs. Williams happy	$19
Cost of attracting 17 new customers	$2,006

Now let's make our economic "facts of life" even more meaningful to each employee.

Understand How Lost Customers Mean Lost Jobs

Assuming that a company pays 50 percent in taxes and earns a profit of 5 percent after taxes, Exhibit 1.2 shows how much must be sold to pay each employee (in four different salary levels) and maintain current profit levels.

EXHIBIT 1.2 Sales needed to sustain a job.

Salary	Benefits	After-Tax Cost	Sales Needed
$60,000	$27,600	$43,800	$876,000
$40,000	$18,400	$29,200	$584,000
$25,000	$11,500	$18,250	$365,000
$15,000	$ 6,900	$10,950	$219,000

LOOK INSIDE

Applying the Mrs. Williams Example to Your Company

Let's take a few moments and go back to the Mrs. Williams example, but instead use your own organization. Suppose that you lose one customer and the other statistics hold true. Take a few moments to calculate the numbers as they apply to your organization. If you work for a nonprofit or government agency where the dollar sales are not a relevant measure, calculate the number of people who may be aggravated or upset with you and your organization. Think in terms of the psychological price that must be paid as you deal with frustrated, angry, upset patrons on a day-to-day basis.

These figures will vary, of course, but no businessperson would disagree that there can be a direct impact on employee jobs. If a $15,000-a-year part-time clerk irritates as few as three or four customers *in a year*, the ripple effects can quickly exceed the amount of sales needed to maintain that job. Unfortunately, many organizations have employees who irritate three or four customers *a day*! Ouch.

TRANSLATING SLOGANS AND GOOD INTENTIONS INTO A STRATEGY

Most companies accept, or at least pay lip service to, the idea that "the customer is the boss," that he or she is a "king" or "queen" (or at least a prince or princess!). They talk about the customer always being right. They say, ad nauseam, that the customer is "our reason for existing" as an organization. Yet despite these claims, how is the service given? Often, not great.

A significant challenge lies in translating such slogans into actions that convey these feelings and beliefs *to the customer*. Even when leaders truly believe in the importance of customer service, they still face the difficulty of getting employees to do what customers want—especially when a customer's request is a bit unusual. The problem gets trickier when you realize that the lowest-paid and least-trained employees are often those who face the customer every day. For example,

- A multibillion-dollar fast-food restaurant places its success squarely in the hands of the minimum-wage teenager taking the orders and delivering the food. The employee turnover in such businesses is huge, requiring constant training of new people.
- A huge financial institution's image is created in the mind of the customer by the entry-level teller who handles the customer's day-to-day transactions.
- A multibillion-dollar government agency is judged largely by the receptionist who answers the phone or greets the customer, thus setting a tone for any transaction. (Many a criticism of the "government bureaucracy" can be traced to a receptionist "getting off on the wrong foot" with a patron.)

> The face of a company is often that of the lowest paid employees who meet the customers.

When you sincerely buy into the value of a happy, loyal customer and effectively communicate that value to each customer, you virtually guarantee your success. When you supervise others, you need to "infect" them with your same positive attitudes and skills.

What If You Are "Just an Employee?"

Businesses benefit from good service, but suppose you don't own a business. As "just an employee," what can you gain from developing service skills? The short answer is that customer service skills are the same skills that bring success and satisfaction to all aspects of life. The best reason for learning the processes that create customer loyalty is that *it will make you feel better about your life and yourself*. Sure, there are solid business reasons as we've already discussed. But ultimately, the personal benefits can be even greater.

The more we commit to giving great service, the more we will get from our association with our company.

It doesn't matter whether we are the company CEO or are working in the mail room, we choose how much we want to give to the organization. Inevitably, the more effort, energy, and commitment we give, the more value we get from our association with that organization. That's a principle of life that has been proven true throughout time. The flip side—giving the least we can get away with—results in unsatisfying relationships and mind-numbing work.

CUSTOMER SERVICE CORE COMPETENCIES

Core competencies are the key skills a business encompasses to provide a service to the customer that are not easily reproduced by others. Core competencies provide a direct benefit to the customer. Creating ongoing superior customer service is an art that begins with employing the right people who have skills such as the ability to display passion, communicate effectively, and exercise flexibility. These people should also develop techniques to work efficiently, harbor a sense of ownership of their jobs, maintain current knowledge, and project enthusiasm and dedication.

Six major core competencies provide a foundation for delivering superior service:

1. **The Ability to Communicate Effectively**

   Every encounter with the customer begins with communication. The ability to send the right message while projecting an enthusiastic attitude reflects good customer service. But communication is a two-way street. The ability to listen and understand customer needs is critical.

   As technology advances, so does the way we communicate. When communicating by email, text messaging, social networks, and so on, the message should project passion on how you service and care for your customers. This is done with effective, personable wording, courteous tone, and friendliness depicting a helpful attitude. We will discuss this in depth in Chapter 5.

   Communicating over the telephone also requires specific skills that project clear understanding, assess the situation, and provide a solution. This requires knowledge, empathy, personal touch, enthusiasm, and your undivided attention in dealing with individual customers. It calls for projecting a "can do" attitude up front by comforting the customer. This will set the tone of the conversation. One warning: Do not promise something you are not able to deliver on and always state what you "can do" not what you "can't do." We'll discuss more on this in Chapter 4.

2. **Acceptance of Ownership**

   People are more engaged in their work when they own the outcome. True ownership within customer service is the relentless pursuit to drive to completion any issue a customer is currently dealing with. In many cases, the customer is simply asking that a situation be fixed. He or she does not want an employee to recite company policy or forward the call to another department. The ability to seize the opportunity to satisfy a customer request in the quickest way possible (or to shepherd the customer's needs to a timely resolution elsewhere) is a **core competency** that marks career success. Creating an environment where customer service representatives are encouraged to take a leadership role will increase the notion of ownership. Employees will respond in a positive way as increased responsibility brings increased personal pride.

3. **The Ability to Use Empowerment**

   Once employees feel a sense of ownership (responsibility) for a job, they must also be given the latitude to exercise authority. Employees at all levels need appropriate autonomy to make decisions *for the benefit of the customer.* Having to gain management approval to make even small exceptions or accommodations can make the service experience unduly cumbersome. It also inhibits employee morale. People enjoy work where they have reasonable authority to make decisions that are best for the customer. Of course, organizations must manage a fine line to ensure that employees are not "giving away the store." But true empowerment provides customer contact people with the latitude to make nimble decisions (even in contrast of company policies) in order to satisfy important customer needs.

4. **The Ability to Manage Knowledge**

   Knowledge management deals with how people in organizations learn new ways to do things and share that learning with others for the benefit of the company. Alert people constantly learn new ways to deal with various customer needs or providing solutions to unique customer issues. Managers need to ensure ways to tap into employee creativity, to give voice to new ideas. Customer service excellence is not a static condition. What "works" today may lose effectiveness as competitors adapt the same ideas, for example.

   People in the organization will shape the extent of knowledge creation and distribution as they facilitate idea sharing, mentoring, brainstorming, and applying ever-changing knowledge that supports a service strategy. In Chapters 10 through 12, we will discuss ways to participate in idea generation for exceeding customer expectations and solidifying a service strategy.

5. **The Ability to Manage Change**

   Once we get beyond the most basic behaviors (like greeting customers, and saying please or thank you, for example), the service environment is fluid and ever changing. Successful people need to be open to and adaptive of change. This can be difficult for people who may stick to the comfort and predictability of the old ways.

   Ongoing service excellence requires flexibility. For change to be successful requires the people to be involved in the process. Building a team to be flexible in a culture of change requires buy-in. To achieve buy-in requires a clear vision of the corporate strategy. The corporate strategy is dynamic and employees must be able to adapt to change to meet corporate goals. A clear vision of change must be repeatedly communicated and must not be oversimplified. We will talk more about **change management** in Chapter 14.

6. **Predisposition for Continuous Improvement**

   Nothing is forever. Even core competencies are likely to evolve or change in relative importance. A prerequisite to any rational improvement is feedback—from customers, employees, and the marketplace. If we don't know how we're doing now, how can we possible improve?

   As we will discuss in Chapter 8, customer feedback is vital for gaining a clear understanding of what your customers want and expect from you. Once the "effect" of your current efforts is identified, you want to formulate all the "causes" that will contribute to the "effect." Things that work should be expanded; things that do not contribute to success should be reduced or eliminated.

   Continuous improvement as a driving core competency is a mind-set—an openness to adapt and experiment. Such willingness is rooted in the awareness that we are not perfect and can always do things better. Every adjustment in what we do should serve one main purpose and that is to stimulate customer loyalty—to make customers want to come back for more and enthusiastically recommend you to others.

   The rest of this book will offer innumerable ideas for honing these core competencies.

THE ULTIMATE GOAL: DEVELOPING CUSTOMER LOYALTY FOR LIFE

The ultimate goal of customer service is to create customer loyalty. Understanding loyalty—what makes your customer loyal and how to measure this—enables a company or person to improve customer-driven service quality.

To best understand what customer loyalty is it is useful to first recognize what it is *not*. Customer loyalty is sometimes mistaken for:

- Customer satisfaction alone. Satisfaction is a necessary component, but a customer may be satisfied today but not necessarily loyal to you in the future.
- A response to some trial offer or special incentive. You can't buy loyalty; you must earn it.

SERVICE SNAPSHOT

Burgers Supreme

Steve and Debby K. owned an independent fast-food restaurant called Burgers Supreme. For more than six years they built up a loyal clientele, many of whom ate there almost every day. Not only did these customers buy lunch at Burgers Supreme, but they also brought friends and fellow workers. Some of the regulars were teased about owning stock in the restaurant, although none did.

The menu was broad, covering dozens of sandwiches, salads, soups, desserts, onion rings, frozen yogurt, and specialty foods reflecting Steve's heritage like gyros and baklava. Everything was prepared fresh. But the loyalty went far beyond good food and fair prices.

Almost every regular customer had the unexpected surprise of having Steve, Debby, or one of their employees say, "This meal's on me." Owners, managers, and even employees were authorized to give free lunches to loyal customers. Obviously that didn't happen every time the customer came in, but it did reflect the owners' belief in recognizing customer loyalty. It also reflected their willingness to empower their employees to give something away now and then.

The counter help at Burgers Supreme learned service behaviors from Debby's example. She was always right there beside them on the firing line. She taught by example and freely dispensed compliments and corrective suggestions. She taught (and modeled) the behaviors as her people greeted customers by name, smiled, cheerfully fixed any mistakes, and kept hustling to make sure the restaurant was clean, even during the busiest lunch hour.

Faced with tremendous competition from national chains like Wendy's, McDonald's, and others who serve similar fare, Burgers Supreme ate their lunch, so to speak, with friendly, individual, personalized service. They didn't just talk the talk of customer service. They walked the walk.

- Large share of the market. You may have a large percentage of the customers for a particular product or service for reasons other than customer loyalty to you. Perhaps your competitors are poor or your current prices are more attractive.
- Repeat buying alone. Some people buy as a result of habit, convenience, or price but would be quick to defect to an alternative.

Recognizing counterfeit loyalty is important. It can lull you into a false sense of security while your competition may be building real customer loyalty.

Customer Loyalty

So, what exactly is customer loyalty? A more reliable definition has evolved in recent years. Considerable empirical research concludes that customer loyalty is best defined as a composite of three important characteristics:

- It reflects *overall satisfaction*. Low or erratic levels of satisfaction disqualify a company from earning customer loyalty. Satisfaction is necessary but not sufficient for gaining loyalty.
- It involves a commitment on the part of the customer to make a sustained *investment in an ongoing relationship* with a company.
- It manifests in customer behaviors, including
  - *repeat buying* (or the intention to do so as needed)
  - *willingness to recommend* the company to others
  - a commitment to the company demonstrated by a *resistance to switch* to a competitor

Some customers aren't really loyal; they just haven't left—yet.

More recent research by the Gallup polling organization validates these elements and takes the concept a bit further by describing customer "**engagement**" as a critical variable. In a 2003 article, the *Gallup Management Journal* questions the intuitively obvious link between loyalty and profitability. The researchers conclude that some kinds of customer loyalty may not be profitable. Specifically, they say that "repeated purchase behavior [that] has been motivated—or bribed—by a company's gifts, discounts, or other purchase rewards" may not be profitable.

Customers may simply be exploiting the company or milking a special incentive. These customers aren't really loyal; they're just customers who haven't left—yet. Similarly, the uncommitted may *appear* to be loyal, but they only remain customers out of habit, convenience, or because it's a hassle to switch to another provider. These uncommitted customers, however, are susceptible to the incentives and discounts competitors will offer them to switch.

If you fail to make an emotional connection with customers, satisfaction is worthless. Gallup concludes that customer *engagement* with the organizations they buy from becomes a priceless resource for those organizations. Several case studies reveal that fully engaged customers—that is, customers who are both satisfied and emotionally connected to a store—visit the store more often and spend more money.

An emotional connection with customers is crucial to building loyal relationships.

One company that acts in ways that truly value customer relationships is Zappos, the Internet marketing giant. In his remarkable book, *Delivering Happiness,* Zappos CEO Tony Hsieh illustrates how the company encourages behaviors that build relationships not just closes sales. "At Zappos [call centers], we don't measure call times (our longest phone call was almost six hours long!), and we don't up sell. We just care about whether the rep goes above and beyond for the customer. We don't have scripts because we trust our employees to use their best judgment when dealing with each and every customer. We want our reps to let their true personalities shine during each phone call so that they can develop *a personal emotional connection* . . . with the customer."[7]

Customer loyalty achieved through establishing positive relationships is the highest goal of our service efforts. Again quoting Hsieh at Zappos, ". . . we're not trying to maximize each and every transaction. Instead, we're trying to build a lifelong relationship with each customer, one phone call at a time."[8]

ANOTHER LOOK

Why Customer Satisfaction Is Not Enough

World-class organizations unleash their potential for growth by optimizing their customer relationships. Organizations that have optimized engagement have outperformed their competitors by 26 percent in gross margin and 85 percent in sales growth. Their customers buy more, spend more, return more often, and stay longer.

Several studies by the Gallup polling organization look at the connection between customer satisfaction and customer loyalty. Data from a leading supermarket chain support the importance of an emotional connection on the frequency of customers' visits and the amount of money they spent during those visits. Shoppers who reported being *less than* "extremely satisfied" visited this chain about 4.3 times per month, spending an average of $166 during that month. Those who reported being "extremely satisfied" but did not also have a strong emotional connection to the chain actually went to the store less often (4.1 times per month) and spent less ($144). In this case, extreme satisfaction represented no added value to the store.

However, when Gallup looked at customers who were extremely satisfied and emotionally connected to the store (what they call "fully engaged"), a very different customer relationship emerged. These customers visited the store 5.4 times and spent $210 a month.

Apparently, not all "extremely satisfied" customers are the same. Those with strong emotional connections visited the grocery chain 32 percent more often and spent 46 percent more money than those without emotional bonds. Their conclusion is that satisfaction without engagement is basically worthless. Satisfaction with engagement (stemming from some **emotional attachment**), however, is priceless.

Probes

1. What does this research suggest about companies that simply measure customer satisfaction?
2. What are the key challenges facing organizations that want to build customer loyalty?
3. What does the latest research say about the connection between customer satisfaction and customer loyalty? Do an Internet search of this topic and find specific statistics.

Sources: Excerpted from William Jasper McEwen and Jakub Henryk Flemming, "Customer Satisfaction Doesn't Count," *Gallup Management Journal*, March 13, 2003; Customer Engagement Unleashing the Potential for Growth, February 3, 2012, *http://www.gallup.com/consulting/49/customer-engagement. aspx.*

FINAL THOUGHTS

Customer service skills provide the most significant arena for career success. Whether you work for a huge corporation or you run a lemonade stand, you live and die by what your customers think of you. Service to internal customers—employees—can be equally important as service to external customers. All the principles of customer service we will discuss in this book can be applied to employee relationships.

Core competencies for customer service are the same as those that determine professional and personal success in many realms. Mastering these competencies will serve you in countless ways.

In careers, your number-one task, regardless of your job title, organizational position, experience, or seniority, will *always* be to attract, satisfy, and preserve loyal customers. Your author welcomes the opportunity to explore these vital ideas with you.

Summary of Key Ideas

1. Business and personal success is almost always dependent upon one's ability to build healthy relationships. In a broad sense, we succeed when we attract and keep loyal customers—people with whom we exchange value.

2. Customers may be called by many names, but all are engaged in an exchange of value. External customers are those outside the company (usually purchasers); internal customers are generally employees or organization members.

3. Customers can become partners through service intimacy and creation of an ongoing relationship. This happens when we are generous and trustworthy, share a joint purpose, speak with truth and candor, mixed with compassion and care, and pursue equality with grace.

4. Positive word of mouth helps any business get and keep customers. E-commerce spreads the news to people's network with unparalleled speed.

5. The impact of lost customers can be calculated many ways, but a simple process is to compute lost sales, the cost of other lost customers who hear the bad news, and replacement costs of getting new customers.

6. While all companies *say* the customer's satisfaction is paramount, many fail to successfully translate good intentions into a workable strategy or specific behavior. This presents a significant opportunity for leaders.

7. Customer satisfaction, although necessary, is not sufficient to create loyalty.

8. Some key elements of loyalty are a customer's general satisfaction, intention to keep doing business with us, and willingness to recommend us to others.

9. Core service competencies—those unique skills that make your work distinctive—include communication effectiveness, job ownership (responsibility), **empowerment** (authority), **knowledge management**, change management, and continuous improvement.

Key Concepts

core competencies	emotional attachment	external customers	service intimacy
cost of a lost customer	empowerment	knowledge management	social capital
change management	engagement, customer	internal customers	word-of-mouth
continuous improvement	exchange of value	ripple effects	advertising

Reviewing the Facts

1. What defines a "customer" (using this term in the broad sense)?
2. What are some attitudes or orientations that define a customer relationship? What factors account for a strengthening of this relationship?
3. In what ways are customer service skills valuable even in nonprofit organizations (or organizations that have no competitors)?
4. Why does word-of-mouth "advertising" work so effectively?
5. How do ripple effects escalate the problem of the lost customer?
6. What three key characteristics define real customer loyalty according to the Gallup organization?
7. What do we mean by an "engaged" customer, and how does this relate to customer loyalty?
8. What characteristics are often confused with customer loyalty but do not represent real loyalty?
9. What are the six core competencies? Give a brief example of each as it applies to your business or job.

Applying the Ideas: Interview Service Providers

1. Interview five people about their customer service attitudes. Specifically, ask them to describe their internal and external customers and ask what they do to best serve.
2. Ask two businesspeople to estimate the typical amount customers spend with them. Then calculate the "**cost of a lost customer**" based on the scenario in this chapter. Ask each businessperson to react to this estimate. Does it seem plausible? Too high? Too low?
3. Describe three businesses that have won your customer loyalty—places you enjoy doing business and are likely to remain a customer. Make a list of what, specifically, causes you to give them your loyalty? (Note: Often it's subtle little things that win you over.)
4. What major corporations that you've heard of seem to be doing the best job of building customer loyalty? In what specific ways do they attempt to build long-term relationships with customers?

Consider this Case

Costco and the Power of High-Quality Relationships

Retailing wholesale club Costco has enjoyed substantial success at building customer loyalty. The warehouse outlets spend almost nothing on traditional advertising but have grown dramatically primarily by word of mouth. In short, enthusiastic Costco customers tell other people.

Costco is a real-life example of how great customer relationships generate economic benefits. More than 80 percent of customers report a willingness to recommend Costco to their friends and associates. The company has grown to almost 60 million members despite spending next to nothing on advertising or marketing. Total sales exceed $76 billion a year. While a typical retailer may carry anywhere from 30,000 to 150,000 SKUs (stock keeping units—essentially the number of products sold), Costco stores have about 4000—only those items where it can provide outstanding value.[9] Sales per store are almost twice those at Sam's Club, its closest competitor. Costco's success funds a generous compensation package for its employees. Employees receive a benefits package virtually unequalled in the industry. Low turnover and long tenure reduce hiring and training costs and boost productivity; they

also contribute to Costco's remarkably low inventory-shrinkage rate,[10] which is only 13 percent of the industry average. The company offers a generous return policy—there is no time limit on returns except for a limit of one year on computer technology items. Costco's earnings have grown at about 12–17 percent a year, over the past decade, even in a difficult economic environment.

Probes

1. Describe any experiences you have had with Costco. Generally are you satisfied when shopping there? Why?
2. Would you describe yourself as a promoter for Costco—someone who would willingly recommend it to friends?
3. How does Costco appear to be aware of the importance of its internal customers? (Use online search to learn more, as needed.)
4. What challenges do you think Costco will face in the future regarding its customer loyalty? How must it apply core competencies to remain successful?

Consider this Case

The Diminished Image of Airline Travel

Once upon a time, commercial flying was thought to be prestigious, adventurous, and fun. Few people would describe it that way today. In the "old days" passengers dressed in their best clothing and enjoyed the pampering of courteous, uniformed "stewardesses" (virtually all were women and most were hired for their attractiveness). All passengers enjoyed complimentary beverages and meals and other amenities such as decks of playing cards, pillows, blankets, and activity books, and crayons and toy pilot's wings for children.

Bit by bit, the industry's landscape changed and the passenger perks disappeared. With rising costs, increased competition, and extensive security requirements, air travel has become a far less pleasant experience. Flying coach is now likened to steerage in the sailing vessels of old. Discrepancies between first class and coach amenities have reinforced for many the strict notion of social class. One airline recently floated the idea of a flight class *with no* seats! Passengers would stand like subway strap hangers. One recent columnist complains that "the airlines have raised group humiliation into an art form."

Chat with anyone at an airport about service changes and you'll get an earful. Many of these changes are not the fault of the airlines, but they get the blame. Whatever happened to "the friendly skies"?

Probes

1. What changes have you seen as an airline passenger? Which of these are most annoying? Which seem to improve service?
2. What does the commercial airline industry see as its most significant challenges? (Use online search.)
3. What do airlines do right to gain customer loyalty? To what extent are these efforts effective?
4. What could airline leaders do to offset the negative impression so many people have of the industry? Site three initiatives that could be taken now that may be the most fruitful?
5. What do you see as the long-term impact of diminished service quality on the industry?

Building a Customer Service Strategy: Your Ongoing Case

To get the most from this book and your study of customer service, apply ideas from each chapter to an organization of your choice. If you are currently employed or have a clear idea of the organization you want to work in, apply the end-of-chapter exercises to that organization. If you prefer, select one of the following hypothetical organization as your application target. Use the same organization throughout your study (i.e., don't use one for this chapter, another to apply ideas from Chapter 2, etc.).

Below are brief descriptions of two hypothetical companies you may select from if you do not have a real-world application. Feel free to add details as you consider service strategies and ideas you could use if you were involved in the company.

1. INDEPENDENT AUTO SALES AND SERVICE (IAS)

Priority goals:

Expand sales and service business, especially via repeat customers and word-of-mouth recommendations.

This mid-size auto dealership sells late model used automobiles, many of which are recently off-lease cars the owner gets from large new-car dealers in a southwestern city. IAS is owned by Stephany and Lee Bergen, a husband-and-wife team. They have been in business for 15 years and have a positive reputation for honesty. Many of their sales come from referrals from past customers. Competing with other new- and used-car dealerships is always a battle. New cars are sometimes being offered with zero interest loan incentives. IAS, however, can almost always offer a much better purchase price, especially on two- or three-year-old cars with some mileage on them.

With a difficult economy and reduced sales of cars, Steph and Lee have decided to emphasize their repair services in addition to sales. They have three full-time mechanics on duty. The service manager is Ray, a man with good skills but not much of a personality. Nevertheless, repairs now account for about 15 percent of IAS revenues.

In addition, IAS has been cultivating additional business-to-business (B2B) sales efforts. They recently got a contract to provide servicing for the vehicles owned by their local city government as well as a major building contractor. This increase in service business has posed some problems due to lack of repair staff. Sometimes Ray promises more than he can deliver or misses deadlines. IAS is recruiting qualified mechanics to meet this need. They are also on the lookout for good salespeople.

2. NETWORK NUTRITION DISTRIBUTORS (NND)

Priority goals:

Build extensive network of satisfied customers and motivated distributors.

NND's customers are both people who use their products (nutritional supplements and health care items) and the distributors who sell for them. As a "network marketing" organization, NND owners Lisa and Tom Fairmont succeed when people in their "downline" (distributors from whose sale they get a small percentage) effectively sell both product and the business concept to other distributors.

One customer service challenge Lisa and Tom face is that they rarely deal face-to-face with their customers. They do recruit new distributors and demonstrate products at meetings and conferences, but most follow-up and sales comes from online, email, text messaging, and phone calls.

NND also needs to differentiate their products from similar ones sold in stores. Personalizing products for the individual needs of customers is particularly important. Their products also cost more than similar nutritionals sold in big box stores or supermarkets.

Finally, NND deals with suspicion of potential customers and distributors who worry about the idea of network marketing (some see it as a pyramid scheme where only the people at the top succeed while others lose money as distributors). Most consumers acknowledge the high quality of NND products but worry about the pricing. They seem expensive relative to some competing products available in stores.

Strategy planning questions

1. If you were an owner or leader in this business, what could you do to help *employees* understand the value of excellent customer service?
2. Who are your external customers and what are their specific needs? (Describe at least three.)
3. Who are your internal customers and what are their specific needs? (Describe at least three.)
4. What are some starting points for developing the core competencies we discussed in your selected business? Be as specific as possible.
5. How could your business apply the ideas in this chapter to build customer loyalty?

Notes

1. Gary Stoller, "Oh, the Humiliation of Flying Today," *USA Today*, January 27, 2012, pp. B1–2.
2. Oracle, "Measuring and Managing Customer Lifetime Value," White paper, August 2006, p. 2.
3. "The 100 Best Companies to Work for," *Fortune*, February 6, 2012, pp. 117–27.
4. Chip R. Bell and John R. Patterson, "When More Is Less: Why Value-added Service Won't Give You an Edge in Tough Times," *www.chipbell.com/articles* © 2009.
5. From a TV blog by Jon Lafayette "Study Shows TV's Impact on Consumer Purchasing Behavior." To conduct the survey, [polling company] Yankelovich asked consumers about television ads that had made an impression on them. Between January 29 and February 10, 2009, 3,002 consumers who had seen a TV ad in the past two months were questioned. The survey measured what action was taken after seeing the ad and whether ads for the same product or service were seen in other media. They also were asked which media most increased awareness and interest or prompted action.
6. Jacques Bughin, Jonathan Doogan, and Ole Jørgen Vetvik, "Measuring Word-of-Mouth Marketing," *McKinsey Quarterly*, April 2, 2010.
7. Tony Hsieh, *Delivering Happiness* (New York: Hachette Book Group, 2010, p. 145).
8. Ibid.
9. Berry Berman, *Competing in Tough Times* (Pearson Education, 2011, p. 72).
10. Shrinkage refers to how much merchandise is stolen or damaged. It often relates to employee morale. Unhappy workers tend to have higher shrinkage rates.

LIFE: Little Things

The first letter in our acronym is "L" for "little things." In any transaction with customers, the little details can make or break you. The attention to detail—even the most subtle detail—when we interact with customers often determines whether a customer will have a positive experience. The next four chapters focus on some of the little things people value. We begin with the behaviors that engage customers—the things we *do* when talking with and assisting people. Some of these behaviors are second nature to us. Others can be learned in order for us to project a pleasing personality. Chapter 3 considers one of the most often overlooked communication behaviors: listening. Chapter 4 will be of particular value to readers who use the telephone in their business. Finally, in Chapter 5 we will look at the little things that make for more successful electronic communication using email, Web pages, and a variety of social media options.

So, let's consider the "little things" worth considering as we strive to provide better customer service.

CHAPTER 2

Use Behaviors that Engage Your Customers

It's All about the Little Things You Do

After reading this chapter, you should be able to

1. Distinguish between behaviors (specific actions) and desirable outcomes, goals, or hoped-for results.

2. Recognize the kinds of behaviors and personality factors that please customers.

3. Apply specific action tips (behaviors) that can convey a positive personality.

4. Recognize and promote organizational behaviors that convey a customer-centered culture.

The Way It Is...the Power of Personality

"G'morning, Hon," "Hi, there!" and a chorus of other greetings ring out whenever customers enter a Waffle House. The ubiquitous southern restaurants are famous for a cheery hello, especially at breakfast time. You never feel like a stranger at Waffle House.

More than 20 years ago, Ferris Beyer opened a bank account near his office. Being new to town, he needed the checking account and the branch office was close by. A week after opening the account, he walked in to make a deposit. He stated, "I'd barely cleared the door when a teller cheerfully called across the lobby, 'Good morning, Mr. Beyer.' I was stunned. She had remembered my name after only one transaction. I remained a loyal customer of that bank for decades, based largely on the personality of the employees."

The Disney organization builds incredible loyalty by providing a "happiest-place-on-earth" atmosphere in their theme parks. People enjoy themselves in large part because the employees (whom Disney calls "cast members") seem to be enjoying themselves. Smiles and greetings are exchanged freely and convey the organization's personality.

Every organization, like every individual, has a personality. This personality is conveyed by countless "little things," mostly verbal and nonverbal communication cues. Some people are unaware of how these cues work—how subtle behaviors send "messages" to others. In this chapter we will talk about the importance of personality-projecting communication behaviors in customer service.

BEHAVIOR AND PERSONALITY FACTORS THAT PLEASE CUSTOMERS

Behavior is, of course, what people *do*. It is conveyed to others via both verbal (using words or language) and nonverbal (without words) communication. Even when no words are exchanged, personality can still communicate loud and clear. A salesperson who ignores a customer, an employee who routinely shows up late, a clerk wearing a "frowny" face, and a repair person who leaves a mess all communicate something. Likewise, the friendly greeter at a store or restaurant, the cheerful voice from a call center, or the associate who always has a smile and a cheerful comment communicates something as well.

While having a good attitude is important, that attitude only becomes apparent to others through behaviors. A behavior is visible—as a colleague once reminded me, "if it can't be videotaped, it isn't a behavior." Behaviors are the ways we communicate to others, and these are the two important rules of communication: (1) *anything can and will communicate*, and (2) *the receiver of the message determines what it "means."* Therefore, your projected personality is in the eyes of the beholder and what may come across as an attractive personality to one may be less so to another. Nevertheless, some behaviors almost always get a good response.

Good attitudes come across to customers via visible behaviors.

The remainder of this chapter looks at some kinds of **behaviors**—of individuals and organizations—that convey messages to customers. This is by no means an exhaustive list of all possible behaviors, but it does reflect ones that associate closely with customer service.

Each customer is likely to encounter two interrelated personalities: the personality of the individual who provides service and the overall personality of the organization. This organizational personality reflects the company's "culture." Culture is a composite of many factors that project the shared values of the people who work there. The culture of a company can strengthen and reinforce individual behavior and, of course, individual behaviors reinforce the culture. For example, if a company is an enjoyable, fun-loving place to work, its people will convey a sense of enjoyment to customers. If the culture is more formal (say, at a law firm or medical facility), this personality—these shared values—may be reinforced by employee behaviors that convey competence and professionalism. (Of course, lawyers and medical-office employees can also be fun-loving and personable.)

*A company's "personality" comes across through its **organizational culture**.*

The CEO of Yum! (the restaurant firm that includes Taco Bell, KFC, and Pizza Hut) talks about creating a "**recognition culture**." The company leaders "regularly and publicly give awards to employees to recognize them for their good work.... [These] awards are not ordinary things, like a plaque or fancy pen." The president recently gave out floppy chickens at KFC and cheese heads at Pizza Hut. The company also has a "recognition band" that plays when someone is being recognized.[1] Clearly recognizing employee accomplishments is a significant value for Yum!. A culture of celebrating is a way this value manifests itself.

Zappos, the Las Vegas-based e-commerce company we mentioned in Chapter 1, has a culture described as "the quirky retailer." Why? The key factor was the company's personality. It has a reputation for flat-out fun while still being rooted in core values. Zappos's CEO Tony Hsieh articulates his "ten commandments," which include "create fun and a little weirdness" and "deliver 'wow.'"[2] Fun and weirdness include parades, pajama parties, happy hours, and shaved heads. Its notion of "wowing" customers includes free returns, quick shipping, sending flowers and thank-yous, and even finding out-of-stock items for customers at competing stores. The company does its best to hire positive people who can create fun and put them where positive thinking is reinforced by the culture.

Southwest Airlines, which has a culture of informality and fun at work, projects an organizational personality very different from that of many of its competitors. This personality has been useful both in attracting customers and in enlisting employees who enjoy working in such an atmosphere. Southwest has fared far better than its competitors in difficult time for the airline industry. Indeed, research studies of the best companies to work for consistently identify "having fun" as a critically important criterion.

ANOTHER LOOK

Nonverbal Communication Differences across Cultures

Nonverbal communication is one way we convey behaviors to others. People see us doing something and extract meaning from our actions. But, the meaning of these cues is in the eye of the beholder—what we project can come across differently in different cultures. People consider nonverbal cues even more carefully when the words we use are unclear, ambiguous, or of a different language. Nonverbal behavior arises from our cultural common sense—our ideas about what is appropriate, normal, and effective in communicating. Different cultures assign different meanings to nonverbal cues such as these:

- *Gestures* (e.g., hand movements, facial expressions) and posture.
- *Silence* (e.g., how long we pause between comments and how comfortable people are with such silence).
- *Proxemics* (ways of relating to space). In conversations, North Americans tend to position themselves about arm's-length apart. The French, Italian, Arabic, and most Latin American people tend to stand closer to each other when talking. Americans become uncomfortable with such "invasion of personal space," except in situations of intimacy.
- *Personal space.* If someone is accustomed to standing or sitting very close when they are talking with another, they may see attempts to create more space as evidence of coldness, condescension, or a lack of interest. Those who are accustomed to more personal space may view attempts to get closer as pushy, disrespectful, or aggressive. Neither is correct—they are simply different.
- *Furniture or other objects.* In some cultures, it would be very rude for a guest to move a chair when visiting an office. In cultures where people hold a high regard for "power difference," large furniture barriers are commonplace. These people may be quite uncomfortable if invited to sit on a couch or around a small table.
- *Emotional expression* (e.g., speaking aloud "wow!" or "that really makes me mad"). Tolerance for the way we express emotions also vary. For example, the

acceptance of slang or even profanity can be different in different cultures.
- *Touch (e.g., hand shaking, embracing—or the lack of these).* Some cultures find it perfectly normal for men to hold hands, for example, a behavior that is considered unusual in most contexts in the United States.
- *Waiting in line (or "cues" as they are called in Europe).* British and Americans are serious about standing in lines, perhaps in accordance with their beliefs in the principle of "first come, first served." The French, on the other hand, have a practice of line jumping that irritates many British and Americans. In another example, immigrants from Armenia report that it is difficult to adjust to a system of waiting in line, when their home context permitted one member of a family to save spots for several others.
- *Physical appearance (e.g., dress, grooming).*

Some elements of nonverbal communication are consistent across cultures. For example, research has shown that the emotions such as joy, anger, fear, sadness, disgust, and surprise are displayed in similar ways by people around the world. There are, however, exceptions. In China and Japan, for example, a facial expression that would be recognized around the world as conveying happiness may actually express anger or mask sadness, both of which are unacceptable to show overtly. The implication of this: Don't assume too much about the meaning of nonverbal messages.

We also tend to differ in areas such as what emotions are appropriate for expression. For example, in the United States it may be more socially acceptable for women to show fear, but not anger, and for men to display anger, but not fear.

The nonverbal cues discussed above are, of course, just a few examples of differences across cultures. To reduce the risk of offending customers, it makes sense to become aware of such differences and work to avoid giving or taking offense at what are simply differences.

Source: Tracy Novinger, *Intercultural Communication* (Austin, TX: University of Texas Press, 2001, p. 65).

INDIVIDUAL BEHAVIOR ACTION TIPS THAT CONVEY PERSONALITY

The rest of this chapter looks at specific behaviors—often little things—that can project powerful messages to customers and that can make or break relationships. Awareness of these alone can improve service, yet some employees are essentially clueless about the impact of their behaviors. And most of us have blind spots to some things we may do that project the wrong message.

Before we consider some "Action Tips" that, taken together, project personality, it is important to understand what we mean by behavior. To change behaviors (our own or those of others) requires recognizing a clear distinction between behavior and attitudes, outcomes, objectives or good intentions. These are often confused. Let me explain.

A behavior is an action that can be observed or measured. It involves doing something explicit. In most cases, a behavior could be videotaped and replicated. Some things we think of as behaviors are not behaviors. For example, "give good service" is not, in itself, a behavior. It is an outcome or goal or desire but not a behavior. What does "good service" look like? Would we all agree on a precise definition? Not likely. We might argue that we know it when we see it, but that makes measurement and training others very difficult. It is better to work toward identifying the explicit actions or skills and then applying these.

Change management experts talk about targeting "**vital behaviors**"—those explicit actions that have the greatest impact—as being critical to effectively influencing change.[3] We may determine, for example, that a vital behavior for building customer relationships is "making customers feel welcome." Is that a behavior? Not really. It's an objective. How exactly are we likely to make them feel welcome? The vital behavior may be to "greet customers who enter our store within five seconds." That is a better description of the behaviors needed. We may even get more specific by defining what we mean by "greet" perhaps with a specific phrase like "Hi. Welcome to Shopper's World."

We will see other examples of specific behaviors throughout this book. Recognize, of course, that we cannot always boil actions down to explicit behaviors; the closer we can get, the more likely we can apply a technique and teach others to do it also.

> "Give good service" is an objective or goal—not a behavior. Behaviors are explicit actions.

ANOTHER LOOK
AT&T Retail Store Employees Focus on 5 Key Behaviors

To create "an extraordinary customer experience that's smart, friendly and fast" employees are taught to use five "Key Behaviors."

The 5 Key Behaviors

1. Welcome customers to the store with a warm, friendly, and genuine greeting.
2. Use the customer's name whenever possible.
3. Give customers your undivided attention.
4. Maintain a positive attitude with every customer.
5. Walk customers toward the door, thank them, and give a warm, friendly good-bye.

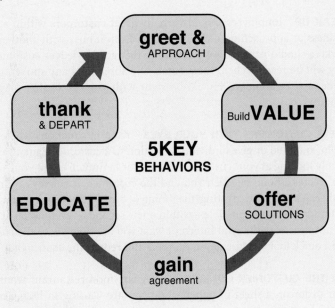

(continued)

Some of these five are specific actions (behaviors); some are more vague and somewhat ambiguous. For example, it is difficult to clearly see "maintaining positive attitude" and even, perhaps, "undivided attention." Employee training elaborates on details of how to achieve congruence with these five, but the five provide easy-to-remember guidelines for all staff and reasonable criteria for evaluating their success. Managers can also use these key behavior guidelines when giving feedback and assessing employee effectiveness.

Source: Ronen Halevy, "AT&T Store Employees 5 Key Behaviors—Good Customer Service?" June 28, 2011. Posted in *Featured News.*

ACTION TIPS FOR MAKING CONTACT WITH CUSTOMERS

The first few seconds of a contact with a customer can go a long way toward establishing a positive relationship. The following behaviors improve the likelihood of a successful interaction.

Action Tip 1—Greet Customers Like Guests

Woody Allen once said that 80 percent of success is just showing up. In customer service, 80 percent of success is treating the customer like a guest who just showed up. When guests come to your home, you greet them, right? You wouldn't ignore someone who comes into your living room. Yet we've all had the experience of being totally ignored by service people in some businesses. A friendly greeting, like that offered routinely at Waffle House, is one of those little things that means a lot. Even in more subdued businesses, a welcome is appreciated.

INITIATE CONVERSATION PROMPTLY   Studies have clocked the number of seconds people had to wait to be greeted in several types of businesses. Researchers then asked customers how long they'd been waiting. In every case, the customer's estimate of the time elapsed was much longer than the actual time. A customer waiting 30 or 40 seconds often felt like it had been three or four minutes. Time drags when you're being ignored.

Customers who are ignored for even short periods feel like it is longer.

A prompt, friendly greeting can help people feel comfortable and reduce stress customers may experience. Why would customers feel stress? Because they are on unfamiliar turf. While employees work there every day, customers are just visiting. A prompt, friendly greeting can help everyone relax and grease the wheels of comfortable interaction.

SPEAK UP   Employees should **verbally greet customers** within a few seconds of entering the business or approaching a work location. Even if busy with another customer or on the phone, workers should pause to say something that acknowledges customers and lets them know that they will be ready to help them soon. The absence of any spoken greeting creates an awkward silence for customers. "Hi. I'll be right with you" is all that may be needed to comfort the customer.

GREET CUSTOMERS WITH YOUR EYES   Even in situations where you may not be able to say "hello" out loud or give undivided attention to a customer right away, you can make eye contact. Simply looking at your customer tells him or her much about your willingness to serve. Eye contact creates a bond between you and the customer. It conveys your interest in communicating further. As with your greeting, the timing of eye contact is important. Make eye contact with your customer as soon as possible—within a few seconds—even if you are busy with another person. It's not necessary that you interrupt what you are doing with the customer at hand. Just a pause and a quick look capture new customers and reduce the chance they'll feel ignored and leave.

GET THE CUSTOMER COMMITTED   A fast-food restaurant would send a clerk out to write your order on a sheet of paper while you are waiting in line. You tell the person what you want, she marks it on a slip of paper, and then she gives it back to you to present at the cash register where the order is called out. Why did they do this? It is a way of **getting the customer committed**. If no one greeted you or wrote your order, you might be more likely to leave, especially if the line seems long, before reaching the register. But psychologically, this strategy makes you feel as if you've "ordered," so you stay in line and follow through with your lunch purchase.

Try to get a customer to do something—physically.

Years ago when personal computers were first gaining widespread popularity, and the behavior differences between the successful and unsuccessful salespeople were striking, the less successful ones rattled off a lot of techno-jargon, apparently intended to impress customers, while their successful counterparts quickly invited the novice computer user to sit down and *do something* on the computer. The principle holds for today's tech-savvy customers as well. Research observations of auto salespeople showed similar patterns. The best car sales reps didn't spend much time talking *about* the car a customer was looking at. He literally tossed them the keys and invited the prospect to test-drive the car. Use behaviors that get customers doing something.

Action Tip 2—Plant Seeds for a Relationship Building

Communicate in ways that create a comfortable platform for relationship building. The best way to start a conversation is to reassure the customer that this is a nice, friendly place to do business. Help them overcome worries about being high-pressured into buying, a major turnoff for many people. Often customers want to browse and get the feel of the place before they commit to doing business. To dispel those worries, use a nonthreatening **icebreaker**. The best icebreaker for the browser can be an off-topic, friendly comment. Some good ones might be:

- Appreciation for them coming in or contacting you (People like to be appreciated!)
- Weather-related or local-interest comments ("Isn't this sunshine just beautiful?" or "Some snowfall, isn't it?" or "How about that game last night?")
- Small talk (Look for cues about the customer's interest in sports, jobs, mutual acquaintances, past experiences, and so on. Then initiate a relevant comment.)

If a browsing customer seems to be focusing attention on a product (say he or she is holding several shirts or is looking at a particular item), the person can be reclassified as a "focused

---

ANOTHER LOOK

On the Stupidity of (Some) Car Salesmen

Fortune columnist Becky Quick unloaded on inappropriate behavior among car salesmen she experienced in her opinion piece, "It drives me crazy!"—a short screed on the stupidity of car salesmen." She relates a lesson she learned when waiting tables as a teenager: Treat every person in a dinner party equally, because you never know who's picking up the bill—and determining your tip. She then goes on to describe her experiences dealing with auto salesmen who ignored her and deferred to her husband—or, in one case to a man she didn't even know who happened to be standing beside her! She then describes other successful women who have been demeaned by thoughtless comments. She cites a situation where Anne Mulcahy, the CEO of Xerox, went shopping for a new Porsche. After test-driving the luxury car, she told the salesman she'll take the car. "After a pregnant pause, he responded, 'Don't you have to talk to someone first?' Her

reply: 'If you don't start working on the paperwork in the next ten seconds, I'll drive 30 minutes to the next Porsche dealer and buy the car there.' "

Many women have experienced inequitable treatment in auto dealerships and shops. This is despite the fact that women were the primary buyers of more than 44 percent of all vehicles last year, and they influenced almost 80 percent of all auto sales, according to CNW Research.

Behaviors that convey a lower status to some customers based on gender, race, age, and so on can quickly damage the customer relationship. Treat all customers with appropriate respect because you never know who's going to pay the bill.

Source: Becky Quick, "It Drives Me Crazy! A Short Screed on the Stupidity of Car Salesmen," *Fortune*, February 27, 2012, p. 56.

shopper." The best icebreaker for the focused shopper is one that is more specific to the buying decision. It may:

- Anticipate the customer's questions ("What size are you looking for, sir?" or "Can I help you select a...?")
- Provide additional information ("Those widgets are all 25 percent off today" or "We have those in other colors in the stockroom" or "We just got those in. They're the latest model.")
- Offer a suggestion or recommendation ("Those striped suits are really popular this season" or "If you need help with measurements, our estimators can figure out what you'll need.")

Be attentive to customers' needs. Give them time to browse if that's what they need, but be responsive in helping them make a buying decision when they are ready. Retail-industry research shows that up to 80 percent of all shopping decisions are made in the store at the point of sale—precisely the point where customers come face-to-face with the employee's and the organization's personality. Reassure customers that you can help them. Ask questions to identify their needs, concerns, or problems. Oh, and *listen* to their responses (more on this in Chapter 3).

Engage your customers at the point of sale.

ACTION TIPS FOR ESTABLISHING RAPPORT WITH CUSTOMERS

Action Tip 3—Smile

As the old adage goes, "You are not dressed for work until you put on a smile." Or, as a more cynical person might say, "Smile—it'll make people wonder what you've been up to." But more importantly, it'll tell customers that they came to the right place and are on friendly ground. Personality is rarely projected without a smile.

Keep in mind that a smile originates in two places, the mouth and the eyes. A lips-only version looks pasted on and insincere. It's like saying "cheese" when being photographed. It doesn't fool anyone. In fact, it might scare them away!

The eyes, however, are the windows to the soul and tell the truth about your feelings toward people. So smile with your eyes and your mouth. Let your face show that you're glad your guest arrived.

Now, in fairness, some people smile more readily than others, and in some business contexts smiling may be inappropriate (at a funeral home, for example). For some people a more serious facial expression is comfortable and natural. But in most cultures, a smile is generally both expected and appreciated when meeting people. If people don't smile spontaneously, they can practice it. This need not be a Cheshire cat, ear-to-ear grin (in fact, that may *really* get people wondering) but just a pleasant, natural smile.

Employees can work on their facial expression as an actor would. If you are a person who does not smile readily, work on it by looking in the mirror and practicing. This may sound a bit weird, but the advantages of smiling may call for such drastic measures.

Action Tip 4—Compliment Freely and Sincerely

It only takes a second to say something nice to a person. Such comments can add enormous goodwill and move people toward a positive experience. Employees should look for opportunities to say something complimentary to their customers and coworkers. Safe ground for sincere compliments includes:

- Some article of clothing or accessories they are wearing ("I like that sport coat!" or "Those shoes look really comfortable. I've been shopping for some like that" or "What a beautiful necklace.")
- Their family ("That's a great family picture" or "How old is your daughter? She's beautiful" or "Your son looks like quite the athlete.")

- Their behavior ("Thanks for waiting. You've been very patient" or "I noticed you checking those items. You're a careful shopper" or "Thanks for being so cheerful. Customers like you make this job much more fun.")
- Something they own ("I like your car. What year is it?" or "I noticed your championship ring. Did you play on that team?")

One important caveat: Avoid any compliments that might be construed as sexually suggestive or condescending.

Action Tip 5—Call People by Name

A person's name is his or her favorite sound. We appreciate it when people make the effort to use our name in addressing us. Just as in the earlier example about the bank teller calling a customer by name, this action can project a company's personality to its customers and build loyalty.

As an employee, introduce yourself to customers and ask their names. If this isn't appropriate (such as when there is a line of waiting customers), note customers' names from checks, credit cards, order forms, or other paperwork and use them in conversation.

People appreciate being called by their names.

Be careful not to become overly familiar too quickly, as some customers may feel it's disrespectful. We are generally safe calling people "Mr. Smith" or "Ms. Jones," but we may be seen as rude calling them "Homer" and "Marge." (This is especially true when younger employees are dealing with older customers.) It's better to err on the side of being too formal. If people prefer being addressed by their first name, they'll tell you so.

Action Tip 6—Ask Often "How Am I Doing?"

Legendary politician and former New York City mayor Ed Koch would constantly ask his constituents, "How'm I doing?" The phrase became his tag line. There is some evidence that he even listened to their answers. After all, he survived as mayor of the Big Apple for many years. We can learn something from the Koch question.

Businesses need to ask that question in as many ways as possible. In addition to using more formalized measurement and feedback systems, employees should demonstrate an ongoing attitude of receptiveness. Being receptive to people's comments and criticisms can be challenging and at times frustrating. It takes a lot of courage not only to accept criticism but to actually request it. Nevertheless, getting a constant flow of "how am I doing" information is a critical key to projecting an open personality. We'll talk much more about getting feedback in Chapter 8.

For now, simply be aware that being open to it is a little thing that can enhance your personality.

LOOK INSIDE

How Often Do You Compliment?

How frequently do you compliment people? To get a better answer, try this: Carry a note card or small notebook and simply tally each time you compliment someone. After each conversation, jot down the number of compliments you included. Do this for a reasonable amount of time—an hour, half day, or full work day.

Then, to build the habit of complimenting, try this: Set a goal to give 10 sincere compliments each day. Keep track.

See what happens. You'll probably see a sharp increase in your personal popularity! People love to be complimented. And, of course, complimenting internal customers (e.g., coworkers, employees) can also help create a supportive and pleasant work climate.

People always appreciate sincere compliments and rarely get enough of them.

SERVICE SNAPSHOT

The Watch Repair Guy

Mr. Stearn ran a very small watch repair shop. The shop was no more than 10 feet square. He was a real expert at repairing time pieces, and his prices were good. Two customers squeezed into his tiny shop. They were both bent over the work counter while Mr. Stearn adjusted the one customer's watch. The second customer stood not more than five feet away from Mr. Stearn for several minutes without ever being acknowledged. It was so uncomfortable that the second customer was just about to step out of the shop and go elsewhere when Mr. Stearn finished with the first customer and finally acknowledged the person waiting.

Mr. Stearn ran a real risk of losing a valuable customer before he got a chance to show what he could do—simply because he made no eye contact and did not take the time to welcome a customer.

Probes

1. What should Mr. Stearn have done when the second customer came into his shop? If you were the first customer would you be upset if he shifted his attention briefly to the second customer?
2. How does this illustrate the principle that little things can mean everything?

Action Tip 7—Say "Please," "Thank You," and "You're Welcome"

At the risk of sounding like a self-help book about things learned in kindergarten, "please," "thank you," and "you're welcome" are powerful words for building customer rapport and creating customer loyalty. Stick with these terms and avoid saying something like "there you go" when concluding a transaction. There is really no good substitute for these traditional terms.

When a customer thanks you, respond with "You're welcome" or, as the Ritz Carlton hotel employees say, "It was my pleasure." Again, stick with these or similar phrases. Do not use the currently popular favorite, "no problem." "No problem" seems to imply that you expected the customers to be potential problems, but dealing with them wasn't as bad as expected. That's not the message you want to convey. Stick with the basics: you're welcome or something equally polite.

Basic courtesy is never out of style.

ACTION TIPS TO COMMUNICATE REASSURANCE TO CUSTOMERS

Action Tip 8—Reassure Customers in Their Decision to Do Business with You

Marketers talk about the problem of **buyer's remorse**—the feeling that a purchase was a mistake. This feeling can set in pretty quickly, especially when people make a large purchase. At the time of sale, service providers can inoculate against buyer's remorse by reassuring customers that they've made a good purchasing decision.

Phrases like "I'm sure you'll get many hours of enjoyment out of this" or "Your family will love it" can help reassure and strengthen the buyer's resolve to follow through with the purchase and, as importantly, feel good about it. A government agency employee might say, "I'll bet you're glad that's over with for another year" or "I'll handle the renewal—you've done all that is necessary." Such reassurance can project your personality in positive ways.

Action Tip 9—Reach Out and Touch Them

Physical touch is a powerful form of communication that can impact customer perceptions of personality. Successful employees often take an opportunity to shake hands with a customer or even pat him or her on the back, if appropriate.

A study of bank tellers shows the power of touch. Tellers were taught to place money or receipts in the hand of the customer rather than on the counter. Researchers found that customer perceptions of the bank rose sharply among customers who had been touched in this way. In a similar study, restaurant servers who touched their customers when serving the food or while handing the customers something found that their tips increased dramatically.

Similarly, studies found that restaurant servers who touch customers received higher tips. Handing a person something or even lightly touching a shoulder while placing a dish before the customer seems to be a little behavior that strengthens the customer experience.

Among internal customers and coworkers, a literal pat on the back can build instant rapport. But don't overdo it; some people resent people who seem too touchy-feely. Recognize different preferences; try touching behavior but be willing to adjust if the person seems uncomfortable or ill at ease. And, of course, the key word here is "appropriateness." Never touch a person in a manner that could be interpreted as being overly intimate or having sexual overtones.

Appropriate touching behavior can help build positive relationships.

Action Tip 10—Discipline Your Self-talk to Enjoy People and Their Diversity

J. D. Salinger said, "I am a kind of paranoid in reverse. I suspect people of plotting to make me happy." If everyone had an attitude like that, as employees we'd look forward to every meeting with every customer. Of course, we quickly learn that some customers do not seem to be plotting to make us happy. Most are very pleasant. Some are unusual. A few are downright difficult.

Although "enjoy" may not look like a specific behavior, it underlies much of what we do. When we come to recognize that every person is different and that each has a unique personality, we can also discover a rich opportunity for personal growth: dealing with the ones who are *not like us*. If we were all alike, it would be a rather uninteresting world. Accept the wide range of diversity among customers and coworkers and learn to enjoy it. Know that people's needs are basically the same at some level and that treating all people as guests will create the most goodwill. We can create goodwill with **verbal discipline**.

To be more accepting of others, focus your comments to others as well as your "self-talk"— those internal conversations in your mind—on the positive, and avoid being judgmental. Instead of saying, "Can you believe that ugly dress on that lady?" avoid comment at all or say in a nonjudgmental way, "She dresses interestingly." Instead of saying, "This guy will nickel-and-dime me to death," say, "This customer is very cost-conscious." Phrase potentially negative comments in neutral tones—even when talking to yourself.

Pay attention to verbal discipline; resist negative comments whenever possible.

At times you'll have to force yourself to avoid the negative and judgmental comments. Accept the challenge and make a game out of it. Sincerely try for one full day to avoid saying anything negative or judgmental about another person. If you make it through the day, shoot for another day. Verbal discipline can become a habit that pays off. You'll find yourself enjoying people more.

We have all read, seen, or experienced heartbreaking examples of people who look and act differently being mistreated. A recent story about a returning military veteran who was disfigured from a war injury made me stop and think about cutting people some slack. This particular story spoke of people who became impatient with the veteran whose ability to complete his transaction was slowed by his injuries. Give diverse people the benefit of the doubt.

People come in all sizes, shapes, ages, and with a wide variety of appearances and behaviors. This variety can make work fun—so long as we back off on judging and treat them like our guests.

People who are different from us are just that: different. Not better or worse. Avoid the tendency to judge; accept the diversity for the richness it brings to our lives.

ACTION TIPS FOR PROJECTING PROFESSIONALISM

Action Tip 11—Pay Attention to Your Dress, Grooming, and Workplace Attractiveness

Experts on decision making talk about the "diagnosis bias"—our propensity to label people, ideas, or things based on our initial opinions of them. In other words, customers make rather quick judgments (diagnoses) about service providers they encounter. From the moment we meet people, we

---

ANOTHER LOOK

Credit Unions Offer Clothing Loans—for Business Wardrobe

Workplace dress codes are a frequent topic for discussion on management blogs and websites. *Credit Union Management* magazine reported some interesting tactics being used to help employees look professional. "To make it easier for employees to dress appropriately, some credit unions offer low or no interest loans for staff to purchase work clothes." Other organizations provide branded clothing with company logos for employees to wear to work. These clothes are not uniforms, per se, but allow the employee flexibility in selecting from a variety of appropriate shirts, blouses, sweaters, and so forth. Although not a new idea, this approach creates look of professionalism and also helps customers distinguish employees from other customers in a business.

Source: Theresa Williams, "Clothing Loans," *Credit Union Management,* January 2012, p. 10.

---

immediately begin to size them up and draw conclusions about them. What we decide about their character, trustworthiness, and ability is largely a factor of first impressions. And, as the old saying goes, you only get one chance to make that first impression. The way they dress is a first clue.

The key word in dress and grooming is "appropriate." Salespeople in a surf shop would look foolish in three-piece suits; an undertaker would look ludicrous in a tank top and shorts. Some organizations issue uniforms to standardize the look of their people. These may be coveralls, full uniforms, or partial uniforms such as blazers, vests, name badges, or logo work shirts. Some employees like these (as they save on the costs of a wardrobe), while some resist the sameness of the uniformed look.

Appropriate dress and grooming conveys important messages to customers.

Determine what level of professionalism you want to convey to your customers; then create a look that projects your competence and your company's personality. Pay attention to the little things that reinforce (or detract from) the look you are trying for. Your customers notice these things.

ORGANIZATIONAL ACTION TIPS THAT CONVEY A CUSTOMER-CENTERED CULTURE

In addition to the individual behaviors previously described, a customer also assesses the personality of the entire organization by looking at group behaviors. The communication rule that anything can and will communicate still applies to these behaviors, of course. The composite result of group and individual behaviors conveys much about the organization's culture. If the customer likes a company's culture, that company is well on the way to building satisfaction and a loyalty relationship. The following are some action tips organizations should consider.

SERVICE SNAPSHOT

Looking Good at the Auto Repair Shop

"Man, some of these guys look scruffy," said Roger, the owner of Furrin Auto Repair Services. He was drinking his morning coffee and looking at his crew of mechanics, each getting to work on repair projects for customers. "I wonder what my customers think of these characters?"

Then Roger struck on an idea. He decided to try an experiment. Since each of his repair people was paid on commission for the amount of repair work done (and often, customers requested a particular mechanic to work on their car), he wondered if customers ask for guys who dressed a little better.

That evening he called the crew together and invited the mechanics to volunteer to change their dress and grooming. He would not require changes, but if they wanted to participate in the experiment, they could do so. Several agreed to cut their hair shorter, shave daily, remove some piercings, and wear clean uniforms, which Roger provided.

The outcome: Those who cleaned up their act to look more like their customers created far more repeat business than the others. People would ask for the better dressed mechanics, while those who chose to dress and groom themselves in the "old way" found themselves getting less work.

Action Tip 12—Consider Your Company's Appearance and Grooming

What does your customer see when he or she comes to your business? Are the facilities attractive and well maintained? Is merchandise displayed in an appealing manner? Are employee desks tidy? Is the customer or employee lounge area clean and tidy? Does the work space look like an organized, efficient place? Are the restrooms clean and well maintained?

A cluttered work area conveys a sense of disorganization and low professionalism. Look around you, and see what your customer sees. If the view is unappealing, take time and spend some money to make the place look good. Be aware that you don't have to be located in five-star offices or the most exclusive retail mall to have an attractive appearance. A friend of mine is Finland named Pauli runs a small custom medical products shop located in a basement. Customers who visit don't expect the Taj Mahal but they are pleasantly surprised by the attention to detail Pauli has put forth to make them comfortable. He provides a well-lit seating area, displays interesting posters, and provides humorous reading materials for adults and toys for children. Rocket science? Of course not, but simply attention to some little things that make customers comfortable—and project the caring personality of this small organization.

The appearance of the store, shop, or office conveys nonverbal messages to customers.

As you consider your organizational appearance, check, too, for barriers. Often people arrange their work space with a desk, counter, or table between them and the customer. While

LOOK INSIDE

How Do You Measure Up?

Below is a list of many of the individual behaviors discussed thus far in this chapter. Using the following scale, evaluate how well you do with each behavior:

N = never; O = occasionally; S = sometimes; M = most of the time; A = always.

Be completely honest. There is nothing wrong with admitting shortcomings. Indeed, it is far more damaging to deny them. After rating yourself on the scale, go back through the list and circle the plus (+) or minus (−) to indicate how you *feel* about your response. If you are comfortable with your answer, circle the plus. If you wish you could honestly answer otherwise.

For each item where you circled a minus sign, write a goal for improvement on a separate sheet of paper. Make this specific and measurable, if possible.

Behaviors	Scale	Goal
1. I promptly greet all customers.	N O S M A + −	
2. I get customers committed to doing something.	N O S M A + −	
3. I compliment people freely and often.	N O S M A + −	
4. I call customers by their name.	N O S M A + −	
5. I make and maintain eye contact with customers.	N O S M A + −	
6. I often ask for feedback to find out how I'm doing.	N O S M A + −	
7. I resist prejudging customers based on their appearance.	N O S M A + −	
8. I always say "please," "thank you," and "you're welcome."	N O S M A + −	
9. I reassure customers in their decisions to do business with me.	N O S M A + −	
10. I smile freely and often.	N O S M A + −	
11. I dress with appropriate professionalism.	N O S M A + −	
12. I appropriately touch customers when possible.	N O S M A + −	
13. I use verbal discipline to avoid negative judgments, thus helping me enjoy people and their diversity.	N O S M A + −	

The Lexus Dealer

When customers bring their automobiles into Lexus of Lindon (and most other Lexus dealerships) for repair, they are invited to wait in a comfortable, well-lighted area near the showroom. In addition to soft couches or chairs, soft music, and interesting reading material, morning guests are also invited to help themselves to donuts, pastries, coffee, and other beverages—all complimentary. The environment and the food make the normally unpleasant task of waiting for auto service not only bearable but actually enjoyable.

---

sometimes this is necessary, it can create a barrier—both physical and psychological—between the customer and the one serving. Companies may establish a better personality by doing the following:

- Invite customers to sit beside a desk with the employee instead of across from him or her.
- Offer a comfortable living room-type atmosphere as a place to meet customers or as a waiting area. (An auto body shop had a waiting room that looked like a living room in a nice home, complete with easy chairs, a TV, a coffee table with recent magazines, and even fresh flowers. That surprised a lot of first-time customers!)
- Do as some auto dealerships have done: Remove all sales office desks and replace them with small round tables. Now the customer and salesperson sit around the table and work together to make a deal. When the table is round, they don't feel as if they are on opposite sides, engaged in "combat" with each other.

Finally, look for customer comfort. Are your customers invited to sit in a comfortable chair? Does your office or store encourage them to relax? Are waiting areas furnished with reading materials, music, or perhaps a TV? Are vending machines or complimentary snacks available? Is the area kept neat? Are restrooms checked regularly and kept clean?

Recently, auto dealers have begun to emphasize ways to make their car lots and showrooms, many of which are decades old, more attractive, and customer friendly. Some now feature landscaped settings with benches and pathways, different display areas for each auto brand, and interactive systems with screens that show how elements like paint colors and upholstery coordinate together. Take a look at your work areas from the customer's viewpoint.

Action Tip 13—Get Customers to Interact with Your Organization

Make it easy for customers to sample the company culture—the organizational personality. We talked earlier about getting customers to promptly order their food, try a new computer, or test-drive a car. Some high-end stores such as Brookstone (which advertises "unique gifts & smart solutions") encourage customers to "test-drive" the latest games, massage chairs, or electronic gadget. Other, perhaps less obvious ways to involve customers with little things may include:

- Personally handing them a shopping cart or basket
- Asking them to begin filling out paperwork
- Inviting them to touch, taste, or sample the product
- Offering coffee, a piece of candy, or fruit while they wait
- Offering a product flyer, information packet, video presentation, or sample to review

If the organizational culture encourages such activities, the customer is increasingly likely to have a positive impression of the company's personality. It doesn't matter so much *what* they do, so long as they begin to do *something*.

Action Tip 14—Correspond Regularly—the Old-Fashioned Way

An athletic shoe store and a rental car agency represent two good examples of the simple idea of correspondence. A week after purchasing some running shoes, customers receive a handwritten note from the store owner simply thanking them for buying. In no fancy prose, it expresses appreciation for the business and invites them to return via a one- or two-sentence message. Similarly, a small city airport car-rental desk has employees write thank-you notes to customers when the desk is not busy. The notes are handwritten on the company letterhead and personalized to mention the type of car rented. They thank the customer and invite them to rent again the next time they are in town. The cost of doing this is practically nil, since the desk is busy when flights come in but then has slow periods in between. Why let employees sit around and waste time when it's slow? Instead, they write these notes and build customer loyalty.

Written messages are becoming increasingly rare in our e-world. Most of us prefer generating an email or instant message. It's efficient and easy. That said, an "old-fashioned" written note may have even more impact because it takes additional effort and is so rare.

An even simpler example of the power of a brief written message is when the employee serving the customer writes "Thank you, Sharon" or "Please come again" followed by their signature. A little thing like this begins to create a bond.

A print shop sends all customers a monthly package of coupons, flyers, and samples, including a motivational quote printed on parchment paper suitable for framing. Additional copies of the quote are available free for the asking. The mailing acts as a reminder of the quality of the work the shop can do as well as a promotion.

Don't let your customer forget you. Another way to make customers remember your company is to send them information about upcoming sales, changes in policies, new promotions, and the like. Keep the customer tied in. Help him or her feel like part of the company, like an insider.

Obviously correspondence can be done electronically so long as you gather customer email addresses. I don't mean to minimize this—it's a great tool. Send customers discount coupons or announcements of special hours for preferred customers via such media. But for special, personal, and important messages, consider the potential advantages of "snail mail."

> "Old-fashioned" written messages still convey a sense of caring.

Action Tip 15—Use Hoopla and Fun

People enjoy working in an organization that has fun. We mentioned Zappos earlier as an example of a company that has grown very rapidly and is seen as a great place to work. Successful companies have regular rituals, whether they are Friday afternoon popcorn, birthday parties,

---

SERVICE SNAPSHOT

Touching the Stuff at the Gap

Some retailers arrange merchandise so that customers can easily pick it up. In fact, they are encouraged to do so even though this may call for more work from employees as they continuously refold and redisplay product. Marketing expert Paco Underhill describes this:

> A trademark of the Gap clothing stores, for example, is that customers can easily touch, stroke, unfold, and otherwise examine at close range anything on the selling floor. A lot of sweaters and shirts are sold thanks to the decision to foster intimate contact between shoppers and goods. That merchandising policy dictates the display scheme (wide, flat tabletops, which are easier to shop than racks or shelves). That display scheme in turn determines how and where employees will spend their time; all that customer touching means that sweaters and shirts constantly need to be refolded and straightened. That translates into the need for lots of clerks roaming the floor rather than standing behind the counter ringing up sales. Which is a big expense, but for Gap and others, it's a sound investment—a cost of doing business.

Source: Paco Underhill, "What Shoppers Want," *Inc.*, July 1999, p. 76.

employee-of-the-month celebrations, or other more creative celebrations. Excellent organizations are fun places to work; they create rituals of their own.

As a manager at a telephone company, Jim initiated frequent sales contests, complete with skits and prizes. Each time a particular product was sold, the service representative could pop a balloon and find inside a prize ranging from a $20 bill to a coupon good for a piece of pie in the company cafeteria. Employees loved it and got involved. The rewards at such events need not be large or costly. The fact that employees are being recognized, even with little things, can be very motivating for them.

Other ideas to promote fun in the workplace include:

- Employee (or hero) of the week/month recognition
- Awards luncheons (include some tongue-in-cheek "awards")
- Win a day off with pay
- Casual dress days
- Halloween costume day
- Family picnics, after-work sports, dinner together

Don't dismiss these tactics as being hokey. Employees at all levels enjoy celebrations and hoopla—and the good cheer can spread to its customers. Of course, be sure the hoopla is not distracting to customers or seen as unprofessional. One company I recently worked with found a need to dial back the Nerf gun combat in the office because clients thought it was a bit too childish. Consider the nature of your customers. How might they view your professionalism?

Have fun and celebrate at work, but maintain an appropriate level of professionalism.

Action Tip 16—Reward the Right Actions

Sometimes organizational reward systems incentivize one behavior while hoping for something else. In other words, the organization *hopes* people will do something—take right actions—but actually rewards an opposite behavior. For example, a company rewards individuals and departments for "never receiving complaints." The hope is that receiving no complaints means the company is doing a good job. In reality, however, you may well be that no complaints are heard because the complaints are simply being suppressed or ignored. Actually complaints are valuable indicators of ways we can do better. The complaining customer can be like a coach, showing us how to improve. Rewarding "no complaints" may be counterproductive.

Here are some other examples of possible reward conflicts where the wrong behaviors may be rewarded and the right behaviors ignored:

- Rewarding employees for fast transaction-handling when the customer may be left uninformed or may resent being rushed. For instance, the restaurant that encourages employees to get the customers fed and out the door may make people who prefer more leisurely dining unhappy. Or, the buyer of electronic equipment who is rushed may leave the store not understanding how to work the features of his or her purchase.
- Encouraging salespeople to cooperate with each other to best meet the customer needs while paying a straight commission to just one salesperson. For instance, salespeople practically trip over each other to approach the new customer before the other guy gets him. So much for cooperation.
- Encouraging employees to send thank-you notes to customers but never allowing on-the-job time to do so. This creates the impression that it really isn't that important.
- Constantly stressing the need to reduce the amount of return merchandise by punishing clerks who accept too many returns. The result: Customers encounter employees' reluctance to take back unsatisfactory products.
- Paying people by the hour instead of by the task accomplished. Hourly wages are simpler to administer, but they basically pay people for using up time!

The organization's reward system needs to be tilted to the advantage of the employee who provides excellent service. Any rewards should be given in direct relationship to the employee's contribution to customer service that is consistent with the company's mission and service theme.

Action Tip 17—Stay Close after the Sale or Transaction

Customers hate a love-'em-and-leave-'em relationship, yet many companies offer just that. Once the sale is made, the customer goes back to feeling like a stranger. The relationship with the customer doesn't go beyond the current transaction. There is little or no incentive for the customer to come back or remain loyal.

Organizational resources should be used to track and contact the customer after the sale. Follow-up systems should support actions such as these:

- Mail thank-you notes.
- Call to be sure the product/service met their needs.
- Send out new-product information or advance notice of upcoming sales.
- Send clippings of interest or newsworthy information that may be interesting to the customer. These clippings need not be directly related to your company.
- Send birthday and holiday cards.
- Invite people to participate in focus groups or marketing research about topics of interest to them.
- Call, write, or email to thank customers for referrals.
- Send employees messages that recognize their work and express appreciation. Build a "recognition culture."

A FINAL THOUGHT

The behaviors of individual employees convey impressions to customers via little things. Often employees are unaware of how they are coming across and, as such, are at a distinct disadvantage. They run a significant risk of annoying or at least failing to impress customers. Broadening our awareness of how other people read our verbal and nonverbal messages is a useful step in improving customer service.

Likewise, just as individuals project their behaviors to customers, so do organizations. The company's collective behavior patterns constitute its culture and may be perceived as favorable or unfavorable by customers and employees. The ways managers and leaders interact with subordinates and associates will have considerable impact on the way all employees behave toward customers. Like it or not, organizational leaders model the kinds of behaviors the company accepts or desires.

Behaviors such as those discussed in this chapter are often unconscious and subtle. As such, they constitute examples of the "little things" principle. Raising our awareness of these little things can go a long way toward building or damaging customer relationships.

Summary of Key Ideas

- Behavior is what people do. It is marked by explicit actions people take, not by attitudes, outcomes, or goals (although those can affect behaviors). Many behaviors are conveyed via verbal or nonverbal communication.
- Individual actions as well as organizational behaviors convey messages to customers which may be positive or counterproductive to the customers' perception of service received.
- Any behaviors (or sometimes the lack of behaviors) can communicate; the receiver of the message (e.g., the customer) determines what the message means. Perception is reality.

- Projecting positive personality depends on both individual actions and the patterns of behavior exhibited in the organization. This reflects the organizational culture.
- Individual behaviors that can improve your customer service skills include applying action tips for (1) making contact with customer, (2) establishing rapport, (3) reassuring customers, and (4) projecting professionalism.
- Organizational behavior patterns that tell the customer about your culture include applying action tips for appearance and grooming of employees, appearance of work areas, frequency and quality of correspondence with customers, getting customers to do something relevant to the buying decision, the use of hoopla and fun to celebrate company successes, reward systems that motivate appropriate employee behaviors, and staying close to the customer after the sale.

Key Concepts

buyer's remorse
getting the customer committed

icebreaker
organizational culture
recognition culture

rewarding right actions
verbal discipline (in self-talk)

verbally greet customers
vital behaviors

Reviewing the Facts

1. What constitutes behavior, and how is it conveyed? How can you distinguish a behavior from an attitude, outcome, hoped-for condition?
2. What are some ways an organization's culture can impact customer loyalty?
3. What are some specific behaviors that project individual personality? How do these reflect the importance of "little things"?
4. How can physical touch be used to project positive personality?
5. What are some factors (patterns of behavior) that project a company's culture? List several examples from the organizations you work in.
6. What are some examples of reward systems that encourage the wrong kinds of behaviors? How can leaders adjust these to reward more positive behaviors?

Applying the Ideas: How Do Behaviors Influence Customer Loyalty?

1. This chapter implies a strong relationship between behaviors (of individuals and organizations) and the likelihood of customer loyalty. Let's test that idea. The following are two simple data-gathering forms. The first lists the behaviors discussed in the chapter and invites customers to rate these. The second form asks three simple questions about customer loyalty. We call this the Customer Loyalty Index (CLI).

    Select five to ten customers of a given business at random. These may be people who frequent a nearby restaurant, customers of a popular store, or even students in the same school.

    Write the name of the company or organization in the blanks on the questionnaire. Make a copy of the following questionnaire for each respondent and administer it to your selected customers. Then score the results as described at the end of the questionnaire.

Write a one-page summary of what you found. To what degree did your samples agree with each other? How do their answers on the first questionnaire relate to the answers on the CLI?

INTERVIEW GUIDE

Part I Behavior Questionnaire

When you last did business with [_____], did the employees there

	Yes	No	Unsure or Does Not Apply
1. Greet you promptly?			
2. Use opening comments to help you feel at ease?			
3. Compliment you in any way?			
4. Call you by name?			
5. Make and maintain eye contact with you?			
6. Ask for feedback from you in any way?			
7. Say "please" and "thank you"?			
8. Reassure your decisions to do business with them?			
9. Smile freely and often?			
10. Appropriately touch you (with a handshake, pat on the back, etc.)?			
11. Present a clean and attractive workplace?			
12. Dress and groom themselves appropriately?			
13. Seem to enjoy working for this company?			

Part II Customer Loyalty Index (CLI)

1. Overall how satisfied were you with [_____]?
   Extremely dissatisfied/Dissatisfied/Neutral/Satisfied/
   Extremely satisfied
2. How likely would you be to recommend [_____]
   to a friend or associate?
   Very unlikely/Not likely/Maybe/Very likely/Certain
3. How likely are you to do business with [_____]
   again?
   Very unlikely/Not likely/Maybe/Very likely/Certain

Scoring

- For Part I of the interview, score 1 point for each "yes" response. The total possible is 14.
- For the CLI, score each item on a 5-point scale from left to right (e.g., the most negative response is 1, the most positive is 5, and those in between are 2, 3, or 4).
- After you have tallied scores for your entire sample of customers (5 to 10), write a brief analysis of the results. Comment especially on the behaviors that most seem to relate to customer service, as your customers see them.

Applying the Ideas: Hooray for Waffle House

The following was posted on a Waffle House blog by a happy internal customer—an employee:[4]

> Hi welcome to the waffle house! There is your official greeting my name is amber i work at waffle house i have for 2 yrs now I'm a grill op. and i love my job. I don't know many people who can be as proud of their job or love there job as much as i do. my whole family works at waffle house. I have 6 brothers and sisters I am the oldest the youngest is 7. my mom is the unit mgr.
>
> I'm a grill op my 16 yr old sister is a grill op my 22 yr old sister is a salesperson, my 16 yr old brother is a

> waffle boy. he drops waffles hash browns etc. my 20 yr old brother is a grill op and my 12 and 7 yr old sisters can't get enough of the place. they come up after school to sweep mop and help do odd and end things. my son 4 yr old son and 3 yr old nephew come to waffle house to eat or help rack eggs all the time. they love it. the owners of our waffle house are so nice and friendly. we talk on! the phone every day. the customers all know us and love the fact that our whole family is there. well at least one on every shift. (it's an invasion! lol.)
>
> As i said before i love my job now i don't know if that's all my waffle house songs brainwashing me or if i really

do lol. just joking. it's the only place a family can eat, talk, listen to music and enjoy the ambiance at the same time, and the show isn't that bad either. so thanks for hearing me out. Oh and the omelet trick is to season your pan w/ nonstick coating and let it set on the grill for a few minutes to get it nice and greasy then drain the grease and go on about your omelet flip. it's all in the wrist. a nicely seasoned pan doesn't hurt either.

Have a great day and come back and see us soon!! (a waffle goodbye) amber grill op since 2001

1. Employees have a dramatic impact on the organization's personality. What does Amber's blog posting say about her loyalty to Waffle House? How does her personality shine through?
2. What elements of personality discussed in this chapter are evident in this blog entry?
3. As a manager of a similar organization, what could you do to encourage the display of such enthusiasm from your staff?

Consider this Case

How Difficult Is It to Treat Someone Well?

Marcia and Lamar had just moved into a larger home and wanted to furnish the family room tastefully but without spending a lot of money. Saturday was the day for their furniture shopping, so off they went.

Their first stop was a deep-discount Furniture Barn.* The place was appropriately named—it looked like a barn—and its merchandise was piled high in irregular heaps. Some was wrapped in plastic from the manufacturer while others were uncovered. Some collected dust. The Barn had a pretty good variety of goods, but the "display" left a lot to be desired. The goods had no posted prices, although the company had a reputation for good deals.

Upon entering the Barn, a middle-aged fellow with a beard, sandals, cut-off shorts, and a sleeveless tee shirt called a greeting to Marcia and Lamar from across the cavernous room where he was stacking merchandise. "Lemme know if ya need help," he yelled from across the room. But that was the last they saw of him. They wandered around the Barn for about 10 minutes before making a hasty retreat, apparently unmissed.

Their next stop was Whooley Furniture* a few miles away. Here the merchandise was displayed attractively and prices were clearly posted on each piece. Anne, a 40-something woman, greeted them and introduced herself when they came into the store. They shook hands and Lamar introduced himself and his wife as they chatted briefly about what they were looking for. Anne invited them to look around, directed them to the family room furniture section, and said that she would be happy to answer any questions. She mentioned that they had a sale on LazyChair brand recliners and showed them where they were. The saleswoman was dressed in slacks, a yellow blouse, and wore a tactful necklace. She was quite attractive, although not a raving beauty. She smiled pleasantly and gave them some space as they strolled through the store.

Marcia and Lamar were on a pretty tight budget and the merchandise at the Barn would have probably been cheaper, but about an hour later they had spent about $2,000 with Anne at Whooley Furniture. Asked by friends why they shopped there, Lamar summed it up: We felt like they wanted our business, and Anne became a friend.

Probes

1. If you owned the Furniture Barn, what lesson would you learn from this case? What actions would you take? Identify several "little things" they could do to better serve the customer without changing their basic "stack-it-deep-and-sell-it-cheap" business approach.
2. In your opinion, how important is the personality of salespeople in a furniture business? Would Anne's approach be advantageous in all kinds of businesses? Why or why not?

*These are fictional organizations.

Consider this Case
Hospitality in the Big City

When people think of "down home" hospitality, big city hotels don't generally come to mind. But this past weekend in New York City, Midwesterners Dennis and Sylvia were downright shocked at just how friendly those big city folks can be.

They arrived in New York on a rainy Friday afternoon. The taxi from the airport took almost two hours, but the driver knew the shortcuts through Queens and gave them a running commentary on the various neighborhoods and explained why he chose to avoid the traffic-choked freeways. He also reassured them that the flat rate fare applied and that he was as anxious as they were to get them to the hotel.

Despite the friendly cabby, their patience was wearing thin as they checked into the Manhattan hotel. But travel exhaustion soon turned to laughter as the desk clerks greeted them warmly and joked about the "liquid sunshine." The check-in process was quick and painless and they were given a choice of several room options. The bellman, a smiling giant of a fellow, welcomed them to the Big Apple and took their bags and got them settled into their room, all the while chatting pleasantly and telling them about the features of the hotel and nearby restaurants.

An hour later, when Dennis and Sylvia decided to go out to dinner, they realized they had forgotten umbrellas and the rain showed no signs of letting up. Overhearing this, the desk clerk offered his own personal umbrella with a smile. All he asked was that they bring it back before he got off duty at midnight "or else I'll have to charge you interest," he joked.

Probes

1. How does this case illustrate the importance of little things and personality?
2. How important is it to defuse unpleasantness even when the problems are not caused by you?
3. Describe any similar experiences you may have had where people surprised you with unexpected pleasantness. How did it feel?

Building a Customer Service Strategy: Your Ongoing Case

Let's go back to the ongoing case you selected. This will be either your current employer, a specific organization you want to work in, or one of the two hypothetical organizations described in Chapter 1: Independent Auto Sales and Service (IAS) or Network Nutrition Distributors (NND). Now consider the following questions as you develop a customer service strategy.

Strategy Planning Questions

1. If you were leading the organization's customer service efforts, what are five key behaviors you would want your employees to apply? Be specific, recognizing that you may not be able to do all things at first. Target the behaviors that would have the strongest impact. (Be sure you are clear about the distinction between behaviors and attitudes/goals, and so on. You want to apply explicit, observable actions whenever possible.)

Key behaviors:

- 1.
- 2.
- 3.
- 4.
- 5.

2. What actions could you take to get others in the organization to do these specific things? Note: consider your answer from two perspectives: What you could do as a manager/boss, and what you could do if you are not the boss but hope to encourage others to do these things.
3. What specific behaviors have you experienced in your roles as a customer in various businesses that seemed especially effective, memorable? Which of these could you apply to your organization?

Notes

1. David Novak, *Taking People with You: The Only Way to Make Big Things Happen* (New York: Portfolio/Penguin, 2012, p. 149).
2. Jeffrey M. O'Brien, "Zappos Knows How to Kick It," *Fortune*, February 2, 2009, pp. 55–6.
3. See, for example, Kerry Patterson et.al., *Influencer* (New York: McGraw-Hill, 2008).
4. This was posted on a pro-Waffle House blog by a truly enthusiastic "internal customer"—an employee!

CHAPTER 3

Listen to Your Customer (a Big "Little Thing")

Better Service Means Getting Your Ears On

After reading this chapter, you should be able to

1. Describe the important distinction between hearing and listening.

2. Explain internal, environmental, and interactional factors that complicate the listening process.

3. Assess your own listening skills and set goals for improvement.

4. Avoid five particularly detrimental behaviors that inhibit effective listening.

5. Employ four simple, positive approaches to enhance your active listening skills.

The Way It Is... How Can You Help Me? Try Listening!

SALESPERSON: "Hi, I'm Jerry. Welcome to Cell Phone Kingdom. How can I help you today Mr....?" [Jerry smiles and shakes hands with the customer but pulls his cell phone off his belt to glance at it at the same time.]

CUSTOMER: "Nice to meet you, Jerry. I'm George Patterson. I just want a very basic cell phone with no fancy bells and whistles, okay? It's for my 75-year-old mother and she isn't interested in a built-in taking pictures or text messaging or fancy ring tones or music. All she wants is a phone that's easy to use and reliable. Oh, and it would be good if the keys were larger and the screen easy to read. Do you have anything like that?"

SALESPERSON: "Sure, we can get her into a nice phone like this model, Jeff. It has some pretty cool features like a built-in MP3 player and a lot of cool custom options. In fact, we have a nice deal on music downloads—unlimited songs for just a flat monthly fee. It's incredible. I can set it all up for her and make it just what she needs. We'll have her texting and sending IMs in no time—people love that once they get the hang of it. I see kids texting all the time. Everybody likes to do that."

CUSTOMER: "You're not listening to me. I want to get her something simple. The woman is 75 years old and not technologically savvy. She wants something simple."

SALESPERSON: "Not a problem, Mr. Peterson. This is real simple. Look you just turn on the feature you want from this drop-down menu on the touch screen and..."

CUSTOMER: "It's Patterson and I don't want any of those 'features.' I just want a plain vanilla phone that..."

SALESPERSON: "I'll check to see what colors it comes in but I don't think we have vanilla. We can get her a nice tan-colored one—that should be close. And it'll have access to our video

> download option. Another nice thing we have going this week is a special deal where we'll load your choice of three games for free—it's included in our free setup. Does she play Angry Birds or FreeCell? I love those games—I can play for hours. One weekend I spent about 20 hours straight. It was awesome. Oh wait, I'm getting a text. Will you excuse me for a minute? I need to answer this and then I'll check our stock for a vanilla-colored phone. You'll want a Bluetooth with that won't you, Mr. Pearson?"
>
> CUSTOMER "No 'Larry.' I do NOT want a blue tooth or any other tooth from you.
> (WALKING OUT All I want is a plain, ordinary, simple, easy-to-use cell phone with
> THE DOOR): big numbers!"

DOESN'T ANYBODY EVER LISTEN?

It looks like Jerry (or was it Larry?) had a problem listening to his customer. George Patterson had some fairly clear requirements for his mother's cell phone but Jerry never quite got it. Was Patterson unclear? Did he seem to use words from a foreign language Jerry didn't speak? It doesn't appear so. Jerry just wasn't listening very well. You might think listening is easy. After all, doesn't everybody do it? Well, yes and no. The fact is that many people are confused about listening effectiveness and how best to do it. For example, listening is sometimes confused with hearing.

Many people are unaware of how to listen most effectively.

Think about a commercial for a product you have no interest in—it's easy to tune out that information, isn't it? You may hear the ad, but you're not really listening. Listening involves mentally absorbing the message. Without listening, the commercial is just noise. As service providers it may be easy to *hear* what the customer says, but great customer service requires great *listening* skills—an ability to absorb and digest what the customer says.

It may strike you as unusual that we would dedicate a whole chapter in a customer service book to listening. Hopefully, by the time you finish reading this, you will appreciate the critical importance of this skill.

ANOTHER LOOK
Four Listening Activities

American communication researchers Lyman K. Steil, Kittie W. Watson, and Larry L. Barker created a model to help better understand the process of listening. They call this the **SIER hierarchy of active listening.** Their approach has held up over the years in helping us understand the relationship between different types of listening. Let's consider how this might apply to the customer service situation described in our opening story.

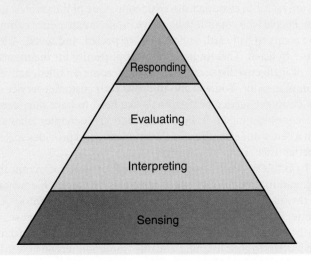

(continued)

The SIER model is a hierarchical, four-step sequence of listening activities:

1. *Sensing.* Active listening begins by hearing and receiving the verbal and nonverbal aspects of the message. The verbal, of course, refers to the actual words; the nonverbal includes such things as tone of voice, accents or speech mannerisms, and, if face-to-face conversation, all the visual cues such as appearance and gestures. Concentration is required in this phase. The message sender should not be interrupted so the message can be delivered in full and adequate detail. The receiver's body language should be positive to help the sender deliver the message.
   (Jerry acted as if he sensed exactly what Mr. Patterson wanted in a cell phone for his mother—but did he really? He greeted the customer but also glanced at his phone, indicating something less than undivided attention. He failed to let Patterson fully describe his needs before jumping to conclusions.)

2. *Interpreting.* The message receiver must interpret and place the message in meaningful context. The customer's experiences, knowledge, and attitudes should be linked to the verbal and nonverbal elements of the message. Interpreting helps insure that the receiver's understanding corresponds to the sender's meaning.
   (Jerry seemed to fail to interpret Mr. Patterson's needs. He apparently could not grasp the possibility that some customers may not want music, games, and videos on her phone—after all, Jerry enjoys these features.

His context was a poor match with the needs of the customer.)

3. *Evaluating.* For active listening to occur the listener must sort fact from opinion. The receiver needs to judge the message based on its strengths and weaknesses and how well the listener likes or dislikes what the customer says. The evaluation phase consists of both logical and emotional components.
   (Jerry seems to evaluate the customer's wants as being somewhat irrelevant. Jerry dislikes simple phones without all the features and can't really imagine how a customer would want such a thing. Patterson's needs don't seem logical to Jerry.)

4. *Responding.* Active listening requires the receiver to respond to the sender. The response provides feedback to the sender on how well the message was understood and encourages further clarification if needed between the two parties. Rephrasing and reflecting the sender's message shows interest and increases understanding.
   (Jerry doesn't respond effectively. He calls George Patterson "Jeff" at one point and misses his last name twice. It soon becomes evident to the customer that Jerry has not listened. He never rephrased the sender's message—it went in one ear and out the other. If he heard the customer's message at all, he discounted it. Either way, he lost the customer due to poor listening.)

Source: Based on descriptions of Larry L. Barker, Lyman K. Steil, and Kittie W. Watson, *Effective Listening: Key to Your Success* (Addison-Wesley, 1983).

This chapter focuses on the nature of listening and the skills individual service providers need to do a better job. In Chapter 8 we will study the processes companies use to get feedback from customers—in other words, *organizational listening.*

POOR LISTENING = THE #1 COMMUNICATION PROBLEM

Applying principles of active listening will make you a better communicator.

The lack of effective listening may be the most common human communication problem—and a significant factor in customer dissatisfaction. One of the greatest gifts we can give others is our attention. People who commit to be active listeners experience communication like never before. Everyone wants to be heard, understood, respected, and loved. A lot of us like to talk and very few choose to listen. Therein lies a huge opportunity for distinguishing yourself from the vast majority of ineffective listeners. When you become a skilled, active listener, you will become a better communicator. You will also improve your customer service skills.

As customer service professionals, we need to have our "ears on" regularly. We need to apply effective listening in dealing with others. This chapter takes an in-depth look at listening, gives you a better understanding of the problems, and provides specific action tips you can apply to be a better listener.

Active listening is much more than just sitting back and letting the talker talk.

Why is this so tough? Ironically, of the four basic communication skills—reading, writing, speaking, and listening—only one is not formally taught. Elementary schools focus heavily on the first three and assume that students are picking up listening. After all, isn't listening really just a matter of sitting back and letting the talker have his or her say?

In the following pages we will explain why listening is so much more important, define some common barriers to good listening, and offer some pointers on how to become a more skillful, active listener. Highly developed listening skills are crucial to success in any relationship—including our

---

SERVICE SNAPSHOT

P&G's Listening Paid Off

Here's a brief trip down memory lane: Procter and Gamble (P&G) was one of the first companies to apply active listening to its customers. In the 1960s, P&G publicized a toll-free 800 number to more actively listen to customer concerns. People staffing those phone lines were trained in active listening. The information they gathered from the customer told them that the average household's weekly laundry increased from 6.4 to 7.6 loads. At the same time, the average washing temperature dropped 15 degrees, caused by the new fabrics introduced to the market. Because of their careful listening, the company created a new product to meet the demand, one that became a hugely profitable market leader—All-Temperature Cheer, now known as Cheer Colorguard.

---

relationships with customers. Few people are really good at listening and those who become good have a significant competitive advantage over others in the world of customer service.

THE DIFFERENCE BETWEEN LISTENING AND MERELY HEARING

Many of us confuse hearing and listening. In reality, they are two different things. The process we call *hearing* is purely a physical activity by which acoustic energy in the form of sound waves is changed to mechanical and electrochemical energy that the brain can understand. All of this has little to do with listening. *Listening* refers to the psychological processes that allow us to attach meaning to the patterns of energy we "hear." All the potential problems, which typically arise from psychological processes—differences in perception, biases, our predispositions, our lack of patience—come into play in the listening process.

Perhaps you are "listening" to music while reading this. Or perhaps you are in an environment where other people can be heard. Are you really listening to those sounds or merely hearing them. The "**cocktail party effect**" provides another example of the difference between hearing and listening. At a cocktail party there are usually several conversations going on simultaneously in the same room. Everyone present at the party is aware of these conversations in that they can be heard. On the other hand, we usually have to make a conscious effort to *listen* to any one of these conversations. We are physically capable of changing all or most of the acoustic energy in the room into electrochemical energy. We are much less capable of attaching meanings to all the sounds—unless we actively focus.

> Hearing is a purely physical process. Listening involves psychology as we attach meaning to what we hear.

WHAT CONTRIBUTES TO LISTENING?

Before we can begin to improve our listening skills, we need to understand the demands placed upon our listening capacities. These demands fall into three categories or elements of the listening process: **internal elements**, **environmental elements**, and **interactional elements**.

Internal Elements Affecting Listening

Listening involves the mental process of attaching meanings to words or sounds we hear. Two preconditions must be met:

1. The words or other sounds used by the message source must be received by the hearer.
2. The listener must possess a set of meanings or referents for these sounds—the words need to make sense.

Trying to hear in a noisy environment, dealing with a static-filled phone line, or encountering people who speak too softly are examples of problems with the first precondition. These can cause a breakdown in the ability to receive the message. Overhearing someone speaking a strange foreign language or with a strong, unfamiliar accent is an obvious example of breakdown of the second precondition. If the sounds have no referent—they don't refer to anything that makes sense to us—we cannot understand. Listening is the way we put sounds and their meanings together to create understanding.

> Through listening we associate sounds and meanings to create understanding.

LOOK INSIDE

What Are Your Listening Habits?

How often do you find yourself relying on these 10 bad **listening** habits? Check yourself carefully on each one, and be honest (no one is grading you).

Habit	Frequency				
	Almost always	Usually	Sometimes	Seldom	Almost never
I get sidetracked by mental distractions (thoughts going on in my head)	_____	_____	_____	_____	_____
I get distracted by the customer's speech patterns, tone of voice, accent, or noises around me	_____	_____	_____	_____	_____
Although I try to recall everything a customer says, I don't take notes	_____	_____	_____	_____	_____
I reject some topics as uninteresting before hearing the customer	_____	_____	_____	_____	_____
I fake listening	_____	_____	_____	_____	_____
I jump to conclusions about a customer's meaning before he or she has finished explaining	_____	_____	_____	_____	_____
I decide that a customer is wrong before hearing everything she or he has to say	_____	_____	_____	_____	_____
I judge a customer on personal appearance and mannerisms, etc.	_____	_____	_____	_____	_____
I ignore or discount a customer's evidence when it sounds wrong	_____	_____	_____	_____	_____
I don't bother to create a comfortable place for the customer to talk	_____	_____	_____	_____	_____
				Total:	_____

How to score:
Give yourself the following scores for every frequency checked:

For every "almost always" : 2

For every "usually" : 4

For every "sometimes" : 6

For every "seldom" : 8

For every "almost never" : 10

Total score interpretation:

Below 70   : You need a lot of training in listening.

From 71 to 90 : You listen well.

Above 90   : You listen exceptionally well.

Environmental Elements Affecting Listening

The listening process is also impacted by factors of the communication environment, which determine what we are able to listen to and what we cannot. These factors can impact our individual ability to listen and our organization's listening capacity, as well. These factors include:

- Our individual listening capacity
- The presence of noise
- The use or misuse of gatekeepers

INDIVIDUAL LISTENING CAPACITY   Our **listening capacity** can be overburdened in two ways: It can be overloaded with too much information or it can be underutilized with too little. In both cases, listening tends to break down.

Listening capacity can be hindered by too much information or too little.

Think about how many messages clamor for your attention every day. You wake to a clock radio and advertisers want you to listen. You catch a little TV with breakfast and newscasters, politicians, and commercials try to get you to listen to what they have to say. On the way to work or school, there are more radio ads. At work or in classes we have meetings and idea sharing and lectures and discussions of all types. You can spend a huge portion of your day listening—or tuning out. Why do some messages stick while others are never heard or soon forgotten?

Listening breakdowns happen when we exceed our listening capacity. Only a finite number of messages can be heard and responded to in any given day; only so many phone calls can be answered at one time. Only so many meetings or conversations can be processed or commercials pondered. Once our capacity for listening has been reached, we develop defensive mechanisms for coping. We select what we will attend to and what we will tune out.

These selection mechanisms, although often unconscious, are normally based on our needs, which, of course, change from time to time. We do listen to auto ads when we are in the market for a car, for example. When our capacity for paying attention to incoming information is overloaded, we will tune out some messages.

When serving customers, our need is to create understanding regarding their needs and wants. Professionalism requires that we, in fact, make such understanding a top priority at that particular time.

Good customer service requires understanding of customer needs and wants.

When our listening capacity is greater than is being used, we may let our mind drift off-topic, potentially missing important information. Most people speak at the rate of about 120 words per minute (except for auctioneers or some disc jockeys), yet a normal capacity for listening—assigning meanings to words—is about 500 words per minute. The problem, of course, is that we listen faster than anyone can talk to us, providing ample time for our minds to wander far afield. Listening to others becomes a tedious task, forcing us to slow down our thinking to stay synchronized with, for example, the customer speaking to us. We will fill the gaps with irrelevant thoughts.

THE PRESENCE OF NOISE   The presence of noise is another environmental element affecting listening. **Noise** refers to those sounds that are irrelevant to the conversation. It is important to note that noise may be either environmental (the sound of machinery, other conversations, buzzers, ringtones) or internal (a headache, our dislike of the person to whom we are listening, preoccupation with another problem). Whatever the source, noise distracts us from the business of listening.

THE USE OR MISUSE OF GATEKEEPERS   One way busy people deal with the problems of exceeded listening capacity and excessive noise is through *gatekeepers*. The term **gatekeeper** refers to one who previews incoming information to determine if it is appropriate to the needs of the person the message is aimed at. If the message appears nonessential, the gatekeeper blocks it from getting to the person. In this sense, a gatekeeper's job is to do some of our listening for us. Managers almost always have at least one gatekeeper. This may be a secretary, administrative assistant, or any other person they turn to for organizational information. In many instances, these individuals determine what needs the manager's attention and what doesn't.

Gatekeepers may filter out messages we need to listen to.

Unfortunately, some managers use gatekeepers to insulate them from customers and other important sources of information. One company CEO, who we will call Phil, is very uncomfortable talking with customers. He was trained as an accountant and has excellent administrative skills—he does a good job keeping records and tracking company data. But when a salesperson asks Phil to call a customer or intervene in a dispute with other employees, Phil looks for any excuse to avoid it. To make matters worse, his company is a small, entrepreneurial firm where every employee should be expected to wear many hats—including customer service. But Phil often delegates to someone else the tasks of listening to customers and dealing with their concerns. His use of gatekeepers (to "protect" him from those pesky customers) is a detriment to his organization's listening ability.

While gatekeeping has its benefits (such as reducing communication overload), it also poses problems. When we finally do get the information, it has been through at least two sets of interpretations, our gatekeeper's and ours. There is a pretty good likelihood that we are listening to a message that has been distorted. Also, our gatekeeper may accidentally filter out messages that we need to hear. The effect is much like the "telephone game" where players whisper a message to several others and the end report is far different from the original.

ANOTHER LOOK

Techniques for better support listening and retention listening

Effective listening is more than just sitting back and letting others talk. It is not passive but rather an active mental process that requires our *attention* and clear *intention*. Intentions generally take two forms: support listening and retention listening. Often we combine both intentions, but sometimes one is more important than the other when dealing with customers.

Support listening involves giving people enough feedback so that they thoroughly express their thoughts. Retention listening emphasizes techniques for capturing information from what is said.

The intent of support listening is to learn, in sufficient detail, what a customer things and feels. This is best accomplished when we avoid speaking except to encourage the customer to elaborate. And, yes, this can be hard! Draw out more details by using non-evaluative responses such as these:

- **"Go on" comments.** "Uh-huh" or hmmm" will trigger further elaboration. Likewise, open-ended questions (that are non-evaluative, not-argumentative) will encourage the customer to go on.
- **Content reflection.** Repeat, mirror, or echo the statement made by the customer in the form of a question. Be care that you don't use a tone of voice that implies a judgment. Instead, simply repeat what the customer said in essentially the same words and wait for further elaboration.
- **Nonverbal encouragement.** Maintain eye contact, nod your head and avoid being distracted to provide support listening.

Retention listening calls for techniques that help you remember and use the information you get from the customer. The following are some tips for better retention listening:

- **Minimize distractions.** Concentrate on the customer. Force yourself to keep your mind on what the speakers is saying and avoid multitasking. Trying to do other things while listening does not work.
- **Recognize opportunities.** Do your best to find areas of interest between you and the customer. Ask yourself, "What's in this customer's message for me? What of this information can I use in the future?"
- **Identify the customer's purpose.** Is the person trying to inform you? Persuade you? Build rapport with you? Entertain you? Then support the customer's goals as best you can. Listen to his persuasive arguments, help establish rapport, enjoy his jokes.
- **Stay alert.** Avoid daydreaming. If the customer speaks too slowly or is a bit boring, force yourself to stay alert. If he or she is inarticulate or has distracting speech habits, overlook them to get to the meat on the message.
- **Listen for central themes** rather than isolated facts. Too often listeners get lost because they focus on unimportant details and miss the customer's main point. Summarize the information under themes: For example, the customer's concerns about value, systems, people problems.
- **Take notes efficiently.** Although not always feasible, taking notes tells the customer you respect the urgency or importance of what they are telling you.
- **Plan to report** the content of the message to someone else. Assume you will have the opportunity to share this discussion with your boss, coworkers, or others. This forces you to concentrate on remembering. It's a good practice technique for any communication.

SERVICE SNAPSHOT

Steph Remembers Sparky

Stephanie Burge owns a used-car business specializing in high-quality cars with a lot of life still in them. And Steph herself has a lot of life in her! She works tirelessly to build relationships with her repeat customers. Literally hundreds of people in her city wouldn't even bother shopping elsewhere. When they (or someone they care about) need a good car, they just go over and see Steph. They know she can be trusted to give them a good deal on a good car.

Part of her secret is she is a really good listener. She remembers people's names, the names of their family and friends, their preferences, and what they like to do. It's not unusual for past customers to just drop by the lot just to chat. She and her husband Lee treat every customer like family. Their conversations seem to pick up where they left off last time—even if it's been months or even years.

The "little thing" that sealed the deal for a continuing business relationship for one customer was when he stopped to look at a spiffy red sports car she had on her lot. Several years earlier he had owned a Mazda Miata which he named Sparky. They had no sooner begun talking about sports cars when Steph asked, "Are you thinking about a replacement for Sparky? I know you've missed that little car." She remembered Sparky! She had been listening way back then and her listening paid off in knowing her customer. And the man drove off in that little red one.

Interactional Elements Affecting Listening

In contrast to noise and other environmental elements of the listening process, the interactional elements go on within our own head. These involve psychological processes that are not as easily identified. To build better listening skills, we need to consider two such psychological elements: **self-centeredness** and **self-protection**.

EFFECTS OF SELF-CENTEREDNESS ON LISTENING   Self-centeredness refers to the degree of "vested interest" we may have in our own point of view. When a difference of opinion arises among people, our vested interest in our ideas can create a listening barrier. For example, if a salesperson feels particularly strong about selling a particular product—for whatever reasons—she may quite literally not even hear a customer's request for a different product. She will be so personally sold on Product A that she will tune out a customer's desire to buy Product B—even when the customer may be better served with Product B. (Remember our opening story?)

It isn't hard to understand why self-centeredness occurs. When we have taken the time to formulate an idea, we usually verbalize that idea in the presence of others, like the salesman in our opening story (*phones should have cool features*). In essence, we have made a public commitment to that position (*I played games on my phone for 20 hours one weekend*), and it becomes awkward for us to change. At the same time, the people we are interacting with have also publicly committed themselves to their opinions (*I only want a simple phone for my mother*). In such cases, neither party is really listening.

Since listening is a psychological process, based on our individual needs, we think and listen from a self-centered orientation. As a result, we don't listen to *what* the other person is saying; we listen instead to how his or her views affect our position. In other words, we are "listening" through a predetermined set of biases, looking for flaws in our "opponent's" views rather than seeking common understanding. We develop a mind like a steel trap—closed.

Too often we find ourselves listening to other people solely for the purpose of finding the weaknesses in their positions so that we can formulate a convincing response. At that point we stop listening and begin to plan what we'll say in response. The other person is still talking and we still hear him or her, but we are no longer listening.

Self-centered listening has a direct impact on the amount of information we receive. Since, in most cases, additional information helps make better decisions, such blocking out of relevant information cannot help but lower the quality of our decisions and our ability to assist customers.

EFFECTS OF SELF-PROTECTION ON LISTENING   Another element affecting the listening process is self-protection. We "protect" ourselves by playing out an anticipated conversation in our own minds before the real conversation ever occurs, to make sure we don't get caught saying something stupid. We figure we know where this conversation is going so we anticipate what we expect to hear and plan our counterargument, rather than listening to the actual message. In essence, then, we are practicing by listening to ourselves listen to others.

Anticipating where a conversation may lead before it occurs can distort meaning.

An old story illustrates this notion of self-protective listening. If you've heard it before, enjoy it again in light of our discussion of self-protective listening:

> *A fellow was speeding down a country road late at night and BANG! went a tire. He got out and looked but he had no jack.*
>
> *Then he said to himself. "Well, I'll just walk to the nearest farmhouse and borrow a jack." He saw a light in the distance and said, "Well, I'm in luck; the farmer's up. I'll just knock on the door and say I'm in trouble, would you please lend me a jack? And he'll say, why sure, neighbor, help yourself, but bring it back."*
>
> *He walked on a little farther and the light went out so he said to himself, "Now he's gone to bed, and he'll be annoyed because I'm bothering him so he'll probably want some money for his jack." And I'll say, "All right, it isn't very neighborly but I'll give you a dollar." And he'll say, "Do you think you can get me out of bed in the middle of the night and then offer me a dollar? Give me five dollars or get yourself a jack somewhere else."*
>
> *By the time he got to the farmhouse the fellow had worked himself into a lather. He turned into the gate and muttered, "Five dollars! All right, I'll give you five dollars. But not a cent more! A poor devil has an accident and all he needs is a jack. You probably won't let me have one no matter what I give you. That's the kind of guy you are."*
>
> *Which brought him to the door and he knocked angrily, loudly. The farmer stuck his head out the window above the door and hollered down, "Who's there? What do you want?" The fellow stopped pounding on the door and yelled up, "You and your stupid jack! You know what you can do with it!"*

How does this illustrate self-protectiveness? The fellow had played the scene in his mind and adjusted what he planned to say because of his fear of being hurt or embarrassed. He was being self-protective.

Actively listen before making up responses in your mind.

Serious listening problems can arise when we engage in conjecture by listening to ourselves listen to others, by anticipating what *might be said* and reacting to that instead of to what the customer is actually saying. Actively listen to your customer before you start making up a dialogue in your head.

Both of these interactional elements—self-centeredness and self-protectiveness—affect the listening process in that they tend to orient our listening behavior toward biased interpretations of messages.

These three elements of the listening process—internal, environmental, and interactional—pose potential problems requiring *active* effort. Listening must be recognized as more than something we sit back and do to kill time when we're not talking. Listening…is not merely hearing; it is a state of receptivity that permits understanding of what is heard and grants the listener full partnership in the communication process. Are your customers full partners in your communication processes?

What can we do to improve our listening skills? A good starting point would be to apply some rather simple action tips designed to break bad habits and strengthen some good ones.

LISTENING HABITS TO AVOID

Most of us didn't become poor listeners overnight; we learned how over a period of time—we develop poor listening habits. Here are some actions we can take to avoid common bad habits.

Action Tip 1—Stop Talking

How is your listen–talk ratio? If you are like most people you talk a lot more than you listen and that can be a problem. You can never become a better listener if you aren't disciplined to be quiet until others have expressed their thought fully.

Set a goal to boost your listen/talk ratio. Listening should typically be two or three times greater than talking when dealing with customers.

Listen two or three times as much as you talk.

Action Tip 2—Go to a Good Place

Sometimes preparing to listen well means going to another location where you will not be interrupted, where it's more quiet or comfortable. *Where* we listen can have an impact on *how* we listen. If your organization has physical barriers between you and customers such as a large counter or desk, consider inviting the customer to sit somewhere more conducive to talking. Executives sometimes run the risk of "hiding" behind their large desks, when coming around to stand or sit where the customer can comfortably interact make a better listening environment.

Find places where you are less likely to be interrupted by other people or by noise. Just the act of inviting a person to a better listening place can signal goodwill and a sincere willingness to understand.

Inviting a person to a better listening play can signal your desire to understand them.

Action Tip 3—Avoid Faking Attention

Faking attention is an attempt to be polite to someone during a conversation and results in what someone called the "**wide asleep listener.**" This is usually accomplished by looking directly at the speaker when you are really thinking about something else, automatically nodding responses, or even saying "yes" and "uh huh" to conversations you have mentally tuned out. When you have agreed to listen to someone, commit yourself to expending the needed effort to listen and give that conversation your active attention.

that all people send out when they are speaking. By looking at the speaker, your eyes will also complete the eye contact that the speaker is trying to make. A speaker will work harder in sending out the information when he or she sees a receptive audience in attendance. Your eyes help complete the communication circuit that must be established between speaker and listener.

When you have established eye and face contact with your speaker, you must then *react to the speaker* by sending out nonverbal signals. Your face must move and give the range of emotions that indicate whether you are following what the speaker has to say. By moving your face to the information, you can better concentrate on what the person is saying. Your face must become an active and contoured catcher of information.

It is extremely difficult to receive information when your mouth is moving information out at the same time. A good listener will *stop talking and use receptive language* instead. Use the *I see...uh huh...oh really* words and phrases that follow and encourage your speaker's train of thought. This forces you to react to the ideas presented, rather than the person. You can then move to asking questions, instead of giving your opinion on the information being presented. It is a true listening skill to use your mouth as a moving receptor of information rather than a broadcaster.

A final skill is to move your mind to *concentrate on what the speaker is saying*. You cannot fully hear a person's point of view or process information when you argue mentally or judge what he or she is saying before the speaker has completed. An open mind receives and listens to information.

If you really want to listen, you will act like a good listener. Good listeners are good catchers because they give their speakers a target and then move that target to capture the information that is being sent. When good listeners aren't understanding their speakers, they will send signals to the speakers about what they expect next or how the speakers can change the speed of information delivery to suit the listener. Above all, a good listener involves all of his or her face to be an active moving listener.

Source: These ideas are adapted from the *Canadian Association of Student Activity Advisors (CASAA) Student Activity Sourcebook*.

Action Tip 4—Be Patient; Defer Disagreement

When a conversation appears to be too uninteresting, too hard to comprehend, or too time consuming to us—or if a customer starts repeating a story we've heard before—we may tune out. Since we know there is plenty of thinking time between the speaker's thoughts, we figure we can switch back and forth between several conversations without losing any information. This assumption is often incorrect and is a mark of poor listening.

Likewise, we may have a response to the customer's "mistaken" point of view. Let them have their say before "correcting" or debating what they say. Perhaps they have a valid argument you have not heard before.

Sometime customers don't know the specialized terminology of your business. Be patient and give them time to express themselves.

Customers can't always communicate to you efficiently. Sometimes they don't know the terminology or exactly how to describe their problem. Be patient. Be sure they have had ample opportunity to express themselves fully before you offer additional information or respectful disagreement.

Action Tip 5—Listen for More Than the Facts

Much of what people communicate are feelings, impressions, and emotions; the actual facts of messages are often wrapped up in these. For example, an employee came to her manager's office, and in the course of the conversation she appeared quite upset about something. When she explained to the manager that her husband had just been terminated from his job, the manager expressed what he thought was appropriate concern and soon changed the subject. Shortly after, the employee abruptly left the office, apparently angry with the manager. He had listened to the facts of what she'd said, but completely missed her meaning.

From the manager's perspective, these were the facts:

1. Her husband was a very capable young executive who was unhappy with his present employer and had been looking around for another company.
2. This couple was young, had no children, and had few financial burdens.

3. Her husband had recently been offered another comparable position which he turned down because it paid about the same as he was currently making.
4. Her husband had just lost his job.

In his listening process, the manager associated the new fact (4) with the facts he already knew (1, 2, and 3) and concluded that there was no real serious problem. The husband would find a new and probably better job soon.

So why did the employee storm out of the office? The manager had **listened only for the facts** while the employee wanted to talk about feelings and concerns she had. She wanted him to listen to what she was *not* saying—that she felt threatened by her husband's loss of the job or that she was embarrassed by his termination. What she needed was someone to share these thoughts with, and perhaps get some comfort from. Many messages convey emotion as well as information. Listening only for the facts is often not enough.

Customers almost always make buying decisions based on feelings and emotion. We don't just pay for the core product but rather seek some emotional gratification out of our purchases. Buying an automobile is rarely simply acquiring a means to transport us from Point A to Point B. We get gratification out of the prestige of a new car or the satisfaction of making a wise purchase. If the salesperson is listening only for the facts, he or she may miss the emotional hook that helps establish understanding—and a better relationship with the customer.

> Messages almost always include both facts and emotions or feelings. Listen for both.

Action Tip 6—Bite Your Tongue before Interrupting

We tend to interrupt people because we get impatient. We want them to get their point across more quickly so that we can jump in and solve it. This, by the way, is a characteristic of men more frequently than women. Women have often been socialized to engage in longer, more supportive sharing of feelings, while men have often been socialized to get to the point and solve the problem. (See the Another Look article below.)

Interrupting in the middle of the message can damage a conversation. Yes, you may need to gain clarification of some points, but wait for an appropriate time to ask for that clarification rather than abruptly interrupting. Hold back on frequent use of questions like "What do you

---

ANOTHER LOOK
Do Men and Women Listen Differently?

Numerous books and studies of differences in communication between male and female communicators lay the blame on socialization. Young girls often communicate to build bonds with each other, to be supportive and sympathetic. Boys tend to communicate in ways that assert their dominance—to compete with others or dominate them in some way. Studies also show differences in listening behaviors.

Studies on gender difference in listening behaviors indicate that minimal responses such as nods, "yes," and "mm hum" are common features of conversation. These responses often lead to male–female miscommunication. For women, a minimal response of this type means simply that she is listening, not necessarily that she agrees with the speaker. She is expressing her supportiveness. For men, such responses are likely to be interpreted as meaning, "I agree with you."

A female speaker who receives only occasional nods from a male thinks he isn't listening. This example explains two common complaints about male–female communication: (1) women who get upset with men who never seem to listen and (2) men who think that a woman is always agreeing and then conclude, when they find the woman doesn't agree, that it's impossible to tell what a woman really thinks.

Of course, such generalizations are just that—generalizations. Some men are supportive and understanding while some women are very competitive and eager to dominate. Gender differences across communication behaviors do, however, hold up when looking at the genders as a group.

Source: Sherron Bienvenu, Ph.D., Management Consultant, Communication Solutions. See more ideas on communication and workplace gender differences at her Web site: *www. ChinUp.net.*

mean?" and "Why do you say that?" until you are sure the customer is finished. Then, if you need clarification, ask for it.

A colleague mentioned a situation where she called a business and stated her name at the beginning of the conversation. Before saying another word, the receptionist asked, "Who?" It was abrupt and unpleasant. The receptionist and her company image would have been far better served if she had waited for the caller to finish and then asked, "I'm sorry, I didn't get your name." Interruptions—especially abrupt ones—can quickly damage customer service.

POSITIVE STEPS TO BETTER LISTENING

Avoidance of poor listening behaviors is only part of the process of becoming a good listener. You also need to take some positive steps to improve your listening effectiveness. In doing so, your customer service skills can dramatically improve. Here are some proactive behaviors that lead to improvement.

Action Tip 7—Reinforce the Customer with Positive Nonverbal and Verbal Cues

Nonverbal behaviors such as eye contact and facial expressions are important to creating understanding.

Especially in face-to-face interactions, nonverbal behaviors are critical. Appropriate responses such as good eye contact, facial expression, appearing concerned, nodding, and reinforcing to show agreement and understanding are examples of nonverbal behaviors that contribute to better listening.

Verbally, we can improve communication by using "continuers" such as *uh huh, I see,* or *I can see why you'd be upset.* These types of comments tend to let the customer know that you are listening and to encourage them to fully express their thoughts.

Action Tip 8—Solicit Clarification

When customers are being unclear, it is important that we tactfully let them know it. We sometimes don't do this because:

- We think we will sound uninformed.
- We think we can figure the message out on our own—eventually.
- We don't want to take the time or expend the effort to make sure we understand.

Phrases such as "help me to understand" can create clarification and better understanding.

By failing to ask for clarification, we rely too heavily on our own guesses in interpreting messages. When you ask questions about the meanings of a message, any implication that you lack knowledge will be more than made up for by your sincere desire to understand. This is flattering to others. It conveys a regard for people who speak to you. When you solicit clarification, ask open-ended questions or use a phrase such as, "Help me understand." For example, "Help me understand. You felt that the service you received was not what you had expected." These comments open the door for further description by the customer.

Action Tip 9—Minimize the Number of Gatekeepers

As previously noted, gatekeepers result in our listening to someone else's version of the message. Whenever possible, avoid sending an intermediary to get the story from the source and then report back to you. Avoid requesting that someone tell his or her story to your assistant and then let that person synthesize the information for you. Get customer concerns directly from the proverbial horse's mouth. The more people the message must go through, the more likely the message will be distorted.

You'll notice this recommendation was prefaced with "whenever possible." A top company executive cannot listen to every customer directly. A manager may be handling thousands of accounts and can be overloaded with too many messages. To reduce information overload, managers should develop a clear policy on which situations need their direct personal attention and which can be satisfactorily handled by others in the organization. Problems that can be handled at lower levels in the organization should be handled at lower levels itself. A customer problem requiring a decision should go only as far as the lowest ranking person authorized to make the decision. And the best companies empower people at all levels in an organization to solve problems.

That said, companies should also have clear **escalation policies**—procedures that tell which kinds of issues or concerns should be referred to people up the chain of command. For example, routine refunds should be authorized up to a certain dollar figure by first-line employees while larger refunds need to be approved by supervisors. Or, escalation may be automatic when a customer feels he has been treated unethically or has been discriminated against in ways that other customers would not be.

Action Tip 10—Try Counterattitudinal Advocacy

Counterattitudinal advocacy (CAA) is a big term for a simple process. It means to take the other person's position—to advocate or express a point of view that runs counter to your own attitude. The objective of CAA is to reduce the degree to which a listener listens through his or her own biases. Counterattitudinal advocacy forces you to listen objectively until you truly understand, rather than to listen only until you think of a response or counterargument.

Here is how CAA works: You, as a listener, simply make a commitment to *restate* and *defend* the position that is counter to your attitude, that is, opposite to your position. Say, for example, a customer feels that the company doesn't care about the environment. You could immediately tell that customer about all the environmentally friendly things the company does, but, using CAA, you hold back. Instead, you honestly try to restate to that customer exactly what you hear him or her expressing. This, of course, includes both the facts and the emotions you think the customer is conveying. Use your own words to express the idea you hear the other

---

ANOTHER LOOK

The Central Role of Listening in Sales for Service Providers

Performance consultant and leadership coach Tanja Parsley takes a closer look at the listening skills needed for a first meeting with a potential client. She asserts that high-performing salespeople:

1. Ask a lot more questions.
2. Allow the client to do most of the talking.
3. Wait much longer before jumping in with a solution.

She goes on to recommend the following questioning structure for service providers, including consultants, to follow when meeting with potential customers. The structure uses (most of) the letters in the word *DISCOVER*.

D—Data questions uncover facts, data, and background about the current state.

Examples:
 –Can you give me an overview of your business?
 –What exposure have you had to our type of services?
 –What is driving you to explore coaching at this point in time?

IS—Issue questions uncover issues, dissatisfactions, concerns, and problems.

Issue questions begin to reveal potential areas where your services may help, but just like in consulting, do not try to "fix" it or provide a solution yet. There are many more questions to ask to uncover explicit needs. Just because someone raises a concern does not mean that the person is ready, willing, and able to use your services. Most consultants and salespeople jump in too soon at this point with solutions.

Examples:
 –If something was not working, what might that be?
 –What challenges are you facing?
 –What concerns are you hearing from others in the organization?

C—Consequence questions uncover consequences, implications, and risks and increase the severity of the problem, making issues more critical.

(continued)

Examples:
  –What's the impact of...(the issue)?
  –What risks are you running if you don't solve this?
  –How might (that issue) affect...?

O—Outcome questions uncover desired outcomes and future states.

Examples:
  –What are your personal goals?
  –What would you like to accomplish in the next year?
  –What would your ideal situation look like?

V—Value questions uncover the value of solving the problem.

Examples:
  –What's the benefit of achieving that outcome (or solving this problem)?
  –What else would happen if you got that?
  –How important is it for you to solve this now?

E—Evidence questions uncover evidence of success for consulting.

Examples:
  –What are your success criteria?
  –How will you know when you are successful?
  –How will you measure success?

R—Rationale questions uncover how a purchasing decision is made.

Examples:
  –How will the decision be made?
  –Who else will be included in the decision-making process?
  –What budget are we working with?

Stay connected and in rapport with your clients when you follow this questioning strategy. When you listen with your focus of attention on your client, the right questions will emerge naturally. Remember, this is not an inquisition; it is a discovery. It is a process that not only deepens your understanding of your client's needs but also creates new insights and "ah hah's" for your client.

Probes

1. How many of the "DISCOVER" questions could apply to fact finding you might do with your customers/clients?

2. Assume that you are selling a company executive on the idea of doing additional customer service training. How could you use this questioning approach to gather information?

Source: Portions of this information are by Tanja Parsley, Parsley and Associates. "Intentional Selling™" and "Discover Dialogue™" are trademarks of Parsley and Associates. See, *www.businesslistening.com/listening_for_sales.php*. Downloaded May 1, 2006.

---

person saying. You may say, "You see our company as being harmful by erecting too many signs that are visually unattractive and make the neighborhood look junky." Then ask if your interpretation is accurate. If not, restate it again until agreement is reached.

What happens is this: By committing yourself to restate and defend someone else's position, you must listen more effectively to that position in order to understand what you are defending. This more accurate listening provides a basis for solving the problem. By articulating a position counter to your own, you force yourself to consider the information that you may have avoided when advancing your own position. You have forced yourself to listen to ideas through someone else's biases. The end result is a better understanding of the entire situation, rather than just your position.

Disagreements can evaporate when we articulate another person's point of view.

This process does not obligate you to cave in to the views of others when you honestly disagree. It simply provides one way of better understanding where those you disagree with are coming from. In some cases disagreements evaporate when we clarify each other's position. We may recognize that we don't really disagree in principle; we are simply expressing similar ideas in different or confusing ways. At any rate, clearer understanding forms a basis for problem resolution.

Action Tip 11—Take Notes

Should you take notes when listening to a customer? Depending on the circumstances, there may be some real advantages to doing so. Note-taking conveys that you are sincerely interested in understanding.

Of course, when taking notes, jot down only key ideas and important facts that may help you to listen and remember more effectively. Don't try to write down everything word for word.

Let the customer see you taking the notes (or tell him or her that you are doing so if you are on the phone). Most customers will be flattered that you are taking their input so seriously. Note-taking can show that you are committed to listening and understanding the customer. Few people would be offended by such a show of concern.

A FINAL THOUGHT

Most thoughtful people recognize the need for careful listening. We spend more time in listening than any other communication activity. Of all the sources of information we have when dealing with customers, listening is the most important. No tool rivals skilled and sympathetic listening for building stronger customer relationships.

How do we motivate others to listen? A cartoon showed the boss talking to employees at a meeting saying, "Now pay careful attention. I'll let you know at the end of the meeting who will write up the minutes." When everyone in the organization begins to listen as though they were going to have to write up the minutes, understanding will advance in a quantum leap.

If we give undivided attention to our customers, coworkers, and associates, we will see a dramatic improvement in our ability to meet customer needs and win their loyalty. Such listening improvement starts at home; it starts with us.

Summary of Key Ideas

- Hearing differs from listening in that hearing is a purely physiological activity while listening also involves the psychological processing of sounds.
- Three types of factors complicate the listening process and pose potential barriers: internal elements within the listener's mind, environmental elements surrounding the communication, and interactional elements which arise especially from listener self-centeredness and self-protection.
- Communication problems can arise from information overload or from underuse of our listening capacity.

- Interactional elements of the listening process encompass the problems of self-centeredness and self-protection.
- To be a better listener, avoid poor listening behaviors such as faking attention, changing channels, listening only for facts, responses that turn people off, impatience, and overuse of gatekeepers.
- To improve listening effectiveness, use these behaviors (in addition to avoiding those previously) listed: Solicit clarification, tactfully use counterattitudinal advocacy, and minimize the number of gatekeepers.

Key Concepts

cocktail party effect	gatekeepers	listening capacity	self-protection
counterattitudinal advocacy (CAA)	internal, environmental, and interactional	listening only for the facts	SIER hierarchy of active listening
escalation policies	elements of listening	noise	wide asleep listener
faking attention	listening	self-centeredness	

Reviewing the Facts

1. How do hearing and listening differ?
2. What is the "cocktail party effect?" What can you do to minimize this effect when dealing with a customer?

3. What are three major elements that complicate listening? Give customer service-related examples of each.

4. What happens when people experience communication overload? Describe at least three ways we respond. How can this be a problem in customer service?

5. What do we mean by environmental and internal "noise"? Give examples of each as they might be found in a customer service situation.

6. How do "gatekeepers" complicate the listening process? What can organizations do to minimize the number of gatekeepers between the customer and top management?

7. What are self-centeredness and self-protection as they relate to listening? Give an example of each in the context of customer service.

8. What is counterattitudinal advocacy and how can it be used to clarify understanding? How can this be used to deal with customer issues?

Applying the Ideas: Discover Your Listening Style

1. Try a Listening Log.

   Try this skill-building activity: Keep a listening log for one full day. As you engage in conversations with people, analyze what you are doing. Identify the number of times you engage in the unproductive habits described in this chapter. Record these in a log. (Be honest and open. We all do these ineffective things and become aware of how frequently we do them can be helpful in improving our listening skills.)

   Which habits seem to pop up in your listening? What can you do to replace these habits with more productive behaviors?

   Write a one-page paper describing what you have discovered about your listening skills.

2. Ask to DISCOVER

   Interview a customer, client, associate, or classmate using applicable questions from the "DISCOVER" guidelines. After the interview, write a brief paper describing how such questions made you listen differently than you normally do.

3. Search It Out: What Do We Know about Listening Styles?

   Use your preferred search engine to see what you can find on the Internet about differences in listening styles. Be creative about your search terms. You may want to start with phrases such as "listening styles," "male–female listening patterns," "listening to customers," and so on.

   Write a brief report about the most commonly described listening problems that are related to customer service. Be sure to document the Web site addresses you access.

Consider this Case

Storytelling Helps Listeners

Let's consider the flip side of good listening for a moment. How can we make it easier for other people to listen to us?

Some things are easier to listen to than others. If we want to be listened to, we can apply some easy tactics to be more engaging by interlacing stories into our conversations. Typically, people enjoy hearing stories or vivid descriptions because these create mental pictures in the mind. Further, storytelling is one of the most effective ways to foster relationships in an organization. Indeed, the whole area of organizational stories has become a fruitful area of research into why some companies do better than others.

Jack Welch, CEO of GE, tells about a young manager leading his first project. As a result of the young man's bad decisions, the company lost $5 million. He went to Jack Welch to apologize and resign. Instead of accepting his resignation, Welch told the embarrassed young manager that the company could not afford for him to resign because GE had just invested $5 million in his education!

Stories about people's antics—heroic or humorous—make for engaging conversation. They are often easier to listen to than other kinds of messages.

A story can be used to change the way people operate in a company. The GE story says several things: that people can make a mistake and still be valuable to the company, that experiments don't always work, and that people are more important than projects. Whatever the interpretation, messages like these free up creativity and encourage experimentation and discovery. It is a reason that Jack Welch was one of the most highly regarded CEOs in corporate America.

Probes

1. Why is it easier for most of us to listen to stories as opposed to other forms of information?

2. What can you do to use stories or vivid anecdotes and thus help others listen?

Consider this Case

The Boss's Great Idea

Mario had barely arrived at the office when his boss, Marilyn, swept into his office and in her usual brusque way said, "Hi, Mario. Good weekend? Hope so. I got this idea: We've been concerned about the way our people never seem to listen to us—or to the customers. So, I was surfing the 'Net and found this little chart. Let's see that we get copies to everybody and maybe they'll listen better. I gotta run. Talk with you later."

Before Mario could respond, she was gone. He smiled to himself and shook his head. "Ah, Marilyn. You always think problems can be solved with simple quick messages. Oh well, no harm looking at this. Maybe it'll get our people thinking about better listening, even if their boss isn't much of a role model," he said to himself.

He then read the chart and noticed a few poor listening characteristics in his own behaviors, although he thought of himself as a pretty good listener. Maybe this chart will provide a wake-up call for our people, he thought. The chart looked like this:

Poor Listener	Effective Listener
Tends to have his or her mind wander with slow-speaking customers	Thinks and mentally summarizes, weighs the evidence, listens between the lines to the customer's tone of voice and evidence
Tunes out if the subject is dry or if he or she has heard it all before	Works to find same value in the comments—what's in it for me
Is distracted easily	Fights distractions, sees past bad communication habits, knows how to concentrate
May take intensive notes, but the more notes taken, the less value; has only one way to take notes	Has two to three ways to take notes and organize important information
Is overstimulated, tends to seek and enter into arguments with customer	Doesn't judge until comprehension is complete
Reacts immediately to logic flaws or emotional words that catch his or her attention	Interprets emotional wording and doesn't get hung up on it
Shows no reaction, energy output	Holds eye contact and helps speaker along by showing an active body state
Judges the customer's delivery—tunes out	Judges content, skips over delivery errors
Listens for facts	Listens for central ideas

Probes

1. What should Mario do to get his employees thinking about the better listening ideas described in the chart?
2. How likely is it that people will recognize and change their behaviors based on this brief message? What else could Mario do?
3. What do you think of Marilyn's listening, based on this brief description? Do you know people who communicate like she did? How do you react?
4. To what extent are your own listening skills reflective of the poor or effective listener described in the chart?

Building a Customer Service Strategy: Your Ongoing Case

Return to the ongoing case you selected. This will be either your current employer, a specific organization you want to work in, or one of the two hypothetical organizations described in Chapter 1: Independent Auto Sales and Service (IAS) or Network Nutrition Distributors (NND). Now consider the following questions as you develop a customer service strategy:

Strategy Planning Questions

Write a plan for enhancing your listening effectiveness while working in this organization. Include specific actions you could take. Build your plan around questions such as these:

1. What personal behaviors can you change to be a better listener? Be specific (and remember our definition of "behaviors" from Chapter 2).

2. How might you (as a leader or as a peer) encourage others to also improve listening skills?

3. Describe any environmental factors in your organization that may be making listening more difficult. Examples might be related to the physical facilities, available communication channels, geographic separation, and so on. How could you improve these?

4. What distracters regularly exist in the organization that hurt listening? How might you deal with these?

5. Does the organization seem to have problems with gatekeeping? If so, what are some specific escalation policies that could be clarified and taught to all employees? Write a list of situations that should require attention from supervisors or managers/leaders.

CHAPTER 4

Use the Telephone Correctly for Good Service

Phone Responsiveness Can Enhance Customer Loyalty

After reading this chapter, you should be able to

1. Know the benefits and drawbacks of telephone communication.

2. Identify your own telephone use attitudes as well as those of your company.

3. Apply specific action tips for what to do and say when dealing with customers on the phone.

4. Employ specific action tips to better express yourself on the phone.

5. Use specific action tips to be more efficient on the phone.

6. Recognize challenges and opportunities associated with building customer relationships with call centers.

The Way It Is... Frustrations of Unresponsive Telephone Use

Hearing a radio commercial for a concert, Sarah called the number to buy tickets. The number was an easy-to-remember 888 toll-free number that had the word "ARTS" as the last four digits. So far, so good. On the first try, the phone rang eight times before she gave up and decided to try again later. On her second attempt, it rang nine times and then a recorded message gave her another number to call. When Sarah dialed that number an electronic voice put her on hold, after which another recorded voice told her to call the first number she had tried!

Petro recently spent 71 minutes on the phone booking a flight with a major airline. The first representative used vocal mannerisms that were difficult to understand. Petro explained that he wanted to fly from Salt Lake City to Amsterdam. The phone rep's first response was, "Do we fly direct from Salt Lake to Amsterdam?" "She was asking me!" Petro exclaimed. He then assured her that he had made that trip a number of times but, because she sounded so unfamiliar with overseas travel, Petro decided to call back. He made up an excuse to terminate the call and called back in hopes of getting another, better informed reservations clerk.

On his next attempt, he spoke with a man who had a very strong foreign accent and was difficult to understand. The man spent the better part of an hour trying to find the flights Petro needed, pausing to explain that "that cannot be booked because it is a point-to-point flight rather than a final destination" or something like that. Petro had no idea what he was talking about with this airfare jargon. Finally, out of the clerk's frustration, he handed Petro off to another representative, a woman with whom he had to start all over to explain his needs. She, however, got the job done and the airline managed to take some $4,000 in sales from Petro. But, they made him work hard to give them his money! Petro ended the call, fully understanding why that airline was in serious financial trouble. Of course, he had no choice but to book by phone because there were restrictions on booking international flights on the Web site and the airline had eliminated all regional ticket offices where he used to speak to an actual human being in person.

Hotel reservation lines, airlines, credit card companies, banks—virtually all companies run their customers through an electronic maze of choices that supposedly make the call more efficient, but often succeed to annoy the caller who simply wants to talk to a human being. By contrast, many consumers do repeat business with organizations where calls are answered by a real person and avoid companies whose phone service is mechanical, unresponsive, or laborious. How about you?

Wise, service-oriented companies regularly improve their phone and net services, but many are succeeding only at angering or annoying their customers when the customer is ready to buy!

KNOW THE BENEFITS AND DRAWBACKS OF TELEPHONE COMMUNICATION

Call centers handle after-the-sale customer care.

People who answer the phones (often working in **call centers**) have been described as the conscripts of the Information Age. "Lined up headset-to-headset, they make pitches, take orders, and provide technical support. They get sworn at, hung up on, sometimes even thanked. But what these telephone-wielding armies really do is tell people about your business."[1] Ironically, these people are often among the lowest paid in the organization, yet they are the voice and image of the entire company to customers.

The telephone certainly can be, as the ads used to say, "The next best thing to being there." In fact, no business can long survive without a phone because, in many cases, a large percentage of their customers make first contact with the company via phone. However, there are two challenges to telephone use that can negate their benefits:

1. *Some employees are unaware of the basics of telephone professionalism necessary to convey a good business image.* People who have been using the phone since childhood may have never polished their business telephone techniques. Everyday casual telephone usage may be inappropriate for business. The result can be customer dissatisfaction and a decline of organizational image.

People answering the phone project the voice and image of the whole organization.

2. *People cannot see the person they are dealing with.* Thus, the phone does not permit most nonverbal communication. Without **visual cues** to reinforce or clarify a message, the listener may be misled or confused.

Phrased another way, each telephone call creates interactions where people are operating blind—without the visual feedback that helps assign meaning to spoken messages. To compensate for this lack of visual feedback, callers create an image of the organization from what they experience—every nuance conveys subtle messages through timing, tone of voice, word choice, and interruptions.

In an attempt to improve efficiency and burnish the image of the organization, an increasing number of companies now have call centers (sometimes called contact centers), where most or all phone calls are directed. But whether dealing with a call center or an individual in an organization, the way the phone call is handled has an impact on the quality of service provided.

Consider this service snapshot story about one incident where a company lost a customer because it forgot (or never stopped to think about) the drawbacks to telephone communication:

This chapter will discuss specific actions and behaviors that can make your phone use more professional and beneficial to customer service. We will first consider some action tips for improving professionalism in your telephone use. Then, you will learn action tips on when and how you can make the most of the telephone, what you should say and do, and how you can best phrase certain messages to assure better customer service.

SERVICE SNAPSHOT

Garth and the Auto Dealer

Garth enjoys working on old cars. A few years ago as he drove to work, he noticed a sports car in an auto dealership's lot. Sensing that such a car would do a lot for his image, Garth decided to inquire about it. He telephoned the dealership. A receptionist briskly identified the name of the dealership and, just as quickly, commanded, "Hold a minute." Fifteen seconds later the receptionist came back on the line and asked, "Can I help ya?" Garth asked to "speak to someone in used cars, please."

"Just a minute," the receptionist replied.

After a pause, a man's voice said, "Hello?"

"I'd like a little information about the Porsche Boxster you have on your lot," Garth said.

"Ya mean the silver one?"

"Yes. Could you give me some information on that car?"

The male voice hesitated for a moment and said, "I think that's the owner's daughter's car. She's been driving it around. Let me check and see what the deal is on it."

There was a long pause. While Garth waited on hold, another male voice came on the line saying, "Hello? Hello?" to which he replied, "I'm already being helped." There was a click as the interrupter hung up without acknowledging Garth's comment.

After a few more minutes, the original salesman came back on the line and said, "Yeah, I think that's the car the boss's daughter has been driving around. If they sell it, they'll want an arm and a leg for it. I think it's a '98 model."

"Well, would you check and let me know if it's for sale?" Garth asked again, getting exasperated.

"Just a minute, I'll ask the owner," he said as he put Garth on hold again. After a few moments, the salesperson again picked up the telephone and abruptly said, "The owner says it's not for sale."

As Garth began to say, "Thanks for the information," he was cut off in mid-sentence by the click of the telephone as the man hung up.

Although this sales representative was probably not being intentionally rude, he sure came across that way. Garth was irritated to the point where he would definitely not do business with this dealership. Have you ever decided to stop doing business with a company because of their minuses on the phone? Many people have.

ACTION TIPS FOR TELEPHONE USE PROFESSIONALISM

Action Tip 1—Check Your Phone Use Attitudes

People tend to have a love–hate relationship with the telephone. Of course, we all know that the telephone can be a powerful tool for sales, information gathering, and relationship building—by receiving and initiating calls, we can accomplish a lot. Yet some people are phone shy. They are hesitant to call others and sometimes hesitant about answering incoming calls. They perceive the phone call as an intrusion on their other activities. Perhaps this attitude is reinforced by the annoyance of dinnertime telemarketers.

> Some people see the incoming call as an annoyance. That call should be seen as an opportunity.

Check your telephone-use attitudes using the self-evaluation that follows. It can help you understand some of your attitudes toward using the telephone. It can also help you improve your telephone techniques by showing what you may be doing wrong.

Action Tip 2—Contact and Compare Your Company

Call the general contact number of your current employer and ask a routine question such as information about office hours or products. Then call a company that you have dealt with in the past as a customer and ask a similar question. What attitude toward communicating does your company's phone use reflect? How does the other company compare?

> A phone call is often the first contact a customer experiences. A good first impression creates a good basis for a positive relationship.

As the old saying goes, you never get a second chance to make a first impression. Callers create first impressions and draw immediate conclusions about the person's (and the company's) efficiency, communication skills, friendliness, and expertise, all in the first few moments of an electronic visit. In short, your courtesy and effectiveness quickly convey unspoken but important attitudes to calling customers.

LOOK INSIDE

How Are Your Phone Usage Skills and Attitudes?

Circle the appropriate letter for each item:
  N = never, R = rarely, S = sometimes, O = often, A = always.
Then read the instructions at the end of the form.

How Often Do You...	
1. Procrastinate calling someone or fail to return a call?	N R S O A
2. Answer the telephone with a curt or mechanical greeting?	N R S O A
3. Let the phone ring, hoping the caller will go away?	N R S O A
4. Save travel time by calling for information ("let your fingers do the walking")?	N R S O A
5. End the conversation by summarizing what was agreed upon?	N R S O A
6. Solicit feedback about your customer service by phone call?	N R S O A
7. Put people on hold for more than a few seconds?	N R S O A
8. Have someone else place your calls for you?	N R S O A
9. Consciously smile as you speak?	N R S O A
10. Speak clearly and in pleasant, conversational tones?	N R S O A

Take a moment to think about your responses. If they signal possible areas for improvement—even minor "little thing" that you might do well to change—jot down your top three ideas or goals here:

-
-
-

Managers should regularly check on their organization's phone skills. They should have people who know how the phones should be handled call periodically and then prepare a brief report. If you are not sure exactly what to listen for, hire a phone consulting firm to gather some good data.

Action Tip 3—Avoid Unnecessary Call Screening

The amount of **call screening** reveals certain attitudes toward phone use. Screening means having someone answer for you, acting as your gatekeeper. The more gatekeepers, the more likely messages will get distorted. Ideally, people should be encouraged to answer their own telephone unless busy in a face-to-face conversation with a customer. Routine screening of calls by a secretary or receptionist often creates caller resentment. The constant use of "May I say who is calling?" is recognized as a dodge—an opportunity for the person to decide if he or she wants to talk or not. Customers get annoyed when there are too many gatekeepers. On the flip side, giving customers your direct line—and actually answering it—can speak volumes about your openness and willingness to serve.

ANOTHER LOOK

Oops! Accessibility Is Job #1

As an administrative assistant at a chiropractic office, I called an insurance company to verify benefits for a patient. Although the call was important, I couldn't reach a human being, only a recording. "Thank you for calling," said the message. "Our office will be closed until two o'clock as we enjoy our Customer Appreciation Week Celebration." This customer didn't feel appreciated at that moment!

ACTION TIPS ON WHAT TO DO AND SAY

Action Tip 4—Answer with Professionalism

When customers do get through to you answer professionally. The first seconds of a call will begin to establish your professionalism. The appropriate way to answer a business call is to simply state your name or your department and your name. Example: "Customer support. This is Nancy Chin." Calling yourself Mrs., Ms., Mr., or a title may sound a bit self-important. Example: "Accounting office, Mr. Silvia speaking." Some people use just their last name, although this can sometimes confuse callers—especially if an unusual or one syllable name. (A manager named Paul Waite found his last-name-only greeting often followed by a very long pause!)

Use of "How may I help you?" (or a similar phrase) following your name tells callers whom they are speaking to, and that you are ready to converse with them. When answering another person's telephone, be sure to identify both that other person and yourself. Example: "Michelle Theron's office. This is Buddy Sampson. May I help you?"

Of course, receptionists would never need to ask who is calling if *callers* would use good business etiquette. Good manners dictate that when we call people, we identify ourselves immediately. Example: "Good morning, Barry Adamson calling. Is Sharon Silverstein there?" Get in the habit of doing this and you will set a good example for others who may realize the advantage of such courtesy.

Action Tip 5—Answer Promptly and Be Prepared to Handle Calls

An answer after two rings or less conveys efficiency and a willingness to serve. When the telephone rings longer, callers get the feeling that you are unavailable and that their call is an intrusion. What is worse is that unanswered callers get the message that you think they are not important.

If your phone system goes to a message announcing a delay in answering, make that message efficient and avoid clichés. One company's answering machine promptly says, "We know your time is valuable and we want to serve you promptly. Calls will be answered in order. We sincerely apologize for this brief delay." That is a pretty good message. We too often hear the more common clichéd phrases such as "All of our representatives are currently helping other customers," which sound more like an excuse than an apology. Make your message efficient (reduce wordiness) and considerate of the caller's feelings.

Have your work area set up for comfortable and efficient telephone use. Place the telephone at a convenient spot on your desk or worktable. Keep your frequently called numbers list current and have material you may need to refer to within reach. Have your computer screen, note paper, message slips, and necessary forms handy. Use a planner system (electronic or paper) that has room to jot down notes about your conversations. Don't scribble notes on random sheets of paper. They'll get misplaced.

Get the caller's name and number as soon as possible and summarize the conversations briefly—especially any commitments you will need to follow up. If you agree to do something for a caller, be sure to record it (in writing or on the computer) and then check it off when completed.

Be sure to record follow-up commitments.

Action Tip 6—Use Courtesy Titles

While calling yourself Mr. or Ms. may sound stuffy, it sounds respectful when you call the customer with such **courtesy titles**. Don't assume that a caller prefers to be called by his or her first name. If in doubt whether to use a first name, call the person by the more formal "Mr." or "Ms." If they prefer the more informal first name, they will say so. It is better to be a bit overly formal than too familiar.

Err on the side of more formal rather than assuming casual address.

Titles and formality can create credibility. If you refer to other professionals, refer to them formally. You'd be a bit thrown off if a medical doctor introduced himself: "Hi, I'm Larry, your brain surgeon." Even if your organization has an informal culture, don't assume that others do. If referring to a company executive, consider using a courtesy title: "I'll get this information to our marketing director, Mr. Kagel, and he'll get back to you by Monday, okay?"

ANOTHER LOOK

Hello, Your Paycheck Is Calling

Communication coach Anne Obarski challenges business-people to think that every time their phone rings, it is their paycheck calling. She also challenges businesses to look at their phone with as much respect and interest as they look at their merchandise, their marketing, and their employees; it is a reflection of their "brand." And reinforcing a brand through every customer touch point can provide the repetition necessary to inspire repeat purchasing decisions.

When you think about your phone calls that way, you are more apt to answer the phone with a little more expectation in your voice rather than disgust. You will start looking at your phone as a sales-building tool. People develop a perception about you within the first few seconds of a phone conversation and their final opinion of you in the last few seconds. Obarski recommends some phone tips that will boost that final opinion to one of an ongoing, positive relationship.

1. *Breathe!* Before you pick up the phone, take a deep breath. Most of us are what they call "shallow breathers." We take small breaths in and out and, therefore, sound tired when we answer the phone. The goal is to sound like you like your job and you are glad they called.

    Practice taking a very big breath and answering the phone at the top of that breath. You will continue speaking on the exhale of that breath and the caller will hear energy in your voice. You can also practice it when you are making a call and start your breath as the phone is ringing on the other end.

2. *Identify yourself.* Give your full name and function or name of your company. Anne answers the phone this way: "Thank you for calling Merchandise Concepts, this is Anne Obarski, how can I make it a great day for you?" Hokey, maybe; memorable, maybe; friendly, you bet. Since she has an unusual last name, she

makes it a point to say it first so that the caller doesn't have to fumble with the pronunciation.

3. *Be sincere.* People call us on the phone to have a problem answered. Whether it is to get driving directions, or hours of operation, or questions about our merchandise or services, they have a question and want it answered quickly, intelligently, and politely.

4. *Listen attentively.* Put everything down when you answer the phone! Easier said than done, isn't it? How many times have you been in your office answering email, talking on the phone, listening to your iPod, and sipping on a Starbucks, playing a game on the computer? Me too. Shame on us. Customers don't like to be ignored and by multitasking, we are not focused on the customer's wants and needs.

    Visualize the person, even if you don't know him or her so that you remind yourself you are engaged in a two-way conversation. If you still have trouble listening, take notes on what the customer is saying. Use a headset, if possible, to keep your hands free. By taking notes you can verify with them, as well as yourself, the important points of the conversation and the action items that need attention.

5. *Outcome.* If the phone call has been successful, you will have established a positive perception about you through your voice, tone, and focus. The way in which you conclude the call will influence how callers finalize their opinion of you. Make that a positive experience by thanking them for calling, reviewing the problem you were able to solve, and then, most importantly, thanking them for their continued business.

Source: Adapted from ideas of Anne M. Obarski, a professional speaker and trainer. For more information, visit her Web site at *www.merchandiseconcepts.com*

Action Tip 7—Thank People for Calling

"Thank you" is the most powerful phrase in human relations. Express appreciation regularly. Some companies use it as a greeting: "Thank you for calling Avis." A "thanks for calling" at the end of a conversation is also a strong customer satisfaction booster. It reassures the customer that you are interested in serving and that the call was not an intrusion.

If a caller is complaining, thanking is still useful. Remember that complainers can be our best friends. They give us feedback that can help us improve and, because they made the effort to call us, deserve our thanks. By saying "I appreciate your bringing this problem to my attention," we shift the conversation from confrontation to a problem-solving tone.

Action Tip 8—Smile

Picture the person you are talking with and treat that person as though you were face-to-face with a friend. Be pleasant, concerned, and helpful. Physically smiling somehow comes through the telephone line via your voice tones.

Keep a mirror by the telephone to remind yourself to smile. If your face looks grumpy or stressed, you are probably coming across that way to the caller. Lighten up and your cheerfulness can be contagious.

A smile can be "seen" through the phone.

Action Tip 9—Be Sure the Conversation Is Finished before You Hang Up

Only on TV and in movies do people hang up a call without closing remarks. Here in the real world it is both polite and useful to tactfully signal the conclusion of a call. If you initiated the call, take the responsibility for ending it. Use conclusion words such as "Thank you for your help" or "That is just what I needed."

If you received the call, be sure the caller is finished. In our earlier auto dealer story, Garth was about to ask the salesperson if the dealership had any other sports cars available, but was cut off before he could. It can be a good practice to simply ask, "Is there anything else I can help you with?" at the end of the call. Or, depending on your company, you might offer additional, specific services or products. Airline ticket agents will often ask if you'll "be needing help with hotel or rental car reservations" before signing off. Of course, that is an attempt to sell more, but it also provides customer convenience and an effective way to signal the end of the call.

Abruptly ending a call sounds rude.

Action Tip 10—Handle the Upset Caller with Tact and Skill

When a caller is frustrated or upset, use additional tact and sensitivity. Here are some additional tips for recovering upset callers. First, recognize that there are two phases to handling upset or difficult people:

Step One: Understand why they are upset or difficult.

The three common root causes of anger/frustration arise from peoples' feelings that

- They are not valued or important.
- They are helpless.
- "It" just isn't fair (whatever "it" may be).

We have all experienced these feelings at some time. Be empathic and recognize that these don't make the caller a bad person but rather a person who is having an unpleasant experience. Try to put yourself in the caller's position.

Step Two: Diffuse the anger or frustration with statements or questions like:

1. *Help me to understand....* This will encourage them to explain why they are upset. Don't try to defend or argue with their perceptions—they know what

they feel, even if it doesn't make a lot of sense to you. Then, let them know that you empathize by saying,

2. *I can understand why you would feel that way.* Do not say "I know *exactly* what you mean" because you probably don't. Instead, convey that you have an idea of what he or she might be feeling. Then ask

3. *What would be a good solution from your point of view?* This begins to shift the conversation away from the venting of emotion toward solution seeking.

Strive to have the caller share the responsibility for finding a reasonable solution to the problem being experienced. When he has made a proposal or suggested an idea that might work, you can begin a negotiating process that can lead to reconciliation—and cooling off—of the caller.

ACTION TIPS FOR EXPRESSING YOURSELF ON THE PHONE

Action Tip 11—Keep Your Conversation Tactful and Businesslike

Have you ever had the experience where, upon telling people your name, they abruptly say, "Who?" Few things make a caller feel less appreciated. If you didn't catch the name, ask politely, "I'm sorry, I didn't get your name, sir. Would you repeat it?"

Keep your comments positive and oriented toward solving the caller's problem or concern. Don't just toss the ball back when you can't immediately help. Don't say anything that makes people or your organization look unprofessional or uncaring.

A LOOK INSIDE

How Do You Defuse Upset People?

We have all experienced conversations that called for special tact to defuse conflict. We have all, also, said things that just didn't "work." Our comments made the situation worse or, minimally, failed to lead to any resolution.

Think back on your experiences. List four or five phrases or words that did not seem to improve the situation. (Examples: "You are wrong," "you cannot be serious!," or use of imperative words that sound like orders such as "don't," "stop," "take a deep breath," and so on. Also, consider sarcastic remarks you may have used.)

Words and phrases that have not worked:

-
-
-
-
-

Next, recall successful cases where you seemed to find just the right thing to say. List five examples of words or phrases that "worked."

Words or phrases that seem to "work":

-
-
-
-
-

Finally, make a short list of taboo words or phrases—ones you will seek to avoid as you improve your skills and professionalism.

Taboo words and phrases to avoid:

-
-
-
-

Here are some other dos and don'ts:

Avoid Saying	Do Say
Who is this?	May I ask who is calling?
What's your name again?	I'm sorry, but I didn't get your name, or May I have your name?
What do you want?	How can I help you?
Speak up, I can't hear you.	I'm sorry, I can't hear you. Could you speak a little louder please?
I wasn't the one you talked to.	I'm sorry, Ms. James, someone else must have helped you earlier.
He's out to lunch.	Mr. Barringer is away from the office for about one hour. Can I ask him to call you back?
You need to call our billing office.	That information is available in our billing office. I'll be happy to connect you. (Or, shall I ask someone in billing to call you back?)
I can't help you with that.	I don't have that information here. May I have someone from our quality service department give you a call?
There's nothing I can do about that.	I'll put that on my calendar for next Tuesday and I'll check on your request again then. Then I'll call you back by 2 pm Tuesday. Will that be satisfactory?

Action Tip 12—Speak Clearly and Distinctly

Today's telephone headsets are quite sensitive. You need not speak loudly. When using a traditional phone, hold the mouthpiece about a half inch from your lips. Whether you answer with your name, the company name, or the department name, speak clearly and distinctly. For example, carefully say "Good morning, Primo Computer Service," "Hello, this is KJQQ radio," or "Scheduling department," followed by your name. Separate the words with tiny pauses.

Tiny pauses between words make your voice more clear to callers.

ANOTHER LOOK

Use Plain Language

Some people think their ability to sling a lot of professional jargon is a way to show how smart they are. The problem is this can be annoying and confusing to customer.

Every organization has its own specialized language. When used "inside," this language is a shortcut for establishing understanding. If used outside the organization where people are unfamiliar with the terms, it is likely to be annoying. Our customers may not understand the jargon or acronyms that we use every day and take for granted. Use plain words that the customer can understand.

Technology-based businesses are especially fertile sources of ever-changing jargon. Similarly, the medical fields use numerous acronyms to quickly describe multiple-word conditions. Customers will understand some terms from such fields but the potential for misunderstanding is often high. It is useful to anticipate that not everyone will understand specialized terms.

On an even more basic level, a diverse customer base often makes it necessary to deal with people who speak different languages. Learning some basic explanations in the language of your customers can be an important way to win the trust and goodwill of foreign-speaking people.

Even if you say these words a hundred times a day, resist the temptation to get lazy or to repeat the greeting in a mechanical, unfriendly manner. Remember that each caller hears your greeting just once, even though you have said it many times. Make it fresh and sincere.

Avoid eating, drinking, or chewing gum while talking to customers. Also avoid turning away from the phone while speaking (unless you are using a headset) and, of course, mumbling.

Action Tip 13—Speak Naturally and Comfortably

Talk to your caller as you would to a friend. Use warm, friendly voice tones and natural spontaneous reactions. If a caller says something humorous, laugh. If his or her tone of voice suggests tension or even anger, it may be appropriate to comment on that: "You sound upset. Is there something I can do to help?"

An animated voice is a tremendous asset. It conveys confidence and high credibility. But even if a person is not gifted with the vocal tones of a professional broadcaster, he or she can do things with the voice that creates and holds listener interest.

Vocal variation in pitch, rate, and loudness combines to project your personality.

The key to holding interest is *variation* in the voice. People cannot pay attention to something that does not change. But we do perk up when speakers adjust their voice. The three things any speaker can vary are **pitch, loudness, and rate**.

Pitch is like a musical quality—the place on a musical scale where the voice tone is. Male speakers tend to have more trouble varying pitch than females. The problem, of course, is that too little variation in **voice pitch** sounds like a monotone. In a word, it is boring.

Another problem is that people try to force their voice into a different pitch. By artificially speaking too low or too high, we create a stage voice that sounds phony. Use your natural range, but experiment with broadening that range, too.

Some speakers do not want to risk much pitch variation. They fear sounding silly. (This fear tends to be more common for men who may want to keep their pitch low to sound more manly.) Failing to vary pitch is like throwing away one of your most useful tools for effective communication.

Listen carefully to good radio or TV announcers, comedians, or other entertainers. You will find that they vary their pitch a lot. Try pushing your range of pitch outward a bit. Go a little higher and a little lower than you typically do, but be careful to not be so extreme as to sound sing-songy (more common in women). Pitch variation conveys personality and helps hold listener interest. Try small changes—you don't need a major makeover—and see how you come across.

Also be mindful of loudness and rate of loudness and rate of your speech. Some people speak very softly and that can be difficult to hear. Let your speech have sufficient volume so that your caller can get what you are saying without straining to hear. Rate of speech is also important. Although this may differ in various parts of the country where the norm is to speak quickly or more slowly, speaking at a pace like what you hear from professional communicators such as news reporters is usually appropriate. Speaking too slowly actually leads to more problems than speaking a bit too quickly. Slow speech gives listeners too much time between thoughts and their thoughts may wander, as we discussed in Chapter 3 on listening.

Action Tip 14—Do Not Let "Dead Air" Happen

"Dead air" is awkward and uncomfortable for callers.

Broadcasters call those awkward gaps when listeners hear nothing as "**dead air.**" Listeners have no idea what is going on and may change stations if the silence persists. The same can happen with a telephone call.

If you need to look up some information, or read some material, *tell the caller what you are doing.* Remember, he or she cannot see you. Use statements such as these to reassure your caller that you are still with him or her:

"I'm reviewing your account now, Mr. Jenson. Let me just check a few figures and I can give you that information in a moment."

"I am pulling up your most recent bills now. One moment please while I look for those charges you are questioning."

"I understand your concern. Ms. Jessop in our billing department can best help you with that. May I put you on hold for a moment? I will see if she is in."

One more time: Always remember that they cannot see you! Always acknowledge comments audibly. Be sure to react to your caller's conversation. Since your callers can't see you and don't receive visual feedback from you, they must rely on your spoken feedback—on what you say—to determine whether you understand what is being said. By frequently saying "yes" or "I see" or "uh-huh" or "I agree" you are providing the needed feedback. Don't let caller comments go unacknowledged.

Action Tip 15—Keep Callers on Track

If a caller digresses into chit chat or nonessential conversation, use a bridging technique to get back on track. This often calls for some creativity, but give it a try.

If your caller says, "I get really sick of this gloomy weather around here. It really gets to you after a while, don't you think?"

You might say, "Well, one way we can brighten your day is to…get this billing problem straightened out…[or] get that new recliner ordered for you…[or] give you the information you've been wanting."

If your caller says, "How about those Broncos last week. They never looked tougher. Payton is still the best passer in the league, don't you think?"

You might say, "They do look good. I hope I can get your game straightened out for you real soon…[or] which reminds me, we need to be looking long and deep into your financial plan…[or] let's tackle this order for you."

If your caller says, "I really appreciate your volunteering with the Special Olympics last weekend. Your company is a big help."

You might say, "Well thank you, Ms. Knowaki. It was our pleasure. Now I hope I can help you find that widgit you called about, too. Let's see. Here it is.…"

If your caller wants to chat on and on, politely take charge, "Mrs. Customer, let me summarize what you've said and then if there is anything else you need to tell me, you can fill in."

If your caller is exceptionally upset, let him or her get it all out before you attempt to interrupt. An interruption will just make the caller angrier. As callers describe their anger, offer sympathetic comments that let them know that you are still listening: "I see" or "Wow, that doesn't sound like we treated you very well," or "I know how upsetting that can be." Then shift to a positive, solution-oriented comment such as "Let's get this fixed for you."

When you have done all you can to handle the customer's need, bring the conversation to a pleasant but efficient close. Try some of these techniques for tactfully closing a conversation even when the caller seems to want to go on:

1. *Summarize the call and what has been decided.* Say, "Let me go over what we decided to do" or "Let me summarize the process for you." Spell out what has been done: "I closed that account and transferred $1,000 to your new fund." "That is all you need to do for now. It has been taken care of."
2. *Speak in the past tense.* "As we discussed" or "That was all the information I needed" or "I'm glad that you called."
3. *Say "Thank you for calling."* This is a universal clue that the conversation is over.
4. *End the call positively by saying,* "I've enjoyed talking with you, Mr. Blanko."

ACTION TIPS FOR EFFICIENT USE OF THE PHONE

Action Tip 16—When Making Outgoing Calls Ask, "Is This a Convenient Time to Talk?"

Too many callers burst into their message when the person being called may be involved in something else or be unprepared—perhaps not having needed information, and so on. If there is any possibility that the person may be busy, ask if this is a good time before you begin.

Always check to be sure this is a good time to talk.

If you asked that question and it really isn't a good time, let the caller know and arrange another time to talk that would be more convenient.

This tip also holds if you don't have information you may need to answer a caller's questions. Be honest and tell him so. Then arrange a callback.

Action Tip 17—Take Messages Cheerfully and Accurately

Many companies now offer callers the option of recording a voice message when the person they are calling cannot be reached. Be sure you know how to transfer a caller to voice mail. If this alternative is not available, be willing to take messages for others the old-fashioned way. Keep a notepad handy to record key words and phrases. Read the message back to the caller to be sure it is accurate. Then be sure to pass the message to the right person.

If your company uses message slips, be complete when filling them out. To avoid possible communication problems, it is especially important to:

1. *Get the full name and correct spelling.* If you don't understand it clearly, ask the caller to spell it for you. Let the caller know why you are asking for the spelling by saying something like, "I want to make sure your message is accurate. Will you spell your name?"
2. *Ask for the name of the organization if appropriate.* The best reason for this is that it may give the message receiver a hint as to the nature of the call. It can also be a way of double-checking if there is a mistake with the number.
3. *Get the full telephone number, including the area code if it's long distance.* If the caller says, "She has it," you can say politely, "I know she can get back to you even faster if I jot your number down with your message."
4. *If the caller doesn't volunteer any specific message, it will save on the callback if you ask,* "Is there any information you would like to leave that may be helpful to Ms. Jones when she calls you back?"
5. *Say, "Thank you," and tell the caller that you will give the person the message as soon as he or she is available.* Say this with assurance.
6. *Note the time and date the message was taken, and add your initials in case there are any questions.*

Action Tip 18—Make Your Greeting Message Efficient

When setting up your answering machine or voice mail to capture messages keep your greeting message current and not too long or too clever. Record your message to be brief. Messages like the following usually work fine:

- *You have reached 555-1131. We cannot take your call now. Please leave a message at the tone. (Note: This message does not identify who you are and may provide privacy and security.)*
- *This is Acme Manufacturing's Warehouse. Our business hours are from 8 a.m. to 6 p.m., Monday through Friday. Please leave a message.*
- *Thank you for calling NuHousing, Inc.—your mobile home leader. Please leave a message and we will get back to you as soon as we can. Thank you.*

Recorded messages may also ask for specific information from callers. ("If you have your account number available, please leave it so we can respond to your request more quickly.") Do not, however, ask for too much. Also, assure the caller that you will return the call and by when.

Avoid messages that sound artificial. For example, a small business that's message say "all of our representatives are currently helping other customers" sounds lofty when the customer knows you have only a few employees. Say, instead, something like "I am in the office today and will get back to you within the hour. You can also contact me via our Web site at StopDirt.com for a quick response." This can also be a good place to thank customers for contacting you as well.

When you as a caller leave a message on another person's machine, be sure to state the following:

- Your name (spoken clearly and spelled if necessary)
- Time and day of your call
- A brief explanation of why you are calling
- Your phone number
- When you can be reached

Here are two examples:

- *This is Jarom Steadman calling. It's 7 p.m. Friday. I have a question about your new Wave Runners. Please call me at 555-3077 after 10 a.m. Saturday.*
- *This is Raul Sancheski—that is spelled S-A-N-C-H-E-S-K-I. I am interested in your job opening for an experienced night programmer and would like to arrange an interview. I have six years experience with a company like yours. Please call me at 555-0819 after 6 p.m. today, Thursday the 4th. Thank you.*

Action Tip 19—Learn to Use Your Phone's Features

The wonderful world of telephone technology is constantly coming up with new features. Unfortunately, like the many people who have no idea how to program their cable TV system, many businesspeople haven't learned to use the many tricks available through their phone system. (Mobile phone manufacturers estimate that only about 5 percent of customers actually read the manual.)

Customer dissatisfaction with a firm's phone call-handling stems from two general classes:

1. Inability of employees to use the features of telephone and voice mail systems, and
2. Shortcomings in treating customers with the highest degree of courtesy.

Customer-focused companies respond to these concerns by providing appropriate training for all employees. Such training boosts customer satisfaction with the firm's telephone responsiveness dramatically.

> Mobile phone company research shows that only about 5 percent of users read the manual.

Action Tip 20—Use the Hold Button and Call Transfer Correctly

The most frequently used features on even the most basic phone systems are the **hold button** and **call transfer**. While putting someone on hold seems easy enough, be careful not to be too abrupt. *Ask* customers if it'll be okay if you put them on hold for (a specific amount of time). For example, "May I put you on hold for about three minutes while I gather that information?" Ideally, you will be back on the phone in the allotted time or sooner. If you need additional time, come online and explain that: "Mr. Rissouli, I'm going to need about another minute to get your file, can you continue to hold?"

When transferring a call to another person, take a moment to explain why: "I think we can better help you if you talk directly to a service technician. Will it be okay if I transfer you to Sarah Booker, our service manager?" One question callers are likely to have when transferred is how much does the new person know about my call. Ideally, the person transferring you will have briefed the person picking up the call. Often this does not happen, however. So, if you receive a transferred call from another employee and you do not know any details about the caller's needs, be open about that. Say something like, "I'm sorry Mrs. Sycamore, but could you take a moment to bring me up-to-date on your needs." Being open about the caller's feelings can be a very nice way to reduce the annoyance of having to retell the story. "I know this can be annoying to have to start over, Mr. Brunno, but could you please help me understand how I can serve you?"

If you are uncertain about the use of your telephone system's features such as call transferring, hold, and the like, take time to read the user's guide or call the service provider. They will be happy to have a representative teach you how to use the system. After all, it is in their best interest to have you using the equipment fully—so that they have a satisfied customer.

Action Tip 21—Plan Your Outgoing Calls for Efficiency

Although small talk is sometimes useful to create a good relationship with callers, strive to make business calls concise without being curt or abrupt. This can be especially important when using portable cellular telephones because both the receiver of the call and the caller are billed for "air time"—the time you use the cellular network. Even for local calls, charges can run 50 cents per minute or more, depending on the time of day.

Plan ahead for call efficiency.

When placing a business call, plan what you will say, preferably in writing. Jot down some notes that include:

1. The purpose of your call
2. A list of information you need to get or give

Be sure to identify yourself and the reason for your call early in the conversation. Businesspeople do not like playing "guess who?" or "guess what?" A good way to kick off a typical call would be to say:

> *"Hello. This is Tina Watson calling from Unicorn Corporation. Is Marilyn Smith in?" Once connected with Ms. Smith, say, "Hello, Ms. Smith. This is Tina Watson with Unicorn Corporation. I need to get some information about your recent catalog order. Is this a good time for you to talk?"*

Notice that the caller here identifies herself, previews what she needs to discuss, and also asks about the person's readiness to talk. If the person is busy and cannot give the call full attention, this provides a chance to offer to call back.

When you need to return calls to people who have called you, schedule them at times they are likely to be in. Be aware of probable lunch hours and long-distance time differences. If you do not, you are likely to play that dreaded game: telephone tag. You keep returning calls and just missing the person who is trying to call you.

Time your callbacks for efficiency. Be specific about when you plan to call a person back. Vague statements like "I'll get back to you on that" may create unrealistic expectations. The caller expects to hear from you within 15 minutes while you meant two or three hours. Instead say, "I'll call you back between one and two this afternoon" and, of course, do it during that time frame.

Action Tip 22—Don't Let the Telephone Interrupt an Important Live Conversation

One of the pet peeves of many customers is when their face-to-face discussion with a businessperson is interrupted by a phone call. If you are talking live to someone, don't jump to answer the phone assuming that the phone call is more important or should be given priority.

If you must take the call, always excuse yourself and, when you determine what the call is about, inform the caller that you have someone with you now and will be happy to call back in a specified time.

Consistently Work to Improve Your Telephone Communications

Good telephone skills are essential for career success in almost every field. Make it an ongoing effort to get feedback about your skill level. Take the opportunity to attend seminars or view training videos that teach new and specialized skills.

If you supervise other people, don't hesitate to critique their telephone skills. Be frank with them if some things they are doing are inconsistent with the tips in this book. Remind them of the critical importance—to the company and to their professionalism—of good telephone skills. They are the voice and image of the company when answering calls.

Be observant. Listen carefully to both the spoken and unspoken messages that may be sent to your callers. Remember that when you use the telephone, your communication channel is limited. There are no visual cues being sent—your callers can't see you. So help them "see" you in the best possible light by your use of winning telephone techniques.

CALL CENTERS: CENTRALIZED PHONE HANDLING

Many organizations have centralized phone-answering services for most customer calls. These **call centers** (sometimes called **contact centers**) should add efficiency and project the best in customer service.

What a Call Center Is

Today's call center is a facility where customer service representatives handle high-volume phone traffic, whether inbound or outbound, using sophisticated telephone and computer technology. Call centers typically serve external customers by answering questions, taking orders, responding to billing concerns, or pitching products and services through telemarketing. For some industries such as financial services, catalog retailing, and travel, call centers provide the primary presale contact point with the customer. For other industries such as consumer products and utilities, call centers are the primary postsale customer care channel. They handle customer questions or concerns. Regardless of when the customer is served, however, call centers have earned their place as an integral part in a modern customer care strategy.

Call centers handle after-the-sale customer care.

Before we had call centers, a company's traditional phone services may have adequately handled customer needs, albeit at a slower pace. As the volume of calls increased, companies either added more desks, phones, and reps or took longer to get back to their callers. Life was slower then, and customers were more patient.

Since then, the pace of business has accelerated from the speed of sound to the speed of light. The current generation of consumers—the Net generation—would never put up with, "I'll get back to you in a couple of days." Today's customers want answers now. Fortunately, for them, technology changed everything, allowing companies to improve the service they provided over the phone and via other electronic technologies.

All the principles of good phone usage apply to call center operators as well as individuals who handle customer communications on the telephone. By designating specialists as call center staff, companies can more easily monitor and more intensively train the people who interface with customers over the telephones.

Sometimes call centers do not, however, provide better service. One common problem is that top management overemphasizes economy at the cost of customer relations. The trend of outsourcing call centers to foreign countries with lower labor costs has often proven shortsighted. In fact, the drive to minimize call times can sometimes be counterproductive. Yes, callers like efficiency, but sometimes being overly efficient trumps the opportunity to build relationships. Zappos.com, the online merchant we have mentioned several times in this book, encourages its call center people to talk as long as the customer wants. By not measuring efficiency metrics (such as call duration) that urge employees to make it quick, the company encourages relationship building, which can pay off in customer loyalty.

ANOTHER LOOK

Today's Expectation of Quick Service

A few decades ago, when customers had questions or concerns about a product or service they would usually call the company and ask to speak to a representative. The operator would patch the caller through to an employee in customer service, who usually worked at a desk outfitted with a phone, some reference materials, a notepad, and a pen or pencil. If the rep could answer the customer's question, she would. More often than not, however, she wouldn't have all the information. She'd explain that she needed to research the issue and ask the caller to please leave his or her name and number. The customer service representative (CSR) would then begin the time-consuming process of rifling through file cabinets and paper records looking for the answers. Assuming the CSR didn't lose the customer's phone number, later that day or even later that week, the CSR would call back with the requested information. The times, they have changed! Such a ponderous process would be totally unacceptable to today's customers. Well-run call centers can facilitate quicker service and better customer relationships. If your company is not working toward better responsiveness, it is likely to lose customers to competitors that are. Consumer expectations require rapid responses.

A FINAL THOUGHT

Telephones, Web sites, texting, and email usage are increasingly important to modern organizations. This chapter focused on specific ideas for better telephone use. (We'll look at the other e-media in Chapter 5.) Customer service professionals need to be aware of the advantages as well as the limitations of these media. Customers who have a poor experience with your company over the phone are highly unlikely to become loyal customers.

Clearly, poor telephone use can have a dramatic impact on a company's success. Whether or not a company sets up separate call centers or other staff members answer customer calls, positive attitudes and winning techniques build stronger relationships with customers and other people important to the organization. Employees who master techniques such as the action tips in this chapter are particularly valuable to the organization. Truly, phone skills are critical to professional success on all levels.

Summary of Key Ideas

- Understanding the pros and cons of telephone use in customer service.
- Ineffective telephone mannerisms can lead to poor first impressions and customer dissatisfaction.
- Apply action tips for telephone, use professionalism such as checking your phone, use attitudes, contacting a company to see how they do, and avoid unnecessary call screening.
- Use plain language when speaking with customers who may be unfamiliar with specialized jargon.
- Apply action tips on what to do and say, including such things as prompt and professional answering, using courtesy titles, thanking, smiling, closing a conversation, and using tact and skill with upset callers.
- Apply action tips for keeping a conversation tactful and businesslike, speaking clearly, being natural and comfortable, and avoiding dead air.
- Apply tips for efficient use of the phone such as asking if this is a good time to talk, taking messages, using efficient greetings, using hold and call transfer correctly, planning outgoing calls, and constantly improving skills.
- Some companies centralize most phone call functions by creating call centers. For such centers to enhance the company's reputation, they must provide excellent customer contact and responsiveness.

Key Concepts

call center	contact center	dead air	visual cues (lack of)
call screening	courtesy titles	hold button	voice pitch, rate, loudness
call transfer			

Reviewing the Facts

1. Compare and contrast the benefits of phone communication versus face-to-face contact with customers.
2. How do attitudes toward using the phone affect one's telephone techniques? What attitudes might you harbor that could make your phone use less effective?
3. What is call screening? When is it appropriate to use it? When should it be avoided?
4. What three elements can speakers vary in their voices to better hold listener attention?
5. What is "dead air" and how can it impact customer relationships?
6. What information should people have on their answering machine messages? What should be avoided?
7. What are the two important factors required to effectively handle irate customers on the phone?
8. What are courtesy titles and why are they important?
9. How can you improve the efficiency of your call use? Be specific.
10. Why is it important to not let a phone call interrupt a live conversation?
11. What are some advantages and disadvantages of call centers?

Applying the Ideas: Try Rewording for a Better Tone

Rephrase the following statements to make the wording positive and tactful. Also strive to solve the caller's concern as efficiently as possible.

1. Bill is out playing golf again. I doubt that he'll be back in the office today.
2. Sarah went to the restroom and then is going to lunch for about an hour or so.
3. Who did you say you were?
4. You say you've been trying to get through? When did you try?
5. Who are you holding for?
6. This is Bobby. What do you need?
7. Hey, sorry about that. I got backed up and couldn't call you back.
8. We don't do that kind of work here.
9. Try again after five, okay?
10. Sally used to work here but we let her go. Maybe I can help.

Applying the Ideas: Hear the Difference

1. Try this simple exercise to demonstrate how voice inflection can change the meaning of what you say. Repeat out loud the following sentence, first just using your normal voice:

   "Henry didn't show up for work today."

   Now restate the same sentence expressing criticism in your voice:
   Next, make it sound like a secret.
   Finally, turn it into a question.
   Next, try saying the following sentence with the emphasis on a different word each time:

   "I think Doris can do that."

   Notice that when you emphasize the word "I," the unspoken message may be "I think she can do it, although maybe no one else thinks so." When you emphasize the word "think" it conveys more uncertainty.
   Listen for the possible unspoken messages as you emphasize "Doris," "can," and "that."
   Notice how these subtle changes in voice and emphasis can convey widely different meanings.

2. Go to the Web using your preferred search engine to locate additional articles on telephone techniques. Report on what you find regarding the changing nature of telephone use in businesses. What are the key trends? How does the use of cellular phones change the ways companies serve customers?

Consider this Case

Critique this Call

The following situation describes a fairly common-place business telephone conversation. In the space provided at the right, critique what is going on, noting both effective and ineffective techniques used by each speaker. Then answer the probe questions at the end of this exercise.

The Story		My Critique
Dallin:	Good morning, marketing department. This is Dallin. May I help you?	
Kristine:	Hi, is this marketing? Oh good. I need to find out some information about your future seminar schedule. Let me see now…[pause] there are several cities where our people might want to attend. [pause] I think I saw a list here somewhere. I know Cleveland is one….	
Dallin:	We do have seminars scheduled for Cleveland, but which programs are you interested in?	
Kristine:	I'm not real sure. My boss just asked me to get a schedule from you. Don't you have a secretary training class?	
Dallin:	Yes. In fact we have three professional secretaries' programs. One is for the new employee and the others for advanced—those with two years experience or more—and one that focuses on advanced office technology.	
Kristine:	Oh, good. Oh, here it is. I found my list of cities. The Cleveland, Buffalo, Denver, and Biloxi offices all seem interested. They said they saw a brochure about your company somewhere.	
Dallin:	Do you have one of our print brochures or have you seen us online?	
Kristine:	No, I haven't seen either.	
Dallin:	Okay. Here's what I think we should do. Please go to our Web site and you'll see the list of cities and dates for our seminars. I'm showing that we will be in Cleveland, Buffalo, and Denver in the next two months, but not Biloxi. Perhaps there is a nearby city your Biloxi people could go to. If you prefer, I can send you a print brochure with the complete list and you can handle the registration by phone or online. Will this be satisfactory?	
Kristine:	Great. Sounds perfect. I prefer the print brochure so I can take it to my boss. Can you shoot that to me quickly?	
Dallin:	I sure will. I'll send several copies via overnight delivery. And I know your people will love the seminars. They're really interesting. Now, can I get your name and address? I'll get this information out to you today….	

Probes

1. What was accomplished by Dallin's greeting?
2. What did Kristine fail to do in her opening remarks?
3. What information did Kristine need to make this a successful conversation? How well prepared was she?
4. How well did Dallin handle the call? What, specifically did he do well?
5. What would you do differently if you were Kristine? If you were Dallin?
6. Did you notice the ways Dallin reassured the customer? Why is that important?
7. How was the overall efficiency of this call?

Consider this Case

Identify the Errors in Garth's Call

Reread the story of Garth's call to the car dealership presented in this chapter. Then describe four or more telephone-use problems that probably led to Garth's irritation and his decision not to do business with that dealer.

Problem 1:

Problem 2:

Problem 3:

Problem 4:

Building a Customer Service Strategy: Your Ongoing Case

Let's go back to the ongoing case you selected. This will be either your current employer, a specific organization you want to work in, or one of the two hypothetical organizations described in Chapter 1: Independent Auto Sales and Service (IAS) or Network Nutrition Distributors (NND). Now consider the following questions as you develop a customer service strategy:

Strategy Planning Questions

1. How could you improve the overall quality of telephone use in your organization? Assuming you have authority to do so, what would you do? Describe specific training you could develop. What suggestions would you have for greeting callers? What are some key phrases you would encourage all employees to use? What taboos—words and phrases you would forbid—might be useful?

2. How could you develop guidelines for handling unhappy customers? Draft such a "cheat sheet" for employee reference. Make it long enough to cover most concerns but not so long that it is too complicated.

3. What kinds of routine calls do your company handle most often? Describe these and offer brief guidelines (or checklists) for handling these in ways that provide excellent service.

Note

1. Alec Appelbaum, "Who's Answering the Phone?" *Gallup Management Journal*, 15, Fall 2001, pp. 2–18.

CHAPTER 5

Use Friendly Web Sites and Electronic Communication

Customer Service in an Online Environment

After reading this chapter, you should be able to

1. Describe the importance of Web-based customer service.
2. Acknowledge the cost advantages of "Webifying" customer service.
3. Recognize key disadvantages of e-service.
4. Identify some tools and approaches organizations can use to make the most of the service potential of the Web.
5. Apply five action tips for avoiding e-service problems.
6. Utilize five action tips for evaluating and growing your e-service effectiveness.

The Way It Is... Why You Should Have a Web Site!

The Internet has become the place for searching and shopping. Every day millions of people access the Internet (or "Web") fully expecting it to provide information about products and services worldwide. We have come to assume that companies have a Web presence. It's gotten to the point where if you're not on the Web, you're not in business. Even small, local businesses have sites if, for nothing else but to show customers where to find them.

The cost of creating and maintaining a Web site continues to come down. Many companies will assist you in creating and "hosting" such sites. Giant tech firm, Google, for example, sends trainers to cities across the country offering free seminars showing businesses how to establish a Web presence.

So, just for the sake of discussion, let's agree that "if you're not on the Web, you're not in business." But being "on the Web" is just the start. How can you maximize this powerful sales and customer service medium? This chapter looks at that question.

Note that rapid technology changes present a moving target for writers of books like this one. Accordingly, this text focuses on fairly broad, widely applicable e-commerce issues. Readers who need to get down into the weedy details should seek advice from active tech professionals.

WHAT IS WEB-BASED CUSTOMER SERVICE?

Listening to World Wide Web gurus talk, you'd think the Internet was made for customer service. Not only is the Web a "perfect" sales channel, but it's an excellent channel for presale and postsale customer support as well. Customers have come to assume that almost every business today has a Web site that will provide some kinds of customer service. Although the telephone is still an important way for people to contact businesses for support, Web sites, email, instant messaging, and e-chat are becoming much more commonplace. Think of your own customer behaviors. Are you quick to check out a company's Web site? Do you prefer email or instant messaging over phone use? Many people are moving in that direction as customer comfort with technology grows. Among today's generation, the majority of whom are being raised with an unprecedented comfort with technology, the service expectations are changing dramatically, as we will discuss later in this chapter.[1]

Let's look at some key characteristics of Web-based customer service where contact can occur in several ways and for several purposes.

Self-serve Common Answers

From the company's perspective, low interaction communication (also known as self-service) is the nirvana of online customer service. Here customers take care of themselves using **knowledge bases**, which are databases of answers to **frequently asked questions (FAQs)**.

Knowledge bases may be structured or unstructured. Structured knowledge bases are organized into a question-and-answer format. Unstructured knowledge bases are repositories of customer interaction, such as email correspondence with customer service or postings on an electronic bulletin board or blog. Such repositories are indexed by key word so that other people with similar concerns can readily find the posting.

Providing such basic information is often the starting point for organizations as they migrate some of their customer support to the Web. Historically, organizations started by creating and hosting a static (unchanging) Web page, something like an electronic version of a marketing brochure. At a most basic level, this includes organizational contact information such as name, address, phone number, and little more. Such a page, while better than nothing, rarely satisfied customer needs.

Online knowledge bases make it possible for customers to answer their own questions. Self-learning knowledge bases constantly update themselves based on customer inquiries.

Characteristically, FAQs include key product questions with short answers, such as:

- How am I billed for Skype mobile™ on Verizon?
- Are your coffee-flavored ice creams caffeine free?
- What can I do about wind noise from my mountain bike rack accessory?
- How do I download video clips for my slide presentations?
- How do I determine if my vehicle uses conventional or synthetic oil?
- What is your pricing policy, do you offer coupons, and will you price-match?

Often the questions are listed at the top of the Web page and hyperlinked to the answers further down the page. (Hyperlinks are those words or phrases that you can click on to get to another place.) Questions would be sorted alphabetically or by the frequency in which they are asked. For common questions, FAQs are both efficient and effective. And for many sites, FAQs are still the norm.

The problem with such static Web pages is that, in order to get an answer, customers may have to wade through a list of the top 100 or so questions hoping to find one that matches or comes close. This is kind of like forcing them to read a book from beginning to end to get a simple answer. Again, this is relatively easy for the organization hosting the FAQs but not efficient for the self-serve customer.

Today's customer expects efficient access to answers.

More sophisticated Web sites can do multiword searches of the frequently asked questions. Some offer a searchable, self-learning knowledge database. Such a database is an online repository of information—the collective wisdom regarding the product or service. And, unlike static FAQs, this knowledge base is dynamic, is ever changing, and enables self-learning. This means that it is automatically updated based on customer inquiries. In this way, the repository evolves with each new question. Customers can search knowledge bases not just by single key words but also by phrases.

Delayed Answers

When customers can't get the answers they need from self-serve sites, they often turn to email or instant messaging (IM). Customer assistance reps look up answers and take turns responding to customer-initiated inquiries. While a few years ago a Web customer may have been satisfied with a 24-hour response to an email, few find this sufficient today. And, of course, the kiss of death to customer service is to not respond at all! Because email relies on one-way communication, the possibility of misunderstanding is high. This delayed communication is neither very effective nor efficient—and certainly fails to meet today's customer expectations.

Email and texting usually increase when customers are having trouble finding answers on their own.

Larger volumes of email result when customers are not able to find answers they need on the Web site. Rather than representing an effective customer care solution, handling a lot of email can be a symptom of an ineffective Web presence.

Live Answers

High-assistance service can be provided by such things as **Web chat** or **live chat**, a more costly but often welcome addition to the customer's service options. When customers began to complain about the slow response times of email queries, companies responded with online chat. With live chat, the customer service representative communicates live (in "real time") with the customer who needs assistance. All messaging is text based—both parties type questions and responses. Often, a complete transcript of the chat session is available to the customer for review. Nineteen percent of U.S. online customers have used live chat to attempt to resolve a customer service issue in a given year.[2]

A variation on chat rooms is the use of **blogs**. A blog is a log or journal maintained by a company or individual. As others participate in sharing thoughts on an ongoing basis, a blog becomes an **online forum** for discussion. Bloggers play a role in shaping a company's discussions and even public image. When many people come together in cyberspace for blogging, they are giving open, unfiltered feedback and other information. Blogs can support service efforts when people share their experiences in dealing with service issues. For example:

- *I had difficulty installing the sprocket on my wingnut until I used a strip of duct tape to hold it in place...*
- *A neighbor of mine sealed his driveway with a mixture of X and Y which gave it a nice, glossy finish.*
- *Whenever you are considering an upgrade to the Model C, first list the key functions you use most. Sometimes the C isn't your best option unless...*

A blog can be an information-sharing site that facilitates customers helping each other. Savvy companies in many industries are turning to blogs as an additional option to disseminating information and service tips.

ANOTHER LOOK

But I Don't *Want* to Chat!

A woman who uses the Web extensively for online shopping reports this irritating situation: When she pauses in her shopping, the company's site pops up a request that she chat online. The company's chat features can answer product questions thus providing better product information. But companies that program their systems so that a shopping customer gets a pop-up invitation to chat any time she stops keystroking may come across as the electronic version of a hard sell. The customer feels pressured to make a decision while she may prefer to explore various products at her leisure.

Companies need to consider the trade-off between selling (pushing the shopper for a decision) and service (addressing customer concerns). Obviously, this distinction is often blurry, but a premature chat request can be annoying.

ANOTHER LOOK

Social Networking Skyrockets

Blogs and chat rooms have morphed into **social networking sites** (SNS) as the largest of which are Facebook, MySpace, LinkedIn, Friendster, Tagged, and others. These link friends and associates of all ages in easy-to-use contact networks. Recent research shows that while popular in many nations around the globe, SNS are used by fully 50 percent of Americans. Other developed countries show similar usage. For example: Israel 53 percent, Britain 43 percent, Russia 43 percent, and Spain 42 percent.

These networks are not just for young people, as some mistakenly assume. The fastest growth segment of SNS adopters is the middle-aged or older user.

The impact of such networks cannot be overemphasized for its customer service implications. Think about it: In past days unhappy customers would tell a few or a few dozen others people about their experience. Today's social networkers can tell thousands—perhaps hundreds of thousands! Fortunately for some businesses, good news can travel fast, too.

Companies cannot afford to overlook the customer service potential of these networks. They need to spread the word about their ability to solve customer problems and get out in front of negative comments.

Source: Pew Research Center, "Texting, Social Networking Popular Worldwide," December 20, 2011, *pewresearch.org/ pubs/2152.*

Following are a few points to keep in mind about using blogs:

- Use blogs as a real-time online conversation. If there's a conversation going on about your issue or organization, you need to be involved in the dialogue.
- Remember the 80/20 rule; 20 percent of the people in the world have great influence on how the other 80 percent think. The 20 percent are actively reading blogs.
- Understand that almost one-third of all U.S. Internet users read online forums, so the potential for communicating about customer service (for good or ill) is high.
- Reach out to bloggers who follow your issues. If possible, have conference calls with them. Engage them.
- Submit posts/comments from your organization's leaders on blogs. It establishes that you are willing and able to be part of the conversation.

Self-serve Personalized Answers

Personalized service—customized real-time data about the customer's specific problem—is the ideal technology-assisted service a company can offer. For example, you just ordered the perfect gift for your mom three days before Mother's Day. You received multiple assurances that the gift would arrive before that special Sunday morning. Now you want to know where your order stands. Has it been filled? If so, where is it? Has it left the loading dock? Is it on a UPS or FedEx truck? These kinds of customer inquiries are simple for Web-enabled tracking systems. The customer enters the tracking number and seconds later knows the package's location.

Personalized self-serve solutions rely on real-time tailoring of Web content to the customer's individual needs. Web pages are dynamically adjusted (frequently changed) based on customer profiles and even customer input. For instance, when a platinum-level frequent flyer checks her itinerary on the Web, she'll see flight status, the in-flight meal menu, and an airport map showing her where the Platinum Club lounge is located in relation to her arriving gate. Economy-class flyers, on the other hand, would see only flight status. Such personalization provides tailored information for frequent flyers, engendering an almost-religious loyalty among those valuable business travelers. The Net-savvy customer expects such personalization and even the opportunity to participate with the company. For example, these customers want not only to choose from options but to suggest additional ones.

Customers are coming to expect personalized options in e-commerce.

ANOTHER LOOK

Customer Service Expectations for Today's Net-Savvy Generation

A whole new class of technology-savvy young people (often called Net-geners) with considerable purchasing power is emerging. Their definition of customer service success goes beyond what has been traditionally expected of businesses.

The norms that guide Net-geners when they shop—and which they are coming to assume from businesses—are strikingly different from what customers have traditionally expected. Some examples:

- Customization: They assume companies will provide them with personalized products or services. They often demand the ability to custom-build or individualize and are rarely content with one-size-fits-all. They want to make it their own.
- Scrutiny: They check out products online or with friends (often via their social networking sites) before they go to the store. Eight-three percent know what they want before going to buy a product. Shopping now involves simply picking up the product.
- Integrity: They are more conscious than ever of company reputation and readily share impressions with each other. Does this company deserve my money? Social networks spread word as do their blogs of the "your company sucks.com"-type.
- Collaboration: They want to participate with companies to make the product or service better and they

expect to be able to do so via open communication channels. Unresponsive or difficult-to-reach companies lose credulity and Net-gener customers.
- Entertainment: They expect companies to make it fun to do business with them. Since 93 percent of kids ages 2–17 have regular access to video games, their tolerance for uninteresting media used by traditional companies won't fly.
- Speed: They want the company to serve them *now*. They assume instant response to requests (like they get when they IM with friends) and sophisticated technology interface. An unresponsive Web site loses the Net-gener instantly.
- Innovation: They want companies to give them the latest, hippest, trendiest products and services. The old model of slow-to-change products (such as the once-a-year model changes of automobiles, for example) is unacceptable.

These norms put a lot of pressure on businesses to get into the swim of a very fast-moving economy. To capture and keep such customers means that less responsive forms of customer service may no longer cut it.

Source: These ideas are adopted from, Don Tapscott's excellent book, *Grown Up Digital* (New York: McGraw Hill, 2009, especially pp. 188–92).

RECOGNIZE DISADVANTAGES OF WEB-BASED E-SERVICE

E-service alone is not, and never will be, a 100 percent, surefire strategy for handling all customer contacts. It is a helpful "platform" for several cost-effective channels—self-service Web, blogs, email, text messaging, and live chat—but, for some customers, e-service will never be a substitute for old-fashioned phone calls and direct contact with customer care representatives. For such people, e-service, then, is "in addition"—another set of channels for communicating with customers. As such, e-service is just one more assistance approach that must be designed, implemented, and maintained. Installing an e-service solution is no small undertaking. It is costly and highly dependent on available technology.

> Poorly managed e-service systems can result in a reputation for bad service.

> Technology applications are moving targets—the rate of change is extremely fast.

The Internet, like most information technologies, is a moving target. The hardware used has a life cycle averaging less than five years before it becomes obsolete. Software life cycles are even shorter, with minor product updates appearing every few months and major updates every 18 months.

Finally, the rush to migrate customer service to the Web and smart phone platforms has produced its share of failed sites and frustrated customers, prompting a not necessarily undeserved reputation akin to the voice-response runaround, where the customer sits on hold listening to tinny elevator music. Poor e-service delivery can substitute one negative stereotype for another. Ignoring the human side of customer service can turn what looks like a low-cost service alternative into a costly mistake.

Expert blogger Shawn Graham sees several shortcomings of customer service tech.[3]

- **Powerful tech, same old wait.** Tech firm Next IT conducted 34 live chat secret shopper sessions regarding four Fortune 500 companies (a home entertainment provider, a rental car business, a national retailer, and a home improvement retailer). The average time for a first response was 5.6 minutes. The average chat session lasted 18.5 minutes—a total interaction time of 24 minutes.
- **Time spent worth it?** Information received in chats was accurate only 60 percent of the time. In addition to accuracy concerns, 55 percent of all questions escalated to a phone call, basically negating the value of the chat.
- **Missed opportunities.** Only a quarter of the customers reported a positive experience.

All this indicates a significant opportunity to improve the quality and efficiency of e-support.

APPLY ACTION TIPS FOR AVOIDING E-SERVICE PROBLEMS

While the Web offers great potential for building customer loyalty, it also can lead to frustration and failure if not done right. By putting the following actions into practice, a company can be well on its way to establishing a positive presence on the Web.

Action Tip 1—Be There and Be Quick

Did you ever log on to your favorite site to do a little online business only to find the site down? It's like showing up at the company during business hours only to find the doors locked. When the site's down, you are closed for business. And to make matters worse, a competitor is only a click away for your increasingly impatient customer. For customers looking for assistance (who are likely to be already frustrated), an inaccessible or slow site can be extremely annoying. Instead of a customer being able to help herself online, the situation usually escalates. Now your company has to deal with three problems: an inoperable site, a frazzled customer, and the customer's original concern.

Or, have you ever found yourself frustrated because a Web site seemed to take forever to open pages? If a page takes longer than a few seconds to load, most visitors won't stick around. With today's lightning-fast Internet connections, a few seconds can seem simply too slow. Customers today won't wait.

Therefore, the first rule of successful e-service is to be there and be quick. When customers hit your company's Web page, they want it to be up. Many companies go to great effort to offer stable, **redundant servers**. (*Redundant* means having backup to ensure that if one aspect of the service goes down, others take over to keep it running.) The goal is 99.999 percent uptime and rapid page-loading times.

Action Tip 2—Make Sites Friendly

Friendliness and general good etiquette should be applied to all customer contacts. Whether in-person, during voice or chat communication, or in printed materials, language should be consistent, simple, and confident and project an eagerness to help. Avoid sarcasm, abrupt one-word answers, needlessly deferring to other departments, and ambiguity.

Customers, especially in older demographics, can often feel confused or overwhelmed by Web-based service applications. Getting the language simple and clear should be a priority for designing and updating the Web sites as well as training the service representatives staffing the site's chat or email functions.

Action Tip 3—Make Site Navigation Simple

Web customer service should be only one click away. Once customers connect to a home page, they should be able to get to the customer assistance page with a single click. And they shouldn't have to scour the home page to find the button, tab, or hyperlink.

Site navigation should be simple and obvious, with a consistent scheme for going from page to page. The customer should always have a way to get back to a specific page or be able to press the back button on the browser to escape. Forcing a customer to stay in a site or wade through a complex maze is counterproductive to good service.

Customers won't tolerate hard-to-navigate Web sites.

Action Tip 4—Respond Quickly

Today's video game generation expects immediate response from their game consoles, desktop computers, and sports cars. Waiting more than two to three seconds for a computer screen to refresh is unacceptable to them.

But such Web site performance is only one dimension of quick response. Even more important is quick turnaround or customer questions. Here again, the bar is rising. Where people were once quite satisfied with a 24-hour response time to an email, today that is way too long. If staffing prohibits quick responses, automatically generated responses should go out indicating that the customer's message was received and tell when he can expect a more detailed response. For something as dynamic as Web chat, the communication should have the pace of a live conversation. Long pauses on the order of five minutes or more may confuse the customer into thinking the chat has been abandoned. Before long, the customer is typing "Are you still there?" in the chat window.

Action Tip 5—Make a Progression of Solutions Seamless

Web-based customer service should provide users with a progression of solutions. If the site's FAQ section does not solve the customer's issue, chat may be the next logical progression. If chat is ineffective or overly burdensome, voice communication with a real person should be readily accessible. Guiding users through that process helps customers feel they are getting closer to a solution. Simple icons such as "Can't find an answer?" or "Click here to chat with a representative" should be easy to find.

Action Tip 6—Provide Human Communication Alternatives

The more high-tech the world becomes, the more some people crave high touch service or non-electronic contact of some sort. In the realm of customer care, the Internet is almost a synonym for high-tech, the opposite of high touch or personal attention. At some point, customers may become frustrated with the various self-serve options or the distant communication of bits and bytes. They will seek human contact. The solution may be to provide several communication alternatives as we have discussed. But ultimately, for some, something as low-tech as the telephone is the best option. Some customers just need the human touch—someone to talk with—and should be given such options.

Display phone numbers on the Web site. Hiding them, although perhaps done to nudge customers to the more company-efficient e-service, can send an unspoken message that "we really don't want to talk with you."

Action Tip 7—Pay Attention to Form and Function

Just because technology can give a company animations, 256 type fonts, and 16 million colors doesn't mean its Web site has to use it all. Customer care sites should be functional and visually pleasing, but they need not be elaborate or incorporate every possible bell and whistle. All this "form" may be distracting, especially when the customer just wants a quick answer.

Successful sites, like those with modern video games, are the result of a team effort. Graphic designers, usability engineers, database administrators, content experts, and programmers all play a part. Form should support function, avoiding jazzy technology for technology's sake while remaining current with the technology expectations of today's customers. The most customer-friendly sites avoid unnecessary clutter, and instead keep the site simple and functional.

SERVICE SNAPSHOT

Wilde Mats and Matting

Erika Wilde runs a Web site selling floor mats to businesses. Her site, *www.StopDirt.com,* is easily available for people needing a wide variety of industrial floor mats and matting products, including custom logo mats. When customers contact Erika's Web site to get personalized information or to describe a problem, she quickly calls them back on the phone. Her upbeat personality makes this immediate and very personalized service even better. It also helps to create "hand-holding" relationships with her customers, who are invariably impressed by the level of personal service they receive. She thus exceeds customer expectations with better information and with her bubbly telephone personality.

Just because a business sells on the Web doesn't mean that it must forego all other forms of communication. Often, the telephone can supplement e-commerce and provide the opportunity to project the human touch.

UTILIZE ACTION TIPS FOR EVALUATING AND GROWING E-SERVICE EFFECTIVENESS

Technology and customer expectations are ever changing. Your company must adapt to such change. The following are some action tips that can evolve your Web service to new levels of effectiveness and give customers a better experience.

Action Tip 8—Track Customer Traffic

The best thing about the Web may be that companies can track anything using available software. Companies can use the services of firms that specialize in "**Web analytics**"—the measurement, collection, analysis, and reporting of Internet data for purposes of understanding and optimizing Web usage. (Examples of top-rated Web analytic companies include Coremetrics, Inc., Unica Corporation, Omniture, Inc., and Mondosoft. Search these for a better understanding of their services and software.)

Analytic data can show them such things as the "**click path**" the customer took to get to the site and whether the customer is a first-time visitor. (A click path is a record of all the URLs or Web addresses the customer clicked on to get to your site.) They can track service resolution and abandonment rates, average site connect time, and frequent requests and much more. If companies want to know where to spend their time to better serve customers, they should track customer paths and then use such analytic data to systematically improve the site. Guessing about these data is a certain way to fall behind in the hypercompetitive world of customer service.

Action Tip 9—Benchmark Service Levels

Benchmarking means keeping careful statistics about existing service levels. Web sites with successful customer care **benchmark** and compare against themselves and against their best competitors. These statistics can then be used to set targets for the future. Typical services monitored include site uptime, average response rate per page request, average time to respond to email inquiries, average time to respond to Web chat inquiries, and number of resolved and unresolved inquiries per day. These data can be gathered automatically but management needs to review them and develop strategies for constant improvement.

Action Tip 10—Teach Your Site to Learn

If the content of a Web site remains the same today as it was last month, chances are it will be able to satisfy only last month's customers. Successful e-service requires learning such things as:

- What customer service solutions work or don't work
- What content is missing

- What click paths end in dissatisfied customers
- What new questions are your customers asking

Some commercial software scours Web activity and automatically updates a company's knowledge base with new content. Whether a company chooses to have its site "learn" via such software or whether it has the content updated by staff, adaptive, dynamic sites let customers know the organization is listening and responding to their needs.

Action Tip 11—Build an Ongoing E-Relationship

Successful human relationships require two-way communication (verbal and nonverbal). Sometimes people initiate communication or behaviors that build the relationship; sometimes they reciprocate to others. Traditional customer service, however, tends to be primarily customer initiated and thus mostly reactive. Yet e-service offers companies additional opportunities to take the initiative—to be proactive. To build an e-relationship, companies can simply offer email notifications to customers. "Notify-on-change" puts the customer's e-mailbox to use. With each change in product, catalog, or content area, the company can automatically fire off an appropriate email to its customer base. Be careful to avoid blatantly selling; stress, instead, solutions to customer concerns.

Companies should be sure to get permission from customers first. Sending unwanted email (**spamming**) can damage a relationship rather than enhance it. If customers do agree to accept notifications, the company should always give them the option with each email to have their name removed from the notification list.

Action Tip 12—End High for Better Loyalty

One common model for providing traditional in-person customer service suggests apologizing for any inconvenience (expressing caring), solving the problem (showing competence), and offering a peace token (providing comfort) such as a small gift or additional points in a customer loyalty program. This last step is designed to leave the customer on a high note, thinking positively about the company. With Web-based customer service, even though the focus is on helping the customer help himself or herself, it still makes sense to make peace, or provide comfort.

Thank customers for visiting and using your Web site. This can help build goodwill and repeat usage.

Before customers log off from a Web site, the company should always thank them for visiting. To rebuild the goodwill (if the customer has had a problem), offer some kind of peace token—a discount on their next purchase, free shipping, or some kind of additional service coverage, if appropriate. You want them to be glad they visited your site.

A FINAL THOUGHT

Today's Web-mediated customer service offers a low-cost approach for many customer transactions. Getting answers to frequently asked questions, checking the status of an order, or even researching the details of an invoice are easy tasks for Internet-enabled customer care service centers. The Web has made building and maintaining customer relationships simpler. We would expect that of technology. But there's the dark side—some Web sites are more complicated and difficult to navigate than a video arcade game. They can, if poorly managed, turn customers off rather than support good service.

Successful companies put considerable thought into their Web sites, blogs, messaging, live chat, and email processes. Few companies today can thrive without an electronic presence. People simply expect to be able to communicate with companies through these media. Take the opportunity to surprise customers with exceptional e-service.

LOOK INSIDE

How Well Does Your Company Use Its Web site?

Now that you've had a chance to explore the Internet's role in building customer loyalty, it's time to see how well your organization is doing. If you are currently working in an organization with a Web site, take a minute and complete the following survey. If you do not work in such an organization, select the Web site of a company you have visited, put yourself in the role of one of the company's leaders, and answer as many of the questions as you can.

	Yes	No	Don't Know
1. Is your Web site dynamic (more than simply a posted brochure)?			
2. Is it easy for your customers to quickly find answers on your Web site to their most frequently asked questions?			
3. Is the FAQ section updated frequently based on customer input?			
4. Do you respond to all customer emails within two hours or less?			
5. Can your customer's input change the content on your site automatically (i.e., do they participate in information sharing beyond the FAQs)?			
6. Does your site offer chat or live call options?			
7. Can your customers track the status of their requests easily on your site?			
8. Can customers get to a human support staffer easily?			
9. Do you monitor how frequently customers return to your site for information?			
10. Is information on your site presented in easy-to-use formats (including video clips, etc.) rather than as only text?			
11. Is it easy for visitors to have updates sent to them automatically by email, text messages, or social networks such as Facebook?			
12. Does your Web site capture and share useful information with your staff so that they may understand and adjust to customer concerns?			
13. Do customers ever praise your company because they found your site especially helpful?			
14. Do you use systematic Web analytics to determine if you are making the most of your Web site's potential?			
15. Do you strive for consistency of messages so that answers you give your customers on the phone are the same as the ones you give them on your Web site?			
16. Do you check for accuracy of advice given and correct it when necessary?			

Scoring:

A "Yes" answer on 10 or more items indicates that your organization's e-service health is excellent. Anything less should prompt you to reexamine some of your online customer service strategies.

Summary of Key Ideas

- The Internet is a potentially powerful avenue for delivering customer assistance. In many cases companies fail to maximize its service potential.
- Online knowledge bases make it possible for customers to answer their own questions. The best of such knowledge bases are dynamic and keep "learning" as they process customer input.
- Email provides delayed answers to customer inquiries. A rule of thumb for exemplary customer service is to acknowledge all customer email and respond to them within two hours or less—usually less. An instant response message acknowledging receipt of the message is acceptable so long as a real follow-up happens in a timely manner.
- Web chat is an adaptation of Internet chat room technology that allows customers and service representatives to carry out two-way communication. Blogs and social network sites can serve similar functions.
- Web analytics and benchmarking (comparing to others) provide data for constant improvement of your Web site's effectiveness. The target is moving!
- Web self-service has a significant cost advantage over traditional customer service channels, such as talking to a live agent on the telephone. That said, some customers still prefer the "human touch" of a real person.
- E-services are not only cost-effective, but they can provide additional benefits such as improved customer relationships. However, poorly managed e-services can nullify any potential cost savings and result in lost customers.
- Successful e-service delivery requires attention to several factors: Web site uptime, navigation ease, etiquette, server speed, personal touch, appropriate site design, benchmarking, traffic monitoring, adaptive knowledge bases, proactive communication, and customer loyalty programs.

Key Concepts

benchmarking
blog
click path
e-service

FAQs (frequently asked
    questions)
knowledge database
live chat

online forum
redundant servers
social networking sites
    (SNS)

spamming
Web analytics
Web chat

Reviewing the Facts

1. Describe in your own words the categories of Web-enabled customer service as discussed in this chapter. What makes the most sense for a business like yours (if you are currently employed)?
2. To what extent is "Webifying" customer service equally important for all types of businesses? Identify possible exceptions.
3. Summarize the advantages and disadvantages of Web-based service.
4. Make an exhaustive list of the kinds of questions you would like answered by Web analytics—by systematic evaluation of date—in order to make the most of a Web service. Why would such data, if readily available, be useful?
5. What are some ways companies can make their Web sites more efficient and ever evolving to provide better service? How have customer expectations about Web sites changed in recent years?

Applying the Ideas: Explore the World of E-Service

1. Pick three of your favorite companies or organizations, locate the home page for each of these organizations, and investigate the online customer service they provide. Do they include most e-service channels such as FAQs, email, and chat? What additional online services are provided?
2. Imagine that you have purchased a technology product. You take it home, hook it up, and find you can't get it to work properly. Select a major vendor, and connect to its customer service Web site. Perform a navigation analysis of the site. How many links did you have to follow to get your problem resolved? Were you able to "serve yourself," or did you have to contact a customer assistance representative? If you were assisted, was it easy to contact a customer assistance representative? Did you use email? Web chat? Telephone?
3. Log on to the customer service site of an established Internet retailing company (e.g., *www.amazon.com, www.overstock.*

com, www.proflowers.com) and also the site of a relatively new entrant to the Web (e.g., a local business such as a martial arts studio or an auto repair shop). Record how long it takes to move from Web page to Web page. (Use a stopwatch if possible.) Send an email and see how long it takes to receive a reply. Compare the performance (speed) of the two e-service providers. Did these organizations meet your need for speed?

4. Find a business or an organization that doesn't have a customer service Web presence. Develop a plan to create Web-assisted e-service capability. Outline what steps would be necessary. You need not flesh out every detail, just the major

decisions and steps involved in the organization in moving some of its customer assistance processes to the Internet.

5. A fascinating Web site is called the Wayback Machine or the Internet Archive found at *www.archive.org*. You can put in a Web address from as far back as 1996 and see how it looked back then.

Select several popular sites or favorites you use regularly. Use the Wayback Machine to see how they have evolved and changed over the years. Then write a description of five key ways each site has changed (or failed to change). What trends can you spot? What does this say about the use of the Web for customer service?

Consider this Case

Weeding Out the Unprofitable Customer

Bruno LeBron was recently assigned as the technology officer for a midsized, business-to-business (B2B) consulting firm. His company offered other businesses help with planning locations for new stores, restaurants, and the like. While great service to clients has always been a core value of the company, Bruno was concerned that his people were spending too much time with e-service to customers or prospects who were not profitable. And, too often, they were gabbing among themselves instead of working efficiently with clients. "How can I get my people to spend time and effort only with the clients who matter?" he wondered.

Then he hit on an idea after reading an online "white paper" about business rules[4] and the Internet. That's it, he thought, I'll put certain rules into place that prevent a lot of wasted time. As he thought this idea through, he decided to have his tech

people configure the call-handling systems so that his employees (1) could not use electronic chat to gab with other employees internally, (2) could not deal with customers outside the employee's assigned specialty, and (3) could handle calls only from clients and potential clients who are deemed as high value. "That should do it," he thought. "I'll minimize the *jibber-jabber* (his term) and keep people focused on real clients and real problems."

Probes

1. To what extent do you think Bruno's approach will work?
2. What are some possible negative side-effects of implementing such a system?
3. If you were Bruno's boss, what would you recommend?

Consider this Case

The Future of the Internet

What does the future of the Internet look like? Many people have written about what has been described as one of humanity's greatest technologies. But, time marches on and technology changes rapidly. For example, while virtually all Internet users used to enter through some portal software such as Microsoft's Internet Explorer or Foxfire's Mozilla. People now access the Net via cell phones, tablets, and other devices, making its reach even greater and its impact quite profound. When experts

are asked if they think that business is exploiting the Internet's full potential, most feel it's barely scratching the surface of what we can do with this kind of communication technology. Experts, for example, say that we can see new product announcements that involve networked devices almost daily. They expect to see many billions of devices using the Net to communicate with each other. This is not just for human communication, which has been tremendously valuable, or human sharing of knowledge, which has also been very valuable, but it can also be used for managing and controlling various devices.

Devices will become able to communicate with each other such that, for example, entertainment systems could be manageable through the Network and even household and office devices can be controlled via smart phones. Once these devices are able to communicate with each other, it means that third parties can build software that services those devices, interacts with them, and manages them. This can add a whole new dimension to customer service.

Probes

1. If, in fact, the Internet can provide many more ways that devices can communicate with each other, what are some implications for customer service?
2. What kinds of new expectations might customers hold regarding online repairs, adjustments, and new features?
3. Describe how such "futuristic" online services might possibly affect an organization you work in or are familiar with. Be creative.

Building a Customer Service Strategy: Your Ongoing Case

Let's go back to the ongoing case you selected. This will be either your current employer, a specific organization you want to work in, or one of the two hypothetical organizations described in Chapter 1: Independent Auto Sales and Service (IAS) or Network Nutrition Distributors (NND). Now consider the following questions as you develop a customer service strategy:

Strategy Planning Questions

1. Review the Web site for your company or for companies similar to IAS or NND. Use the "Wayback Machine" found at *http://archive.org/web/web.php* to look at the progression of the Web site. Write a report covering the major improvements made over time.
2. Develop a plan for further improvement of the above Web site based on the ideas discussed in this chapter. Include a plan for prioritizing the steps you recommend.
3. Research the expansion of the use of mobile communication devices as these affect your chosen business. How could the company better provide service via smart phone or tablet apps, better TXT capabilities, and the like. If you are reporting on your own (real) company, include findings from an interview with someone in the organization involved with technology planning. What are their priorities?

Notes

1. The author acknowledges the work of Dr. Christopher G. Jones, Professor of Accounting at California State University—Northridge for developing some of the material for this chapter.
2. Forrester Research data cited by blogger Shawn Graham in "The Dismal State of Web-Based Customer Service," August 15, 2011, *www.shawngraham.me.*
3. Graham, The Dismal State of Web-Based Customer Service.
4. An example of such a "white paper" is one by Jackson Wilson, "Business Rules and the Internet: The Good, the Bad, and the Ugly." Vendor whitepaper published February 1, 2006, *http://callcenter.knowledgestorm.com/search.*

LIFE: Insight

The second letter in our acronym is "I" for "insight." Customer service professionals (and hopefully that includes all of us) greatly improve their ability to build customer loyalty gaining insight into two areas:

1. potential turnoffs customers may experience, and
2. changing trends in dealing with customers and their needs.

Attention to these concerns can head off the kinds of problems that leave the customer feeling less than satisfied or even mistreated.

The next two chapters focus on these insights and how professionals can minimize the potential damage to relationships felt when our company fails to deliver the best in service. Chapter 6 focuses on ways we can identify and deal with potential turnoffs that can reduce loyalty. Chapter 7 discusses insight into emerging trends that may be changing the landscape in customer service. The idea of these chapters is to stimulate thinking about these concerns and generate ideas for ways we can avoid damage to our loyalty-building efforts. So, let's consider the "insights" we need to develop to provide consistently exceptional customer service.

CHAPTER 6

Recognize and Deal with Customer Turnoffs
The Customer Keeps Score

After reading this chapter you should be able to

1. Sharpen your insight into the pet peeves customers have about poor service.

2. Categorize customer turnoffs as stemming from value, systems, or people problems.

3. Understand that reducing customer turnoffs may be the best form of advertising.

4. Appreciate how great value arises from moving people beyond satisfaction in their **"zone of indifference"** into the category of loyal customer.

The Way It Is...Breakdown on the Highway

A cross-country traveler tells this story:

On a recent cross-country trip, my tire blew out on the Ohio Turnpike south of Toledo. It was 6 p.m. on Friday, the temperature hovered in the upper 90s, and traffic was heavy. The right rear tire blew like a bomb, and I limped onto the median to dodge the constant flow of rumbling semis. I called the American Automobile Association's (AAA) hot line on my cell phone. I was greeted by an unsympathetic monotone who mechanically sought my membership card number, expiration date, address, home phone number, complete description of my car, my mother's maiden name, and the middle name of my oldest grandchild or some such stuff. (A slight exaggeration, but that's how it felt.) All the while I am attempting to explain to her the imminent danger of being crushed by a big rig roaring by at 80 mph.

"Exactly where are you?" she asked. I tried to explain my general location. That wasn't good enough. I'd need to give her an exact mileage marker. So I trekked up the median in 98-degree heat, screaming into the cell phone over the roar of the trucks, until I could see a mileage marker. She then told me that a tow truck would be there "in 45 minutes or less" and that I was to jump out of the car when I saw him coming to flag him down. This, apparently, so that he would know which white Lexus with a blown-out tire in the median at mileage marker 68 of the Ohio Turnpike was mine.

Fifty minutes later I called for an update. "Any possibility that the truck will actually get here today?" I asked. A different, and more sympathetic, service rep answered this time; and after going through the membership card info all over again, he told me he would "check to see if they'd received my call!" I waited on hold for four minutes. I was not encouraged. He then, to his credit, at least apologized ("I'm sorry about the wait. The truck was called to an accident up the road.") and promised me the truck would be there in "25 minutes or less." I waited.

This story has a happier ending. The truck driver—Paul, it said on his shirt—was a very nice man. He immediately apologized and told me he was literally 50 miles away when he got the call. He then jumped to work on my tire and I was on the road again. I also had a pleasant surprise: My newly purchased

---

car had a full-size spare tire mounted on a matching wheel. I was anticipating one of those crummy emergency donuts and a trip to the tire store before I could continue my travel. Thank you, Lexus!

Paul was a lifesaver. If I had attempted to change the tire myself, I would have lost it when discovering the special socket for the locking lug nuts. Paul knew his stuff, and I somehow felt secure in the shadow of his huge towing rig. We chatted pleasantly and he worked efficiently and, although the "45 minutes or less" turned out to be an hour and 18 minutes, I was saved as a Triple-A customer by a tow-truck operator named Paul from Toledo, Ohio.

But there were moments when AAA ran a serious risk of losing me, a customer since 1984. Paul's behavior overcame the indifferent telephone behaviors of the AAA employees. And Lexus moved me one step toward customer loyalty by providing a real spare tire.

We have all experienced customer service that leaves something to be desired. While virtually all companies tout their great service, customer turnoffs inevitable pop up with individual companies and sometimes with whole industries.

If ever we have a witnessed a textbook case of a great industry morphing into a panoply of customer service debacles, just look at commercial air travel. Customer turnoffs range from unfair and undecipherable fares to petty (and often arbitrary) charges for baggage, schedule changes, substandard overpriced food, and the list goes on. A once pleasurable travel option has become a veritable fountain of customer complaints.

Another industry whose reputation has generally suffered from service problems is the cable TV providers. The term "cable guy" has become a punch line reference to poor service, overcharging, and all manner of annoyances. Of course, it is unfair to paint a whole industry with the same broad brush. Brighthouse Networks, which serves areas of Florida, has a strong reputation generally. But even they face the everyday challenge of providing consistent service excellence. A couple who recently moved to Florida had heard many positive references to Brighthouse and even greeted the installer telling him how much they were looking forward to the company's service. The installer looked baffled—like he had never heard of such high expectations from a customer. Unfortunately, he failed to live up to the expectations having done a poor job that required several return visits from other Brighthouse technicians. When the customer called to report problems, they received exceptional telephone support: positive, upbeat, helpful call center people. Unfortunately, the repair people (some of whom were independent contractors hired by Brighthouse) did not always measure up to the sunny dispositions of the call center folks. On balance, Brighthouse seems to be a good company, but even their emphasis on service sometimes fails to measure up. One significant challenge for any organization is to produce consistent, turnoff free service—a huge order. Everyday disappointments plague many customers, even in today's so-called "service economy."

BE AWARE. BE VERY AWARE—RECOGNIZE PET PEEVES ABOUT CUSTOMER SERVICE

Try this: With a group of people—the larger the better—ask for a show of hands in response to the question "Can you remember a poor experience you have had as a customer?" Then ask "Can you remember a great experience you have had as a customer?" Typically, people will very quickly raise hands for the first question and take a few seconds longer to respond to the second one (if they respond at all). The point is that negative experiences—turnoff, as we'll call them in this chapter—stick in our mind and are quickly remembered.

Any time you gather a few people together and ask them to describe some pet peeves about their experiences as customers you'll get an earful. Virtually all of us can recall situations where we feel we were treated poorly, or where we bought products or services that just didn't measure up.

Customer service training sessions often begin by having the group talk about specifically irritating experiences and generate a list of gripes. You may find it useful to articulate some of your own pet peeves. Take a moment to make a list of *specific* things about customer service that turn you off.

LOOK INSIDE

My Pet Peeves in Customer Service

Quickly list 10 specific turnoffs you experience as a customer. What kinds of things irritate you when doing business? Think about several customer contexts: retail, repair services, restaurants, government agencies, and so on. Cite examples and be as specific as possible about what exactly irritates you. Don't just say "poor service" or "low quality."

1. _____
2. _____
3. _____
4. _____
5. _____
6. _____
7. _____
8. _____
9. _____
10. _____

Extensive research would predict that some of these turnoffs may be on your list:

- Being ignored or receiving rude or indifferent service
- Having to wait too long
- Repair work that did not fix the problem
- Products with defective parts or parts missing
- Advertised sale items that are not in stock
- Merchandise prices not marked, forcing a price check at the cashier
- Dirty facilities (especially restaurants or rest rooms)
- Bad acoustics, noisy environment
- Phone calls put on hold or forcing you to select from a long menu of choices
- Employees lacking product knowledge (and who may try to bluff the customer)
- High-pressure sales tactics
- Employees talking down to you or using confusing jargon
- Inflexibility when you make a request

Everyone has examples of irritating experiences as customers.

Do you see some of your pet peeves on this list? Most people will, although there are many other possibilities, as well.

GAINING INSIGHT: WHAT TURNS CUSTOMERS OFF?

Winning a battle requires knowing the enemy. The first tactic in our quest to win at customer service is to know what turns people off. What kinds of things can lead to a serious risk of losing a customer, associate, or employee—perhaps forever?

"What kinds of things do turn customers off?" Research by your author analyzed almost 2,000 open-ended comments. The data identified three categories of customer turnoffs that disqualify organizations from earning loyalty: value, systems, and people. We will elaborate on these categories in this chapter. The data also revealed that the following 10 turnoffs accounted for 97 percent of all comments cited by the study's participants: [1]

VALUE TURNOFFS: These include such things as:

- Poor guarantee or failure to back up products
- Quality not as good as expected
- Price too high for value received
- Overly complicated or difficult-to-use products

SYSTEMS TURNOFFS: These include such thing as:

- Slow service or help not available
- Business place dirty, messy, or cluttered
- Low selection or poor availability of product
- Inconvenient location, layout, parking, or access

PEOPLE TURNOFFS: These include the kinds of behavioral things we discussed in Chapter 2 such as:

- Lack of courtesy, friendliness, or attention
- Employees who lack knowledge or are not helpful
- Sloppy appearance, poor grooming, or annoying mannerisms
- Distracting clothing, piercing, or tattoos

Follow-up interviews and further study seem to confirm that these categories provide a useful framework for identifying root causes of customer dissatisfaction. Let's look at each in more depth.

Value Turnoffs

A fundamental turnoff for customers is the feeling that they receive poor value from a product or service. In short, shoddy products or sloppy work can put customers through the roof.

POOR QUALITY RELATIVE TO PRICE CAN BE A VALUE TURN-OFF   Value can be simply defined as *quality relative to price paid*. If you purchase an inexpensive, throwaway item at a discount store—say a 79 cent pen—you may not be upset if it doesn't last very long. But buy a $79 gold fountain pen (probably called a "writing instrument" since it costs so much) that leaks in your shirt pocket and you'd be furious.

If you sign a contract for a gym membership and personal trainer but the trainer is tone-deaf to your particular needs, you'll experience a value turnoff. If you make a major purchase of an automobile, appliance, computer, or professional service and it quits working or fails to meet your needs, you will experience a value turnoff.

> Value is a function of a product's quality relative to its price.

TOP LEADERS DEFINE THE "VALUE PROPOSITION"   The major responsibility for providing customers with appropriate value (and avoiding value turnoffs) lies with the top leadership of the organization. It's the executive decision makers in a company who determine the products or services that will be sold. They define what marketers call the **value proposition**—what the company intends to exchange with its customers. In a one-person enterprise, the owner determines the quality/pricing formula which defines value. If you run a lemonade stand, you determine how many lemons and how much sugar you will use. (Ideally, you check with your customers to see how they like it.) If you start an auto sales business, you will need to choose if you want to sell Hyundai or Lexus, Ford or Lincoln. You may opt for a new car dealership or a preowned car lot that specializes in low-cost, basic transportation. If you offer tax preparation services, you will need to decide whether you hire clerks who input data into software programs or certified accountants who can advise clients on tax planning.

Any of these strategies can work fine but the perception of value (product quality relative to price) may be different in the eyes of your customers.

While other people in an organization can affect value, the top leaders bear the major responsibility for ensuring an appropriate value proposition. The responsibility for minimizing value turnoffs lies with them.

Systems Turnoffs

Say the word *systems* and many people think of computers or phones. In the context of customer service, however, the term *systems* is broader than that. The term is used here to describe any *process, procedure,* or *policy used to "deliver" the product or service to the customer.* Systems are the processes we use to get value to our customer. When seen like this, systems will also include such nontechy things as:

- Company location, layout, parking facilities, phone accessibility
- Employee training and staffing
- Record-keeping or order-writing systems for handling customer transactions
- Policies regarding guarantees and product returns
- Delivery or pick-up services
- Merchandise displays
- Customer follow-up procedures
- Billing and accounting processes

Systems turnoffs have to do with any process, procedure, or policy associated with getting goods and services to customers.

MANAGERS ARE RESPONSIBLE FOR ORGANIZATIONAL SYSTEMS   The responsibility for minimizing system turnoffs lies with managers in most organizations. This is because systems changes often require spending organizational resources (e.g., for new locations, remodeling, additional staffing and training, and added delivery services) which must be authorized by managers. Nonmanagement employees can and should be involved in suggesting systems changes, however. Management can get some of its best change ideas from employees at all levels. But ultimately, a manager must initiate and provide resources for a systems/process change.

System turnoffs must be addressed by managers who have the authority to spend money to fix them.

How important are systems? While every organization needs systems for doing business in a consistent and orderly manner, some people argue that the majority of customer service

---

ANOTHER LOOK
Distracting Web sites Diminish Value

Sometimes less is more. Many businesses add so many bells and whistles to a Web site (or a print document, for that matter) while overlooking how this can damage the viewer's experience. This "design overkill" may actually make the user's job more difficult rather than seamlessly getting customers needed information. Usefulness takes a back seat.

For example, he first thing you see when you open up the Web site of a Pizza place in a major city, is an animated status bar telling you that the Web site is loading. Okay. I think we kinow that. Then, a red ball bounces up and down as text displaying the restaurant's name juts randomly across the page. Finally, the full Web site opens.

Next, customers are greeted to a photo of a street scene of crowded patrons along with a list of menu options which make a loud "blip" noise when you move your cursor over them. This visual business serves no real purpose.

Conspicuously absent from this first look at the website is what the customer usually wants! The three most vital pieces of information—the restaurant's hours, a phone number, and where the place is located—require multiple clicks and some tenacity.

For most customers, a flashy animation exploding across the screen (with sound effects, no less) is an irritating distraction from finding out simple information about a business. Customers may well experience a turnoff that does not bode well for building a relationship. Don't let the "form" overwhelm the "function" for your customer.

Source: Adapted from "Overdesign Is a Major Customer Turnoff," on a blog by Steven R. Jolly, Tuesday, February 21, 2012, *http://www.srj.net/blog/2012/2/21/overdesign-is-a-major-customer-turnoff.html.*

turnoffs are caused by systems mistakes or the illogical application of systems. The converse, however, is true as well.

LACK OF CONSISTENCY IS OFTEN A SYSTEMS TURN-OFF Business consultant Michael Gerber believes that systems may well be the most important key to business success. He cites hamburger giant McDonald's as an example. In an excerpt from a brochure advertising Gerber's "The E-Myth Seminar," Gerber describes working with a client named Murray, who was so tied up in the day-to-day work of his business that he failed to grow a successful company. Gerber calls this episode "The Day I Fell in Love with McDonald's." His description helps us better understand the importance of good systems.

> When my meeting with Murray ended, I was exhausted. I had pages of notes, hours of conversations swirling in my head, and a long drive home. I needed a few minutes to collect my thoughts. So, I pulled into a McDonald's to grab a bite and sort out my notes.

He goes on to talk about being confused and not knowing where to start with his client Murray's company. Murray loved his product and had big dreams for the future. But Gerber felt that something was wrong, something he couldn't put his finger on. And then it hit him:

> Maybe its fate, but that day was the first time I was in a McDonald's twice in the same day. Suddenly, from the corner of my eye, I watched a lady approach the counter, and the young girl who was serving asked if she could take her order. Nothing out of the ordinary. But there was something about what happened that caught my interest. It was both what she said and her manner of saying it.

He goes on to say that he'd been to McDonald's restaurants from coast-to-coast, was served by all types of employees, and, regardless of where he was or who served him, felt comfortable, because he knew what to expect and felt in control of his experience. He goes on to conclude that

> at that moment I knew the secret of McDonald's success. Wow! What an amazing discovery. Instantly I could see that this secret can work in any business... The essence of the secret... that they have a system for everything. Regardless of who is working on a shift, the entire staff is taught the system.... There is no indecision. No confusion. No hesitation. No sour faces. No frustrated looks. Everything works like a well-oiled machine.

Gerber's observations illustrate the importance of effective systems in any business. It is clear, effective systems that can create comfort and confidence for both employees and customers. Failure to design and train people on effective systems not only negates the usefulness of systems but can result in customer service turnoffs.

> *Creating and maintaining consistently excellent systems is a major responsibility of management.*

To repeat an important reminder: "Systems turnoffs" refer to much more than technology. In the context of customer service, "systems" encompass a wide range of factors ranging from product selection, business location, policies and procedures, customer convenience and comfort efforts, staffing, employee training, and, of course, technology systems as well. As you can imagine, systems problems include a multitude of sins.

> *Systems turnoffs involve much more than just technology glitches. They arise when company processes irritate or inconvenience customers.*

When transactions are unnecessarily complicated, inefficient, or troublesome for people as customers or employees, they experience systems turnoffs. Complaints about long lines, slow service, poor selection, untrained employees, workplace appearance, and poor signage are examples of systems problems.

> *Making things too complicated for customers can cause systems turnoffs.*

ANOTHER LOOK

Customers Turn Off When You Make Them Log In

Does your company "run like clockwork"? Are your accountants pleased with how smoothly everything moves along? Are your managers content with how customers are managed throughout your system? If so, watch out! Customers are often left frustrated by a company's smooth-running and standardized, but inflexible, policies. Your present methods may include policies and procedures that are convenient for the company, but utterly frustrating for your customers.

One common example: Do you make customers register an account in order to leave comments on your blog, access information, or shop? You could be driving them away. A study by Blue Research for Janrain found 86 percent of respondents get annoyed by having to create new accounts on Web sites, an increase of 10 percent from the same survey last year. While 14 percent complete the registration despite being annoyed, more than half (54 percent) say they either leave the site or don't return again, and 26 percent go to a different site.

Source: April 16, 2012, *http://janrain.com/news-articles/customers-turn-when-you-make-them-log-survey-says/*

Consultant Ron Kaufman tells of a poor service experience that he said was "enough to make me wonder whether anyone is listening at all!" For example, there's the case of "The Conference Rate" at Hilton Hotel in Los Angeles:[2]

Kaufman was making arrangements to attend a large Conference in Los Angeles. As a frequent flyer, he had many award coupons offering a 60 percent discount from usual hotel rates. He called Hilton Hotels in California to make his reservations.

The reservations clerk was infinitely helpful. First, she took my name, then my contact numbers. She confirmed the dates, my room preference and credit card number. She asked if I was a Hilton Honors Club member, which I was not. She signed me up on the spot and then remarked: "Now that you are a Hilton Honors Club member, I can offer you an even lower rate, and an upgraded Towers room on a higher floor. A fruit basket will be waiting for you upon arrival." I was delighted. And my special discount rate was just US$85 per night.

In signing off, I said, "Thank you for your help. I am looking forward to staying at the Hilton during the conference." "The conference?" she shot back quickly. "What conference are you attending?"

I replied that I was attending the American Society for Training and Development's 50th Annual Conference at Disneyland. She said quickly, "Mr. Kaufman, if you are attending a conference during your stay, you must use our special conference rate of US$112." I laughed at her proposal and stated that I was happy with the special rate she had already confirmed on my behalf. "Oh no," she repeated. "If you are coming for a conference, you must use the special conference rate. We have a block of rooms set aside for conference participants on a lower floor. These rooms are specially reserved for the people who are attending the conference."

My protests were to no avail. She checked with her supervisor, who concurred. "I'm sorry, but that's our policy," she said without much concern. I surrendered to her insistence, listened as she cancelled my Hilton Honors Club reservation, declined to have her book me back into the same hotel at the higher conference rate, and hung up the phone in disbelief.

I called right back. I reached a different reservations clerk and made another reservation. I used my frequent flyer award coupon and the new Hilton Honors Club membership number I had received in the previous phone call. This time I kept my mouth shut about attending any conference!

I paid just US$85 when I went to Los Angeles. I enjoyed the Hilton Towers room and enjoyed the complimentary fruit basket upon arrival. No thanks to Hilton's absurd policy and customer-unfriendly procedures, though.

Somewhere deep inside the marketing department of Hilton Hotels, yield management professionals have carefully calculated the maximum rate they can, and will, charge participants at an international conference. Meanwhile conference participants are also thinkers, communicators, and frequent flyers ... real-live customers! Hilton Hotels, are you listening?

REQUIRED LOG-IN MAY BE A SYSTEM TURNOFF   More businesses are recognizing the frustration for customers when they are required to log-in in order to shop. When you walk into a department store, clerks don't ask for your name and password before letting you shop. A common online procedure has become a systems turnoff for many customers.

Of course, the requirement to have customers register before shopping has advantages which many customers appreciate. For example, if you expect to do repeat business with the company (say, you plan to keep shopping on Amazon.com), their having your shipping information and your credit card number provides quick checkout convenience. But customers should not be forced to do so. Companies need to think through the trade-off between what's potentially good for the company (customer data for possible marketing, convenience in fulfilling an order, etc.) with what's good for the customer (ease of use, quick service, etc.). At least allow the option of shopping without registering.

Turnoffs arise when company benefit outweighs customer benefit. If the company forces customers to do something solely because it benefits the company, the turnoff likelihood will be high.

SYSTEMS TURNOFFS INCLUDE EXCESSIVELY SLOW SERVICE   Research shows that a Number 1 turnoff for many customers is slow service. One of the first frustrations people cite is slow service or having to wait. We live in a society that values speed and efficiency and that resents things that slow us down.

Employees who lack the knowledge to answer customer questions and organizations that have just one person capable of fulfilling a key function are likely to deliver slow service. Telephone menus that are unnecessarily complicated (press 1 for such and such, 2 for so and so, etc.) may annoy customers if they slow down the service. Repetitious paperwork requirements (such as requiring that you complete name/address/SS number, etc. of every form) or lack of convenient parking or accessible locations can lead to needlessly slow service and are examples of systems problems.

Company systems determine the speed of service because they involve staffing, layout of the business, accessibility, efficiency of delivery, employee-efficiency training, and so on. Once again, the responsibility for implementing and maintaining effective systems lies with a company's management because decisions to add personnel, provide additional training, change locations, implement new delivery methods, or even rearrange the office layout require spending money.

Customers are easily turned off by inappropriately slow service.

AUTOMATIC BILLING MAY BE A SYSTEMS TURN-OFF   Companies love to have people agree to automatic billing or renewals of service contracts. On one level, these can provide a convenience to customers, but for some they result in renewed services the customer may no longer want or need. Gym memberships or newspaper or magazine subscription—even charitable donations—that automatically bill the customer can accumulate leaving customers frustrated or upset. Yes, you can keep a customer using fine print renewals but you do so at the cost of damaging the relationship. It has become a common occurrence for people, when reviewing their credit card statements, to be surprised by an unnoticed auto-payment for something no longer wanted.

People Turnoffs

Our third category, people turnoffs, almost always arises from communication problems. Employees who fail to communicate appropriately, both verbally (with words) and nonverbally (without words), can quickly irritate a customer. Some examples of people turnoffs are as follows:

- Employees who fail to greet or even smile at a customer
- People who give inaccurate information or convey a lack of knowledge

- Employees chatting among themselves or allowing telephone interruptions while ignoring a customer
- Behaviors that project a rude or uncaring attitude
- Sales tactics that come across as high pressure
- Work locations that appear dirty or sloppy
- Employees who are dressed inappropriately or have poor grooming
- Employees with body piercing, tattoos (although such personal choices may be appropriate for certain clientele)
- Any communicated message that causes the customer to feel uncomfortable

All Employees Are Responsible for Minimizing People Turn-Offs

Communication turnoffs often result when employees are ignorant of the kinds of "messages" they are sending to customers.

Employees at all organizational levels can create satisfaction versus motivation, often unconsciously. In most cases these turnoffs arise because people fail to understand how they come across to other people. Everyone interested in having a successful career would be wise to become constant students of communication. Even the most subtle or unconscious behaviors can communicate the wrong messages and result in lost customers.

People turnoffs make customers feel discounted. They arise when employees who represent the company project inappropriate behaviors, indifferent attitudes, or mechanical tone (as we discussed in Chapter 2). People turnoffs include such things as rudeness, poor nonverbal behaviors such as lack of eye contact, inappropriate dress and grooming, autocratic bosses, and any behaviors that convey a low level of caring or consideration for others.

Responsibility for reducing people turnoffs lies with every employee. Often people are unaware of how their behaviors communicate. Training can help raise awareness, but ultimately the individual staff member will decide how he or she will interact with customers and other employees.

HIRE GOOD PEOPLE-PEOPLE   Because teaching specific behaviors is often difficult, hiring people with good attitudes and interpersonal skills is especially important. Some successful employers constantly recruit people they have seen working in other customer situations. When they meet a person in another business who gives them great service, they encourage that person to join their company. One man who owns a chain of restaurants carries extra business cards to give to people he gets to meet in other transactions. When such a person does a great job selling him shoes or handling a billing problem, he hands them a card and asks them to contact him if they ever want to consider another job. Notice that these people may have no

---

ANOTHER LOOK
Business-to-Business People Turnoffs

A study by consulting firm McKinsey & Company looked at actions of sales reps that actually turn off their B2B customers (business to business). A survey of more than 1,200 companies in the United States and Europe found these traits to be destructive to business relationships:

- Too much contact: 35 percent
- Lack of knowledge about their own or competitors' products/services: 20 percent
- Lack of industry knowledge about usefulness of product/service to customer: 9 percent

- Sales style too aggressive: 8 percent
- Customer forgotten/ignored after the sale: 8 percent

Other turnoffs mentioned included inconsistent sales teams, slow response, too little contact, and no single point of contact.

Source: Adapted from McKinsey & Co., *http://www.cfo.com/article.cfm/14501405*, June 2010.

experience in the restaurant business, but their customer service skills are "**transferrable**"—they can be taught the specifics of the restaurant business. What they bring to the job are excellent service skills and attitudes.

People communicate the way they do because they have learned that behavior. Changes come slowly and only with considerable effort. The best way to change communication behavior (or help others do so) is by raising awareness, modeling new behaviors, having people try the new behavior, and reinforcing the improvement. Companies can benefit from using scripts or scripted phrases and from clearly identifying **communication taboos**—certain messages, terms, and nonverbal behaviors that are unacceptable. Typically such taboos include crude or profane language, degrading comments about others (including competitors), or slovenly appearance.

In fairness, some people are unaware of how their behaviors come across to others. They may be tone-deaf to the ways they communicate or fail to communicate. Training can help raise awareness, but ultimately the individual staff member will decide how he or she will interact with customers and other employees. Hopefully, they will realize the impact of poor skills on their career and their organization.

Here is a brief recap of the three turnoff categories as applied to the road-trip experience described at the beginning of the chapter:

> Companies benefit from identifying certain communication taboos—words or phrases that should be avoided.

Value Turnoffs	Systems Turnoffs	People Turnoffs
Had paid my dues for years and never used AAA's road service before. Was not sure I was getting a good deal.	Policy of saying "45 minutes or less" was initially reassuring, but when the deadline was not met, it was a turnoff. Required much information before allowing the driver to explain his problem.	Unsympathetic tone of voice, no expressions of empathy.

In the case of the Ohio Turnpike road trip, factors that initially were turnoffs (tone of voice, uncaring attitude, demands for information, and inaccurate promises about response time) were mitigated by the good service of a dedicated employee: the truck driver who was personable, friendly, and reassuring. He worked with expertise and efficiency. And personality!

And that is largely the point of this discussion. Turnoffs happen. By recognizing and categorizing them, companies can assign responsibility and attack them.

Know That Reducing Turnoffs Is the Best Advertising

No company can succeed if it lets turnoffs aggravate its customers to the point where they quit doing business with it. A typical company will lose 10–30 percent of customers each year because it turned them off. This touches off a treadmill-like scramble to replace the lost customers with new customers—an effort- and cost-intensive process. Employee turnover—loss of internal customers—is often a result of turnoffs as well. A far more efficient process is to keep and build upon the current customer base.

Customer and employee loyalty is like an election held every day, and people vote with their feet. If dissatisfied, they walk (sometimes run) to a competitor. When customers cannot realistically switch to another company (in the case of a public utility or government agency, for example), they do anything within their power to get even, starting with complaining loudly. And if those turned-off customers are employees, they respond by producing shoddy work, undermining their supervisors, aggravating their coworkers, and creating all sorts of mischief and counterproductive activity.

> Customers "vote" with their feet—they'll quickly go to a competitor if your service comes up short.

To sustain repeat business, a company must generate positive word of mouth by reducing the turnoffs and exceeding customer expectations. People talk to others about a service

---

Word of mouth is still the best form of advertising.

experience when it is exceptional or out of the ordinary. Bad news travels faster and further than good news. A company can have the best products available. But if it fails to develop insight into potential customer turnoffs and provide a positive customer experience, few people will notice the difference between that company and its competition.

CREATE LOYAL CUSTOMERS

Thinking about customer turnoffs is particularly important when we consider that the correlation between mere customer satisfaction and loyalty is rather tenuous. Even satisfied customers may be neutral toward their relationship with a business. They may feel little or no sense of **engagement** and the littlest thing can push them over the edge toward dissatisfaction. Service levels may meet their needs adequately but fail to motivate their continuing loyalty. Just as motivation researchers discovered long ago, satisfied workers are not necessarily motivated workers. They may be satisfied because they don't have to work very hard or because they like fooling around with their coworkers—even though they accomplish little. Satisfied workers are not necessarily motivated workers. Likewise, satisfied customers cannot be assumed to be motivated repeat customers. Things are okay but there is little to engage the customer in the long run.

The Zone of Indifference

Actually, customers who are satisfied may be *inert*, not motivated to buy more or strengthen their business dealings with a company. Their satisfaction simply means the *absence of dissatisfaction*, not the motivation to become a loyal customer. A "zone of indifference" lies between the dissatisfied and the motivated (see Exhibit 6.1).

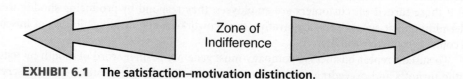

Dissatisfied — Satisfied — Motivated

Zone of Indifference

EXHIBIT 6.1   The satisfaction–motivation distinction.

The challenge, then, is to get customers beyond satisfaction to *motivation*. This is best done by responding to customer perceptions and expectations.

Value the Importance of Service Recovery

Despite the best efforts of customer-savvy people, problems inevitably will arise. Problem situations should not be viewed as tragic, but as opportunities to further solidify customer loyalty. Anyone can give good service when customer transactions go smoothly, but it is precisely when special needs or problems arise that customer skills are put to the test.

Why do customer problems often provide opportunities? Because the payoff for recovering potentially lost customers is actually an *increased* likelihood that they will be loyal to you—they are more likely to be motivated according to our model. It sounds strange, but studies have shown that a customer who encounters a problem with a company—and has that problem addressed promptly and effectively—will be even *more likely to remain loyal* than a customer who never had a problem. Even in cases in which the customer's problem is not resolved 100 percent in his or her favor, the loyalty still increased. Just the fact that the problem was acknowledged and addressed seems to be the key variable in strengthening the customer relationship. This is a powerful argument for opening the communication channels with customers.

An old saying claims that "people don't care how much you know until they know how much you care." A genuine sense of concern for customers must be on the bedrock of any organization's customer loyalty efforts.

> Showing customers that you truly care is fundamental to building loyalty.

Customer Loyalty Grows When Service Is Your Core Business

Having a "service department" should be seen as a redundancy. Every department exists only to serve its customers, internal and external. Customer turnoffs arise when companies make service something less than an integral part of their operating philosophy. When companies seek to isolate service as some special function or program, the results will be disappointing. Service begins to be meaningful when it is an internal dynamic—when service is the underpinning of the enterprise.

> Service must be seen as the very essence of your business, not a side function.

Customers are quick to see the depth of a company's commitment to service. The organization that truly distinguishes itself in the eyes of its customers remains rare. Most companies have not made enough of an impression one way or another for their customers to even think about them, much less to share these thoughts with others. That element of loyalty—recommending a company to others—is lost because of undistinguished service.

Earn Your Customer's Loyalty with Three Steps

How can we help a customer step outside the zone of indifference and become a "raving fan" of our company? Three steps can provide the essence of a sound strategy:

1. Continuously sharpen insights into areas where you may be falling short.
2. Reduce or eliminate value, systems, and people turnoffs.
3. Exceed customer expectations to create a positive awareness.

The first step in reducing or eliminating turnoffs is to persistently recognize their existence. Categorizing potential turnoffs as value, systems, or people helps identify who should shoulder major responsibility for dealing with each.

How can we tell if we are turning off customers? The short answer is to put yourself in the shoes of your customers. Objectively assess the way they are treated and compare this with how other companies may be treating them. As Yogi Berra said, "You can observe a lot by just watching." Once you assess the possibility of a turnoff, the second step is to fix the specific problem quickly and to the degree that is possible.

We will discuss the third step in a sound strategy in Chapters 10–12. For now, think about the importance of playing defense—of consistently taking all reasonable steps to reduce any

> ### SERVICE SNAPSHOT
>
> ### Monika's Attitude of Service
>
> Monika works at a medium-sized credit union. In her two years there, she has won repeated awards and bonuses for her effectiveness as a teller and member-services representative. Her supervisor consistently ranks Monika's work as outstanding and her opportunities in the financial service industry look rosy. When asked about her customer service "technique," she laughed and said she doesn't really have a technique; she just tries to treat people the way she'd want to be treated. "I try to anticipate anything that might be annoying or uncomfortable for my customers and fix it before it becomes a problem. Sometimes that's as simple as saying 'I'm sorry you had to wait so long—we are a bit busy today.' People seem to appreciate that you acknowledge little problems."
>
> Monika pays attention to little things, avoiding people turnoffs as much as possible. When members (what credit unions call their customers) approach her desk, she immediately looks up and greets with a smile. If she's busy helping someone else, she still makes eye contact to acknowledge the customer and let him or her know she'll be available in a moment. She is especially good at handling transactions quickly and efficiently without rushing the customer. When asked how she prepared for her career, she stated that when she was a little girl her favorite toy was a cash register. She loved to play store and keep Monopoly money in a special section in the cash drawer. She even used to iron her play money to keep it crisp, she laughed!
>
> Technique aside, Monika projects a friendly, helpful attitude. She works hard to keep current on changes in systems and procedures. She knows that her customers value quick, efficient service "although some of them like to chat—which is fine." She loves her job and her customers. Serving others with professionalism and skill has its own reward, she says.

Insight into potential turnoffs is essential to service improvement.

potential customer turnoffs. This may sound like a tall order—after all, people can always find something they are unhappy with—but it is essential that we ferret out the kinds of turnoffs your customers may be experiencing. This insight is invaluable.

SOME FINAL THOUGHTS

Repositioning customers from that reasonably satisfied "zone of indifference" into the category of motivated, loyal fans requires vigilant insight into what may be turning them off. Look for value, systems, and people turnoffs and determine who in the organization can best deal with each. Value and systems problems require management attention, but employees at all levels can and should be aware of possible people turnoffs.

The analysis of potential turnoffs must be an ongoing process, not just occasional or haphazard actions. Even the best organizations make mistakes. When (not if) we make mistakes that leave the customer unhappy, we need to view these as opportunities for fixing our value proposition, systems effectiveness, or people behaviors to solidify our relationships with customers. Often such fixing requires attention to little things (yes we are back to that point).

Summary of Key Ideas

- Everyone has pet peeves about the ways they are served (or not served). Often, these are little things that have a cumulative effect in creating a dissatisfied or, minimally, an indifferent customer.
- Reducing turnoffs can be the best form of advertisement. It can also help move people out of the "zone of indifference" toward being motivated, loyal customers.
- Customer turnoffs can be usefully categorized into value, systems, and people problems. Value and systems problems are best addressed by company leaders; everyone can help eliminate people problems primarily through improving interpersonal skills.
- Value is a function of the apparent quality of a product or service relative to its cost.
- *Systems* refers to much more than just technology. Systems include anything involved with getting the product or service to the customer. Systems turnoffs arise from problems with procedures, policies, technology, training, staffing, locations, facilities, and systematic actions.

- People turnoffs are almost always communication problems. Employees communicate inappropriate "messages" by their words or nonverbal actions.
- Service recovery seeks to win back customers when they have had a disappointing experience. Customers whose problems are addressed by the company will actually be more likely to do repeat business than customers who never have a problem.
- Regularly identifying and working to reduce possible customer turnoffs can provide a basis for building customer loyalty.

Key Concepts

Communication taboos	People turnoffs	Value proposition	Zone of indifference
Engagement	Systems turnoffs	Value turnoffs	Transferable skills

Reviewing the Facts

1. Look back on your own experiences as a customer and identify situations when little things have made a difference in your buying decision. Identify examples of places you have stopped doing business. What little things pushed you out of the zone of indifference into the dissatisfied range? Be as specific as possible and remember that often dissatisfaction comes from a series of truly small, almost insignificant turnoffs. Categorize these reasons for leaving according to the three turnoffs described in this chapter.

2. Describe in your own words the three categories of customer turnoffs. Give five specific examples of each.

3. What do we mean by a "value proposition"? What are some of the questions one should consider when defining a value proposition? Who determines what that proposition will be for a given company?

4. What specific actions can companies take to best identify potential turnoffs? How does classifying them as value, systems, and people turnoffs become useful to organizational leaders?

5. Why do customers whose problems are addressed and rectified become even more loyal? What do we mean by a "value proposition"? What are some of the questions one should consider when defining a value proposition? Who determines what that proposition will be for a given company?

Applying the Ideas

1. Let's go "mystery shopping." One way we can get a clearer understanding of customer turnoffs is to observe, in a systematic way, specific behaviors in places we do business. This is called "mystery shopping" or "secret shopping." It can be an excellent way to identify possible turnoffs customers may be experiencing. In this exercise we are focusing mostly on people turnoffs.

    Assume that the behaviors described on the Sample Mystery Shopper Form (Exhibit 6.2) are important to you as a customer (and the absence of them turns you off). Make copies of that form and try a little mystery shopping. Here is how:

    a. Select a minimum of four businesses of the same type (retailers, restaurants, banks, auto dealers, etc.) to visit as a mystery shopper. Your task will be to pose as a potential shopper seeking information. You may want information about account types from banks, details on a particular computer or appliance from electronics stores, information about a particular automobile, and so forth. Then plan to visit these businesses posing as a customer.

    b. Be yourself during these visits. Don't attempt to act. Respond naturally to the employees. Maintain an open and unbiased attitude. Carefully observe what the company does well or poorly. Don't go in with a chip on your shoulder—with the attitude that you'll catch them doing something wrong—and don't overemphasize the negative. If you can't remember whether the employee did or did not do something positive, assume that he or she did.

    c. Immediately after each visit, complete an evaluation form. (In real-world mystery shopping, you can and probably should modify this data-gathering form to make it more appropriate for the specific type of businesses you will be visiting.)

    d. When you have gathered your data from four or more locations, compile a brief report describing what you found. Identify key turnoffs (by category), if possible. Comment on things done well and opportunities for improvement.

e. Write a brief report on what would you do to reduce possible turnoffs and improve the service if you owned this business? Prioritize the steps you would take. Be specific.

2. Search it out: Use the Web to identify turnoffs. Go to your preferred Internet search engine and search for information on what turns off customers in a particular type of business. Describe the nature of and number of sites that deal with this topic. How well do these sites identify or categorize the kinds of things that turn customers off?

See if you can categorize the most common turnoffs using our value–systems–people distinction? If you find other kinds of turnoffs that don't seem to fit into these three categories, identify a new category or discuss why they don't fit. (Recognize that some turnoffs can fit into more than one category.) Prepare a one- or two-page report summarizing the results of your search.

Sample Mystery Shopper Form

Name of business: _____ Date & Time: _____

Employee's name (if available):_____ Task: [what you are shopping for]

	Did	Did Not
A. When you entered, did the employee		
1. Look up, make eye contact?	_____	_____
2. Smile with a genuine smile?	_____	_____
3. Acknowledge you with an appropriate greeting?	_____	_____
4. Make you wait too long before helping you?	_____	_____
B. While assisting you, did the employee		
5. Project a positive, helpful attitude and willingness to assist?	_____	_____
6. Pay full and undivided attention to you?	_____	_____
7. Deliver accurate and speedy, but unhurried, service?	_____	_____
8. Ask you if there is anything else he/she can do for you?	_____	_____
C. Given the opportunity to offer or introduce other products, did the employee		
9. Acknowledge or identify other things that may meet your needs?	_____	_____
10. Offer further information or introduce you to others for more info?	_____	_____
11. Ask you for your business?	_____	_____
D. When the transaction/visit was over, did the employee		
12. Thank you for coming in?	_____	_____
13. Invite you to come again?	_____	_____
14. Offer a friendly goodbye?	_____	_____
E. At any time during the transaction, did the employee		
15. Ask for your name and/or call you by name?	_____	_____
16. Make you feel like a valued customer?	_____	_____
Score one point for each "did" answer. **Total:**	_____	_____

General comments or observations: What was particularly good or bad about the shopping experience?

EXHIBIT 6.2 Sample Mystery Shopper Form.

Consider this Case

The Auto Inspection Center

D'Arcy takes her car to a local inspection and emission station in her town. These inspections are required in her state and, generally, the process is relatively painless. The technician checks out her car while she fills out a simple form.

Last Tuesday, she decided to stop on the way to work to get this chore finished in time to get her license renewal sticker by the end of the month. "I'm in luck," she said to herself as she approached the open garage doors, "nobody in line ahead of me." The sign said to wait at the shop entrance. This she did, for several minutes. She could see three employees. Two were engaged in an apparently personal conversation; they were laughing and joking. The third person was standing off to the side of the shop smoking a cigarette. All three people glanced at D'Arcy, but ignored her.

After several minutes, the fellow having a smoke came to her car and said, "You here for an inspection? You're gonna have to wait a few minutes." As he started to walk away, D'Arcy said, "I really need to get to work." He said, "Yeah, okay. Hold your horses. I'll get you the paperwork." He then walked to the back of the shop and appeared to join the conversation with the other two employees, while he shuffled through a stack of papers that had accumulated on the greasy desk. The phone rang and he took the call, which sounded like a personal conversation that lasted several minutes. He finally turned back to D'Arcy and said, "Pull your car into the second bay."

Probes

1. How would you feel if you were D'Arcy?
2. If this inspection station was a government agency, is customer service really important? The customer really doesn't have a choice, so why expend efforts to give better service?
3. What types of turnoffs are displayed in this case?
4. If you were the manager of this facility, what might you do to reduce potential customer turnoffs?

Consider this Case

Mac's Stack It Deep, Sell It Cheap

Devon MacGregor, known to his many friends as "Mac," jokes about being true to his Scottish heritage when he opened his warehouse-style store selling odd lots and large quantities of basic household staples. Mac and his partner, Donnie Antonio, talked for many hours as they planned the new company launch. Donnie felt they would be better off setting up a more traditional retail store with attractive merchandise displays, lighting, and a "classier" looking place. Both men had recently graduated from State University and were committed to building a successful retail store, but they needed to get agreement on the focus of their business.

"It's all about value proposition, Donnie," Mac said. "If we try to be all things to all people, we'll be competing with all the big boys. We can't be a Walmart or a Target. We're little guys. We need to give people something different, and the best way to do that is to give great deals. Our customers are cost-conscious. Let's stick with our stack 'it deep, sell it cheap' philosophy." After considerable discussion, Donnie came to agree and that is the direction they decided to take.

Probes

1. If Mac and Donnie stick with this value proposition, how might that affect customer service? What are the pros and cons from the customers' perspective?
2. What expectations would you have as you went to shop at their store? Be specific—what would you expect it to like?
3. How can they best stick with their value proposition? What should they avoid?
4. Is customer service in such a low-cost operation less important than it would be in a full service retailer? Defend your answer.
5. How could Mac and Donnie best avoid customer turnoffs? Exceed customer expectations?

Building a Customer Service Strategy: Your Ongoing Case

Let's go back to the ongoing case you selected. This will be either your current employer, a specific organization you want to work in, or one of the two hypothetical organizations described in Chapter 1: Independent Auto Sales and Service (IAS) or Network Nutrition Distributors (NND). Now consider the following questions as you develop a customer service strategy:

Strategy Planning Activities

1. Create a mystery shopper evaluation form that would be applicable to your company. Start with the relevant items from the sample form on page 106 but delete items that are less important or not applicable. Add company-specific items. Be careful to avoid making the evaluation form too long. It can become unwieldy and will produce less effective data. Better to target the most significant items while making the form fairly easy to use.

2. Pretest the evaluation by having several evaluators use it and report their reactions. Based on such feedback, revise the form as necessary.

3. Administer your revised form to gather real data about your company and competing or similar businesses.

4. Write a report of your findings including tabulations from each measured item.

5. Conduct a debriefing meeting to discuss results of your mystery shops. Categorize turnoffs and assign responsibility for minimizing each. Be specific about the appropriate actions to be taken.

Notes

1. Kristen B. DeTienne and Paul R. Timm, "How Well Do Businesses Predict Customer Turnoffs?: A Discrepancy Analysis," *Journal of Marketing Management,* 5(2), 1996, pp. 3–10.

2. Excerpted from "Don't Let Your Systems Drive Your Customers Crazy!" by consultant/trainer Ron Kaufman, found on his Web site, *www.ronkaufman.com,* 2003.

CHAPTER 7

Insight into Emerging Trends in Customer Service

A Peek into the Future

After reading this chapter, you should be able to

1. Explain how, in addition to insights into what may turn your customers off, you need insight about how customer expectations are changing.

2. Better understand the importance of personalization, or "one-to-one" customer service.

3. Recognize some of the social and economic shifts impacting customer service for the future.

4. Apply some of the new interactivity options for marketing to individual customers.

5. Recognize that some important aspects of customer service will remain consistent.

6. Consider some new interactive marketing options.

The Way It Is (Going): Oh, the Changes We Are Seeing!

"Look at that," Roland said to Mandy as they entered the coffee shop near their office for a morning latte. "Everybody in here seems to be electronically hooked up. If they aren't texting or on cell phones, they are on the net working on something. This is like an office away from the office. Could you imagine seeing this even a few years ago?"

Roland is Mandy's 60-something boss and a good friend. Mandy is thirty years younger, but even she is impressed with the technology changes in the space of her career.

"I hate to sound like a geezer, but this whole tech-crazy world of ours is making my head spin. I remember when there were no ATMs at banks—I used to go into the bank and actually talk to people! We didn't have laser printers or cellphones. I can even remember when most televisions didn't have remotes! We had to get up and change the channel," he said a bit wistfully. "No one had a personal computer let alone a—what do they call it?—a 'tablet'." Roland shook his head as they ordered their coffee.

Then Roland said, "I had a funny experience last week when I went to Cleveland. I checked in to the hotel through a kiosk. There wasn't even a desk clerk. I sort of missed the friendly greeting of an actual human, but it did speed up the process. I talked to the manager the next day and he asked how I liked the kiosk check-in. I told him I appreciated the speed, but kinda missed the human touch. I guess I should be getting used to it. Even this old dog is starting to use smart phone aps—often to bypass humans! I do like connecting with my airline to check in online, change seats, and check departure and arrival times."

As they went to a table, Mandy said, "It really is amazing how tech can impact customer relationships—at the individual level. It's so easy to create an individual 'customer feedback loop'. My favorite businesses seem to easily tell their customers apart and remember them—and specifically what they want. Some of my friends get worried when a web site "recommends" things to them based on their recent past searches. But, to be honest, I often find that useful."

"And I really like how businesses can make and deliver a single, customized product or service—cost efficiently—to an individual customer. That has got to be great for the customers. Sort of the ultimate in individualized customer service."

"It sure ties in with what we have been focusing on at work—the idea of developing relationships with specific customers, differentiating one from the next, and treating each customer as a separate, identifiable, participant in the commercial relationship," said Roland.

"We keep talking about how our business 'values its customers' and how they are our 'principal asset'. It seems to me like this way of interacting with customers is really important. I think people are coming to expect it," said Mandy.

"If we are serious about really centering the business around individual customers," Roland said as he sipped his coffee, "we better learn to get and respond appropriately to the feedback we get from each. People are assuming a level of customization of products and services to their individual wants, and if we don't give them that we're going the way of the VCR and TVs without remotes!"

"Amen, Roland. We better get more creative, and soon," said Mandy.

Much of this book is structured around the acronym LIFE and the I in that acronym stands for insight. In the previous chapter we discussed the importance of insight into what might be turning your customers off. In this chapter we will consider insight into future directions—and new expectations—for customer service.

The term *insight* refers to understanding some changing realities about relationships and behaviors in the context of customer service. Three particular areas of change are having significant impact on customer service and loyalty: enhanced personalization, evolving **customer demographics**, and increased transparency.

PERSONALIZATION   Customers will no longer tolerate being treated as one of a demographic category. They won't accept a "one-size-fits-all" mentality. They will demand—and get—individually customized products and services. Successful companies will adapt to these new demands. They will thrive by exceeding customer expectations in "**goodness-of-fit**." They will master the art of treating each customer as an individual with special needs and wants.

CHANGING DEMOGRAPHICS   Demands of various age categories and ethnicities continue to evolve and customer service must be aware of and in sync with such changes. Younger people become active consumers at earlier ages and with increasing sophistication. At the other end of the age spectrum baby boomers are changing the image of active 60-plus buyers. The global economy requires businesses to be more aware of a broad range of cultures. The demands for individual understanding will continue to be complicated by the ethnic mix of customers and employees. These changed demographics can and will call for insight and responsiveness from successful companies.

TRANSPARENCY   How companies do business can no longer be hidden. Customers' access to pricing information, profit margins, and competitive comparisons are just a click away via the Internet. Attempts to be unduly secretive reduce trust while enlightened companies are doing just the opposite—becoming increasingly open and trusted.

How customer service is likely to be impacted by changing personalization, demographic needs, and transparency all this is the central theme of this chapter.

COMPANIES NEED TO ENHANCE "ONE-TO-ONE" PERSONALIZATION OF CUSTOMER SERVICE

The ability of today's technology to make one-to-one customer relationships possible may well be a master key to better service. In the past, keeping track of customer names and addresses, sales data, and personal preferences was a laborious and time-consuming process.

Most companies have gone far beyond keeping such customer data on note cards in a file box. Today's computers and **point-of-sale electronic data gathering** devices are commonplace and customers assume such personalization. We can now track individual preferences, poll customers about their needs, and customize services and products to meet those needs. Personalization may result in stores offering discount coupons to the customer at the checkout counter. If the customer buys a six-pack of Pepsi, the scanner generates a coupon for 50 cents off on Frito-Lay potato chips. (Frito-Lay is a division of PepsiCo.) People can also get coupons emailed to them for products they buy. For example, *Just for Men* hair-coloring products target their registered users and send them $1 off coupons via email. The customer can simply print the coupon and save a buck. The latest wrinkle is the handheld mobile phone that will provide discount coupons that can be transmitted electronically to the cash register at checkout. Customers increasingly expect such services.

Media changes have made big differences in the ways organizations communicate among their own members (internal customers) and with the world outside (external customers). In addition to the obvious speed and efficiency advantages of today's media, there are other considerations that have an impact on customer relationships. One of the most significant trends is in the increasing ability to efficiently generate personalized, one-to-one messages tailored to the needs and wants of individuals, especially customers, coworkers, and associates.

One-to-one, individually tailored messages can now be sent to huge audiences.

Communication experts have long recognized that (1) the more we know about our message receiver(s) and (2) the more we personalize a message to the receiver(s)'s wants and interests, the more effective we will be in communicating and building relationships. Customers no longer tolerate blanket approach. They expect to be communicated with as individuals. Technology applications make this easier.

We should not underestimate the power of **customized messages** in business and professional communication. In an organization's marketing function, for example, we have seen a major shift from mass marketing—sending the same messages to a large number of people in hopes that some of them will respond favorably—to individualized marketing where we send a unique personalized message to each person. Rudimentary versions of this personalization began with Word Processing, which gave us the ability to produce "merge" letters that include personalized sections interspersed with the generic message. Today, mass mailers routinely take advantage of this ability to personalize sales letters, sweepstakes entry forms, and even the envelopes they are sent in.

But companies go way beyond that. Today's technology lets us easily include past buying information and personal preferences to convey a sense that we know and understand our customer.

Today's media go beyond the simple merging of names and addresses.

Successful online retailers have taken personalization to higher levels. Amazon.com, for example, automatically tracks what you buy and recommends complimentary products. They tell you that "other customers who bought [what you bought] also bought..." Online retailers also track gift purchases you have made, making it easier to send another gift to that same recipient. Social networking sites pop up ads for products you have considered in earlier Internet searches. While such personalization may feel vaguely creepy to some who fear lost privacy, most of us take this kind of pinpointed marketing as a common fact of modern life. Companies that don't offer such customer assistance are at a disadvantage. They may be foregoing opportunities for strengthening relationships.

Indeed, we are progressively moving toward one-to-one marketing that can create long-term *relationships* with customers and provide for a wide range of their needs. Past marketing communication media such as mass media ads or junk mail sought the goal of gaining a larger *share of the market*. If, for example, your store accounts for 10 percent of all the men's wear sold in your town, mass marketing will try to get that up to 12 or 15 percent. The assumption is, of course, that a larger share of market means more profits. This, however, is becoming less of a sure thing. Mass advertising's cost-effectiveness is questionable and its results have dropped. It costs more and more money to get a new customer into your business using traditional approaches.

ANOTHER LOOK

Five Ways to Make the Most of Customer Insights

Research supported by IBM Corporation and the Pepper and Rodgers Group identify six ways companies can sharpen and focus their insights into customer needs and wants, thus creating the opportunity for delivering better service.

1. *Identify granular attributes* about customers (e.g., life-stage changes) that marketing and customer service departments can use to improve communications and offers. ("Granular" refers to the highly individualized characteristics as opposed to generalizing common traits to groups of people.) The better you know customers on an individual basis, the more targeted your offers will be.

2. *Integrate social and other unstructured data* with traditional enterprise feedback and transactional information to develop a multidimensional view of each customer. Social and unstructured data include qualitative reviews or expressions of likes and dislikes. This differs from "enterprise feedback," which tends to be raw numbers about sales, number of returns

or complaints, customer demographics, and so on, usually gathered automatically via software systems.

3. *Leverage* customer intelligence to deliver more targeted communications, which can help strengthen the customer–company relationship. Don't just wait for the customer to contact your company—reach out with specific offers.

4. *Amp up customer intelligence* by adding analytics (measures) and executive dashboards (graphic displays of the findings that can be easily digested by decision makers) to determine which marketing campaigns are most effective with certain customer groups and why.

The common theme, of course, is the need for getting to know customers as individuals, not just as categories. The better we know them, the better we can serve their needs.

Source: These ideas summarize some key findings of research by IBM and the Peppers & Rogers Group as reported in a white paper published in 2012.

The one-to-one marketing instead focuses on understanding individual customers as much as possible and responding to their needs. A men's wear store today may do very little mass advertising and still be very profitable by personalizing the relationship and keeping close to its individual customers. They seek to meet all their clothing needs. Likewise, a bank, credit card company, or credit union may expand its services to eventually handle all their customers' financial needs. This is called getting a larger **share of the customer** (some call it "**share of the wallet**") and has been found to be very profitable.

> One-to-one marketing builds relationships that allow businesses to earn a larger share of the customer's business.

One-to-One Opportunities with Internal Customers

The one-to-one principle holds for internal customer relationships too. Managers who keep closely attuned to their employees' preferences, talents, and wants build long-term relationships that can be mutually beneficial to the company. A fully utilized employee is the counterpart to the fully served customer. Motivating employees increasingly calls for individualized incentives and opportunities. Employees, like customers, want to be engaged in the business and, more than ever, expect to be participants in the workings of the organization. The clear-cut wall between management (decision-makers) and employees is crumbling as companies see the advantages of greater employee participation in a wide range of decisions. Workers who so engage tend to be more satisfied and fulfilled.

In the area of employee perks, the best companies often offer "cafeteria" style benefits programs—approaches that give their employees choices among options. While some employees may value day care assistance as a benefit, others with no children may opt instead for a company-provided health club membership. While some eagerly take advantage of college tuition assistance, others may select flex-time working options. The key concept, once again, is one-to-one personalization to best meet individual needs.

Managers today are increasingly aware of individual employee differences in other ways as well. With the evolution of management theory, employees are no longer seen as interchangeable parts in a company machine but rather as unique individuals. (Do you see a theme here?)

Best managers get to know employees, understand their needs and wants, just as enlightened companies do with customers. They ask; that is, they open the communication channels in all directions. The top–down, boss-telling-employee-what-to-do approach works no better than the company-telling-customers-what-they-want approach.

And, of course, on the social, friendship level, knowing about and addressing the interests, needs, and wants of friends have always been a major factor in building rapport and life-long relationships. Interactivity—the two-way flow of information—is the key.

Effective managers ask employees about their wants and needs; they don't assume.

Two-way communication about individual needs is a key to building any effective relationship.

Use Interactive Options Now Available

Today's communication media typically combine the power of computers to allow such one-to-one relationship building on a larger scale. These media have the following characteristics:

1. They are *individually addressable and highly adaptive* to unique needs. They permit messages to be fully tailored to each customer, not just superficially modified versions of a form letter.
2. They are *interactive*, creating two-way, not one-way communication. They make it easy for customers to give their feedback and reactions to messages.
3. They are *affordable and powerful.*
4. They make things *easier* for people.

Technology truly has made the world smaller. The cost of communicating across town and across the continents has never been lower. Internet telephone services such as Skype.com allow us to talk with people across the globe for little or no cost. To make things better, we can even conference call over the Net. A U.S.-based Finnish professor talks regularly with his family in Helsinki, often pulling in business associates in Singapore and Ethiopia. Calls from every continent are commonplace and affordable.

Web sites can easily use video rather than just written text or pictures.

Are such media available to the typical businessperson or professional? More than any time in history, the answer is an unqualified yes. Even the smallest business or individual proprietorship can afford much of today's technology. We are steadily moving toward more effective one-to-one service in business and the professions, supported by electronic media that can individualize messages.

Likewise, customers can participate in promoting or denigrating the service companies give. Social networks make it simple to spread the word—often with pictures or video clips—about products and services. In the past, customers may have been disappointed with the presentation of a restaurant dinner. Today, that lack of plate-appeal may show up as a photo on Facebook.

COMPANIES NEED TO UNDERSTAND SHIFTING DEMOGRAPHIC NEEDS

Aside from technology, service professionals need insight into other noteworthy changes affecting business and customer relationships today. On the social and economic scene, we see substantial demographic shifts. Workforces are increasingly diverse—made up of people from a wide range of economic circumstances, cultures, religions, and both genders. Today's workforce consists of more nontraditional family units with single parents, multigenerational households, and other life-sharing arrangements, each with unique needs. We have an increasingly educated workforce and its people are less tolerant of mindless, repetitive work. Likewise, customers will not tolerate having to jump through hoops to do business with us. Employees expect to be more involved in organizational decisions, to have their input considered. These internal customers will not stand for anything less than engagement opportunities. Failing to provide such opportunities will sentence companies to the profit-killing treadmill of hiring and training new employees as the current ones slip out the back. And guess what, external customers want to influence organizational decisions, too. They don't just want to buy from you; they also want to engage with you.

Customers (especially those of the "Net generation") expect to have their input considered as companies develop products and services.

The shifting social conditions of customers have stimulated demand for new and different products and services. Working couples have come to value shopping efficiency and convenience. Ethnically diverse neighborhoods have caused restaurants serving many kinds of food to flourish. Upscale fast-food and take-home cuisine have become the mainstay of some busy families. Increasingly popular meal preparation kitchens where customers can prepare multiple meals for future use (e.g., "My Girlfriend's Kitchen," "Dinners to Go," and Publix super markets' "Apron's Make-Ahead Meals") are providing a service that meets needs of busy people.

Politically, organizations face increasing government regulations, most of which reflect levels of social awareness previously not considered in the business world. Customers expect to see a diversity of people from all backgrounds, persons with disabilities, and gender equity in most companies. Likewise concern for the environment, employee health and safety, and even emotional well-being have become hallmarks of today's successful businesses. Caring companies attract and keep better employees (internal customers) which can help them succeed in the marketplace. Most companies are aware of "green" issues: recycling and ecologically friendly packaging. In short, customers have come to expect different kinds of satisfaction that go beyond the core product or service. Insight into such shifting expectations is critical to ongoing service success.

The customers and employees we work with today are different in composition than they were a decade ago. Some significant sociological changes have taken place in the recent past and will continue well into the twenty-first century.

People are more mobile. Changing jobs is commonplace and employees' (internal customers) expectations are far different from a generation ago. Rarely does a worker sign on with a company out of school and remain there throughout his or her career. We are quick to change jobs if an employer fails to provide opportunities for engagement and meaningful work.

Another trend is the aging population. With the oft-discussed "baby boomer" generation (people born after World War II, between 1946 and 1962) growing older, many new services are being offered to this huge demographic consumer base. Today's 60-year-olds are far more active than in past generations. "Sixty is the new forty," proclaim many sociologists. Active, engaged "seniors" have caused many organizations to rethink their strategies for working with customers and employees who may remain vibrant for many more years.

Ironically, marketers have been obsessed with the "golden" demographic segment of 18–49-year-olds. The growth projections for this market make that less of a sure thing. The projected growth in the U.S. 18–49 segment over the next 10 years is 0.8 million, while the projected growth in the 50-plus segment over the next 10 years is 22 million.[1] Companies offering services that appeal to these aging populations will likely thrive.

All these kinds of factors put pressure on companies to be alert, innovative, and willing to change to meet changing consumer demands. There are no calm waters for businesses in the twenty-first century. The landscape is more like a white-water river and leaders need to be alert and agile. Today's service practices may well be inappropriate for tomorrow's customer.

COMPANIES NEED TO GRASP THAT CUSTOMERS EXPECT TRANSPARENCY AND TRUST

A new book by Don Pepper and Martha Rodgers makes a compelling case for the idea that earning the trust of customers is a huge competitive advantage.[2] The authors begin the book with an anecdote about USAA, the insurance and banking company based in San Antonio, Texas. USAA caters to military personnel and their dependents. Immediately after the first Gulf War in 1991, the company sent out refund checks to several thousand customers who had been serving in the

Products and services that help busy working families more efficiently are often attractive options.

Customer demographics evolve, and insight into such changes should help steer a company's service strategy.

war. The idea was that since they were overseas they couldn't drive their cars and therefore it was unfair to charge them for auto insurance.

Obviously, USAA was not required to do this, but they did it citing their cultural value of treating customers the way you'd want to be treated if you were the customer. Of the checks sent out, nearly 2,500 of them were sent back to the company! Grateful customers told USAA to keep the money and just "be there when we need you." Can you imagine the trust-building value of this kind of customer relationship? Could you imagine how you could compete against such an open, trustworthy company? Can you imagine the loyalty of customers who were treated this well?

Pepper and Rodgers go on to build a case for the importance of "**trustability**"—a quality that goes beyond being just trustworthy. Trustable companies do more than just post accurate prices, maintain good quality and reliability, and do what they say they will do. They exceed expectations for **transparency** and openness.

> Companies that build "trustability" benefit from increased customer loyalty.

An important insight for customer service professionals is that transparency—that is, being open and honest—is not just good business but, to a large degree, inevitable. People can and will discover most of what companies try to hide or deemphasize. People understand the need to make a profit and will not begrudge a company doing so. What they will no longer tolerate is taking unfair advantage of customers. Cases in point include such commonplace, but often unfair, policies as:

- Mobile phone carriers that profit from getting customers into the most expensive (and often locked-in pricing plans)
- Health clubs that hold customers to long-term contracts even when the member's circumstances make it so that he can no longer use the facilities
- Special pricing available to new customers that is not made available to existing, loyal customers
- Wide discrepancies in prices for the same service based on ever-changing cost manipulation such as airline or concert seats sold via different outlets or at different times
- Companies that automatically renew subscriptions or services unless the customer explicitly stops them. (While sold as a convenience, such continuous billing—sometimes long after the customer needs the service—has become an annoyance to people who fail to notice or don't go through the hassle of canceling.)

Trustability is damaged when the company's profitability (or convenience) is put ahead of customer needs and wants. Lower trust ultimately kills customer loyalty.

UNDERSTAND THAT SOME THINGS REMAIN CONSISTENT

Having said all we have about technological, economic, social, and organizational change, we must also acknowledge that many aspects of the customer satisfaction process remain the same. In particular, key psychological and behavioral factors have changed little. Human and organizational needs remain largely the same. A basic sense of caring, concern, and competence will continue to play a critical role in building customer satisfaction and loyalty. In fact, for some, the advent of so much technology has rekindled a hunger for the old-fashioned human touch. That is one reason the Gap clothing stores (among others) display products on large tables that become easily messed up. Customers get involved by feeling the merchandise and straightening up the table gives an opportunity for the clerk nearby to interact with the customer. Getting people actively *doing* something generates relationship building and enhances interest.

Even among technology-based companies, the human touch resonates with customers. People who buy tech-based products and systems online often get frustrated when they find that setting them up is more complicated than expected. This poses an opportunity for the smaller, local computer retailer who offers personalized setup, even if the price is a bit higher. Large retailers are increasingly offering such assistance with services such as the Geek Squad services of Best Buy stores. Web retailers who follow up with personal phone calls can also build loyalty, especially if the caller has vibrant telephone skills as discussed in Chapter 4. Human contact will never be replaced by even the most sophisticated technology.

Demand for Fair Value Remains Constant

Likewise, the demand for fair value will always remain. People want fairness in exchanges, good value for their money. Companies that profit from inflated prices, confusing rate structures, hidden charges, and unreasonable penalties will not survive long term. Examples of what Fred Reichheld, author of *Loyalty Rules!* and *The Ultimate Question,* calls **bad profits** include those which may generate short-term income at the cost of long-term customer relationships. Some examples of "bad profits" may be

- Inflated shipping charges such as for goods bought on the Internet
- Excessive penalties for changing services (such as cell phone contracts)
- High premium prices for certain seasonal goods or popular options (air fares inflated during holiday season, high-priced accessories)
- Complex pricing schemes that dupe customers into spending more than necessary (over-priced "service contracts" or extended warrantees)
- Inappropriate products sold to trusting customers
- Lack of pricing transparency creating the impression that others are getting a better deal
- Special offers to new customers that is not available to existing, loyal customers
- And, of course, in one of the most self-destructive industries, commercial airlines, pile on added charges for bags (even carry-on's in some cases), seats with better leg room, and earlier boarding.

Examples of bad profits are easy to find when companies put more emphasis on maximizing short-term revenue than on building sustained customer relationships. Bad profits are corrosive to relationships; good profits create and sustain them. In short, bad profits are those earned at the expense of customer relationships. Going beyond customers, relationships of any type will be damaged when people feel exploited or unfairly treated. By contrast, relationships are strengthened when exchanges are fair and equitable. In the future, people will increasingly demand totally honest service relationships.

The Need to Satisfy Individual Customer Needs and Wants Remains Constant

You probably have heard someone describe a super salesperson as one who can sell anything to anyone—the proverbial ice cubes to an igloo inhabitant. The old conventional wisdom taught that dynamic sales skills are the ticket to success. If the salesperson could give a decent presentation of the product and dazzle the consumer with an amazing close, then the consumer would buy. That was it: transaction complete.

In our day, a new protocol is on the rise. Although presentation and closing are still important to the sales process, an even more vital element supersedes both of these—the ability to tailor products and services to individual customer needs and wants. Today's consumers face an unprecedented number of choices. In today's global economy, consumers have hundreds of places to go to buy the very same product. What makes the customer choose which business to buy from? To what degree are choices based on quality, price, convenience, or on customer service? How do you decide where to buy clothes, groceries, automobiles, electronics, and other consumer goods? How can retailers overcome the trend of customers checking out a product in a store and then buying it online? What is most important to you as a consumer?

Today's consumers face an unprecedented number of choices. Value, systems, and people will tip the scales for one business over others.

There is no mystery in the answers to these questions. A consumer will go where he or she gets the most value, the most efficient and helpful systems, and the most trustworthy and personable transactions. It is that simple. For a business to understand its customers' perception of value, systems, and people, it must establish and maintain a relationship with those customers.

The Need for Relationship Marketing Remains Constant

Companies may argue they have the best quality product around at great prices. The fact is that customers have gotten used to having quality products at good prices. These things are givens. They alone cannot readily distinguish one business from the competition.

But, customers continue to expect less than optimal service. Why? Because that is what they've been getting in the past. They have a list of pet peeves from experiencing poor service. Can you see the enormous opportunity that exists for building a strong competitive advantage through service that truly exceeds their expectations in positive ways?

Customers in a free-market economy expect good products at reasonable cost. This is a given. What they don't always expect is great service.

Think back to when you were a child. Do you remember a corner grocer or a candy store manager? Did he know who you were or who your parents were? A typical comment from the grocer might have been, "Hi Jarome, it's good to see you. Did you have a good vacation to the Grand Canyon?" Or from the candy store manager, "Hello Anika, last time you were here you tried the red licorice. Can I get you the same thing or would you like to try something different?" This is relationship marketing—having a one-to-one relationship with your customers. Every company—from a *Fortune 500* to a local baby-sitter—can utilize relationship marketing with just a bit of training. In fact, relationship marketing is only limited by the creativity of the people in the company.

Relationship marketing opportunities are limited only by one's imagination.

With the use of creativity, the opportunity to exceed customers' expectations extends well beyond just calling someone by name. While that is a great start, consider additional possibilities.

The Need to Prioritize Customer Share over Market Share Remains Constant

Progressive companies are coming to see the wisdom of focusing on share of customers rather than share of market. Let's talk once again about the important concept of **customer share**. Consider the following two competing flower businesses:

- The owners of The Flower Bucket have worked very hard, with a mass-marketing focus, in order to get a good piece of the market. They calculated they achieved about a 20 percent market share. In other words, for every dollar spent on flowers in their market, The Flower Bucket gets 20 cents.
- The owners of flower business Smell Good Flowers, on the other hand, have worked very hard to gain a relationship with every one of the top purchasers of flowers (those who buy flowers on the most consistent basis). They estimate that they have a 20 percent *customer share*. That is, for every 10 customers who buy flowers, 2 of them buy flowers from Smell Good 100 percent of the time.

Which company is better off in the long run? Remember, who Smell Good Flowers focused on, the customers who are frequent buyers—the top customers of the industry—those who buy the most flowers. Therefore, Smell Good enjoys much greater efficiency in their marketing—its customers are the best customers to have. They know them and they massaged their relationship to gain even more of their flower business. They win.

If a company can truly win over the top customers, its chance of survival is much better than just having a percentage of the market. Managers need to think of the present value of a customer's future business. A few examples illustrate what I mean: Super-successful auto dealers teach employees the importance of thinking about the present value of future business. Car dealerships can easily calculate the potential: If an average car costs about $25,000, and if people buy on average 12 cars, then the total sale is $300,000. Add service and parts and each customer of a dealership could be worth about $332,000 in sales. The numbers are not far-fetched. Nor do they include the impact these customers may have on other potential customers.

In a television interview Walmart's CEO David Glass said that his company had calculated the lifetime cost of a single lost customer at about $215,000. Similar estimates for a loyal supermarket customer show each one to be worth an average of $3,800 annually, a figure that is growing as food becomes more expensive. Over the course of a lifetime, this could easily add up to more than $150,000 in sales. Furthermore, a businessperson who frequently flies to different parts of the world could easily spend over $50,000 annually on air travel. This customer could be worth over 1 million dollars in revenue for an airline. This is what we mean by present value of future business.

> Present value of future business is an estimate of the total a customer would potentially spend with you.

With these kinds of long-range dollar thinking, who wouldn't give priority to customer share rather than a market share? The customer you already have is significantly more likely to buy from you again, while ever-scrambling for new customers drains your marketing budget and energy. Remember, though, the only way to increase customer share is to build a relationship with your customer and to enhance your customer's satisfaction and loyalty.

Thanks to computer databases, even small shops are able to collect information and use it for retention of their customers. For example, gift shop owners can send out reminder cards to certain customers. A reminder card may read as follows:

> *Hi, Mr. Joblinski: On March 29, last year, you remembered Jenny's birthday by sending her [a gift]. Here are some other gift ideas you might consider for Jenny this year. Please call or go to our Web site to place an order. We will make sure Jenny has a beautiful gift on her special day. Thank you for your business. We look forward to hearing from you.*

When Mr. Joblinski calls, he must only tell the flower shop what flowers to send. Jenny's address, telephone number, and available times for delivery are already in the computer database. Likewise, the customer's credit card number is on file and can easily be confirmed and used.

Think how you could exceed expectations with these kinds of techniques. Why not do as a gift catalog company does using its database? The company implemented a new program that offers the following services: They will

1. Store and fulfill your orders of gifts to your friends and relatives up to 15 months in advance.
2. Deliver the gift on the day specified. The customer will never again miss any important date.
3. Bill the customer's credit card only when the gifts are sent. Send an invoice to the customer for each gift charged to the account within five working days.
4. Send a reminder postcard to the customer before the gift is sent out explaining whom the gift is going to and what the gift is. (So when the recipient says thank you, the customer knows what he or she is talking about.)
5. Send all customers an updated catalog that will have all of the previous years' names preprinted on the order sheet. The customer can add any new names to the bottom.
6. Provide a 24-hour telephone number and Web site access for any changes or updates the customer may have.

With the use of a database, the information needed to do all this is stored easily; and the catalog store employees most likely have less work than they did before the service was implemented. An additional benefit is that the managers can see almost exactly what their sales revenue will be in the near future, thus helping financial planning for the company.

To add an interactive dimension to this service, the company includes two short questions on the customer order form. They ask customers what they would like to see our catalog service include in the future. And what are some additional products you would like us to have in our gift catalog? Bingo! Customer preferences and expectations are revealed.

Insights into these ever-changing expectations are critical to maintain competitiveness and service success.

SERVICE SNAPSHOT

Special Service for Best Customers

Hertz Car Rental knew they had problems when people were getting upset about having to wait in long lines to get their rental cars. Many businesspeople travel very tight schedules and need to have a car quickly. Hertz knew that unless they took action quickly, they would lose many of their most valuable and frequent renters. Hertz launched a special service—the #1 Gold Club—for those who needed their rental cars quickly. The #1 Gold Club members can call ahead of time to reserve a car. When the member gets off the plane, a shuttle is waiting for the customer at the curb to take him or her to the car. The shuttle driver can welcome him or her by name and explain the shuttle trip is just two minutes. The shuttle drops off the customer at the reserved car. The engine is running, the trunk lid is open, and today's issue of the *WallStreet Journal* is on the front seat. The member gets in the car and drives to the gate where he or she shows his or her driver's license and #1 Gold Card. No lines. No hassle.

The successes of this approach lead other auto rental companies to offer similar accommodations. Some offer the preferred customer the option to pick any car they want. Frequent travelers often get streamlined service on airlines (with special lines for first-class and frequent flyers as well as special security lines) and hotel guests get upgrades and special features. What can your company do to offer special consideration to your very best customers? The future "gold card" customer will expect something more.

A FINAL THOUGHT

Insight. That is the key word as we seek to stay abreast of ever-changing customer service realities. Accurately forecasting the future is, of course, a tricky business. Often we are limited by our preconceived ideas or our inability to think, as the cliché goes, "outside the box." Even our customers may not know what they want. Henry Ford is famous for saying that if he had asked customers what they wanted they would have said a faster horse. Nevertheless, maintaining great customer service calls for constant evolution. Today's service innovation can quickly become tomorrow's minimum requirement. Being ever-sensitive to possible customer turnoffs and changing industry standards is fundamental.

The future looks exciting for people and organizations willing to change to stay competitive. Changes are often driven by technology although some organizations may choose to minimize technological innovation. They may decide to keep doing things the old-fashioned, down-home way as they do now. That's an alternative strategy that may appeal to people who don't much care for all this new-fangled techy-stuff. In some business contexts, lo-tech may be fine. But for most organizations, embracing technological capabilities is a logical choice. Having the insight necessary to decipher customer wants and needs should be a high priority for service professionals.

Companies will need to give some hard thought to their **value proposition**. What exactly do they want to offer customers? It is possible to do business the old ways, to run the mom 'n pop store or restaurant just as it's been run in the past decades. But even among staunch traditionalists, customer demand for change may become a clamor. Even in Ye Olde Gift Shoppe with the 1890s theme, customers expect to be able to use their credit cards and probably even look at inventory online. Unless the shop has another gimmick, they will face a lot of pressure to upgrade to current customer demands.

Some customers are concerned about the impact of technology on privacy and the potential for intrusion into personal lives. For example, a few years ago a failed promotion offered free computers to people so long as the company can gather infinite data about every click of the mouse made on that computer. In a sense, those customer would have been selling their privacy for the price of a PC. These customers may resist some of the techniques we've discussed but would be open to friendly, informal personalization found in local, neighborhood stores or shops.

Whatever strategy your company employs, from having highly sophisticated intelligent-system databases to jotting down handwritten notes on customer preferences, one-to-one, personalized customer service and relationship building must stand as its cornerstone. Cultivate your insight into the future of customer service.

Summary of Key Ideas

- Insight—the ability to monitor and understand an ever-changing customer service landscape is critical to success.
- Future success in customer service will depend on companies' abilities to adjust to various changes (many of which involve technology shifts). Some such shifts will dramatically change the nature of products or services offered. Others will call for adjustments in marketing and service delivery approaches.
- "Trustability" of a company is becoming increasingly important to customers. Organizational decisions that undercut transparency and trust will damage relationships; actions that build trust will strengthen customer loyalty.
- Companies can, using technology, personalize products or services to individual customers rather than marketing to demographic groups. While personal service has always been possible, technology makes it feasible on a wide scale and with large customer bases.
- Demographic changes will also impact the future of customer service. Successful businesses will need to be cognizant of changes in customer expectations and needs as dictated by the buying power of rising ethnic groups, age categories, and genders.
- Developing an ability to seek insights is an important customer service skill. Expectations about the quality of the customer experience are ever-changing. Awareness of and adapting to such change expectations is a hallmark of service excellence.
- Among the ever-changing business landscape lies that which remains the same. People want to experience caring, concern, and competence in their business dealings.

Key Concepts

bad profits	goodness-of-fit	share of the customer (or share of the wallet)	"trustability"
customized messages	point-of-sale electronic		value proposition
customer share	data gathering	transparency	

Reviewing the Facts

1. Some breakthrough products and services have literally changed the world. The automobile, the telephone, the Internet, and countless other inventions have historically shifted the ways people live and work. But shifts in ways of doing business have also had dramatic impact on lives throughout history. Self-service shopping, online sales, overnight shipping, 24/7 business hours, and globalization of services such as call centers are other examples. Look back and list three major shifts you are aware of. For each, describe three or more ways these shifts impact customer service?

2. Among the most important determinants of customer satisfaction is the availability of feedback. We gain clearer insight into what customers want and don't want by systematically processing all types of feedback. Describe five ways today's organizations and individuals can sharpen their insights by using customer feedback.

3. Describe one or more specific examples of how businesses you know are using one-to-one communication to build a stronger relationship with you. (Note: Often these are little things done to build rapport and loyalty.)

Applying the Ideas

1. How are changing customer demographics affecting your business? Select a business and write a paper describing at least three demographic changes that are or will soon impact its effectiveness. How might the business react to these pressures?

2. Log on to the Internet and search for information related to the notion of personalized services or "one-to-one" marketing and service. What are companies doing to take advantage of such personalization? Write a brief report on what you find.

3. Read the opening chapter of the Pepper and Rodgers book *Extreme Trust*, which is found at this url: *http://www.extremetrustbook.com*. Identify similar examples of situations where companies have taken dramatic actions to build higher

levels of trust. Then identify examples of experiences you have had with organizations that have become less trustworthy, in your opinion. How could the lower-trust examples be reversed to create higher customer trust. (Don't forget that you may use internal customers as well as external customers in your examples.)

4. Log on to the Internet and see what you can find about demographic shifts that may affect customer service. Write a brief report that answers these questions: What are the most significant shifts in your country, state, or local region? What do online sources suggest about adjusting to such demographic changes?

Consider this Case

Back from the Future

Many of you readers will have never seen a telegram, but most are familiar with the history. In 2006 Western Union delivered its last telegram. The telegraph industry's life was taken, definitively and brutally by technological change. For more than 150 years, the telegram stood for immediacy and importance. It was an icon for urgency. But now, Western Union has closed down its telegraph service around the world. Email, instant messaging, and faxes are the new technologies the telegram could not survive. So, Western Union has reconfigured itself into a business primarily dedicated to wiring money.

The shift from teletype and telegram to the new technologies represents one aspect of what some business consultants term a "paradigm shift"—a discontinuity in the otherwise steady march of business progress. There are many more examples of a lesser scale. Think about the music business. Some people alive today can remember the advent of radio and TV. Many have seen the evolution from vinyl records to 8-track tapes, to cassettes, to CDs, and now to MP3 and i-Pods. Once-thriving music stores have shut down or converted to vintage shops specializing in those odd antiquities—records!

While once a hot business, "video" stores are virtually gone. Having made the transition from videotape movies to DVDs, they continue to face the competition of Red Box-type vending machines and other delivery

systems that allow customers access to movies without leaving the comfort of their homes such as on-demand movies through cable, satellite, and cellular phone systems.

Looking further back in history, the automobile was another discontinuity, one that radically transformed both the economy and society. When the automobile first appeared, it seemed to be merely a horseless version of the well-known carriage. No one could have predicted the consequences of the automobile's introduction. Who would have imagined that a noisy, smelly, unreliable machine would eventually be responsible for the creation of suburbs; the fractionalization of families; and the growth of supermarkets, malls, and the interstate highway system? For that matter, who among us pictured the day when automobiles routinely included more electronics than the early spacecraft or when on-board electronic communication systems can call for help or open an accidentally locked door?

Probes

1. How has technology shifted in your adult lifetime? What are the most significant examples reflecting these kinds of paradigm shifts in recent years?
2. What future shifts do you envision? Be creative in describing possibilities.

Consider this Case

Welcome to an Exceptional Hotel

On his way back to his home in San Francisco from a business trip, Michael decided to stop for the night in a little hotel overlooking the Pacific. When he arrived at the reception desk, quickly a well-dressed woman appeared and welcomed him to the hotel. Within three

minutes from the greeting, he was ushered into his room by the bellboy. The room was decorated with plush carpeting, white-on-white bedding, natural cedar walls, and a stone fireplace. The fireplace grate had oak logs, rolled paper, and matches waiting to be used.

After changing in his room, Michael walked to the restaurant. The hotel receptionist had made him reservations for the restaurant at the time of his checkin. Michael was immediately shown to his table upon arrival—even though others without reservations were waiting. When he got back to his room that night, the pillows were plumped up, the bed was turned down, and there was a fire blazing in the fireplace. On the night stand was a glass of brandy and a card that read, "Welcome to your first stay at Venetia. I hope it has been enjoyable. If there is anything I can do for you, day or night, please don't hesitate to call. Kathi."

In the morning Michael woke up to the smell of coffee. When he went into the bathroom he found a perking coffee pot. A card by the pot read, "Your brand of coffee. Enjoy! K." Michael had been asked the night before at the restaurant which brand of coffee he preferred. Now it was bubbling in his room. Michael heard a polite knock on the door. When he opened the door, he saw *The New York Times* lying on the mat. When Michael had checked in, the reservationist had asked him what paper he preferred. Now his preferred paper was at his room for him to read.

Michael explains the service at the hotel has been exactly the same every time he has gone back. But after the first visit, he was never asked his preferences again.

Probes

1. In what way is this a great example of relationship-based customer service? How does it differ from the customer experience at other hotels you are familiar with?

2. By "learning" his preferences, the hotel management was able to manipulate a common experience into one that was very personal for Michael. What else might a hotel do? Be creative in brainstorming possibilities.

Source: Adapted from a story told in Michael E. Gerber, *The E Myth Revisited* (New York: HarperCollins Publishers, Inc., 1995, pp. 188–92).

Building a Customer Service Strategy: Your Ongoing Case

Let's go back to the ongoing case you selected. This will be either your current employer, a specific organization you want to work in, or one of the two hypothetical organizations described in Chapter 1: Independent Auto Sales and Service (IAS) or Network Nutrition Distributors (NND). Now consider the following questions as you develop a customer service strategy:

Strategy Planning Questions

1. What changes do you anticipate coming that will affect your business? Describe the top three changes that could destroy your business or leap-frog it into new levels of success.

2. Calculate the lifetime value of your customer using today's dollars. Develop a strategy for capturing more "share of the customer." What policies, processes, actions, or changes would you plan to keep your organization healthy and prosperous?

Notes

1. Southeastern Institute of Research, Inc. Boomer Project, 2006 (*www.boomerproject.com*).

2. Don Pepper and Martha Rodgers, *Extreme Trust: Honesty as a Competitive Advantage* (Penguin Press, 2012).

PART 3

LIFE: Feedback

The third letter in our acronym is **F** for "feedback." The only way to monitor and improve the quality of customer interaction is via feedback. Soliciting, digesting and using customer feedback is the major subject of Chapter 8. Chapter 9 shows how we can build upon feedback received to recover potentially lost customers—to win them back.

An ongoing feedback loop provides the basis for ongoing relationships. Feedback provides the data needed to improve and strengthen such relationships.

So, let's consider the crucial roles of feedback and customer recovery as we strive to provide better customer service.

Get Customer Feedback
The Customer Can Be Our Coach

After reading this chapter, you should be able to

1. Validate why feedback is so important.

2. Understand that feedback receptiveness is a crucial characteristic of successful people and companies.

3. Identify the varying levels of importance that companies place on customer feedback.

4. Recognize seven ways feedback cards can lose their effectiveness.

5. Calculate a "Net Promoter Score" and explain why this is an important feedback tool.

6. Apply behaviors that reinforce rather than challenge customer feedback.

7. Act on complaints in productive ways.

8. Apply four ways to proactively seek out feedback information.

The Way It Is...Pop's Café Takes Feedback Seriously

Andre's favorite eatery is Pop's Café. Located a few blocks from his downtown office, Pop's has the best home cooking, complete with fresh-baked biscuits. The owner of the restaurant (yup, his nickname is actually Pop) personally greets each customer, and the food is delicious. One day, as Andre paid for his meal, Pop asked if everything was okay. Andre half-jokingly mentioned that the biscuits weren't as warm as usual. The owner immediately handed his money back.

"Oh no, Pop, I can't take my money back—the biscuits were okay," said Andre as he tried to pay him, "the meal was fine, just not quite as great as it usually is." But Pop would hear nothing of this and refused to accept payment. Andre continues to be a regular customer and frequently introduces his friends and business associates to Pop's.

A restaurant owner's demonstration that he wants only 100 percent satisfied customers strengthened Andre's allegiance to Pop's Café. Pop really wants feedback—positive or negative. And when he got some negative feedback (in this case a mild complaint) he acted on it immediately.

Hearing and addressing customer complaints is a crucial tactic in building customer satisfaction and loyalty. Organizations have several options for collecting customer feedback, some of which are more effective than others. We'll look at some of these options in this chapter, but the prerequisite to choosing a method is that companies must genuinely want to receive feedback, even when it may be uncomfortable. The best companies jump at opportunities to hear from their customers—especially the complaining ones.

WHY FEEDBACK IS VITALLY IMPORTANT

At its most basic level, feedback is crucial to any kind of improvement. While positive feedback is nice—we all love a compliment—it is usually the *negative* feedback that helps us the most. Despite people saying "I always welcome your feedback" most of us, as individuals and companies, need to work to overcome the "feedback hurts" mentality. Of course, it isn't always pleasant to hear negative comments about what we are doing. Sometimes our feelings get hurt, our ego is wounded, or the feedback strikes us as uninformed or even stupid. That said, let's consider a shift in our perspective.

Most people need to work at not being offended by feedback.

View Feedback as a Form of Coaching

Try this: Think about feedback as a form of *coaching*. When we work with a coach, he or she is constantly giving us negative feedback—and we appreciate it. A golf coach, for example, will correct the way you hold or swing the club and you're delighted to get the negative feedback. In fact you pay for all these "complaints."

The principle is the same in our business or personal life. We need feedback (which often takes the form of complaints) to improve our performance. It makes us better at what we are learning to do. Customer service skills are all about constant learning and the customers are our coaches.

Customers can coach us to better performance.

Complaints Are Valuable Feedback

Dissatisfaction happens. What we choose to do about what makes others dissatisfied can make all the difference in creating customer and employee loyalty. To do something constructive about dissatisfaction, we need to get even the silently dissatisfied customer to speak up by creating open communication channels.

Open communication occurs best when people feel that their opinions are valued and that they will not be "punished" for expressing them—they may even be rewarded. Companies earn loyalty by participating in dialogue—by making it safe for customers to speak up.

Most people find expressing a complaint to be an unpleasant experience. It's uncomfortable and a bit intimidating. People generally want to maintain cordial relationships and fear that complaining will upset others. Our job, then, is to let people know that we are sincerely open to their comments—negative or positive.

Commitment to Feedback Varies

Companies (and people) have differing levels of commitment to feedback gathering, as shown in Exhibit 8.1. While most of us will accept it from a coach or consultant, we may be less eager to open ourselves up to broader input.

Some companies get feedback reluctantly. They know they should do it but their heart isn't in it. The first level of feedback commitment is **reluctant-compliant**, where companies may offer customers a "feedback card" but the effort is halfhearted. They neither encourage customer feedback nor enthusiastically act on the information received. They do little to make it easy for customers.

Some companies reluctantly go through the motions of gathering feedback.

The second level of feedback commitment is **active listener**. These companies are genuinely open to hearing from customers—using the term "hearing" to refer to any form of input, not just spoken words. They make it quite easy and they respond, thus reinforcing the customer's willingness to share perceptions with them.

The third level of feedback commitment involves taking customer comments and measuring and tracking them. These companies apply **metrics-conscious** techniques—they quantify as much data as possible and use that data to make organizational decisions. They keep score over extended periods and refer to these data regularly to motivate employees, correct weaknesses, and generally look for better ways to meet customer service objectives. So, where is your company?

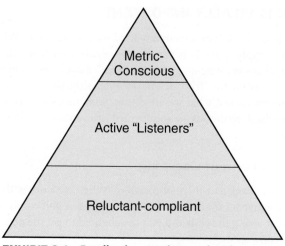

EXHIBIT 8.1   Feedback commitment levels.

Getting Input at the Point of Contact

Most companies (even the reluctant-compliant ones) have some sort of formal feedback system, ostensibly to gather data that could make service better. The simplest system invites customers to fill out a feedback card. The way the cards are designed and what companies do with them when received will have a major impact on whether customers will use them. In too many cases, businesses make such cards available but are half-hearted at best about getting them, and even less enthusiastic about doing something based on the feedback received. They offer the cards to create an illusion that they want to hear from customers—they are among the reluctant-compliant organizations. They probably feel they should be doing *something* but their heart isn't really in it.

Feedback cards have limited value as feedback gathering devices.

Collecting feedback cards can show historical trends and even measure customer loyalty rates if well designed. But the information they provide is often too little, too late, and too broadbrush. The time to gain specific, useful insights from an unhappy customer is at the point of contact and at the time of the problem. For a rapidly growing number of people, the Internet (or, within many companies, an intranet) provides the easiest way to give feedback. Some people prefer direct communication with an organization's employees, the telephone, or letters. Creating a climate in which people will give real-time, on-the-spot feedback is almost always more effective than printed customer-feedback cards, telephone follow-ups, or focus-group sessions.

ANOTHER LOOK

Tracking Your Net Promoter Score

Managers have long sought easy-to-gather data that can indicate how well they are doing with customers. In his book *The Ultimate Question*[1] Bain & Company consultant Fred Reichheld advocates a now widely used technique for evaluating loyalty and long-term organizational success.

In short, Reichheld argues that the most critical thing we need to know about our customers is the likelihood that they would recommend us or our organization to friends or colleagues. The most useful way to tabulate such information is to have customers respond to the statement "I would recommend [the company] to others" on a 10-point scale ranging from 1 (not at all likely that I would recommend) to 10 (extremely likely that I would recommend). The scores given determine if that customer is a detractor, passive, or a promoter.

If the person responding checks 9 or 10 on the scale, they are *promoters*—customers who are loyal and enthusiastic; if they check 7 or 8, they are *passives*—customers who are satisfied but unenthusiastic; and if they check 6 or

(continued)

below, they are *detractors*. They are quite unhappy with the service or quality or are perhaps trapped in a bad relationship. From these data we calculate a **Net Promoter Score (NPS)**.

Managers can calculate the NPS by applying the formula $P - D = NPS$, where P and D are the number of promoters and detractors. Here is a simple example of how to calculate an NPS:

Suppose you have 100 customers on a given day and all 100 agree to mark a ballot grading the statement on a 1–10 scale. You add up the following responses:

- 15 people give you a score of 10
- 20 people give you a score of 9
- 20 scores of 8
- 20 scores of 7
- 10 scores of 6
- 10 scores of 5
- 5 scores of 4

Calculating the NPS, you would add the 9s and 10s (total of 35), ignore the 8s and 7s, and subtract the scores of six or below (total of 25), giving an NPS score of +10. This, incidentally, is approximately the average score for U.S. companies.

Another example gets a different result. Suppose you get these scores from your 100 customers:

- 2 scores of 10
- 8 scores of 9
- 20 scores of 8
- 20 scores of 7
- 20 scores of 6
- 15 scores of 5
- 10 scores of 4
- 5 scores of 3

The 9s and 10s = 10; the 6s and below = 50. This would be a net promoter score of –40. That is a poor score and should provide a wake-up call that service or product quality needs serious improvement. This is not an unrealistic score, by the way. Some major banks, airlines, and other out-of-favor companies do get such low scores. The (not at all simple) challenge for organizations is to improve their service quality which will be reflected by improvements in their Net Promoter Scores.

NPS can be a valuable indicator of the overall customer service an organization is giving. If a manager were to measure just one indicator, this may be the most robust number. It is easy to use and provides a good measurement of how customers see your service and product quality.

Why Should Companies Be So Concerned about Getting Feedback?

Surveys by the U.S. Office of Consumer Affairs[2] and other research organizations concur in reinforcing the importance of actively soliciting feedback. This is because of the following:

- On average, one customer in four is dissatisfied with some aspect of a typical transaction. They may not be terribly upset, but some part of the interaction with the company was less than 100 percent excellent.
- Only 5 percent of dissatisfied customers will bother to complain to the company. The vast silent majority would rather switch than fight. They generally take their business elsewhere.
- In past years, a dissatisfied customer would tell, on average, 12 other people about a company that provided poor service. This figure was estimated before social networks and extensive electronic communication became commonplace. Today, of course, unhappy customers can post their complaints to thousands of people with a simple keystroke.

Today more than ever, people can broadcast their complaints.

Let's translate those statistics using even the most conservative estimates: If 25 percent of your customers are unhappy with some aspect of your company's service but only 5 percent of that 25 percent bother to complain (yet each unhappy customer tells a dozen others) the impact can be devastating. For simplicity, let's say a company serves 100 customers a day. Twenty-five of them are somewhat dissatisfied, but the company hears only one or two complaints. That may sound good to management until they realize that the 23 quiet ones are likely to tell 274 other people (or announce to several thousands via social networking) about the unsatisfactory service!

The **ripple effects** can be devastating. Only by being open to complaints or concerns can companies turn this lemon into lemonade. Gathering and paying attention to customer and employee complaints is the first and most crucial step in fixing problems to maintain customer loyalty. You really must *want* to listen to people's concerns, and you really must make it easy for people to give you feedback. Avoiding feedback is, as someone once said, like being an ostrich. An ostrich can bury its head, but he always leaves the other end exposed.

Increasing the number of complainers heard from can be a benefit to companies.

Although it may sound counterintuitive, companies can and should *increase the number of complainers they hear from.* Handling complaints from two or three dissatisfied people can save 30, 40, or perhaps hundreds of possible defections. Furthermore, these complaints can teach the company what it needs to know to improve. (Unfortunately, many companies reward managers who get the fewest complaints, assuming that this means they are doing great work. Just as likely is the possibility that they are obstructing honest feedback.)

The best news of all is that customers who have their complaints handled well are increasingly likely to do business with the company again. The willingness of unhappy customers to consider doing repeat business with you jumps from as low as 10 percent to about 80 percent *if* their concerns are addressed. This seems to be the case even if their complaints were not resolved in their favor.[3] You may not be able to totally fix the problem (e.g., if customers complain about slow service you cannot give them back their time) but they will give you credit for trying (perhaps by giving them a small token acknowledging the inconvenience). This point is worth repeating since it provides an overall rationale for getting and responding to customer feedback.

When an organization creates a dialoguing process with customers and employees, those who participate can become the company's best friends—even when complaining. To make the most of such dialoguing, you need to

- Make it easy for people to voice complaints (as well as compliments, suggestions, and questions).
- Act on input quickly and efficiently.

REINFORCE, DON'T CHALLENGE THE CUSTOMER

You create a good feedback climate by reinforcing customer behaviors, not by challenging them. The natural tendency may be to react to complaints with some defensiveness. Instead, we should react with encouragement. Suppose you call an auto dealership service manager to tell him of a funny noise coming from your car after the dealer had just serviced it. Instead of asking a bunch

---

ANOTHER LOOK

Feedback Data Worth Having

Analyzing customer opinions can provide valuable insights but these insights can not be easily gained—especially when gathering qualitative—nonnumeric—data. Best practices in aggregating and using customer opinions call for creativity and care in analysis of what customers are saying.

Analyzing qualitative comments can be especially important business-to-business (B2B) relationships as contrasted with business-to-consumer surveying. In B2B, there's generally more time. It's a different kind of relationship. Business-to-consumer interactions tend to be quick, and in many cases the consumer loyalty may be driven simply by price. Because there is so much choice, and it is so easy to click away or walk across the aisle, B2B relationships often involve more complex relationships based on meeting unique customer requirements. For example, a B2B

customer may have just a few sources of a raw material or specialized legal service. In such complex relationships, feedback efforts make greater use of unstructured questions—open dialog questions. In the past, practitioners had to go through the answers manually. While laborious, this kind of qualitative data provide the area with the most gold, where companies can find insights haven't perceived or predicted they would say.

Newer analysis tools are being constructed around "driver questions"—questions that will help you understand the reasons someone gives for their feedback. Knowing the drivers of consumer evaluations helps leaders connect the dots and make change.

Text analytics software now makes such analysis more efficient. Gathering data that go beyond the numbers is feedback worth having for better customer service.

of questions about the kind of noise, or, worse yet, implying in some way that the noise may be your fault, he immediately says, "That's not good. We better get that fixed for you." You didn't have to explain, justify, or diagnose (although later he tactfully asked for some additional details about the nature of the noise). You told him of your complaint, and he immediately projected an attitude of "Let's get this fixed for you."

Avoid challenging customer complaints. Instead take a "let's fix this" attitude.

A quick response that acknowledges the customer's problem and conveys a willingness to work toward solutions will go a long way toward building loyalty.

Be Sensitive to Your First Reactions

The first comments out of your mouth when a customer begins to complain will largely determine the quality and quantity of feedback you will get. Like the auto-service guy, make those first comments positive, helpful, and solution oriented.

Avoid acting defensively and making unnecessary demands for details. Accept the fact that the complaint is legitimate because it *is* real to the customer. Don't justify, or even try to explain, your reaction until you hear the whole story. Customers don't care that the factory has been backlogged or a supplier's products have not been of high quality. None of that matters. You need to *own* the customer's problem, not pass the buck.

Customers don't care about company problems, they want their concerns met.

In face-to-face situations, maintain eye contact and use nonverbal behaviors that show your interest in hearing it all. Be careful of facial expressions that may convey skepticism, boredom, or anything that may discount the customer's concerns. If your contact is by phone, avoid dead air or prolonged silences, as we discussed in Chapter 4.

Avoid any comments that would be construed as challenging the customer. If you suspect that the problem may be caused by customer misuse of the product, wait until the whole complaint is expressed and then ask some tactful questions about how the customer is using the product. The issue is *not* whether the customer or the company is "right." The productive

---

ANOTHER LOOK

Seven Deadly Sins of Feedback Cards

Too often, companies use feedback cards as an easy way to get customer insights and, perhaps, as an alternative to having to deal with customers face to face. (Again, this is a typical approach of reluctant-compliant feedback gatherer described above.) Here are seven ways such cards fall short of being effective:

1. Customers strongly tend to fill out a card only when they are extremely upset or extremely happy. Customer experiences in the larger gray area in between will seldom generate enough interest to give us usable feedback.
2. The card is not readily available. Sometimes customers have to ask for a card—and they generally won't, unless they are particularly upset (see 1, above).
3. Some cards have too many questions and use check boxes or rating scales that may be irrelevant to the customer's current concern. If the restaurant service was too slow, customers don't want to have to answer a bunch of questions about food temperature, ambiance, cleanliness, and so on.

4. Some cards are too open ended. They may be essentially a blank form that invites customer comments. This requires a lot of work from the customer who may find it difficult to express the problem in writing.
5. Customers may not know what to do with the card when it is completed. Some cards fail to have prepaid postage or even an address, thus requiring the customer to deposit it in a designated box. Or, worse yet, some cards require the customer to put postage on it before mailing!
6. The card fails to reassure customers that you really want this feedback, encourage people to complete it, and thank customers who use it.
7. The card mixes marketing surveys with customer service questions. In addition to scales for rating service, the card may ask for information about how the customer first found the business, age or income demographics, postal code information, and so on. While such data may be useful for marketing, it should not be a part of a customer service feedback card unless absolutely necessary.

attitude is one of cooperation and problem solving. As previously discussed, you create a good feedback climate by reinforcing customer behaviors, not by challenging them. If customers face a debate or argument every time they voice a concern, they will quit giving feedback.

ACT ON COMPLAINTS IN PRODUCTIVE WAYS

You successfully open the door to receiving useful negative feedback. Now, what can we do to act on customer complaints? Two fundamental steps can lead to a successful resolution and enhanced customer loyalty.

1. **Feel the Customer's Pain: Empathize**
   Recognize that upset customers are likely to be disappointed, angry, frustrated, or even in pain—and they blame you to some extent. Typically they want you to do some or all of the following:

   - Treat them with respect and empathy
   - Listen to their concerns, understand their problems, and take them seriously
   - Compensate them or provide restitution for the unsatisfactory product or service
   - Share their sense of urgency; get the problems handled quickly
   - Avoid further inconveniences
   - Punish someone for the problem (sometimes)
   - Assure them the problem will not happen again

   Respond to complaints with **empathy**. This means sincerely considering how you would feel if you were this customer. Express this understanding with comments such as, "I'm sorry you were disappointed" and "I can see why that would upset you." Be sensitive to wording and be honest in your reactions. You may say "I've never seen that kind of problem before" but be sure to add "but I see why you'd be disappointed" or similar comments.

   Sincere empathy can go a long way toward satisfying customer needs.

2. **Do All You Can to Resolve the Problem**
   Take whatever steps you can to solve the immediate issue. If the product is unacceptable, get them a replacement. If an employee was rude, apologize immediately and do whatever you can to repair the relationship.

SERVICE SNAPSHOT

How to Kill Off Feedback

The following text that appears on a Web page shows how *not* to solicit feedback. Under the "Customer Feedback/ Feature Request Area" we find this: (Note: The company's name has been changed).[4]

Customer Feedback/Feature Request Area
Tell us what's on your mind (good or bad!)

Thank you for your interest in giving X-corporation feedback for the current as well as future versions of our products. It is with your suggestions and comments that we can continue to work to produce products which meet the needs of our end users.

*** *You will Receive No Response with This Form* ***

This form is for feedback/feature request submissions only. Please do not submit sales questions, support questions, or email unsubscribe requests to this form as you will not receive a response.

In addition, please review the Top Customer Questions [on our Web page] as we have noticed that many feedback submissions are regarding one or more of those issues.

I understand that I will not receive a response to my feedback and would like to continue to the feedback form.

Probes

1. How would you feel about giving feedback that the company will not respond to?
2. Does this feedback page make you want to do business with X-corporation?

Sometimes, an acceptable solution to a problem will be perceived differently by different people. Don't always assume that you know what the customer wants. In most cases, a good tactic is to simply ask the complaining person what he or she would regard as an appropriate solution. More often than not, the person will request something perfectly reasonable and perhaps even less drastic than the company would be willing to do. Do what is requested, and the problem is resolved.

OTHER PROACTIVE WAYS TO GET FEEDBACK

Fishing for feedback should be assumed to be an everyday activity. Ongoing *naïve* **listening** is more of an attitude than a strategy. As its name implies, this kind of listening conveys that you don't know—are naïve—about what customers want. Your task is to invite them to explain it to you. You do this by creating an atmosphere of cheerful receptiveness to customer comments, even—*especially*—comments that might not be pleasant to hear. In prompting customers to share what they're thinking, use open-ended questions to get the most information.

Cheerfully invite customers to explain their feelings or concerns.

Open-ended questions cannot be answered with a simple yes, no, or other simple response but instead encourage a considered, meaningful response. For example, restaurant servers who ask an open-ended question like, "How else can I make your dinner enjoyable?" will get a broader range of responses than one who asks the more common, "Do you need anything else?" ("No") or "Is everything okay?" ("Yes").

ANOTHER LOOK

The Allegiance Technologies™ Active Listening System

Allegiance Technologies has developed a Web-based "active listening system" (ALS) that provides an exceptional turnkey customer and employee dialoguing tool. After you read this, take a few moments to go to *www.Allegiance.com* and look at the system's demo.

Allegiance Technology gathers four kinds of customer input: complaints, compliments, questions, and suggestions. This input is directed to the client company while the complaining customer can remain anonymous if he or she wishes to. The system also provides measures of customer loyalty and satisfaction before and after the company responds to the feedback. The person filing a complaint is also asked what he or she would like to see the company do to remedy the situation. In this way, the customer or employee is drawn into a dialogue and enjoys engagement with the company. The feeling of engagement goes a long way toward earning allegiance and building confidence in management. Allegiance Technologies sells three versions of the ALS—one for customers, one for employees, and one for partners. All three versions follow the same general format. Client organizations subscribe to the hosted service, which is modestly priced—less expensive than the cost of developing a similar in-house system.

By having a neutral third party acting as a conduit between the customer (or employee) and the organization, frank and open communication can be achieved. Any feedback can be submitted anonymously; the person giving the feedback need only provide an email address to Allegiance, not to the client company. This anonymity feature makes the system especially useful for employees who may fear retaliation. (It can be useful for government-mandated processes for facilitating whistle-blowing on company misdeeds.)

Customers or employees who do not have Web access can submit feedback by telephone, at kiosks, or in person. Designated representatives then enter the comments in the system.

Timing is critical when you get customer or employee input. Early recovery is far easier than letting a bad situation fester and then trying to fix it. Act on complaints quickly, tactfully, and efficiently using a three-step process of (1) feeling empathy, (2) resolving the problem, and (3) offering something more to exceed what the customer anticipates.

Efficiency of responses is easily monitored by the ALS. In both the customer and employee versions, a built-in clock provides metrics that indicate how long it takes to respond and close out a dialogue. Managers can quickly determine the status of any input and, if necessary, provide resources needed to make response times acceptable. Nothing impresses people as significantly as quick follow-up.

ANOTHER LOOK
Encouraging Continuous Feedback

To generate a continuous, ongoing flow of good feedback, apply these simple tips:

- Listen—don't explain or justify. Avoid being defensive. Learn to withhold your response. While someone criticizes you it is not the time to explain or justify your actions, even if you feel the criticism is unwarranted or stems from a misunderstanding. Listen now, explain later. Being defensive stifles your feedback. It tells others you are more interested in justifying yourself than in understanding what they are saying.
- Use the feedback as an opportunity to obtain more information—especially specifics. Honest questions will support and encourage the continued flow of feedback. For example, say, "That's very helpful. Tell me more. Is there anything else I should know about that?"

- Express an honest reaction. You certainly have a right to express your feelings about the feedback received. You may well say "I'm a little surprised (or frustrated or disappointed) you had that experience, but I can see your point" or "I'm not sure what to say. I never even thought of that, but I will from now on." Be careful to not sound like you are judging the person. Accept his or her perceptions at face value.
- Thank the person for providing feedback. Let him or her know that you realize how risky giving feedback can be, and express your appreciation for their efforts.

Using these kinds of communication behaviors gives you the opportunity to avoid turning off future feedback that could be valuable to you.

In addition to being open to customer-initiated feedback, companies should also reach out for feedback. Four systematic ways to do this are as follows:

- Focus groups
- Explorer groups
- Customer surveys
- Mystery shoppers

Try Focus Groups

Focus groups have been widely used in marketing and can also provide customer service feedback.

Focus groups have long been used for marketing research, and they can play an important role in understanding customer and employee expectations as well. Although some marketing consultants may disagree, there's no great mystery to how focus groups work, and any intelligent person could run one effectively.

Here is the procedure for creating and getting the most from a focus group:

- Select a sample for your customers or employees to join with you in the focus-group session. Don't just pick people you know or customers you like. You may, however, want to be sure they are among your better customers by qualifying them according to their influence or how much they spend with you.
- Formally invite the customers or employees to participate, telling them when and where the focus group will meet, as well as how long the session will take. Let them know the reason: that you are attempting to better understand their needs and how you can better be of service to them.
- Limit your focus group to not fewer than five or more than a dozen people. Ask customers to confirm their attendance, but expect that some will not show up. Fifteen confirmed reservations will generally get you 12 actual participants. Follow up with phone calls to confirm attendance.
- Reward focus-group participants. Give people something for their participation. For example, a company may give focus-group participants merchandise, a gift card, a free dinner, or even cash. The value of the gift should be at least what the participant would earn for an hour of creative work.

When running the focus group:

- Set the stage by having someone from top management moderate the group.
- Create an open atmosphere where participants will feel comfortable giving you all kinds of feedback. Be polite, open, encouraging, and receptive.
- Avoid cutting people off when they're making a critical comment, and do not, above all, be defensive of the way you're doing things now.
- Keep any follow-up questions open ended. Don't interrogate or imply judgment of a participant's comments.
- Acknowledge compliments that group members may express, and thank the contributor for the compliment. Then make a statement such as, "We're happy to hear that we are doing things you like. Our major purpose here is to identify ways we can do a better job in meeting your needs. How can we do even better?"
- Limit the group to a predetermined amount of time; typically a one-hour or 90-minute (maximum) session works best. Focus-group sessions that are any longer than that will start to lose people's interest.
- Record the entire focus-group session and transcribe key notes for review. As you analyze the results of the group session, look for key words that might tip you off to what customers are looking for.
- At the end of the focus-group session, of course, be sure to thank the participants for all of their input.

The critical key to successful focus groups is the careful analysis of the information you receive. It may be necessary to transcribe, word for word, the entire discussion and to read this transcription carefully. This can be laborious but the careful processing of such qualitative data can lead to important insights about customer/employee perceptions that might never come out in other feedback sessions.

Use Explorer Groups

Explorer groups go to other businesses to see how they do things. When you hear about a great idea another business is using, send out an explorer group to scope it out. One retailer known for exceptional service encourages employees to take a company van and visit the scene of a great service idea used by another company. They take notes and discuss possible implementation in their store. Explorer groups need not be sent only to direct competitors; often totally unrelated businesses have great ideas you can use.

Another way to gather great data is to "explore" how your own organization is serving customers by being a "customer." Call the company and listen to the impression created by the person answering the phone. Is this what your customer is hearing? How do you like it? Then visit other locations or areas in your own organization and see how you are treated.

Explorer groups are forms of **observational research**, which is most effective when carefully planned. Before going exploring, decide what you are looking for. Limit the exploration. For example, if you are looking for better ideas on merchandise display, focus on that rather than other factors such as employee behaviors. If you are interested in how a competitor handles training classes for its customers, check out the classes, not pricing strategies or other factors.

Sending employees out to explore what others do can be fun and rewarding.

Exploring can be fun for your employees. Many will enjoy being "sent on a mission" to gather ideas and insights. Listen carefully to their observations and thoughts about implementing these in your organization.

Use Customer Surveys

Customer surveys are systematic ways of asking a series of questions to determine what the respondents—and, if the sample is random, many of your customers—think. Selecting a representative sample is critical to the accuracy of the survey. A **random sample** means that any customer has an equal chance of being selected for surveying. A **stratified random sample** means that a certain category of customers has been selected and that anyone in that category has an equal chance of being surveyed. For example, a bank may decide to survey higher net-worth customers—say those with more than $300,000 in assets—to gather their impressions about service. Assuming it is impractical to survey every one of the people in that demographic, they will seek to randomly select a sample of people who fit that description. If proper selection techniques and statistical analysis are used, the sample should accurately represent the thinking of all people in that category.

Customer surveys must be carefully designed in order to be effective feedback tools.

When you conduct a customer satisfaction survey, what you ask the customers is important. *How, when,* and *how often* you ask these questions are also important. However, the most important thing about conducting a customer satisfaction survey is what you *do* with their answers.

THE MECHANICS OF ASKING FOR CUSTOMER SURVEY INPUT

You can use a number of techniques for asking your customers whether or not they are satisfied with your company, your products, and the service they received. Among the choices are as follows:

- Face-to-face interviews as they are about to walk out of your store or office
- Telephone surveys calling customers at home or work
- Mail questionnaires they complete and send back to you or (more commonly) email surveys they respond to online. Personalize emails to avoid spamming laws and keep the survey brief and easy to complete
- Written surveys handed to customers with a mail-back envelope or a drop box
- Internet-based surveys that invite customers to go to a Web site to complete a brief form. Typically, companies give some incentive (such as a future discount) to people who take the time to do complete the survey

WHEN TO CONDUCT A CUSTOMER SATISFACTION SURVEY?

The best time to conduct a customer satisfaction survey is when customers have recently completed a transaction with you and the experience is fresh in their minds. If you delay, responses may be less accurate. Customers may forget some of the details, color their answers because of confusion with other visits, or even confuse you with some other company.

WHAT TO ASK IN A CUSTOMER SATISFACTION SURVEY?

One school of thought advocates that you only need to ask a single question in a customer satisfaction survey such as, "Will you buy from me again?" The Net Promoter scale discussed earlier uses just one response, "Would you recommend us to others?"

While this minimalist approach is a tempting way to reduce your survey to this supposed "essence," other researchers argue that you can get additional useful information without imposing on respondents. Just as with the use of simple yes–no (versus open-ended) questions, it is too easy for customers to answer yes to the "Will you buy from me again?" question whether they mean it or not. You want to ask other questions in a customer satisfaction survey to get closer to the expected behavior and to collect information about what to change and what to keep doing.

You may well decide to ask the basic customer satisfaction questions:

- How satisfied are you with the purchase you made (of a product or service)?
- How satisfied are you with the service you received?
- How satisfied are you with our company overall?

And ask the customer "loyalty questions":

- How likely are you to buy from us again?
- How likely are you to recommend our product/service to others?
- How likely are you to recommend our company to others?

If you give the respondent choices to mark in response to these questions, be certain that you cover all possible choices. The specific design of survey questions goes beyond the scope of this book. However, the KISS (keep-it-simple-surveyors) principle is a good guideline.

One useful tip is to *not ask questions at all*. Instead, give customers a series of statements followed by agree–disagree scales. For example:

Please circle the number that best reflects your degree of agreement with the following statements: 1 = strongly disagree, 2 = disagree, 3 = neither agree nor disagree, 4 = agree, 5 = strongly agree

1.	**The business office is conveniently located.**	**1 2 3 4 5**
2.	**The tellers in the bank are generally friendly.**	**1 2 3 4 5**
3.	**The manager is readily available if I need to speak with him or her.**	**1 2 3 4 5**
4.	**Product prices are fair.**	**1 2 3 4 5**

Be sure that each survey statement deals with only one variable. For example, avoid saying "the business office is attractive and well-staffed" because it may be one or the other but not both. Likewise, "prices of company products and services are excellent" may confuse a respondent who thinks product price is fine, but services are too high.

Using this technique for the "big three" loyalty questions, you might ask people to agree or disagree (again using the five-point scale) with these statements:

- *I am generally satisfied with _____ company.*
- *I intend to continue doing business with _____ company as the need arises.*
- *I would recommend _____ company to others.*

If you did no more surveying than these three items, you could develop a fairly reliable indicator of where you stand with regard to customer loyalty. Note that the third item is the NPS questionnaire scale.

You may, of course, also want to drill down with more pointed questions about what customers like and don't like. If you suspect, for example, that waiting time is a potential turnoff for your customers, ask about it. Use "I feel that I am served promptly" followed by agree–disagree scales. Likewise, any potential turnoff that you get wind of (whether regarding value, systems, or people) may be worth looking into more deeply.

Many surveys offer unstructured space for customers to add comments. These open-ended responses can be useful and also provide relief for respondents who feel that the survey does not cover areas of importance to them.

HOW OFTEN SHOULD YOU CONDUCT A SURVEY?   The best answer is "often enough to get useful information, but not so often as to annoy the customer." Modern technology has made asking for feedback easier and has led to "**feedback fatigue.**" Such fatigue can happen when companies generate email feedback requests (or follow-up phone calls) every time a customer uses its service or buys its products. This can be annoying and possibly result in distorted information. If the response rate (the percentage of people who fill out the survey) drops, you may be inducing feedback fatigue. Give your surveying a rest.

Also, the frequency with which you conduct a customer satisfaction survey should depend on how often you interact with your customers. If you sell automobiles (or similar major purchases) a feedback request is usually appropriate. If you sell small items and see your customer every few days or more, asking for survey feedback after every transaction will quickly become

Keep surveys simple and concise. Don't overburden respondents.

Avoid surveying too much. Customers can develop feedback fatigue.

annoying. If you suspect that surveys are becoming annoying to customers just ask them if this is the case. A comfortable and honest dialogue with customers strengthens relationships.

WHAT TO DO WITH ANSWERS FROM A SURVEY?   Regardless of *how* you ask customers for their feedback, *what* you ask them in the customer satisfaction survey, and *when* you survey them, the most important part of the process is what you *do* with their answers. Gathering data only to ignore it is a waste of organizational time and energy—a mark of the reluctant-compliant feedback gatherer. Don't survey just to go through the motions.

Compile the answers from different customers and look for trends. Consider analyzing for differences by location and/or product. If the survey reveals weak areas act on the information you gathered, using the data to prioritize tasks. Work first on turnoffs to fix the things the customers have complained about. In addition, investigate their suggestions to improve the company and products in those areas that mean the most to your customers.

Finally, look for ways to show people how their responses are appreciated and are being acted upon. That may take the form of individual responses to the customers if appropriate or simply be fixing the things that they tell you need to be fixed. Use your company newsletter or other forms of communication to express appreciation for feedback and to show how customer input is being used to improve the company for the benefit of customers.

Use "Mystery Shoppers"

Mystery shoppers (sometimes called secret shoppers) are hired evaluators who visit or contact companies posing as customers to assess how they are treated. Typically a mystery shopper works as a contract worker for an independent research agency. The agency is hired by retail firms, restaurants, and similar businesses to provide an objective evaluation of their customer service and possibly other aspects of the business.

Mystery shopping can help you understand your business from a customer perspective.

Mystery shopping has become a big business with many firms offering these services. If you Google "mystery shoppers" you will get more than 2 million hits. Many are for firms offering mystery shopping services, and many are advertising for people to do the shopping. Yes, you actually can get paid for shopping.

Mystery shoppers can help companies know what their customers experience, and can inform companies about things that need improving. Armed with the right information, businesses can make necessary improvements. Shopper findings are used in developing employee training materials, for improving business operations, for improving product quality, and for comparing one location to another.

The reports from mystery shoppers are also used to point out positive things. Shopper findings are used to help identify store locations and employees due rewards for outstanding customer service or cleanliness. Secret shoppers are sometimes even allowed to reward employees on the spot for meeting certain criteria. It can be fulfilling for a shopper to hand an employee a certificate for a paid day off for doing a great job!

One challenge faced by mystery shopping is the problem of reliability—are the observations consistent? For example, does slow service or messy facilities look the same to all observers? Although firms train shoppers extensively, subjective elements enter into the evaluations made. One shopper may rate a characteristic as a 5, while another may see the same characteristic as a 3. Who is right? And how does a manager convey critical comments to employees if it's pretty much one person's word against another? The shopper may report a rude clerk, but the clerk denies it. Who is right?

Enter the latest advancement in mystery shopping: use of digital video. Several firms now offer hidden camera visits by evaluators that tape the actual experience in living color. One such firm, Human Touch Consulting (*www.HumanTouchConsulting.com*), visits thousands of businesses (including many fast-food restaurants) to gather video footage. Actually, it is no longer "video" per se, but images that are digitally recorded and stored on a computer. The evaluations are streamed via the Internet back to the client organization within 48 hours of the mystery shop. The action is filmed through a camera lens mounted in a button on the evaluator's shirt. The evaluator has a tiny computer taped under his or her clothing that records both visual images and sound.

Hidden video recording is being widely used to improve the accuracy of mystery shopping.

The beauty of such technology is that the camera eliminates the subjective judgment of the shopper. Once shot, the video can be edited and sent to a client organization within a few days, all via the Internet. Managers in the restaurants can then sit down with employees and invite them to view the tape. The manager can simply ask "How do you think you did with that customer?" and sit back and listen. The employee gets the benefit of exceptionally clear, robust data—feedback that he or she may use to improve service skills.

The video shopper can also pan the dining room, parking lot, and counter area to give an unbiased assessment of cleanliness, the lack of which is a huge turnoff in the restaurant business. In short, this approach gives managers and employees exceptionally detailed and objective feedback.

A FINAL THOUGHT

Capturing and using feedback is critical to success. If, for some reason, you cannot apply the ideas in this chapter (perhaps you do not have organizational authority), there is something you can do: Simply maintain a **complaint log** to capture ideas from customers. The shortest pencil is better than the longest memory. At a minimum, develop a habit of jotting down descriptions of feedback received (especially complaints) and the actions taken to resolve them. Volunteer to describe ideas you gathered in regular staff meetings or informal conversations with colleagues. Invite others to discuss how the situation was handled or brainstorm other ways it could be done.

Create a file (electronically or hard copies) where you collect your notes or comments. Look at these files periodically to learn from the feedback received and actions taken to deliver better customer service. Doing this helps keep a focus on the importance of feedback in maintaining constant service improvement.

Summary of Key Ideas

- Many people dislike negative feedback, which can be embarrassing or hurtful. It is human nature to try to avoid it.
- Feedback is a form of coaching that can teach us to be better at what we do. A complaining customer can be our best friend.
- Companies have varying levels of commitment to feedback: reluctant-compliant (they get it because they feel obligated to), active listener (they are open and receptive), and metric-conscious (they systematically process and measure it over time).
- For some organizations, *increasing* the number of complaints heard may be an effective strategy. If the amount of feedback received is low, something may be blocking customers from speaking out.
- Feedback cards are a relatively unproductive way of getting customer input, although they are better than nothing. The design of the card will impact the quality and quantity of feedback received.

- Calculating a Net Promoter Score (NPS) is a simple process that provides good metrics about a critical measure of satisfaction: the likelihood that people would recommend your business or organization.
- How we react to customer complaints will determine whether we get additional "coaching." Our first response is important. Avoid putting the customer on the defensive, instead of simply accepting the criticism.
- Four systematic ways to proactively seek out feedback are focus groups, explorer groups, surveys, and mystery shoppers.
- Customer surveys work best when the instrument is carefully designed and administered to a random sample (or a stratified random sample) of customers. Repeated administration of surveys is useful so long as the customer is not inconvenienced or annoyed.
- Feedback fatigue is a fairly recent but increasingly common problem. When people are too frequently

asked to complete a feedback form (usually online or via email) they get tired of it.

- Focus groups gather unstructured observations and opinions from customers or potential customers. Explorer groups evaluate the ways other companies do things.
- Mystery shoppers use observational research techniques to reflect the kinds of experiences your customers have when doing business with you. The latest approach to this uses hidden video to gather particularly robust data.
- Regardless of organizational authority, you can keep simple notes of service challenges in a complaint log. Share these and brainstorm ways to better build customer loyalty in your organization.

Key Concepts

active listener	explorer groups	mystery shoppers	random sample
complaint log	feedback fatigue	naïve listening	reluctant-compliant
customer surveys	focus groups	Net Promoter Score (NPS)	ripple effects
empathy	metrics-conscious	observational research	stratified random sample

Reviewing the Facts

1. Describe in your own words the reasons many companies fail to get enough negative feedback.
2. How can organizations become more open to feedback? What kinds of employee training would help? What would you tell your employees about feedback importance if you were the boss?
3. Explain the concept of Net Promoter Score. Why is this score important? How can managers use this number to improve service?
4. Describe the three levels of feedback commitment. Select three companies or organizations you are familiar with and describe which level they seem to be using.
5. Describe the relative advantages and disadvantages of focus groups. How can they be useful? How could they go wrong?
6. What are some advantages of explorer groups? How could they go wrong?
7. Summarize the most important factors in creating a valid survey. What are some ways that surveys can go wrong? How can data potentially be distorted?
8. What are the rules of thumb on how often customers should be surveyed?
9. What are mystery shoppers and how can such feedback processes provide useful data? What should managers avoid when employing this feedback technique?

Applying the Ideas: Getting Customer Feedback

1. Suppose that you own a retail shop. Design a feedback card that could be used to gather useful feedback. Describe how you would implement this system. Who would get the cards? How might you encourage customers to use it? What would you seek to avoid?
2. Focus on an organization you now work in. This could be a business, church or civic group, student organization, or even a class. Write a brief paper describing the feedback receptiveness in this organization. Do the leaders seem eager and willing to get feedback? Have they put mechanisms in place to gather feedback? Are they reluctant-compliant, active listeners, or metric-conscious?
3. Select a company or organization for which you can survey a sample of customers. (You might want to use your college class as an organization.) Create a simple NPS ballot and ask at least 10 customers to complete it. Calculate the Net Promoter Score. How do you think this score compares with other similar organizations? Justify your answer.
4. Plan and conduct a focus group for an organization. Describe how you prepare it, invite the right participants, conduct the session, and process results. How did it go? What did you learn? What would you do differently next time?
5. Go to the Internet and look at the Web site for Allegiance Technologies (*www.Allegiance.com*). Look through the description of their active listening system and report on its capabilities. Then Google (or use a similar search engine) "customer feedback systems" and see what you find. How do these systems compare? Based on this research, which system would you choose for your organization?
6. Visit the Web site for Human Touch Consulting, the firm that offers digital video evaluations of company experiences (*www. HumanTouchConsulting.com*). Write a brief paper describing the advantages and disadvantages of this approach. Search online for other companies that offer similar services and compare them.

Consider this Case

The Disgusting Restaurant

Traveling across the country, Paul and his friend Randy often stopped at restaurants with familiar brands. One advantage of this is that the menu and often the service quality are likely to be consistent and familiar. Occasionally, however, they were disappointed. A breakfast stop at one such restaurant was extremely unpleasant. Although the menu was the same, the restaurant was disgustingly dirty. Paul was so upset, and he visited the company's Web site to register a complaint.

After inputting a lot of required personal information (name, address, email, phone number, time, date and location of the visit, etc.), Paul described his concern and even took the time to assure the company that he was a fan—he frequently visited their stores. Part of his message said,

> *I am a fan of* [the company's restaurants]. *I eat there regularly and love my local store in* [his home town]. *It's clean and well run. So I was SHOCKED at how utterly filthy the* [town and state] *store was. Honestly—I have never been in a dirtier restaurant. Ever. Disgusting. They are really hurting your brand and that disappoints me. BY FAR, MOST* [of your restaurants] *are super—This one really, really needs some management attention.*

Paul immediately got this email response:

> *Thank you for visiting* [company's] *website. Below is your email which has been submitted to* [our] *Customer Response Center. While replies to this e-mail cannot be received, should you need to contact us again, please feel free to contact us through* [company web site.com]. *Thank you.*

A few days later, Paul got another email that said this:

> *Hello Paul:*
> *Thank you for taking the time to contact* [company] *to share a recent experience at one of our restaurants.*
>
> *First, I hope you'll accept our apology for this unsatisfactory visit. It's always our hope that*

> *your visits will be pleasant ones. Because we want to make sure that your experience is properly investigated, we need to verify the address of the restaurant you visited. From your contact, we were unable to determine this.* [Note that in the original message Paul identified the restaurant as located at Exit 177 off Interstate 80 in a particular town and state.] [The company] *is a franchised organization and as such, we'd like to forward your comments to the franchise owner of the restaurant you visited so he or she can take appropriate action. Please call* [company's] *national customer satisfaction toll-free line at 1-800-555-6227 to give us the address of the restaurant you visited. We will then follow up on your comments.*
>
> *Again, thank you for taking the time to contact* [company]. *We hope we have the opportunity to serve you in the future.*
>
> *Angela*
>
> [Company's] *Customer Response Center*

Probes

1. How easy does this company make it to get feedback from customers? What could they do differently if they are genuinely interested in hearing from customers?
2. What is the effect of their requirement that Paul call them with an exact address (considering that there is only one restaurant located at that Interstate highway off ramp)? What message does that requirement send?
3. How do you react to the company's excuse that this is a franchised restaurant and (by implication) that they have no responsibility for cleanliness standards?
4. If you were in a leadership position with this large organization, what would you do to improve the ways they handle such feedback? Be specific.

Consider this Case

Fear of Feedback

A business magazine article on customer service began with a quote that said, "The biggest obstacle to knowing what customers really think about us is fear. We fear they'll tell us our product or service stinks, that we're horrible people, and that we should never have set foot on earth."

Danica, a marketing manager for a mid-sized technology firm, read this opening paragraph and thought, that is so true! We have got to get more proactive about getting and using good feedback. Too many of my people are afraid of feedback. They seem to be tuning out that type of painful feedback—and we need it if we are ever going to grow this business.

Danica was a good amateur golfer and she knew the value of coaching. Her game had improved dramatically since she had hired a coach, Roy, a rather crusty fellow who was quick to point out when she was doing something wrong. Sometimes Roy could be annoying—such a stickler for detail—but he had helped her improve her game to a much lower handicap. Danica thought, maybe I need to look at feedback from customers in the same way: occasionally painful, but almost always useful.

The article she was reading described an Australian beer company that did a great job of using customer feedback to make company decisions. They even asked customers to help determine marketing plans and names for new products—the operational decisions usually made by executive committees. In many ways, the brewery has turned ownership of the company over to customers—and this had caused a lot of positive word of mouth for that company.

Another example described a toy retailer that sends out weekly surveys to its database of 6 million customers asking them to rate their recent store experience, including the cleanliness of the bathrooms! Company founder attributes her company's dramatic success to its intense focus on gathering customer feedback.

Wow, Danica thought. That's what I want to see happen in my company. We have to get more proactive about gathering customer feedback. Waiting for it to arrive on its own is fraught with peril. To know what customers are thinking, we must *ask*.

Probes

1. How does this case reinforce the ideas in this chapter? How is feedback like coaching?
2. If most of Danica's customers communicate with the company only via the Internet or phone, what are the best steps she can take to enhance feedback gathering? Be specific about a plan of action.
3. Assume that Danica's company has been "reluctant-compliant" about gathering feedback—its employees go through the motions but are not very committed. What steps could she take to change to a more aggressive feedback focus?

Source: Some material in paragraphs 4 and 5 were excerpted from Ben McConnell and Jackie Huba, *Fight the Fear: The 10 Golden Rules of Customer Feedback* appearing in *MarketingProfs.com*, March 2004.

Building a Customer Service Strategy: Your Ongoing Case

Let's go back to the ongoing case you selected. This will be either your current employer, a specific organization you want to work in, or one of the two hypothetical organizations described in Chapter 1: Independent Auto Sales and Service (IAS) or Network Nutrition Distributors (NND). Now consider the following questions as you develop a customer service strategy:

Strategy Planning Activities

1. Consider the arguments for and against the three levels of feedback receptiveness discussed in this chapter. Select a reluctant-compliant, active listener, or metric-conscious focus and present a case for applying that approach.

2. What mechanisms would you, as a leader, put in place to gather the appropriate level of feedback needed for organizational success? Be specific and detailed.

3. Develop an effective customer survey instrument that would best meet the needs of your company. Make it detailed enough to gather important data without burdening customers. Pretest your survey by asking a group of people similar to your customers to fill it out. Ask for their feedback regarding the survey's clarity, ease of use, and overall effectiveness. Edit a new version of the survey instrument based on comments from the pretest.

4. Use the Net Promoter Score approach to gather information from employees or colleagues. To what degree do the results

show loyalty or lack thereof? If the score is lower than you would like, ask (using open-ended questions) for ideas that would motivate them to be even more loyal. Identify two or three specific actions you could take to enhance the likelihood of employee loyalty.

5. Write a general description of how open you believe your organization's people are to negative feedback. Include your personal feelings. What do you and others do to block the reception of good feedback? Again, be very specific.

Notes

1. Fred Reichheld. *The Ultimate Question* (Boston: Harvard Business School Press, 2006), p. 21.
2. These U.S. Office of Consumer Affairs statistics are quoted in [no author] *The Customer Service Manager's Handbook of People Power Strategies* (Englewood Cliffs, NJ: Prentice-Hall, Inc., 1999), p. 3.
3. Ibid.
4. *http://www.dataviz.com/eforms/feedback/generalfeedback. html*. Downloaded March 3, 2006.

CHAPTER 9

Recover the Potentially Lost Customer
Building Trust and Lasting Relationships

The Way It Is...the Importance of Customer Recovery

On average, companies lose half their customers every five years. This fact shocks most people, including most top executives who have little insight into the causes of the customer exodus, let alone the cures, because they do not measure customer defections, make little effort to prevent them, and fail to use defections as a guide to improvements.

Another study's scary statistic says that unhappy customers will continue to voice their dissatisfaction for up to 23 years. Can you recall product brands or companies you won't touch because of a negative experience years ago? I know people who refuse to buy Exxon gasoline because of a tanker oil spill more than 30 years ago. I know people who refuse to consider auto brands because their father had a "lemon" a generation ago. And I bet you can recall a restaurant you have not been back to in many years after a bad experience or sick tummy.

No company can afford to have its brand dissed in the marketplace for decades. No company can thrive while losing half its customers every five years, although that's the average across most industries. Leaders would all agree, but surprisingly little attention is paid to addressing customer defections. About 80 percent of marketing budgets are devoted to acquiring new customers, even though it costs three to five times more to replace a lost one than to keep an existing customer. Companies could get dramatically better results from simple efforts to hang on to the customers they already have. **Customer recovery**—the effort to satisfy unhappy.

UNDERSTAND THE CASE FOR CUSTOMER RECOVERY

Customer recovery can substantially impact profitability. Studies indicate that money and effort invested in recovering lost customers come back to the company many times over. Numerous organizations calculate that customer retention efforts return $2 for every dollar invested. In addition, "recovered" customers give the airline *more* of their business after they have been won back. This is consistent with the rationale for gathering good feedback discussed in Chapter 8. A saved customer tends to be a better customer.

By contrast, unrecovered customers do a great deal of damage. Various surveys conclude the following:[1]

- 60 percent of those who read about a bad customer service experience online stop or avoid doing business with the company involved
- 79 percent of customers who have a negative customer experience told others about it
- 85 percent said they wanted to warn others about their bad experience

- 65 percent wanted to dissuade others from doing business with the offending brand
- 76 percent indicated that word of mouth had influenced their purchasing decision.

Many companies miss a huge opportunity when they fail to proactively seek to recover lost customers—to repair damage to customer relationships. The problem starts with the fact that many companies don't even know how many customers they are losing. Service expert Jill Griffin of *loyaltysolutions.com* cites a nationwide study that found that up to 50 percent of marketing and sales managers could not identify their company's percentage of annual customer loss. Those who thought they did know their firm's defection rates said it averages 7–8 percent, when in fact, their companies were losing 20 percent or more of their customers every year.

Another national study showed that 43 percent of sales managers and 47 percent of marketing managers said they did not conduct **defection interviews** thus depriving their companies of insight about root causes of defection. And even when companies do interview departing customers, they may not get the real reasons. Studies show that newly departed customers are often reluctant to tell why they left. They may be embarrassed to explain why they're leaving. Instead they will give an easy reason for defection, like "I am moving" or "I don't need the products anymore." It's often better to wait a month or two to get the real facts. Getting accurate exit interview information can be challenging unless gathered with sensitivity. You need to win the defecting customer's trust (which has probably been damaged) in order to gain honest responses.

A study by Paramus, New Jersey-based Marketing Metrics, found firms have a much better chance of winning business from lost customers than from new prospects. The research found the average firm has a

- 60–70 percent probability of successfully selling again to "active" customers,
- 20–40 percent probability of successfully selling to lost customers,
- and only a 5–20 percent probability of making a successful sale to new prospects.

If you win the customer back, they enter a second life with you. This **second life cycle** (the recovered customer) can differ greatly from the "first life cycle" of the same customer in at least four ways:

1. The recovered customer is already familiar with the products and services you offer. You don't have to teach him or her about what you can do.
2. You are likely to have more data about the likes and dislikes of this particular customer than about any first-time customer and can offer a more targeted service.
3. The customer may feel flattered by your efforts to win him or her back. This can often lead to sales greater than that generated by newly recruited first-time customers.
4. The length of the "prospect phase" and the "new customer phase" would arguably be shorter in the second life cycle than in the first one. The customer will become acclimated to doing business with you more quickly.

We talked in Chapter 6 about the importance of reducing turnoffs. These efforts are worthwhile, but reality tells us that we cannot predict with certainty (let alone prevent) every possible customer complaint. In short, dissatisfaction happens. What we choose to do about it can go a long way toward creating customer loyalty. It's not always easy, but saving customers can be enormously profitable. Effective complaint handling begins with the right attitudes coupled with the skills we'll discuss in this chapter.

MAINTAIN HEALTHY ATTITUDES ABOUT CUSTOMER RECOVERY

The best attitudes stem from the desire for a win-win relationship with the customer. Both parties want to feel good about the business transacted. This is not necessarily a "customer is always right" attitude. The issue is not whether the customer or the company is right. The attitude is one of cooperation and problem solving that won a loyal customer.

Companies that do not aggressively work to recover lost customers miss a huge opportunity.

Customer recovery isn't always easy, but it is tremendously profitable.

"The customer is always right" may not be a good motto. Better to think about win-win relationships, not who is right and who is wrong.

In addition to a problem-solving rather than blame-setting attitude, service recovery is best handled when seen as an **attitude of opportunity** rather than a painful chore. Granted, most of us would prefer not to hear about customers' dissatisfaction. That's human nature. But given that dissatisfaction does occur, an attitude of accepting the opportunity and challenge can be useful. Customer complaints are opportunities to cement relationships. The vast majority of such relationships are worth saving, although occasionally—I stress *occasionally*—we need to let go of the chronic complainer, as we'll discuss later in this chapter.

Always see customer complaints as challenging opportunities to cement relationships.

An attitude of opportunity begins with an understanding that complaints are triggers for improvement. There can be no positive change without negative (corrective) feedback. And much of corrective feedback comes to us disguised as complaints.

No one likes to hear complains, but they are truly opportunities for possible change, not reasons for defensiveness. Carefully track the number of complaints and resolution. More important, complaints must be relayed to the appropriate organizational areas to minimize re-occurrences. Remember that a rising number of complaints is usually a sign of success, not failure. Often, complaining customers are the ones most committed to a band. British Airways found that 87 percent of customers who complained did not defect.

Defensiveness against feedback is the enemy of improvement.

Defensiveness is the enemy of improvement. To succeed at customer service, we need to work very hard to reduce defensiveness and focus on how the dissatisfied customer can be our best friend!

ANOTHER LOOK
Action Ideas to Deal With Difficult Customers

Upset customers are liable to have strong feelings when you, your product, or your service lets them down and they'll probably want to "dump" these feeling on you. Deal with the feelings before concentrating [only] on solving the problem.

Here are 5 action ideas that deal with the customers' human needs:

1. *Don't let them get to you.* Customers may make disparaging and emotional remarks using incendiary language sometimes—don't rise to the bait. They are upset and may say things they don't mean. Cut them some slack. Concentrate on listening nondefensively and actively. Don't acknowledge their out-of-line comments.
2. *Listen—listen—listen.* At the risk of beating this horse too much, apply the ideas on listening discussed in Chapter 3. Look and sound like you're listening. The customer wants to know that you care and that you're interested in his or her problem.
3. *Stop saying sorry.* "Sorry" is an overused word; everyone says it when something goes wrong and it's lost its value. How often have you heard—"Sorry about that, give me the details and I'll sort this out for you". Far better to say "I apologize for..." And if you really need to use the *sorry* word, make sure to include it as part of a full sentence. "I'm sorry you haven't received that information as promised Mr. Smith." (It's also

good practice to use the customer's name in a difficult situation.)

4. *Empathize.* Psychology studies conclude that empathy is an instinct, hardwired into the human brain. We instinctively feel for other people. In dealing with customers, empathy isn't necessarily about agreement; it's only acceptance of what the customer is saying and feeling. Basically the message is "I understand how you feel." Obviously this has to be a genuine response; the customer will realize if you're insincere and they'll feel patronized. Examples of empathy response would be "I can understand that you're angry" or "I see what you mean." Again, these responses need to be genuine.
5. *Build rapport.* Sometimes it's useful to add another phrase to the empathy response: Include yourself in the picture: "I can understand how you feel" or "I don't like it either when I'm kept waiting." This has the effect of putting you on the customer's side and builds rapport. Some customer service people get concerned with this response as they believe it'll lead to the question "Then why don't you do fix it?" The majority of people won't make unrealistic demands if they realize that you're a reasonable and caring person.

If they do, then continue empathizing and tell the customer what you'll do about the situation. "I'll report this to my manager" or "I'll do my best to ensure it doesn't happen in the future."

LOOKING INSIDE

What Are Your Feelings about Dealing with Difficult Customers?

Below is a list of words that may describe the ways you feel about dealing with upset customers. Select the five that best describe your general feelings. When you have finished this chapter, review these words to see if you have some better ideas on how to deal with these emotions. Discuss your results in a small group, asking for their feedback on how to deal with the feelings you have.

afraid	confident	foolish	relieved
angry	confused	frustrated	sad
anxious	contented	glad	silly
apathetic	distraught	hesitant	uncomfortable
bored	eager	humiliated	uneasy
calm	ecstatic	joyful	wishful
cautious	elated	nervous	
comfortable	excited	proud	

My top five:

1. _____
2. _____
3. _____
4. _____
5. _____

Probes

1. How can you reframe these feelings—change the negative into potential positive—when adopting an attitude of opportunity?
2. To what extent are these feelings irrational or unreasonable? Is it possible that some may reflect fears or discomfort that you could learn to manage? Give an example of what you might do.

DEVELOP YOUR RECOVERY SKILLS

To reduce the negative ripple effects of "unrecovered" customers, we need to develop **recovery skills**. As the name implies, we try to recover the potentially lost customer. We can do this best by applying the following ideas:

Feel Their Pain

The first step in developing recovery skills is to recognize that upset customers are likely to be disappointed, angry, frustrated, or even in pain, and they blame you to some extent. Typically they want you to do some or all of the following:

- Listen to their concerns and take them seriously.
- Understand their problem and the reason they are upset.
- Share their sense of urgency; get their problem handled quickly.
- Compensate them or provide restitution for their dissatisfaction or inconvenience.
- Eliminate further inconvenience.
- Treat them with respect and empathy.
- See that someone is punished for the problem (sometimes).
- Assure them the problem will not happen again (to them or others).

You may not need to do all of these things in every situation, but typically the upset customer requires several of them. Feel their pain.

Clarify and Do All That You Can to Resolve the Problem

Ask for clarification of customer concerns but don't interrogate, which can make customers act defensively.

Be certain that you have a clear understanding of the customer's concerns or needs. Ask appropriate questions to clarify exactly what the problem is, but don't interrogate. Phrases such as "help me understand" or "can you tell me exactly what happened" convey a sense that you are genuinely interested in helping.

Once you have a clear understanding of the nature of the problem, move to fix it as expeditiously as possible. Customers appreciate any efforts you expended to solve their problem quickly. If a product needs to be replaced, do it now. If something needs to be repaired (or repaired again), give a high priority to scheduling such repairs. If a delivery has to be rescheduled, do it immediately and confirm it with the customer. Share the customer's sense of urgency. People will appreciate anything you can do, especially if you can do it quickly.

Go Beyond: Offer "Symbolic Atonement"

Although this sounds like a religious term, we are really talking about something more down-to-earth. Symbolic atonement simply means giving something to the customer to make up for the problem he or she has had. It is voluntary—you are rarely required to give back—and shows a sense of caring. Often it cannot fully repair the damage, but it symbolically indicates that you are trying. It's the "something extra" you give to appease the customer and help win him back.

Give the upset customer some symbolic repayment for his or her problem.

This atonement is called symbolic because, in some cases, you cannot fully repay the customer. For example, if a person complains about having to wait 15 minutes on hold, you cannot give her back those 15 minutes. But you can give some token that recognizes her inconvenience. You cannot fully repay a customer who has to take time and energy to return a faulty product, but you can give him something to express your appreciation that he went to the trouble.

What other kinds of things can we do to make up for customer problems? Chapters 10 through 12 of this book will deal in much more depth with this topic. Meanwhile, to give you a few examples of symbolic atonement, here are a few possible ideas that could be seen as going the extra mile with a complaining customer.

- *Offer to pick up or deliver the goods to be replaced or repaired.* Auto companies got a lot of mileage out of offering to pick up recalled cars for product defects rather than have customs bring them in.
- *Give a gift of merchandise to repay for the inconvenience.* The gift may be small, but the thought will be appreciated. Things like a free dessert for the restaurant customer who endures slow service or extra copies of a print job to offset a minor delay are examples. It's the thought that counts.
- *Reimburse for costs of returning merchandise such as parking fees, etc.* (Mail-order retailers often pay all return postage fees to reduce customer annoyance and inconvenience.)
- *Acknowledge the customer's inconvenience and thank him or her for giving you the opportunity to try to make it right.* A sincere apology can go a long way. Make the wording of the apology sincere and personal. Say "I'm sorry you had to wait," rather than "The company regrets the delay." Empathy can be expressed with statements like, "I know how aggravating it can be to…" or "I hate when that happens, and I'm sorry you had to go through…"
- *Follow up to see that the problem was handled.* Don't assume the customer's difficulty has been fixed unless you handled it yourself and have checked with the customer to see that the fix held up.

If you don't have the authority to do what's needed to save the customer, become his or her advocate. Go to bat for the customer with your boss.

You may not have the authority to do all of these things (although many of these cost practically nothing). But you can go to bat for the customer with your boss. Just your being the customer's advocate can help reduce much of the problem. If all goes well, you should feel a genuine sense of satisfaction after handling an unhappy or irate customer.

SERVICE SNAPSHOT

MarketingProfs.com Recovers a Lost Customer

A few years ago I subscribed to an online newsletter called MarketingProfs. After several months of use, I decided it wasn't particularly useful to the research I was doing at that time. I noticed that I was being billed a small monthly charge on my credit card, but didn't think much about it until I recently tried to log in. When the system wouldn't let me in, I emailed the publisher. To my amazement, I received a prompt, friendly, and personal reply. And, although the problem was caused by my own mistake, they took responsibility for it. Here is my original email and their response:

My Original Message:

To: *support@marketingprofs.com*

Subject: Question/Comment from General Website Form

I am unable to access this site despite being billed every month. It's been a while since I tried, but I need it now.

Their Response:

(I received the following response *within an hour* from their "Customer Service Samurai.")

Subject: MarketingProfs access

Hi, Paul—

It looks like you hit the "unsubscribe" link in one of our emails many moons ago. That removed you from our member list, but back then, it didn't actually stop your monthly Premium billing. I'm not sure how that could have happened.

I wish I could reverse all of those charges, but our credit card system won't let me issue credits on transactions that are more than 90 days old. Here's what I'm going to do for you instead:

1. I'm reinstating your membership. Your password is still xxxyzz.
2. I'm canceling your monthly Premium status so that the billing will stop.
3. I'm upgrading you to a Premium Plus member (normally $199/year).

Now you will have access to ALL of our Premium content on the website, including our virtual seminars. You'll start receiving the newsletter again, as well as announcements about upcoming seminars. Our next one is on Thursday, and it's about search engine optimization.

Read about that seminar here:

http://www.marketingprofs.com/newprem/library/default.asp

Your Premium Plus membership is good through February 12 of next year. I hope this arrangement is satisfactory, and I'm very sorry about the glitch with your old membership.

Contact me directly if there's anything else I can do for you!

Regards,

Shelley Ryan
Customer Service Samurai
www.MarketingProfs.com
Premium hotline @ (888) 572–7934

Needless to say, MarketingProfs did everything right. They responded promptly, explained and solved the problem, and offered symbolic atonement in the form of the Premium Plus membership. Well done, Shelley.

Look Back and Learn from Each Situation

When a difficult customer situation has cooled, review it with an eye toward improving your skills. Think about how you used your recovery skills, and ask yourself questions like these:

- What was the nature of the customer's complaint? Was it generated primarily by value, systems, or people turnoffs?
- How did the customer see the problem? Who was to blame; what irritated the customer most; why was he or she angry or frustrated?
- How did I see the problem? Was the customer partially to blame?
- What did I say to the customer that helped the situation?
- What did I say or do that seemed to aggravate the situation, if anything?
- How did I show my concern to the customer?
- What would I do differently?
- Do I think this customer will do business with me/us again? Why or why not?

Making careful notes of your responses to these questions can build your confidence and professionalism.

Understand Your Own Reactions If the Customer Is Still Not Satisfied

Often you can professionally recover an unhappy customer, but not always. People are not always agreeable or even rational, so sometimes you too get upset. Working with customers involves what organizational researchers call **emotional labor**. This term means we sometimes need to do things that we don't much feel like doing. For example, our job may call for us to be upbeat and pleasant even when we don't feel that way (and we all have our less-than-chirpy days). Professionalism requires that we do everything possible to avoid letting our anger or frustrations damage our interactions.

Listed below are the key things to remember:

- *If you try your best to satisfy the customer, you have done all that you can do.*
- *Don't take it personally.* Upset people often say things they don't really mean. They are blowing off steam, venting frustration. *If* the problem was really your fault, resolve to learn from the experience and do better next time. *If* you had no control over the situation, do what you can, but don't bat your head against the wall.
- *Don't rehash the experience with your coworkers or in your own mind.* What's done is done. Recounting the experience with others probably won't make their day any better, and rehashing it to yourself will just make you mad. You may, however, want to ask another person how he would have handled the situation.

Building service skills is an ongoing professional activity. Looking back on both positive and negative experiences can be very fruitful in providing guidance for future actions. Learn from your successes and your failures.

ANOTHER LOOK

Handling Complaints of Four Customer Types

Typical companies are likely to face at least five types of complainers. Each type is motivated by different beliefs, attitudes, and needs. Consider the following definitions of the types of complainers, how one might respond to them, and the danger of not handling complaints effectively.

The Meek Customer. Generally, will not complain. These are among that large silent majority that feels uncomfortable confronting the company. They are still likely to express their complaints to others with whom they feel more comfortable talking.

Our response: Must work hard at soliciting comments and complaints and act appropriately to resolve complaints. Fish for their feedback before a mild annoyance becomes a major complaint.

The Aggressive Customer. Opposite of the meek customer. This type person readily complains, often loudly and at length. They don't hesitate to make a fuss in front of others.

Our response: Listen carefully to be sure you understand the complete problem. Agree that a problem exists and indicate what will be done to resolve it and when. Avoid meeting their aggressiveness with your own. Speak softly and avoid inflammatory language that only serves to fire them up more. The Aggressive Customer does not respond well to excuses or reasons why the product or service was unsatisfactory, so give them straight talk.

The High-Roller Customer. Expects the absolute best and is willing to pay for it. Likely to complain in a reasonable manner, unless a hybrid of the Aggressive Customer.

Our response: Is interested in results and what you are going to do to recover the customer service breakdown. Always listen respectfully and actively and question carefully to fully determine their cause. Ask "what else?" and correct the situation. Like the aggressive customer, the high-roller customer is not interested in excuses.

The Rip-Off Customer. The goal is not to get the complaint satisfied but rather to win by getting something the customer is not entitled to receive. A constant and repetitive "not good enough" response to efforts to satisfy this customer is a sure indicator of a rip-off artist. Fortunately, such people are rare.

Our response: Remain unfailingly objective. Use accurate quantified data to backup your response. Be sure the adjustment is in keeping with what the organization would normally do under the circumstances. Consider asking "What can I do to make things right?" after the first "not good enough."

HANDLE THE OCCASIONAL CUSTOMER FROM HELL

"Stubbornness is the energy of fools," says a German proverb. Sometimes we need to draw the line between upset customers with legitimate problems and excessively **chronic complainers** who consume our time with unreasonable demands—the dreaded "customer from hell." These folks can create emotional *hard* labor for us!

Here are some action tips for dealing with these challenging people:

Action Tip 1—Be Sure This Really Is a Chronic Complainer

Step one in dealing with such people is to be sure you've got a chronic complainer. When you've tried the normal recovery approaches and nothing seems to work, look for the following telltale signs of CCs:

- They always look for someone to blame. In their world accidents don't happen: someone is always at fault, and it's probably you.
- They never admit any degree of fault or responsibility. They see themselves as blameless and victims of the incompetence or malice of others.
- They have strong ideas about what others should do. They love to define other people's duties. If you hear a complaint phrased exclusively in terms of what other people always, never, must, or must not do, you may be talking to a chronic complainer.
- They complain at length. While normal complainers pause for breath every now and then, chronics seem able to inhale while saying the words, "and another thing…"

Action Tip 2—Know What to Do with This Guy (or Gal)

When you are certain that you are faced with that occasional chronic complainer (they really are quite rare, fortunately), try these techniques:

- Actively listen to identify the legitimate grievance beneath the endless griping. Rephrase the complainer's main points in your own words, even if you have to interrupt to do so. Say something like, "Excuse me, but do I understand you to say that the package didn't arrive on time and you feel frustrated and annoyed?"
- Establish the facts to reduce the complainer's tendency to exaggerate or overgeneralize. If he says he "tried calling all day but as usual you tried to avoid me," establish the actual number of times he called and when.
- Resist the temptation to apologize, although that may seem to be the natural thing to do. Since the main thing the complainer is trying to do is fix blame—not solve problems—your apology will be seen as an open invitation to further blaming. Instead, ask questions like, "Would an extended warranty solve your problem?" or "When would be the best time for me to call you back with that information?"
- Force the complainer to pose solutions to the problem, especially if he doesn't seem to like your ideas. Also, try putting a time limit on the conversation by saying something like "I have to talk with someone in 10 minutes. What sort of action plan can we work out in that time?" The object of this is to get him away from whining and into a problem-solving mode.

Action Tip 3—Take a Break, Cool off, Reflect

High-stress customer contact employees need breaks. Emotional labor is very hard work. Its difficulty is not limited to just handling complaints. Card dealers in Las Vegas casinos receive frequent breaks because managers recognize the stress they face. They serve people who may become very emotional (high or low) and need to keep a sharp edge so that they don't become emotionally drained, thus affecting their work accuracy. Representatives who handle complaints and knotty problems may get great satisfaction out of helping people, but they do so at a fairly high emotional price.

Take a break after particularly challenging encounters. Allow yourself to cool off—to detach from the episode—and to think back on what happened with an eye to learning from it. Don't beat yourself up for what happened—that serves no useful purpose. But do learn from it.

HANDLE A NASTY COMPLAINT LETTER OR EMAIL

Today's customers don't write letters very often, but when they do it reflects a significant effort. Perhaps because they are fairly rare, a letter carries considerable impact. Letters provide a graphic and tangible reminder of a customer's dissatisfaction. It makes sense to respond to them and to document what you've done.

Respect the time and effort the complaining customer exerted.

Email complaints are becoming increasingly common. Email has become the medium of choice for many customers. It is quick an easy, although it still requires writing—an activity that is not all that easy for many people. So we need to respect the effort expended and respond.

This notwithstanding, many written messages go unanswered! You have probably had that experience yourself. Letters seem to evaporate and emails to companies have a tendency to fall into a cyber world black hole. And when they do, the unhappy customer gets much more aggravated.

So, rule number one for letters and email complaints is this: *answer them!*

If you choose to respond to a letter or email with a phone call (this may positively surprise your customer), be certain to have the original message in front of you and to refer to the specific points as written. If you answer a letter/email with a letter/email of your own, be certain that your message conveys an attitude of problem solving, projects goodwill, and exhibits professionalism

Be an effective writer by applying the same human relations skills you would use in a face-to-face encounter. Specifically, be especially sensitive to people's feelings, interests, wants, and needs. Failure to do so creates unnecessary strains on a relationship. The fact that a letter or email is a hard copy of a conversation makes it especially important that it be tactful. A poorly written document will come back to haunt you.

ANOTHER LOOK
Just How Hard Can It Be?

By Sherron Bienenu, executive consultant

How hard can it be to answer an email, to say thank you, to simply *respond*?

Are you on the receiving end of "dead air"? Is your email box empty (well, except for spam)? Do you feed "black holes" with your work? Read and commiserate with me.

Are you guilty? *Please* read—for the sake of your career.

Just How Hard Can It Be?

A noted female author emailed me to inquire about a presentation coaching before her national tour. I responded immediately. She agreed to an arrangement and suggested dates. Then, she didn't answer my next email *or* the one after that. I had apparently dropped all my work down a black hole. How hard would it have been to write, "Thanks, but I've decided to do something else"?

A woman I met at a networking luncheon emailed me about my training programs. I replied immediately with

several options, including suggestions about other trainers. I spent about half an hour researching her question and crafting my response. She didn't bother to acknowledge receiving the information. How hard would it have been to say "thanks"?

Let's count the keystrokes:

1. Reply
2. t
3. h
4. a
5. n
6. k
7. s
8. Send

Now, how hard is that?

Don't get me started on how long it often takes to receive thank-you notes after shipping wedding gifts

(continued)

or giving birthday presents or hosting dinner parties—or how many people never acknowledge what you did for them at all.

A manager with the Human Resources Department of a large, national telecommunications company called to say that they had a "communications problem." They hired me to conduct an extensive communications audit. At the end of the process, I submitted a report that included several recommendations, but the first two (and significantly the largest) were these:

1. Return your phone calls.
2. Answer your emails.

Really.

I could go on and on. Okay, I will go on and on. My husband and I took my mother to special buffet brunch at Marriott Hotel on Mother's Day—her choice. Brunch was, well, adequate. On the way out, there were three staff people at the door with no other guess around. I said, "Thank you." None of the three even acknowledged us. First of all, they should have been the ones to express their appreciation. If they were a bit classier, something like "Thank you for choosing the Marriott for your Mother's day celebration" would have been appropriate. Being ignored was not. How hard would it have been to thank us?

Another one of my pet peeves: The retail clerk who never meets your eyes but takes your money, hands over a receipt, and then mutters, "There you go." How much effort goes into an additional "thanks"? One small syllable. I often find myself saying thank you to them, to which they too often say "no problem." Gee, I didn't realize I had potentially been a problem.

One last story really disappoints me. A former colleague and mentor (whom I have often used as a role model and positive example in books and speeches) wrote to ask me about suggestions for improving the business communications program at his university. Over several emails and a telephone conversation, we discussed one or two visits and maybe a speaking engagement. Then all conversation stopped. No return call or email. Nothing. How hard would it have been to tell me that they decided to make other plans, to pursue other options? He's not my role model any longer. And I checked his Web site. He didn't die.

Second questions: Why the lack of common courtesy? I used to say "Raised by wolves," but that's not fair to wolves. A colleague was lamenting the tacky professional dress of job applicants and cried, "Where are their mothers?" Ah, but in some cases, their mothers have no manners, either.

So How Do People Learn?

Learn by watching. Do not, however, use "watching" as an excuse ("No one sends thank-you notes anymore!"). Watch the right people, the successful people, the people who make you feel good about yourself when you are with them. They are usually the people who respond to you, acknowledge you, give you credit, and thank you.

I hear other excuses coming: "She makes me feel inferior because she does everything well," and "he makes me uncomfortable because he remembers so much about me." Did you ever consider that they do their homework to learn about you or work a little harder to do things well?

Yes, it takes hard work to produce great work. It takes some effort to initiate a small act of kindness. It takes a *little* effort to remember a birthday and send a free e-card. It takes very *little* effort to answer an email. It takes almost *no effort at all* to say those two little words: "Thank you."

If you have been cheering my viewpoint throughout this column, then you probably do respond and do say thank you. Please understand that knowing you and doing business with you is a please—for everyone. We all appreciate the time you take and the work you do. It makes us feel good that you are conscientious about your relationships. We will work harder for you because you treat us right. Thank you.

Source: Sherron Bienvenu, PhD Communication Solutions Newsletter June 2005. See *www.ChinUp.net.* Reprinted with permission.

USE HUMAN RELATIONS SKILLS TO CONVEY APPROPRIATE TONE

Let's consider a few principles of human relations with an eye toward how these might apply in phrasing messages to unhappy customers. Below are six action tips for applying fundamental human relations principles to bolster customer relationships. The first and perhaps most basic principle concerns the other person's self-interest.

Action Tip 4—Remember that People Are Strongly Interested in Themselves

It is the nature of the human being—and all other known creatures, for that matter—to be concerned with and motivated by their own personal needs, wants, and interests. This self-centeredness, or egocentricity, is normal and not particularly harmful unless carried to the extreme, where it overwhelms any caring about others. People are often socially conditioned to not say it our loud, but there is constant background music in everyone's mind that says

Every person's primary
motivation is self-interest.

You can turn a person's
natural egocentricity into
an advantage by recogniz-
ing his or her needs.

The receiver-oriented
communicator thinks of
the other person first.

"what's in it for me?" Always think carefully about the other person's view of **"WIIFM"** when expressing ideas or encouraging action. This other-centeredness is fundamental to persuasion and human relationships.

When people speak or write, they reflect this egocentricity in their language. Every fifth word written or spoken by a human being is I or one of its derivations—*me, mine, my, we, ours, us.*

The point here is that service providers can turn this egocentricity into an advantage if they recognize the customer's needs. Effective communicators learn to express concern and appreciation for the views of others in all their messages.

Action Tip 5—Use Receiver-Centered Messages

One important way to reflect consideration for another person is by phrasing your message in terms of that person's viewpoint. Expressing the appropriate viewpoint involves much more than just selecting certain keywords. A genuine receiver viewpoint causes the tone of a letter or email to reflect a sincere interest in the other person. Self-centered writers and talkers think of themselves first. Receiver-oriented writers think of and convey their messages in terms of what the message receiver wants or needs.

One "red flag" that you should look for are the words *I, me, my,* or the plural *we, us, our* found in abundance in your messages. Second or third person (*you,* or the impersonal, *one*) often conveys more receiver interest and objectivity.

Please don't conclude that you should try to eliminate the use of I and its variations. To do so may be impossible in some cases. In other cases, your efforts may result in rather tortured syntax and excessive wordiness. Besides, the use of *I, we,* or *me* does not always indicate a self-centered viewpoint. For example, the person who says "I hope you will be happy with this product" is not really violating a receiver viewpoint even though the sentence begins with the word *I.* The overall tone and sense of caring for the other person is far more important than simply avoiding the use of first-person pronouns.

Look at the following sample sentences and see the difference in the tone of the receiver-oriented version compared to the "I-centered" one:

I-Centered	Receiver Viewpoint
We require that you sign the sales slip before we charge this purchase to your account.	For your protection, we charge your account only after you have signed the sales slip.
I have been a sales professional for 22 years.	My 22 years' experience as a sales professional provides a strong background in understanding customer concerns.
I am sending your report back to you for an update.	So that you may update this report to the most current version, it is being returned to you.
I'd like to show you this life insurance plan.	As a young father, you'll be interested in a life insurance plan tailored to families with small children and a limited budget.
I need you to fill out the application form and get it back to me.	As soon as you can complete the application form, we can get you …

Phrasing ideas in terms of the receiver's viewpoint conveys an interest in the other person and recognizes the principle of good human relations.

Action Tip 6—Talk with People as Individuals, not Groups

We can improve the tone of communication by phrasing our information as though talking to individuals, rather than groups. A personally addressed business letter, for example, singles out a reader for individual attention. Such a letter conveys a more sincere regard for the specific person than one addressed to "Dear Customer" or "Dear Fellow Employee."

Avoid the "blanket tone"—attempting to talk to people as a group rather than as individuals. When a message makes a person feel lost in the crowd, the **blanket tone** is responsible. For example, consider the blanket tone in the excerpts below:

Blanket Tone	More Personal Tone
When a thousand requests are received from prospective customers, we feel pleased. These requests show that our product is well received.	A copy of the booklet you requested is being sent to you today. Thank you for requesting it.
The cooperation of our charge customers in paying their accounts is appreciated. By paying on time, they allow us to give better service.	I certainly appreciate your paying the account. Your prompt payment allows us to give you better service and keep prices down.

Strive to express ideas in terms of the individual's benefit. One way to do this is through direct address or "this means you!" statements. Each day we see examples of this approach in television and radio commercials. The announcer "personally" addresses each of the several million people who may be listening and attempts to make each one feel that he or she is spoken to as an individual. Direct address shows your receivers how your message applies to them and how it can meet their individual needs in some way.

Action Tip 7—Give People Positive Information

Positive language often conveys more information than negative language. It also tends to be more upbeat with a more pleasant tone. Rather than telling a person what is *not* or what you *cannot* do, focus on the positive—what *is* or what you *can* do. If you say, "I *cannot* give cash refunds on sale merchandise," it conveys only negative information. It does not say what you can do; it only rules out one of the possibilities. On the other hand, the positive statement "I can arrange to have the product exchanged for another model that may better serve your needs" conveys more specific and positive information.

Positive language also has a more pleasant ring to the ear. Yet many common negative phrases still creep up in customer service such as:

We *regret* to inform you that we cannot...

We have received your *claim*...(*claim* has a negative connotation for most people)

Your *failure* to maintain the servicing schedule...

We *regret* that we cannot permit...

To illustrate the difference in tone between positive and negative word choices, here is an example: A corporate executive wrote to a local civic group that asked if they could use the company's meeting facilities. To soften the refusal, however, the executive decided to let the group use a conference room, which might be somewhat small for its purpose, but was probably better than no room at all. Unfortunately, the executive was not sensitive to the effects of negative wording. She wrote thus:

> *We regret to inform you that we cannot permit you to use our company training room for your meeting, because the Beardstown Ladies' Investment Club asked for it first. This group has a standing date to use our place the third Thursday of every month. We can, however, let you use our conference room; but it seats only 25.*

A review of the message clearly brings out the negative words (*regret, cannot, seats only 25*) first, while the otherwise positive message (you can use the conference room) is drowned out.

A more positive way of addressing the same situation would be this tactful response:

Although the Beardstown Ladies' Investment Club has already reserved our company training room for Thursday, we would like to suggest that you use our conference room, which seats 25.

No negative words appear in this version. Both approaches convey the primary message of denying the request and offering an alternative, but the positive wording does a better job of building and holding goodwill for the company.

Let's look at some examples of negative and positive sentences. Note the tone of each. (The negative words are in italics.)

Negative Wording	Positive Wording
• You *failed* to give us the part number of the muffler you ordered.	• So that we may get you the muffler you want, will you please check your part number on the enclosed card?
• We *regret* to inform you that we must *deny* your request for credit.	• For the time being, we can serve you only on a cash basis.
• You were *wrong* in your conclusion, for paragraph three of our agreement clearly states…	• You will agree after reading paragraph three of our agreement that…
• We *cannot* deliver your order until next Wednesday.	• We can deliver your order on Wednesday.
• You are *not allowed* to park in the employee lot but must use designated visitor spots.	• You are welcome to park in our visitor's lot.

Action Tip 8—Avoid an Abrasive Tone

Abrasiveness refers to an irritating manner or tone that sounds pushy or critical. To determine if you tend to have an abrasive personality, you might ask yourself questions given in Look Inside:

SERVICE SNAPSHOT

Let's Treat Our Guests Like Criminals

The following notice was placed in the information folder at an Atlanta motel. Talk about negative wording!

IF ITEMS ARE STOLEN FROM THE ROOM!!!!!!!

25 INCH TV = $275.00

REMOTE CONTROL = $7.00

COFFEE MAKER = $25.00

RADIO ALARM CLOCKS = $17.00

HAIR DRYERS = $22.00

ICE BUCKET = $6.00

IRON = $28.00

IRONING BOARD = $25.00

BLANKETS = $25.00

BEDSPREADS—King = $75.00 Queen = $65.00 Full = $55.00

SHEETS—King = $18.00 Queen = $15.00 Full = $13.00

MICRO/FRIDGE = $290.00

PHONE = $30.00

INTERNETCORDS = $7.00

Probes

1. What negative message does this convey to guests?
2. Don't you think $275 for a cheap TV is a little high?

LOOK INSIDE
Do You Have Abrasive People

- Are you often critical of others? When you supervise others, do you speak of "straightening them out" or "whipping them into shape"?
- Do you have a strong need to be in control? Must you have almost everything cleared with you?
- Are you quick to rise to the attack, to challenge, to say no?

- Do you have a strong need to debate with others? Do your discussions often become arguments?
- Do you regard yourself as more competent than your peers? Does your behavior let others know that?
- Do you have a "short fuse" that causes you to lose your temper?

The abrasive personality will tend to communicate in a manner that can be irritating to others. Try to recognize in yourself whether you have a strong need to control or dominate other people or a tendency to have a knee-jerk reaction to things others may say. If you suspect that you do, it would be important for you to make an extra effort to soften the tone of your communications.

Assertiveness and abrasiveness are different. To be assertive is to be pleasantly direct.

Keep in mind that there is a major difference between being abrasive and being assertive. Assertiveness simply means that you express your feelings and observations in a normally phrased manner that is nonthreatening to other people. For example, instead of saying to someone, "You don't make any sense," the assertive person would say, "I'm having a difficult time understanding what you're saying." Or rather than saying, "Deadbeats like you burn me up," the assertive person might say, "People who consistently make late payments cause us a lot of extra work and lost revenue." Few people get offended by the assertive individual. Indeed, one definition of assertiveness is "being pleasantly direct."

Assertiveness means being pleasantly direct.

Action Tip 9—Be Appropriately Assertive but Not Aggressive

Many people confuse assertiveness with aggressiveness. **Aggressive behaviors** differ in the following ways:

1. *Aggressors communicate from a position of superiority.* Aggressive people feel that they know best or must get their way at almost any cost. They see communication situations as win-lose, meaning that they either get their way or they have lost. And if they lose, someone else has won! The idea of compromise or a decision whereby all parties benefit or win is foreign to them.
2. *Aggressors can be indirect, manipulative, or underhanded.* The aggressive communicator may not be the person with the big mouth. Sometimes aggressive people use tricks and manipulation such as false emotion or false roles designed to get their way.
3. *Aggressors set themselves up for retaliation.* Aggressive communicators eventually face adversaries. By being less than authentic, they spin webs of deception that get more and more confusing. Like habitual liars, they eventually lose track of what they told whom.
4. *Aggressors use a lot of judgmental or emotionally charged terms for emphasis.* The aggressive communicator thinks that strong language is clear but fails to see how it can create barriers to understanding. Emotional language almost always generates emotionally worded responses.

Assertive behaviors avoid these problems by being honest and authentic. They are based on beliefs such as the following:

1. *One should have high self-respect for one's own ideas and abilities.* Assertive communicators know that they are valuable. Their time, talents, and efforts are to be respected. They take a back seat to no one, although they do recognize and respect other people's different abilities.

2. *It is important to respect other people.* They see people as having a wide range of experiences and know that we can all learn something from another person. They know that organizational titles or social status do not guarantee people a right to the best ideas. People need people and can gain much from others.

3. *Win-win solutions can be found for many problems.* The purpose of communication is to create understanding, not to beat out another person. Conflicts or challenges need not be couched in win-lose terms. A fresh perspective or creative twist can often be found to create solutions that leave no one as a loser.

4. *Consensus is best created by direct and honest expression of points of view.* The assertive person wins by influencing, listening, and negotiating, not by manipulating.

5. *Honest, open relationships eliminate the desire for retaliation or distrust.* Communication does not get tangled in a web of game playing. Openness begets openness. People are more comfortable with assertive communicators. They can be trusted.

6. *Emotionally charged language is seldom effective.* Using strong, judgmental words hampers the resolution of problems or the creation of understanding. Neutral, descriptive terms are better. They will not turn listeners off.

Rather than relying on assertive and aggressive communication, some people are simply passive. They communicate ineffectively because they do not really care much—they are *apathetic.* They have chosen to stay out of a particular discussion. Do not confuse passiveness with assertiveness.

ANOTHER LOOK
Calming Hostile Customers

A hostile, angry reaction usually follows a certain pattern if it is handled skillfully. This pattern is called the **hostility curve**, illustrated in Exhibit 9.1. It is important to thoroughly understand each step of the hostility curve:

1. Most persons are reasonable much of the time. They function at a *rational level*. At this level, you can reason with them about things.

2. When irritations pile up or a specific incident provokes a person, he or she will *take off*, blowing off steam, possibly becoming abusive, and in general expressing a lot of hostility. Once the person leaves the rational level, there is no use trying to get the person to be "reasonable."

3. This taking-off stage cannot last forever. If not provoked any further, the hostile person just runs out of steam and begins to *slow down*. He or she may feel embarrassed for making a scene.

4. At this point, you can say something *supportive*, such as, "Things can be awfully frustrating when you're under so much pressure" or "I know this has been an upsetting experience for you." In addition, you must be supportive in your nonverbal behavior. Being supportive does not necessarily mean agreeing, but it does mean letting the other person know that you understand his or her feelings.

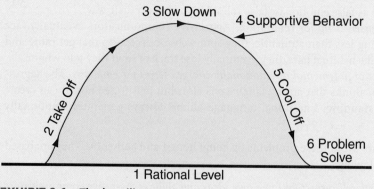

EXHIBIT 9.1   The hostility curve.

(continued)

5. Your supportive comments will usually help the hostile person *cool off*. He or she can come back down to the rational level.
6. Once the person has returned to the rational level, you can begin to *problem solve* with him or her about what caused the anger. Persons are in a mood to problem solve when they are rational, not when they are at the top of the hostility curve.

Probes

1. Why is it important to help an upset customer cool off before trying to solve the problem?
2. How can you best help him or her through the hostility curve? What specific things could you say? What should you avoid saying or doing?

A FINAL THOUGHT

Customer complaints are opportunities for building customer loyalty. Sure, complainers can be annoying, but they can also be your best friends. They can point out ways to improve and strengthen your business like no one else will. That's valuable intelligence for the competitive battlefield. Use it to recover the potentially lost customer, and, in doing so, improve your business and your career success.

Apply good principles of human relations and communication skills to move toward successful recovery of potentially lost customers.

Summary of Key Ideas

- **Customer retention** requires positive attitudes toward problem solving but not necessarily an oversimplified "customer is always right" mind-set.
- The key issue in customer disputes is not who is right or wrong, but rather how all parties can cooperate to solve the customer's concerns.
- A customer complaint is an opportunity to cement a relationship and create customer loyalty.
- Recovery skills are necessary to career success and will be regularly used in business.
- The key skills in recovery involve feeling the customer's "pain," doing all you can to resolve the problem, and then going the extra step via "symbolic atonement."

- After doing your best to deal with a customer problem, it is useful to review the episode and learn from it.
- The best way to handle the occasional chronic complainer is to understand his or her motives and then get the person to propose an acceptable solution.
- Effective communication uses human relations principles such as receiver self-interest, receiver-centeredness, individual treatment, and positive information.
- Abrasiveness is a drawback to customer relations, while assertiveness leads to better problem resolution.
- Three action tips describe specific actions for dealing with difficult complainers.
- Six action tips for applying human relations principles can enhance your customer recovery skills.

Key Concepts

abrasiveness	blanket tone	defection interviews	messages
aggressive behavior	chronic complainers	emotional labor	recovery skills
assertive behavior	customer recovery	hostility curve	second life cycle
attitude of opportunity	customer retention	reader self-interest	WIIFM

Self-Test Questions

1. In customer disputes, who is right or wrong is not the key issue. What overriding issue is more important?

2. What are the three important steps needed to recover the potentially lost customer?

3. What are some of the telltale signs of a chronic complainer? What special customer service techniques can be used when you are faced with a chronic complainer?

4. What human relations principles can we apply to improve our written communication?

5. Compare and contrast assertive versus aggressive behavior.

6. Describe in your own words key ways to apply principles of human relations to improve the likelihood of maintaining (or repairing) customer loyalty.

Application activity Defusing and Recovering the Unhappy Customer

Read the following brief case. Then get another person to role-play the part of the unhappy customer. Practice responding to his or her concerns in a constructive manner that could lead to recovering this customer. If possible, videotape your role-play and review the tape to identify nonverbal and verbal behaviors.

Before you get into this activity, look carefully at the language used to describe the situation. What problems do you see concerning the tone? How could you express the viewpoint of the two parties in more constructive terms? When role-playing, work through the "hostility curve" in Exhibit 9.1.

Consider this Case

A Hot Traveler and a Hot Motel Manager

The Motel Manager's Story

A big arrogant-looking fellow from a city several hundred miles away has just checked into your motel. He gives the impression that he is a big-shot government worker. He addressed the desk clerk in a grumpy and condescending manner and grumbled about the fact that he was stuck in this low-level motel—the only one in town—while he usually stays at the Ritz or "minimally a Marriott." After a short visit to his room, he storms into your office, claiming his air conditioner is faulty. You have recently spent $475 to repair the unit in his room. You are certain that he must have banged it with his fist and that he is responsible for the trouble with the unit. You are not about to let him push you around.

The Traveler's Story

You have just settled into a rather dumpy motel, the only one in this godforsaken town in the middle of nowhere. You are sweaty and tired, and wish your boring job didn't include travel to rural areas where there are no decent motels. It is mid-August, and it's hot. You flip on the switch to the air conditioner; there is a buzz, a hum, and a slight rattling sound. After several bangs with your fist, the rattling stops, but the air conditioner puts out only slightly cooler airs. After cussing like a wounded pirate, you storm back into the motel manager's office and inform him that he runs a cheap, dumpy, and poorly-cared-for motel. You demand that he immediately rush to your room and repair the damn air conditioner.

Probes

1. After role-playing this case with another person for a few minutes, invite the person to tell you what he or she is feeling.

2. Discuss exactly which words or actions you each found most offensive. Which words or actions moved you toward resolution of the problem (if any)?

3. How would you handle this situation if you were the manager?

Consider this Case

Customer Retention Done Right?

Sherry is an active online shopper. She and her husband recently moved into a new home and most of the new furnishings came from her skillful searching of various Web sites. She got very good at ferreting out quality products at bargain process. One of her purchases was a lamp for the living room. It looked exactly right on the Web site and arrived quickly. The brushed metal lamp had a globe shaped like a Champaign flute which made the lamp unobtrusive and a perfect look for the living room.

Some minor assembly was required, but when Sherry turned on the lamp she discovered that it did not have a dimmer switch, just an off–on switch. Sherry was sure she had read the product description carefully (she always did) and that it was to have a dimmer. She contacted the retailer and expressed her disappointment in no uncertain terms including the phrase "this product is misrepresented on your Web site."

The response from the retailer was immediate. An employee emailed back that she was sorry the product did not fully satisfy and said that she had contacted the manufacturer and would get some additional information soon. Within an hour the retailer sends another email saying that the manufacturer refused to replace the switch saying that the lamp has always had an off–on switch. The manufacturer further said they didn't feel a need to replace the product, implying that the customer was too fussy.

The retailer, however, felt differently about customer retention. Her email told Sherry that there had, indeed, been a misstatement on the Web site's product description. They further said that they had corrected the Web site and offered to take back the lamp (and pay for all shipping) or to give Sherry a $50 refund so that she could either purchase a dimmer switch at a hardware store or use the lamp as is, perhaps with a smaller bulb. The retailer again apologized and expressed its desire to keep doing business with Sherry.

Probes

1. How would you be likely to feel if you were Sherry?
2. How does the contrast between the manufacturer's inflexibility and unwillingness to accept responsibility contrast with the retailer? Which is likely to build customer loyalty?
3. What does this short case say about company attitudes toward customer retention?

Building a Customer Service Strategy: Your Ongoing Case

Let's go back to the ongoing case you selected. This will be either your current employer, a specific organization you want to work in, or one of the two hypothetical organizations described in Chapter 1: Independent Auto Sales and Service (IAS) or Network Nutrition Distributors (NND). Now consider the following questions as you develop a customer service strategy:

Strategy Planning Activities

1. In the beginning of this chapter, we said that "most top executives have little insight into the causes of their customer exodus, let alone the cures, because they do not measure customer defections, make little effort to prevent them, and fail to use defections as a guide to improvements." Write a one-page action plan showing how you could seek to change this as a leader in your organization?
2. Develop a policy statement for your employees that describes how your company feels about customer recovery. Limit this to a few sentences or bullet points which can be easily remembered and referred to by you and your staff. Begin this statement with: "We at [name of your organization] believe that…" Include a general description of actions you will take to recover customers.
3. Research recently lost customers. Contact via phone, email, or letters, a sample of customers you have recently lost (or suspect you have lost). Invite them to have an open dialogue with you about their complaints, reasons for defecting, and so on. Compile the responses and discuss them with your colleagues. What actions could you apply to recover these customers? How can you avoid future customers from defecting for the same reasons? Plan to make this a regular, systematic activity.
4. After gathering data on recently lost customers, ask your colleagues or department staff to estimate how many they think have been lost. Is their estimate reasonably accurate? If not, how can you help them understand the extent and impact of lost customers on the organization?
5. Hold a meeting to explore ways to engage all employees in customer retention efforts. How can your people feel engaged in this process? How could you adjust the rewards system to support these efforts?

Note

1. Ongoing survey results show varying numbers but all indicate similar consensus: As we have said repeatedly in this book, unhappy customers tell others about negative experiences which, in turn, impact the company's reputation and likelihood that others will do business with them. The data cited here are from Don Pepper and Martha Rodger's *Extreme Trust,* © 2012, p. 51.

PART 4

LIFE: Expectations

The fourth letter in our acronym is "E" for "expectations." Understanding the role of expectations in creating and maintaining customer relationships is crucial to service success. Psychological theory supports the notion that customers whose expectations are exceeded in some positive ways may feel some need or desire to give back—to strengthen their relationship with the person or organization that seems to be giving them more than anticipated.

The next three chapters focus on ways we can exceed customer expectations. Chapter 10 discusses the concept of value and ideas for creating an enhanced sense of value for customers. Chapter 11 deals with ideas for exceeding expectations in the quality and ease-of-use of information given to customers. The vast majority of products and services we buy today have an informational component—some information accompanies them or is necessary for the customer to benefit from the product. This provides an opportunity for exceeding expectations in that realm. Chapter 12 addresses opportunities for exceeding expectations in convenience and timing—an area that is arguably the most frequently cited turnoff.

When you have studied these chapters, you will be better equipped to create "A-plus service"—customer service that surprises and delights customers. This is a critical key to creating customer loyalty.

CHAPTER 10

Exceed Expectations with Value
Build Customer Loyalty with A-Plus Perceptions of Value

After reading this chapter, you should be able to

1. Define what constitutes A-plus value in the minds of customers.

2. Understand intrinsic and associated value which can affect a customer's loyalty to you or your company.

3. Apply seven categories of actions to enhance the customer's perception of value.

The Way It Is...Finding Value in Unusual Places

Some years ago a *Wall Street Journal* article sang the praises of the public toilets in Suwon, South Korea. The city is so proud of its exceptional toilet facilities that it gives weekly tours to show them off to tourists. The public restroom is inside a building with the sloping wooden roof of a traditional Korean pavilion. Guests are invited to try out its heated toilet seats, examine the sinks, and take pictures...Violin music plays in the background, and small paintings of the Korean countryside hang on the walls...The facilities have bouquets of flowers (both fake and genuine), automatic faucets, sliding stall doors for the disabled, and solar-powered heat. Speakers pipe in Vivaldi's "Four Seasons," Korean palace music, or recordings of chirping birds."[1]

While this level of service may seem far-fetched, it illustrates a fundamental point about the things we value: The perception of value is highly subjective, but people know value when they experience it. While long-term durability or utility is often seen as the ultimate value, companies generally cannot wait the many years needed for their customers to recognize that long-term value. What companies can do is focus on creating an enhanced *sense* or *perception* of customer value, just as the city of Suwon did with its exceptional toilet facilities.

DEFINE A-PLUS VALUE: WHAT IT IS

Poor value is a major form of customer turnoffs, along with ineffective systems and inappropriate people skills. On the flip side, exceptional value or, more accurately, exceptional *perceptions of value* is one way to create customer loyalty. We can build customer allegiance by giving them something that exceeds what they anticipate (what I call A-plus service)—an enhanced *perception* of value.

Marketing scholars define **perceived value** as a "subjective perception of the tradeoff between multiple benefits and sacrifices, relative to competition...This definition highlights not

> A basic definition of value is the perception of quality relative to cost.

only the benefits gained, but also the sacrifices or investments that a customer makes to gain the benefits. The difference may be positive, resulting in customer perceived value, or negative, resulting in customer perceived worthlessness."[2]

Several key ideas stand out in that definition. First, value is *perceived.* This means that it is individual and personalized. What you may find to be valuable may be worthless to me, and vice versa. Second, value arises from some trade-off between the benefits gained and the costs (sacrifices or investments) expended.

A more simplified definition of perception of value is a person's sense of a product or service's *quality* (benefits it provides to us) relative to its *cost.* For example, if you purchased a cheap throwaway product, say, an inexpensive disposable camera that costs less than $10, and the picture quality was not quite up to studio quality, you probably would not be overly upset. The camera's quality, relative to its cost, is what you anticipated—you expected snapshots, not professional portraits. If, however, you spent $900 for a deluxe camera with many professional features, you would have high expectations for the quality of the pictures the camera would produce. If the pictures were no better than those produced by a cheap camera, you'd have a right to be upset. You would have a *diminished* perception of the camera's value.

Likewise, if you gave a kid a few dollars to mow your lawn and he didn't get it exactly right you'd chalk it up to a learning experience. Your perception of value would be satisfactory—you got what you paid for, and probably what you expected. But if you hired an expensive lawn-care professional and the work wasn't up to snuff, your perception of value would likely be reduced or diminished because you didn't get what you expected, considering what you paid. You expect to get what you pay for; and the more you pay, the more you expect.

Recognize the Cost of Diminished Perceptions of Value

The history of commerce is filled with examples of how once-valuable goods diminished in value. At one time whale oil was a valuable commodity, telegraph service was a vital service, and brick-size mobile phones were all the rage. The markets changed and the old became worthless. Sometimes even good companies let their quality slip, and customers eventually catch on to the quality deficit. A company's failure to perceive and then respond to customers' diminished perceptions of value (the opposite of A-plus) can destroy a company.

Here is one historical example: In the 1980s and early 1990s, Volkswagen (VW) Corporation of America saw its sales drop by 90 percent from its 1970 high of over half a million cars a year to less than 50,000 in 1993. What happened?

Much of VW's competitive advantage in subcompact cars evaporated when competitors (especially the Japanese manufacturers) engaged in extended conversations with their customers and used feedback received to develop appealing features. While VW engineers knew the "right" way to position a steering wheel, Japanese compacts offered adjustable tilt wheels. While VW was certain that its radios were "just fine," competitors responded to customer desires for multispeaker stereo sound. Little automotive details like cup holders and power locks—features not really central to the core product of reliable transportation—provided a competitive advantage to companies that listened to their customers. VW didn't listen to its customers nearly enough. As a result, customers began to perceive VW as offering less value. By the early 1990s, Volkswagen of America was fighting for its life. Fortunately, VW learned from this experience and has produced a remarkable turnaround. By the late 1990s, the company regained its traditional position as one of the most innovative and successful auto manufacturers, and the company is now solid. But it almost didn't make it after having paid a terrible price for its indifference to customer wants.

A *USA Today* "test drive" article[3] reviewing Nissan's lowest-priced automobile illustrates how value expectations have risen. While, ostensibly, an automobile's primary function is to transport people from one place to another, we have all come to expect something more. The article on the new Versa model car was fairly balanced once you got past the first few paragraphs (designed to hook the reader, no doubt) which bemoaned the "riot of creaks from the instrument

ANOTHER LOOK

Of Wine and Corks and Perceived Value

Wine makers know that screw cap bottles are better and cheaper than the traditional cork. Yet it is impossible to change to such caps. It may be because buyers would equate screw caps with inferior wine. It may be because the whole event of wine drinking requires the cork.

How can this (perception of value) be changed?

1. It is possible that the transition could be made if the screw caps were very expensive in the first place—for example, enameled. If such caps became collectors' items, then the transition might be accomplished. Here the changed perception, from seeing screws as less desirable to more desirable, is an example of the direct blocking of the "cheap" image.

2. We might go in exactly the opposite direction. We could sell exactly the same wine at two prices: £12 with the usual cork and £10 with a screw cap. People would now set out to convince themselves that the cork was not that important a part of the event of wine drinking.

3. Another approach would be an education campaign to show that corks could go bad and could leak, whereas screw caps could not. This would be less effective than either of the other two approaches— making screw caps either dearer or cheaper—but could be combined with either.

It is almost impossible to delete or block a perception pattern. Another pattern needs to be set up to lead values in a different direction.

Source: Edward de Bono, "Perceived Value: When Considering Value, Perception Can Be as Important as Reality," http://www.thinkingmanagers.com/management/perceived-value.php. Downloaded March 20, 2006.

panel" and "the back seat that was as uncomfortably firm as a park bench," among the other negative comments. These criticisms surface despite Nissan's U.S. general manager asserting that the Versa is "one of our most trouble-free cars." Even the writer acknowledges later in the article a number of positive characteristics for this intentionally stripped-down model.

The challenge for the Versa is probably not competing with other low-cost new cars but rather with comparably priced but better equipped used cars. About a third of the article focused on what it calls "things of importance, rather than indulgence, that you sacrifice" on this vehicle. These "things of importance" are power windows, power locks, power mirrors, and the like. What are today being described as important was not long ago regarded as luxuries. Basic transportation is not enough; the expectation bar has been raised and anything lacking these kinds of features is seen as lacking in sufficient value.

Companies need to be aware of the constantly raising value bar. People demand and expect good value. The snake oil salesman may sell some product in the short-run, transaction-based business. But the likelihood of an ongoing relationship with customers who receive poor value is nil. Good value is a minimum, enhanced value is a competitive advantage.

CREATE AN ENHANCED SENSE OF INTRINSIC AND ASSOCIATED VALUE

Perception of value is based on how customers view both intrinsic and extrinsic or, associated factors. Understanding these factors is the starting point for creating A-plus value experiences for your customers.

Intrinsic Value of the Product Itself

Intrinsic value arises from the core product or service itself. Does it meet customer needs, do what it's supposed to do? This form of product value may not be immediately evident in some cases. We may assume a product is adequate because it seems to work, but the true extent of its value—especially its durability—may not be clear for some time. For example, a truck buyer may not fully appreciate the value until the truck has a hundred-thousand care-free miles on it. Similarly, the intrinsic value of a legal document an attorney prepared may not be fully evident until it holds up in court. The intrinsic value of a house painting job becomes apparent only when it still looks great years later.

The first-time car buyer may be delighted with his very basic transportation (think teenager getting his first set of wheels), but this delight diminishes as the buyer comes to expect more (like power windows or locks). One man reported that he was very disillusioned with a new car because it didn't have an outside temperature indicator like his last one did. This rather insignificant (in the bigger scheme of things) feature was so annoying that the man traded the car in shortly after purchase.

In customer service training sessions your author asks participants to describe products or services that have exceeded their expectations in terms of intrinsic value. People often respond by mentioning unusually reliable products like John Deer lawn tractors, Sony TVs, Kirby vacuum cleaners, certain appliances, Craftsman® tools, and the like. Companies are also publicizing their intrinsic value. Toyota once ran a series of television commercials that a driver stepping out of a 10-year-old truck perched on top of a mountain. The actor looks into the camera and announces that he has over 300,000 miles on his truck. The implication is buy a new truck and it'll exceed your expectations for long-term value. More recently, Ford and Chevy are trumpeting the longevity of their trucks in advertisements, even seeking testimonial stories from long-term owners. We can all think of products with high intrinsic value that have lasted a long time and earned our brand allegiance.

Value takes on another dimension for intangible products or services. With these products, accuracy and attention to detail of the service provider may be the hallmark of value. A public utility, cable provider, or financial institution that gives customers consistently accurate, easy-to-read statements may be giving A-plus service. A repair shop that fixes things quickly and correctly at a reasonable cost will have a favorable perception of **intrinsic value**. The company that makes it easy for customers to contact it and then responds quickly to fix any errors or problems will also be perceived by customers as high in value.

The opposite conditions create immediate and often lasting negative perceptions of value. Electrical blackouts, phone service interruptions, and cable TV quality problems project a sense of poor reliability that can have negative repercussions on whole industries. Here's an example: The phones stopped working at the national reservation center of LOT Polish Airlines in New York a few years ago. The airline called the phone company's problem line at 9 a.m. *Eleven hours* later, after the reservations center had closed for the day, repair technicians arrived. Before all was fixed, the center was without phone service for 33 hours. Without phones, LOT was essentially out of business, and an 11-hour response time was, needless to say, inexcusable. The intrinsic value of the telephone company was clearly lacking.

Another often-cited incident of a catastrophic example of service failures is when JetBlue Airlines held nine planes full of passengers on the tarmac at JFK Airport for six or more hours during an ice storm in early 2007. Although other airlines experienced similar "hostage passenger" situations, the JetBlue case got the most publicity and directly resulted in the dismissal of the company's CEO and founder. There is a personal side to these kinds of service disasters in addition to that suffered by the customers.

Stories of poor intrinsic value can be dramatic and destructive to customer relationships, but what about the advantages of excellent intrinsic value?

Credit card companies offer varying degrees of service. Associates I have talked with favor the American Express Card and Discover Private Issue. They perceive higher intrinsic value in these products for two reasons: They give airline miles or cash back, and when the customer needs to call either of these they can speak to a live person almost immediately. Other cards linger in the wallet because, when they have a problem, the company forces its customers through a maze of telephone switching that is annoying and time-consuming. Access to a live-person contact enhances the perception of intrinsic value.[4]

Still another example of intrinsic value is the personal touch provided by some banks to their key clients (whether individuals or corporations). Each client is assigned a personal banker—a bank executive who is willing to meet personally with the client to oversee his or her financial needs. The status of having a personal banker is premium value for many people.

Associated Value

Associated (or extrinsic) value goes beyond the core product. It is associated with the product, but it is not essential to it. Associated value involves more than whether an automobile starts and drives reliably or the degree to which an Internet service provider stays up and running. It encompasses the entire customer experience with the company.

Remember that value is *perceptual.* Since perception, by definition, is different for different individuals, some people may be turned on by a company's extrinsic value efforts while others may regard them as nothing more than what is expected or, worse, as unnecessary fluff.

Companies need to create conditions that improve the likelihood of customers seeing extrinsic or associated value favorably. Some ways companies seek to enhance these perceptions include the following:

- Packaging
- Guarantees and warranties
- Goodness of product fit
- Memorability of product experience
- Uniqueness and shared values
- Company credibility
- Add-ons

In the remainder of this chapter, we will look at examples of how each of these extrinsic-value enhancers can create an A-plus situation for customers and increase the likelihood of loyalty.

SEVEN WAYS TO ENHANCE THE PERCEPTION OF VALUE

We can build customer loyalty with the creative application of the following techniques for enhancing the perception of value. These approaches, of course, may vary in effectiveness, but companies serious about customer loyalty would be wise to consider each as part of an ongoing process of offering A-plus value.

Build A-Plus Value with Packaging

Packaging can enhance the perceived value of a product—or service.

Imagine going to a hardware store to buy a power drill. There you find a stack of the particular model you want. All but one of these is in its original package. What is the likelihood that you would select the one without a box? Zero, right? You will undoubtedly buy one in a box even knowing that you'll throw the box away when you get home. The box—the package—enhances the perception of value.

A business associate occasionally passes along books he thinks will be useful. Sometimes, he simply hands off a copy of a recommended book. On a few occasions, he enhances the value of his gift by writing a friendly note in the book or by gift wrapping it. The core product is the same (it's the same book!), but the gift-wrapped packaging and personalization enhance its perceived value.

This illustrates the "little things" principle we talked about in part one of this book. Tiny differences make the extrinsic value of the product greater.

If your business sells intangibles, don't overlook possible packaging. If anything, packaging enhancements can be even more powerful when they are completely unexpected. But how do we package an intangible? Here are a few examples:

A successful insurance sales representative gives his clients their policies in an attractive leather portfolio, which can be used to store other important papers. He goes a step further by engraving the client's name on the portfolio. His clients keep the leather binder for many years—the associated value of his product lives on.

If your customers receive only documents in exchange for their money (often the only tangible product associated with a service such as life insurance), give some thought to packaging these papers in an attractive or useful manner. Or add some tangible items that might relate to

---

SERVICE SNAPSHOT

Vik Wool of Iceland

While doing consulting work in Iceland, Arnie shopped for some Icelandic wool gifts for his daughters. After receiving adequate but nondescript service in several shops, he found one store in Reykjavik called Vik Wool that had particularly friendly employees and a nice selection of knitted gloves. Arnie selected two pairs and a few other small items. When the clerk rang up my goods, she wrapped each gift in a small, hand-knit sack tied with a ribbon. The little sacks were made of knitting remnants from their factory. The packaging of these inexpensive gifts far exceeded what he had anticipated. Other stores set the expectation with generic plastic bags; Vik Wool exceeds customer expectations of value with the beautiful knitted wool sacks.

---

your services. A cellular phone company sent its best customers a road-travel gift set. It included a thermos, Starbucks coffee, and some snacks. Financial and educational institutions often give tokens of appreciation that tie in with their intangible products. For example, schools give leather notebook folders, USB jump drives, or writing instruments of various types.

Upscale department stores or boutiques have long known the value of attractive gift wrapping. Customers love it—especially customers like your author who is all thumbs when it comes to wrapping gifts. But any organization can enhance its packaging and thus increase the customer's perception of value.

Build A-Plus Value with Guarantees or Warranties

Would you be likely to see a product with a lifetime warranty as having higher value than a similar product with only a 30-day warranty? Most people do. Jack, a producer of video and DVD tape training programs, used to tell customers that these tapes were unconditionally guaranteed for 30 days. If they felt the programs did not meet their needs, they could return the programs within 30 days and get a full refund. Then he began to think about enhancing this sense of value and changed that guarantee to *forever*. If the customer ever felt the product did not meet his or her needs, it could be returned for a full refund.

> Long-term or lifetime warrantees have a higher perceived value than short-term ones.

Jack found that, with the unlimited guarantee period, the percent of goods returned was unchanged. In fact, with the 30-day guarantee, he may have actually been encouraging refund requests by setting a target date. The customer who had the product for 25 days or so may have felt some urgency to make a decision—and sometimes that decision was to send the product back. A lifetime guarantee eliminates the motivation to act now, thus reducing the likelihood the customer will return the product.

If your product has good intrinsic value, the return rates for short-term guarantees versus long-term or lifetime guarantees will be virtually equal.

Nordstrom's department stores have earned a tremendous amount of good publicity from their no-questions-asked, unconditional return policy. The oft-repeated (old) story of the fellow who returned a set of tires to Nordstrom's (a store that doesn't sell tires!) has had incredible positive ripple effects. The tale has become legend and, when written about in Tom Peters and Robert Waterman's 1982 best seller, *In Search of Excellence,* caught the eye of millions of readers, many of whom are exactly the kind of customers Nordstrom's caters to. The cost of granting the request of one

LOOK INSIDE

How's Your Packaging?

Consider the products or service that your company offers. How effective is your packaging? Are your goods displayed in attractive ways? Do you bundle related products or services in attractive ways? What can you do to spruce up your packaging?

unreasonable customer bought incalculable advertising. Ironically, in some countries, government regulation forbids lifetime guarantees! The American catalog company Lands' End has a simple and reassuring motto for shoppers: *Guaranteed. Period.* Some shortsighted competitors in Germany took Lands' End to court. They claimed this guarantee was unfair advertising and got the court to agree that this guarantee policy was "economically unfeasible" and therefore amounted to unfair competition.

That is a classic case of thinking small and not understanding the value of A-plus service. Lands' End responded to the court ruling with a set of ads in German newspapers and magazines poking fun at the ban. One ad pictured a common housefly with the caption "one-day guarantee." Another showed a washing machine, guaranteed six months. Other companies facing similar bans (Zippo lighters, Tupperware) have dropped their lifetime guarantees but are benefited from the publicity. Zippo ran ads in British papers proclaiming, "A guarantee so good the Germans banned it."[5]

You can surprise a customer with generosity or you can quibble over the fine print in a guarantee, thus missing an opportunity to exceed expectations.

Your company can quibble over guarantees or it can take advantage of A-plus value perceptions by being generous and open. Consider as a cost of doing business the occasional customer who takes unfair advantage of a generous guarantee. Pleasantly surprise the large majority of your customers by offering generous guarantee terms. Go beyond what the customer anticipates and reap the reward of customer loyalty.

One final point about guarantees is that they also project trust. By offering the enhanced value of an exceptional guarantee, companies are implying that they trust their customers to be fair in dealing with the company. Will some people take unfair advantage of a generous guarantee? Perhaps. But the positive side of extending this valuable trust to customers far outweighs the cost of the occasional dishonest person who, for example, uses a product for a long time and then demands a refund. Extend this olive branch of trust and the customer will be likely to establish a trusting relationship with your company. Ultimately, such trust is an intangible measure of value.

Build A-Plus Value with Goodness of Product Fit

Goodness of product fit means thinking one-size-fits-*one*. Personalization, not a simplistic classification of people into demographic groups, permits real relationship building. The danger of categorizing individuals is illustrated by a letter to the editor of a well-known business magazine, written by a 13-year-old girl who said she "often enjoys reading [the] magazine." She was responding to an article called "Girl Power!" in which the magazine described what girls her age were "into." The young lady's articulate response explained that she was not at all like the profile offered in the article. She also criticized *Seventeen, YM, Teen,* and the other magazines for thinking much the way that business magazine does: that girls can be broken down into a demographic group, that "our minds consist of very little more than boys, shopping, makeup, boys, clothes, and shopping."

Think of customers as individuals, not demographic groups, to enhance value through "goodness of product fit."

Taking the concept of goodness of fit to new levels, *mass customization* is all the rage in modern manufacturing. Companies are creating products just the way the customer wants them. Some clothing manufacturers can custom-make jeans to the exact measurements of individual customers. The Internet is a popular medium for custom orders. Auto manufacturers now routinely let potential buyers customize a vehicle. For example, Ford Motor Co. lets buyers "build your own Ford" from a palette of options. Golfsmith.com crafts custom-fit golf clubs based on questionnaire responses. The average person can buy custom clothing at an affordable price, made-to-order music CDs, even personalized vitamins on the Net. Many economists believe that if you don't mass customize, you're going to lose business in today's marketplace.

When companies offer menus of product characteristics for customers to select from, they can create **industrial intimacy**. This "intimacy" comes from better understanding the specific needs and personal wants of customers. Ultimately, the key is to focus on what is important to the customer and, so long as this still permits the company to make a profit, give customers exactly what they want.

Customer relationship management, enabled by technology, gives businesses almost unlimited opportunities to personalize products for their customers, building greater industrial intimacy. CRM software crunches an enormous amount of data and gives specific recommendations for personalizing customer contacts. Here is a hypothetical example:

Suppose that you are in a financial services business, like a consumer bank or credit union. If your organization is using CRM software, customers who call or visit your office would deal with a person who knows a great deal about them. If George Customer calls your office with a question about his mortgage, your employee would key in the customer's account number. The **intelligent systems** (sophisticated computer programs that diagnose patterns of data) would display a series of dialogues your employee could use—word for word—to explain customer options and perhaps sell additional products.

The software system gathers and digests mountains of data about the individual customer and about people like him (demographic data). The system may have information about cars he owns, their price range, and the ages of the cars. It may also factor in data about George such as the fact that he is 55 years old, he is recently divorced, his kids are grown, his mortgage is almost paid off, his Buick is four years old, and he recently changed jobs after receiving a substantial payout from his previous employer. If you were a financial institution, wouldn't you want to know this?

All this data can suggest additional products appropriate to George, thus helping build a stronger relationship. Companies provide A-plus value by offering products that fit perfectly with this customer's needs. This can be a significant way to exceed customer expectations.

One large mortgage company that uses such a CRM system has had tremendous success in increasing the close rate for additional products. Previously, 4 percent of customers contacting the company purchased additional products. After implementing the system, which provides explicit prompts for customer representatives, the close rate jumped to 38 percent.[6]

The benefit of such additional sales is obvious, but the customer service element is equally important. This marriage of technology and customer data can build relationships, develop industrial intimacy, and ultimately enhance customer allegiance.

It is worth noting that customer relationship management (CRM) uses various approaches to collect data. Some customers, however, balk at being forced to give companies a lot of personal information. Supermarket preferred-shopper programs, which reward customers with discounts when they allow the store to scan their coded card, are meeting resistance from people who don't want to carry a special card or who resent the deep discounts available only to those who sign up. But companies should be careful to not throw out the baby with the bathwater. Some form of CRM that helps tailor products to individual customers can be very helpful in creating A-plus value.

Sophisticated customer-contact-management products are becoming less expensive and more readily available. Even small businesses can learn more than ever about customer needs, wants, and preferences by gathering appropriate personal data. CRM systems reflect the most advanced form of technology-enhanced relationship building. But even manual systems that make notes of customer preferences can move companies toward enhanced customer value.

To provide A-plus value, your company may need to be implementing such one-to-one customer service. People don't want to be treated like pieces of demographic data. People have unique, individual needs and wants. A-plus value is personalized value. It involves doing all you can to be sure the products or services you offer fit the needs of the individual customer, not just some large demographic group.

Build A-Plus Value with Memorable Experiences

People remember what they *feel*—their emotional responses—much better than they remember what they see or hear. Salespeople have long been taught to "sell the sizzle, not the steak," meaning that the emotions attached to the product are key triggers in buying decisions. Experiences associated with a customer relationship can tap into the feelings that solidify that relationship.

> People remember emotions long after they have forgotten what they have seen or heard.

A highlight of many a kid's birthday celebrations has been a trip to a Chuck E Cheese restaurant. These pizza emporiums are something else; they go beyond the traditional description of a restaurant. The food is adequate, but the experience is, well, something kids go nuts over. It's a carnival atmosphere with all kinds of exciting sights and sounds. Providing customers with an *experience* may well be the highest level of economic value.

ANOTHER LOOK
Daddy Date Night at Chick-fil-A

Here's an example of A-plus service created with an experience: On February Valentine's Day some Chick-fil-A restaurants redecorate with tablecloths, candles, and specially prepared menus. Dads bring their daughters without the rest of the family in tow for a special experience.

Creative restaurant managers offer unexpected experiences. Some stores set up a maître-d station, some have their staff in tuxedos, and some offer limo service (rides in the parking lot). Most offer a rose for the dad to hand his daughter and lots of extra attention to service. On this night, you get table service, not counter self-serve.

Chick-fil-A sweats the details to make the experience memorable and shareable. For example, when dad is seated and the daughter is still giggling after someone pulls her chair out for her, the customers notice two placemats on the table. There's no special offer on them, rather they have just questions—questions for the daughter to ask the dad and questions for the dad to ask the daughter to generate interesting conversation.

Many a daughter discovers that her dad is cooler than she thought—and that is exceeding expectations with experiences that trigger emotions that will be long-lasting.

In today's developed countries consumers have most of the tangible goods they *need*. (Maybe not all they *want*, but what they need.) People who have benefited from economic good fortune have about all the luxury cars, quality clothes, flat screen TVs, and trendy coffees they can handle. (Arguably, today's middle-class folks in Western cultures live better than royalty in decades past.) Even in times of temporary economic downturns, people today are using discretionary income to enjoy experiences such as entertainment, travel, cruises, spas, and wellness or retreat centers.

Smart companies are connecting with their customers through experiences. An experience occurs when the company's core products are used as props to engage individual customers in a way that creates a memorable event. Examples of events include live entertainment at restaurants and coffee-shop chats at bookstores. Sporting events and competitions may place the company's products in the background, but the customer receives value from the event itself. Ties to the company are likely to follow. An upscale coffee shop is not just a place to get a beverage—it has become, for some people, an office/meeting place. Denise Wymore who is a marketing consultant and author wrote her latest book entirely at a Wi-Fi friendly Starbucks. Says Denise:

> When I ask audiences who Starbucks targets—people don't say "coffee drinkers." Starbucks serves coffee to be sure. But they don't target coffee drinkers. They target me. I'm writing this in a Starbucks right now. I have a bottle of water (no coffee) and a chocolate dipped macaroon. Yum. I bought the water because the chalkboard sign behind the cashier said that the proceeds will go to help children in third-world countries get clean water. I support that.[7]

(We'll talk more about adding value with shared values, such as supporting clean water, in a moment.)

A word of caution, however, is in order: When creating extrinsic A-plus value using customer experiences, don't let the core product go bad. Planet Hollywood was a red-hot restaurant chain in the mid-1990s, only to crash when people realized that the glitzy experience of possible celebrity spotting was not worth eating the substandard food. The company largely forgot about its core product—the food. Experiences can enhance the sense of value so long as the core product maintains its good quality.

Even the best of associated value cannot make up for a poor core product.

Build A-Plus Value with Uniqueness and Shared Values

An enhanced sense of value can stem from a company being perceived as unique or novel. Much of this uniqueness arises from the personality or culture of your organization. Ben and Jerry's ice-cream business projects a sense of culture based on the liberal political values of its founders and its sense of civic responsibility to Vermont. (The ice-cream-plant tours are the most popular tourist attraction in the state.) Their theme was consistent throughout the history of the company (until it was sold to a large food conglomerate) and had been the subject of books, articles, and television magazine shows.

Southwest Airlines (SWA), an airline that has maintained good customer relationships despite turmoil in its industry, continues to convey a charming quirkiness that reflects its founder, Herb Kelleher. The airline started as a scrappy little outfit and has grown into an aviation powerhouse in part because its customers like the people who work there. SWA hires people based on their upbeat attitudes. The interview process and new-employee orientation is uniquely tailored to help people fit the corporate culture. New employees engage in a scavenger hunt to find answers to company-orientation questions, for example. It is noteworthy that SWA is the one of the few U.S. airlines to be continually profitable in the early years of the twenty-first century.

Competitor JetBlue has similarly created a cult of fans with its customer-friendly features. (Founding JetBlue CEO David Neeleman once worked for Southwest and learned much from that experience.) Ben and Jerry's, SWA, Home Depot, numerous hi-tech firms, and many other companies offer their internal customers—their employees—A-plus value by inviting participation in their uniqueness and shared values. JetBlue reservations clerks work out of their homes (allowing flextime hours) in part to honor the corporate commitment to valuing family-friendly work–life balance. North Carolina-based SAS software offers a huge range of perks to employees (fitness centers, day care, health clinic, discounted country club, to name a few) that reduces employee turnover to low single digits in an industry where 20 percent or more of workers leave similar companies every year.

Customers will often go out of their way to support companies that share their **values**. Talk-show hosts such as Rush Limbaugh, Sean Hannity, and the late news commentator Paul Harvey have been credited with launching many popular brands because listeners, who share their views, feel they are getting enhanced value from companies that agree with them. Of course, the flip side to this is that customers who don't agree with the tie-in may deflect. In 2009 many companies received huge government "bailouts" that some consumers felt were unnecessary or unfair. Some customers declared they would not buy from companies that took taxpayer handouts.

> Customers gain a sense of increased value when companies or corporate sponsors support their shared values.

Political, church, civic, alumni, and charitable groups often band together to promote or support certain organizations. This bonding may range from partnering with credit card companies to having the organization's logo on the cards, to having cell phones with a hockey-team logo, to purchasing Girl Scout cookies. The opportunity to share in an affiliation, an interest, or a cause can be an enhanced sense of value for customers and employees. On a more local basis, customers become loyal to companies that make them feel comfortable. They patronize organizations that reflect their values and preferences. A small local bookstore with friendly, helpful employees, a comfortable atmosphere, and, perhaps, book recommendations from its staff can compete against the large book retailers. Even the enormous pricing advantage of the world's big-box discount stores cannot compete with the highly personalized camaraderie of shared values offered when well-run local businesses offer A-plus value. People do and will pay a premium for exceptional extrinsic value. The "little guy" can compete against the large low-price providers if he offers something the big guy cannot offer—some higher value.

Build A-Plus Value with Credibility

Customers also feel they receive extra value when dealing with companies that have exceptional **credibility**. A critical dimension of value is the *degree to which customers trust* a company or organization. Failure to follow through on commitments and other deceptive practices can (and should) damage a company. Of course, sometimes this too is perceptual. You may feel you explained a policy or guarantee to the customer and he interpreted it differently. You think you communicated openly and she sees your limitations as unnecessary fine-print nitpicking. Keep pricing and restrictions simple and understandable for customers.

> Communicate clearly with customers to enhance your credibility.

While many industries are simplifying and bundling services for flat or simplified fees, the airlines are doing a poor job in this area. The fare restrictions and the enormous price discrepancies damage credibility. On any given flight, you will find passengers who have paid up to 10 times as much as another passenger for the same service: transportation from point A to point B. You may be delighted with your $300 fare, while the guy next to you paid $1,000 or more, depending on when the ticket was booked and a lot of other factors. In short, the airlines' fare systems are unintelligible to their customers and foster a lack of trust. Understandably, airlines defend the current system as necessary (and put a great deal of effort into maximizing revenue based on complex pricing models) but customer frustration is a reality. Better transparency and more understandable fares would boost the industry's "trustability."

Speaking of airlines, they would do well to avoid frequent-flyer-type fiascos. Yes, such programs have been successful from a marketing perspective, but they have also been the source of many customer annoyance. Too often, frequent-flyer programs are confusing and perceived as untrustworthy. While programs captivate customers by enticing them to fly the same airline, the promised rewards come only with a lot of strings attached. Customers who accumulate miles too often find that the promised free tickets or service-class upgrades are simply not available. Further, the miles required for free travel is subject to the airline's discretion. Customers commonly pay 65,000, 80,000 miles or more for a single coach ticket while the airline ads hype free travel for cashing in only 25,000 mile credits. The value of the promised reward has degraded.

What the airlines also do not freely tell is that each flight has only a few award-travel seats. They don't mention blackout dates, upgrades that cannot be offered from a certain class of tickets, and a lot of other limitations. In short, they shoot their corporate trustability in the foot with lavish promises that are too often not delivered. In fact, seats available for reward travel average about 6 percent—six seats out of a hundred. The glut of frequent-flyer points held by people has led to less value per point. An estimated 60 percent of all frequent-flyer miles are "earned" by people who don't even fly—they get them for using credit cards.[8] The airlines made a deal with the devil with their tie-ins with credit card companies and now face the need to reduce the number of seats available since such seats generate no revenue for the airline.

People have tried to redeem frequent-flyer seats by booking months in advance only to be told that the flight was sold out. When a quick check on the Web shows many empty seats on that flight, airline credibility takes a dive. Airlines insist that they are not trying to make it hard to redeem miles for tickets, but with planes carrying record numbers of passengers, the demand for free seats far exceeds the space available.

Be open and honest about pricing and restrictions or risk damaged credibility and missed opportunity to create an enhanced sense of value.

What can your business learn from the airlines? Consider the pitfalls of frequent-customer programs carefully. A company's credibility can be damaged by making inflated offers it cannot fulfill.

Following up on commitments made is also crucial to building trust with customers. Here is another true-life example: A few years ago, Marcy purchased a rather pricey six-month-old used car from a dealership that touted itself as a "no-dicker, full-service auto consortium." Among the many frustrations she experienced, she was given just one key to the car and promised that they would get her another because they had lost the backup. After repeated phone calls, she finally gave up, took the car to another dealership, and bought the key—along with several other missing parts like the CD-changer cartridge and all the owner's manuals. She had to go to the right dealership in another city and buy the parts that were missing from her car! The aggravation of getting anything out of the original dealership became more than she could handle.

That dealership may think it "won" since Marcy quit pestering them, but the price they paid in damaged credibility returned to bite them. She takes every opportunity to tell other people (including students she teaches in her large university classes) about this poor value experience. That dealership, despite a good location, a reputable brand, and its promise of providing "a new kind of less-hassle buying experience," went out of business within less than a year.

The solutions to the kinds of trust problems described above are to not offer incentives you cannot provide or to make good on your word. Those are the only choices.

On a more positive note, we all prefer to do business with people who have high trustability. A scrupulously honest handyman who fixes things around a client's house earns the right to a

---

Complicated fares and the perception of inequity among passengers hurt the credibility of airlines.

Don't let the value of loyalty incentives degrade.

There can be no A-plus value without credibility.

house key so that he can work while the client travels. He can be trusted to do good work at a fair price. An auto or appliance dealership that always follows through with fair pricing and impeccable attention to meeting its commitments creates a trust-based bond with customers. Trust is a powerful form of A-plus value. It is fundamental to building loyalty.

Build A-Plus Value with Add-Ons

One of the simplest ways to surprise customers or employees is to give them something unexpected—or sell them something else they may need. When a shoe-store clerk gives you a shoehorn with a pair of new shoes or when he asks if you'd like to try padded inserts or a pair of lifetime-guarantee socks, he is using this A-plus value approach. Sometimes add-ons are sold; sometimes they are given away. Both can be effective. A clerk at a supermarket hands customers a few chocolate kisses with the receipt, an unexpected thank you. The hotel checkin desk has a basket of complimentary apples or a plate of fresh-baked cookies. The paint-store salesperson checks to be sure buyers have caulking, sandpaper, perhaps a drop cloth.

> Add-ons may be given away or sold. Either type can have high perceived value.

Employees who receive unexpected tangible rewards at work experience A-plus relationships. A surprise free lunch, a few movie tickets, flowers, impromptu celebrations, and the like all build employee allegiance. SAS Corporation in North Carolina (which I mentioned above) started their extensive array of perks with a tradition of passing out M&M candies on Wednesdays. The folks who work at a Ryder truck rental location enjoy Friday afternoon barbeques. Add-ons need not be expensive. The little-things principle certainly applies.

An old anecdote tells of the differing popularity of competing ice-cream-cone shops. In one, the servers put a large scoop on the cone and knock off the ice cream that hangs over the edge. In the second store, the server puts a scoop of ice cream on the cone and then adds a bit more. Guess which one creates the best customer satisfaction?

The best kinds of free add-ons are those with high perceived value and low cost to the business. For example, gas stations that give away a free car wash with fill-up are offering something that costs them a few cents (water and soap—not counting, of course, the cost of the equipment), but their customers receive a service with a perceived value of four or five dollars (often the price is printed on the coupon). Free popcorn or drinks given away with DVD rentals cost a few cents but have a much higher perceived value—really high, when compared to the price of movie-theater popcorn!

Obviously, this A-plus opportunity area ties in closely with its marketing counterpart, add-on sales. Marketers have long recognized the value of trying to sell current customers something else so long as they are already buying. This can backfire if it's too pushy,[9] but most customers will not resent low-key inquiries about the need for other products. The hardware salesperson who checks with the customer to be sure he has the right tools is not going to be resented. And the company may well sell some additional products.

A very creative add-on came out of a customer service seminar a few years ago. A woman attending the session owned several quick-lube shops. When people bought a full-service oil change, she did what her competitors had been doing. She checked all fluids, washed windows, checked tire pressure, and vacuumed the car's interior. But then she had this add-on idea: She ran a CD head-cleaning disk through the customer's sound system. We all know that cleaning the CD player this way makes for better sound, but most people never get around to it. After running the cleaning disk, she inserted a preprinted card into the CD player noting that the heads had been cleaned courtesy of her company. This add-on cost practically nothing (truly a "little thing"), but provided a clear and distinctive A-plus for her customers.

Central to the philosophy of add-ons is the belief that you cannot give away more than you eventually receive. That is a tough concept for people to accept. But, at some philosophical level, you need to be comfortable with the belief that what goes around comes around, or, put another way, you win when you "pay it forward." In fact, that is fundamental to all the A-plus loyalty-building tactics. You really will benefit from generosity. Take the leap of faith and reap the rewards of greater customer and employee loyalty.

A-Plus Value and Your Employees

The principles for creating A-plus value not only work for customers but also apply to employees—internal customers. Companies with strong employee allegiance regularly use these kinds of ideas to surprise their people—to exceed their expectations with little things.

Wegmans supermarkets have an exceptional reputation for being a good place to work. Company leaders openly state that "our employees are our number one asset." That could sound like a cliché except for the fact that Wegmans backs it up with countless examples supporting their notion that "happy, knowledgeable, superbly trained employees create a better experience for our customers." One in-store baker marvels that "they let me bake whatever I want," illustrating how much they trust their people to make good decisions. The Western New York-based Wegmans sends employees on trips to where their fish come from (sometimes Alaska) and where some meats originate (Montana). This is a direct application of A-plus value for internal customers.[10]

Virtually every type of A-plus value can be applied to employee relations with powerful results. Employees who receive small tokens of appreciation respond as positively as do other types of customers. Employees who enjoy the shared experience of working in a good company, who appreciate the credibility of the organization, who recognize the company's efforts to fit people to the best job for them, and who are offered unexpected value will be loyal to the company. Loyal long-term employees make economic good sense.

Get all members of the organization thinking about ways to utilize little things to create A-plus value. The payoff in customer and employee allegiance can be enormous.

A FINAL THOUGHT

Products and services have intrinsic and extrinsic, associated value. Exceeding customer expectations with an enhanced sense of value can be a powerful way of tipping the balance in favor of your company (or in favor of you as an individual). A key term is *perception*. At some level, customers will sense that you are offering something more when you give A-plus value.

It's the little things that mean a great deal. You need not give away the business. Simply adding some of the characteristics we discussed in this chapter can provide that value-enhancing customer experience that leads to loyalty and repeat buying.

Summary of Key Ideas

- A customer's perception of value includes a product or service's internal (core) value and external or associated value. Often the associated value includes how the overall buying experience feels.
- An enhanced perception of value is likely to increase a customer's likelihood to be loyal to the company.
- While the intrinsic (core) value of a product must be satisfactory, the extrinsic (or associated) value can go a long way toward exceeding customer expectations. It is often little things that enhance this sense of value—subtle factors that distinguish one company from another.

- Seven categories of actions that can enhance the customer's perception of value include packaging, guarantees (warrantes), goodness of product fit, "memorability" of product experience, uniqueness and shared values, company credibility, and add-ons.
- Your credibility (or "trustability") will be impacted by its willingness to be open, honest, and trustworthy. Some manipulative attempts at buying customer loyalty (such as with frequent-user points, etc.) can lead to disappointment or a decrease in trust. A-plus value requires credibility.

Key Concepts

credibility
associated (or extrinsic)
   value

goodness of product fit
industrial intimacy
intelligent systems

intrinsic value
memorable experience

perceived value
shared values

Reviewing the Facts

1. What is the difference between intrinsic and extrinsic value? Give three examples of each from three different kinds of businesses.

2. Describe a brief example of each of the seven tactics for enhancing the customers' perception of value described in this chapter. Try to use examples other than the ones mentioned in the text. Be creative in describing what companies could do.

3. How might a company selling intangible products or services use packaging to enhance the perception of value? Come up with one or more ideas for a public utility, a bank, an insurance agency, and a government office.

4. Some people argue that experiences are the highest form of value. Defend or oppose that general position. Use examples of your own experiences, as appropriate.

5. Review the daddy–daughter date night experience offered by Chick-fil-A. How could other companies tie in family activities? Give three to five examples including details of the event.

6. How can smaller companies use A-plus value to better compete against larger companies that have a pricing advantage? Select a small business and describe some things it could do to compete successfully. Be specific.

7. Create a list of possible add-ons for each of the following kinds of businesses. Remember that the best add-ons have a high perceived value and relatively low cost to the company. Be realistic about what these companies might be able to give or sell customers to A-plus value.

An appliance store	A Web-based retailer of pet food
A man's shoe store	A sporting goods store
A community bank	An auto tire shop
A budget-priced motel	A dentist's office
A massage therapist	A coffee shop

Applying the Ideas

1. Identify three companies you do business with because you appreciate their social, religious, or community values. Identify what values you find attractive and describe how the companies are supportive of those values. Write a brief paper summarizing these points.

2. Imagine that you are planning to open a restaurant in your home town. Write a one-paragraph description of what that restaurant will be like and describe at least five ways you would intend to exceed customer expectations (compared with competing restaurants) in the area of value.

3. Visit at least three different businesses of the same type. For example, go to three different banks, shoe stores, office equipment retailers, and auto repair shops. Write a brief paper comparing each of these similar businesses in the light of their application of the A-plus ideas we discussed in this chapter. How successful was each at enhancing their sense of value? Which (if any) of the techniques we discussed did they employ? What would you suggest they do to further their efforts to exceed customer expectations with value?

4. What do companies do to provide A-plus value for their employees? Use your Internet searching skills to discover at least five innovative ways companies enhance value for their employees. Look for tactics that go beyond the typical compensation or benefits packages. What creative ways do companies surprise their employees by giving A-plus value? (Hint: A good place to start may be at the *Fortune* magazine site, where they publish articles on "The Best Companies to Work For" annually.)

   Write a brief commentary on how you would react if your company were to offer such A-plus incentives. Would they be likely to make you more loyal? If you are not currently employed, how would you respond if your school offered special value incentives?

Consider this Case
Big Companies Buy Small Brands with Big Values

Even in challenging economic times, consumers have shown they are willing to pay a premium for "natural" products, organic foods, green-friendly products, and the like that carry a cost premium. Such values-oriented companies that make them feel good, and big marketers want a piece of this profitable trend.

In 2000, the large agribusiness conglomerate Unilever bought the flavorful Ben & Jerry's ice-cream company. Today, the company ads remind customers of shared values when they promote family farms, a dairy source for Ben & Jerry's ice creams. Colgate bought 84 percent of Tom's of Maine, the all-natural personal care brand based in Kennebunk, Maine. Tom's was a small company with a social responsibility message. French cosmetics giant L'Oreal bought London-based retailer The Body Shop, a personal care chain known for its avoidance of animal testing and its support for human and animal rights causes. Large companies recognize the added value the customer of these formerly small companies received.

Many customers today appreciate the notion that what's good for you and good for the planet is the ultimate win–win. Being a consumer of companies that share your values can make you feel selfless.

Probes

1. What are some causes that you believe deeply in?
2. What companies or organizations support those similar beliefs?
3. To what extent do you feel more inclined to do business with these supportive organizations? What factors influence your loyalty to them as a customer (external or internal)?
4. Are there companies you will always try to avoid because of some extrinsic value perceptions such as disagreement with their policy stands and so on? Could they win you back?

Consider this Case
Customer Engagement Builds Value

Dave and Andy opened their gym, Elevate Triathlon Training, a year ago. Both are active triathletes and they found that many fitness trainers, although good at giving patrons a healthy workout, were unaware of the special needs of endurance athletes such as those training for Ironman competitions. Workouts for triathletes are a lot different from what bodybuilders do.

Business was slow for the first few months but grew on the basis of word of mouth within the growing community of triathletes. As they became more well known and the business grew, Elevate began to sponsor minitriathlons (held indoors during the winter months) and to participate in race Expos at local races.

Dave decided that a focus group to get client ideas would be a worthwhile investment. He hired a professor of communication from the local university and asked him to hold a series of meetings with invited customers. Clients who participated were given a certificate for a free massage.

Dave decided to sit in on the feedback groups. The facilitator invited people to express criticisms of the gym, but few did. Most felt that it is a friendly place and they enjoyed the nonthreatening feeling of a gym where they could work out to their own fitness level and feel no pressure to put on a show for others, a criticism often heard about local competitors. A few people suggested ideas for improvements such as replace the gym's one coat rack with shelves where people could stow their coats, keys, and cell phones while they worked out. Another suggestion was that they put up bulletin boards to display pictures of members competing and post sports items for sale. Unfortunately, the owners never got around to actually doing any of these things.

A few months after these feedback sessions, Patrick announced that he was dropping his Elevate membership and trying another gym. Andy was surprised and asked Pat why. "To be honest," Pat said, "I guess I was a little disappointed that any ideas I have ever given for improving the place seem to be ignored. You guys are doing okay but it doesn't seem like you value your clients' input. I'd hoped to be more involved in growing this business with you."

Probes

1. What perceived value seems to be causing Patrick to drop his membership?
2. How does the lack of responsiveness to customer input reflect missed opportunities for creating A-plus value?

3. What could Dave and Andy do to build feelings of engagement with their customers using the kinds of ideas discussed in this chapter?

Building a Customer Service Strategy: Your Ongoing Case

Let's go back to the ongoing case you selected. This will be either your current employer, a specific organization you want to work in, or one of the two hypothetical organizations described in Chapter 1: Independent Auto Sales and Service (IAS) or Network Nutrition Distributors (NND). Now consider the following questions as you develop a customer service strategy:

Strategy Planning Activities

1. Identify some core values of this organization as best as you can. What do they believe in (beyond organizational success or profitability)? How might their revealing these values to customers and employees create opportunities to exceed expectations? How can they translate core values into actions to produce A-plus value, thus strengthening relationships?
2. Do some creative thinking about possible ideas you could apply to create A-plus value using the seven areas described in this chapter. Describe at least three ideas for each:
   • packaging, guarantees (warrantees)
   • goodness of product fit

   • "memorability" of product experience
   • uniqueness and shared values
   • company credibility
   • add-ons
3. Consider ways to get employees of your organization involved in generating A-plus value ideas. How would you do this? Be specific about the following:
   • What you would teach employees before soliciting their ideas?
   • Who would be involved in idea-generating sessions?
   • How you would collect and process ideas (specifically)?
   • How often you would gather ideas?
   • How people might be rewarded for participating in the process?
4. What would be necessary for your organization to engage in ongoing A-plus idea generation? How could this become part of the culture of the company? How could you get buy-in from participants and what should you do to avoid turning people off to the process. Be specific.

Notes

1. Michael Schuman and Hae Won Choi, "Suwon's Restrooms, Once the Pits, Are Flush with Tourists," *Wall Street Journal,* November 26, 1999, p. A-1.
2. Hanna Komulainen, Tuija Mainela, Jaana Tähtinen, and Pauliina Ulkuniemi, "Exploring Customer Perceived Value in a Technology Intensive Service Innovation," University of Oulu, Department of Marketing, Oulu, Finland, Proceedings of the 20th Annual IMP Conference, September 2–4, 2004, Copenhagen, Denmark.
3. James R. Healy, "Base Versa Sings Like a Bird: Cheap, Cheap, Cheap," *USA Today,* February 27, 2009, p. 5B.
4. Access to live help overlaps with another way of exceeding expectations, A-plus Information, which we discuss in Chapter 11. Some efforts fit into more than one of our categories.
5. "Lands' End Guarantee Verboten in Germany," Salt Lake City, *Deseret News* (AP), September 25, 1999, p. B-1.

6. Interview with Randall Myers, senior knowledge engineer, Sterling Wentworth Corporation, Salt Lake City, October 2004.
7. Denise Wymore wrote her book, *Tatoos: The Ultimate Proof of a Successful Brand* (2006) entirely at her local Starbucks coffee shop, *www.denisewymore.com.*
8. *www.frequentflyer.com.au/press/theage20Mar05.htm*
9. A 2010 study of sales rep behaviors in business-to-business relationships revealed that "too much contact" was criticized by 35 percent of respondents and "sales style is too aggressive" by 8 percent, *www.cfo.com/*
10. David Rohde, "The Anti-Walmart: The Secret Sauce of Wegmans Is People," *The Atlantic,* April 10, 2012.

CHAPTER 11

Exceeding Customers Expectations with Information
Make Directions Simple

After reading this chapter, you should be able to

1. Understand the nature of A-plus information and how it relates to customer loyalty.

2. Know five ways of producing A-plus information.

3. Recognize informational barriers to customer entry in e-commerce.

4. Select Informational media carefully.

5. Use techniques to enhance message clarity.

6. Create and support user groups.

7. Pay special attention to A-plus information in e-commerce.

8. Evaluate your A-plus information efforts with communication audits.

The Way It Is... Informational Surprises, Good and Bad

When Thomas bought an Acura automobile a few years ago, he received **A-plus information**—the dealership exceeded what the customer anticipated in the area of information. Based on his purchasing experience with dozens of cars, Thomas anticipated that the salesperson would tell him to read the owner's manual in the glove box to figure out how to use the various accessories and features of the car.

Instead, the Acura sales rep spent about 30 minutes with Thomas—after the sale—showing him how each of the car's features worked, how to set technology options, where to check and add oil, how to find and use the jack, spare tire, and tool kit, and how to maintain the car's finish. The sales rep then programmed the radio to Thomas's favorite stations. In short, he gave Thomas the detailed information he needed to make the most of his purchase, and he gave that information using an unexpected medium: personal instruction. This far exceeded any previous experience this customer had had with auto dealerships.

New cars today have unprecedented levels of technology, causing people to see cars as computers on wheels. Although this expansion of onboard computers offers cutting-edge products, it also has a downside: Customers need, more than ever, sufficient information to use the product. Lexus dealers (among other luxury brands) offer classes to customers on how to use the auto's computer tech. Failing to provide enough training has its costs.

Recent J.D. Power rankings of auto quality found that customers faced challenges in adapting to the electronic features of new cars, despite overall improvement in automobile quality. High-quality scores posted by most automakers were tempered by a growing number of complaints about in-car technologies. Customer expectations for ease of use such as voice commands, ability to update their Facebook status, look up directions or check the weather forecast—features readily available on cell phones and computers—seemed to work less well on built-in equipment in their cars and trucks.

In 2012 Ford Motor Company, which had been aggressively installing dashboard touch-screen equipment in its mainstream models, saw its brand drop from fifth in the overall J.D. Power quality rankings to 23rd. This drop was because customers reported numerous problems in their MyFord Touch systems.

This is a perfect illustration of a conundrum faced by many businesses: More sophisticated products require clearer customer information. Failing to clarify leads to dissatisfaction while companies that do good in exceeding expectations regarding information can gain a leg up.

A nontechnology-related A-plus information experience happened a few years ago when a 12-year-old boy, Jimmy, had knee surgery. After the surgery he was referred to a physical therapist. Jimmy's parents anticipated that the therapist would show him how to exercise the knees to aid in recovery. She did this, but also added some small touches that exceeded what the parents expected. She photocopied pictures of each exercise, wrote his name on the pages in large red letters, taught him how to do each exercise, gave him her home phone number, and encouraged him to call with any questions. She also called him the next day to see how he was doing. Little things? Sure they were. But the composite of these little things went beyond what the parent had an anticipated and created an A-plus experience.

The online retailers are learning about the importance of A-plus information—some doing better than others. A friend's recent online purchase through an online merchant resulted in an unsatisfactory exchange of information. The company sent a message saying the order would be shipped within three to four days. However, the order did not arrive as promised. When the customer inquired about when she could expect the merchandise ordered, she was again told inaccurate information—information that promised shipment that did not happen. A few days later, the customer found the product she ordered—valued at several hundred dollars—on her doorstep, having been left out in the rain all night—all this because the company failed to give correct and timely information.

A recent experience with another dot-com merchant also failed badly in the information area. While the company's Web page touted special next day delivery service at no extra charge, the merchandise ordered on Monday still had not arrived on Friday. The customer's email to the company went unanswered. He finally called and was told that part of his order had been shipped and the back-ordered portion would be shipped in two days. A day later he received the following email message addressed to "Dear Valued Customer" (shown exactly as he received it):

> The following item(s) within your order #WO3690775 have been updated, and now have the following status:
>
> | | |
> |---|---|
> | SKU # IN-2027 | -Processing; |
> | SKU # TQ-1010 | -Shipped; |
> | SKU # VS-1135 | -Shipped; |
> | SKU # UE-1003 | -Shipped; |

Does this make any sense to you? The company's message uses internal jargon and numbers that mean nothing to the customer. Customers don't refer to products ordered by SKU numbers, and the status report of "processing" tells nothing. The opportunity to A-plus customers with useful information is obviously a foreign concept to this company. For that matter, communicating with any clarity also seems to be a low priority.

RECOGNIZE THE NATURE OF A-PLUS INFORMATION

A company can deliver A-plus information—that is, exceeding expectations—by communicating in ways that are more timely, clear, interesting, or creative than its customers anticipate.

Every product, service, or purchasing experience has an informational component. If you buy a can of soup, its label is likely to include nutritional data, preparation tips, and recipes. Vehicles, tools, appliances, and electronic equipment have detailed owner's manuals. Lawn care services are likely to tell you how often to water or fertilize your grass. Athletic equipment comes with exercise guides or perhaps with a DVD showing how to get the best results from the product. Customers have come to expect to receive such information.

Virtually every product has an informational component—something communicated to the customer.

ProFlowers.com

In fairness, some e-tailers are getting it right. Online florist ProFlowers.com, for example, tells the customer when the ordered flowers were picked up from the distributor, when they were delivered, and even who accepted the delivery. In doing so, ProFlowers is creating the standard in the young and quickly evolving online business world. Customers are quickly coming to expect that e-tailers will send immediate acknowledgments, telling the precise status of order, the shipping date, and costs. Companies that fail to meet this level of service will soon be left in the e-trade dust.

Joanna's recent experience with ProFlowers reinforced her loyalty. A Christmas wreath order for her sister in Iowa was scheduled for delivery December 15. ProFlowers called her on the 12th and left a voice message asking her to contact them on their toll-free line. When Joanna did, they apologized profusely for a failure to get the order faxed to their Iowa distributor and advised her that the shipment would be late by one day. They then waived the shipping charge.

Probes

1. How does this description of ProFlowers compare with other online retailers you have worked with? Did they seem to be better or less effective?
2. How does ProFlowers use the idea of A-plus information to exceed customer expectations?

Understand the Special Informational Demands of E-Commerce

For e-commerce, timely information on the status of customer orders is especially important to customer retention and loyalty. Online customers may feel left in a vacuum if the company does not communicate efficiently, clearly, and in a timely manner.

One ingenious application of timely information timeliness is provided by Domino's Pizza. The company that pioneered the idea of pizza delivery some 40 years ago continues to be on the cutting edge of customer convenience—and information. Introduced in 2008, "Pizza Tracker" (Figure 11-1) now lets customers literally track their pizza from the moment they place the order until it leaves the store en route to them. What's more, Domino's vows that its online tracking system—for phone or online orders—is accurate to within 40 seconds.

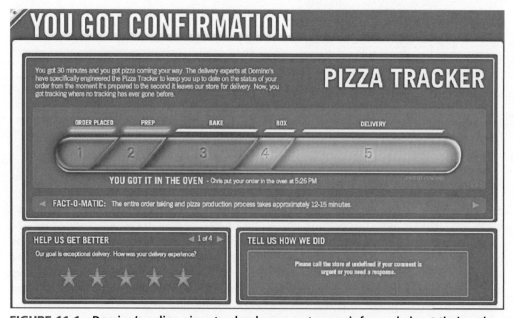

FIGURE 11-1 Domino's online pizza tracker keeps customers informed about their order.

"We're filling that black box of uncertainty—'Has my pizza been forgotten?'—with information and entertainment," says Chris McGlothlin, technology chief at Domino's.[1]

Pizza tracker is fun to watch. It has colorful graphics and a chatty, conversational tone that really does keep the customer informed. Yet some critics grouse that "I guess they'll sell a ton of pizzas to people with no social life who are sitting in front of computers."[2]

The U.S. insurance industry seems to be making an effort to improve on customer responsiveness. Industry data reveal the following:[3]

- Responsiveness to inquiries improved to where only 19 percent of queries were left unanswered, down from 36 percent in a year earlier.
- For those that did respond to user inquiries, 30 percent of surveyed firms provided a response after two days; and 54 percent provided a response within one day.
- Fourteen percent provided a response in less than an hour; 26 percent provided a response in one to four hours, 16 percent between one and two days.
- Most companies acknowledge receipt of an inquiry quickly. Eighty-one percent of surveyed insurers utilize some form of rapid acknowledgment such as email auto-responders; 16 percent issued an acknowledgment within two hours, and only 3 percent didn't acknowledge inquiries at all.

Any way you slice and dice these statistics, companies have a significant opportunity for improvement. Companies that improve upon response times and quality of information given will be likely to please their customers.

As Woody Allen once said, "eighty percent of all success is just showing up." Being available and responsive to customers is a precondition to giving A-plus information. While it is encouraging that some companies are getting better at that, too many still fail to provide even the most basic information in a timely manner to customers.

As e-commerce becomes more sophisticated, companies will continue to find ways to respond in more timely and effective ways. Such responsiveness will become the expectation and companies that fail to meet or exceed that expectation will suffer customer dissatisfaction.

Information handling provides an opportunity for surprising customers. A-plus information happens when customers receive timelier, clearer, or more useful information than they anticipated. The same applies to employee communication, of course. When workers feel well informed and involved in their company, loyalty increases.

Domino's pizza tracker exceeds customer expectations with timely, clear, and useful information.

Customers increasingly expect prompt—very prompt—responses to their inquiries.

KNOW HOW TO PRODUCE A-PLUS INFORMATION

Let's look now at some specific ways to create an A-plus information experience for customers and employees. This chapter will get you thinking about several categories of A-plus information ideas including **informational hand-holding**, **media selection**, **message clarity**, **information accessibility**, and **user groups**. There may, however, be other variations that you can creatively apply.

Provide Informational Hand-Holding

As discussed above, the explosive growth of electronic commerce provides a golden opportunity to exceed what customers anticipate with A-plus information. The young and rapidly changing e-commerce world offers a wide range of service levels as many companies work to figure out how to do it well. Customers are just beginning to develop loyalties to certain e-tailers and are bookmarking select Web sites on their computers. Until customers feel completely comfortable about the information they receive on the Net, they are likely to examine merchandise on the Net, and then purchase it offline at brick-and-mortar retailers. Although improving, customers still say they aren't filling electronic shopping carts because they don't get enough hand-holding on the Net. We can assume that people are getting increasingly comfortable with e-commerce, but there will always be a substantial number who prefer the kinds of information they get from

---

ANOTHER LOOK

Barriers to Customer Entry

═══

Some e-commerce experts contend that Web sites turn away more business than they realize. These are the typical barriers they routinely put in front of potential customers:

Barrier 1: Requiring Too Much Information from Visitors

Many sites require an exorbitant amount of information to register users at all. People are increasingly reticent to disclose personal information and Web sites that require too much lose customers.

Barrier 2: Make Users Repeat Themselves Often

When you've asked users a question once, you should always know the answer. The more often a customer needs to repeat himself, the dumber your Web site seems.

Barrier 3: Make Users Enter Order Numbers, Promotion Codes, or Other Obscure Pieces of Information

Sometimes sites have ads for special discounts on the home page which require the user enter a promotional code during the checkout process. Sometimes there is no way to copy and paste long codes into the correct box during checkout. That's a frustrating annoyance customers should not have to experience.

Probes

1. Describe situations where you have faced similar inconveniences on the Web.
2. How does this article relate to A-plus information? What are some opportunity areas you might use?

---

human contact. Getting useful, reassuring information into the heads of customers should be an important part of the development of any e-commerce efforts.

Opportunities to improve customer hand-holding aren't just for electronic commerce. Better organizations of all types are increasingly sensitive to customer discomfort and are doing things to reduce it. Companies that have personal guides, personal shoppers, and private bankers are doing additional hand-holding. Companies that have exceptionally friendly receptionists or folks at the door who greet and keep customers informed of matters of interest to them are doing hand-holding. Managers who maintain legitimate open-door policies and are receptive to employee concerns are doing additional hand-holding for their internal customers. Company leaders who give customers their home phone numbers and invite them to call if they have problems of concerns are doing hand-holding, too.

Look carefully at your company. Are you providing informational opportunities that make customers and employees comfortable and confident as they do business with you?

Select Informational Media Carefully

When providing customers with information, consider various media options—written documents, DVDs, online helps, and the like. Media should be chosen on the basis of **communication effectiveness**, not just efficiency. Let me explain.

Communication *efficiency* is a simple ratio of the costs of communicating relative to the number of people reached by the message. If a message is extremely simple (a no parking sign, or widely distributed memo announcing a price change on a particular product, a simple cooking tip or recipe), we can get away with an efficient medium such as a flyer, label, or simple instruction sheet. But, as soon as we go beyond such simple messages, communication effectiveness becomes more important.

> Communication efficiency is a simple ratio between the cost of sending a message and the number of people "reached."

Communication *effectiveness* is different from communication efficiency. *Effectiveness* is achieved when the message is

- *received* by the right people (and not others),
- *understood*,
- *remembered* for a reasonable amount of time, and
- *used*.

Effective media are seldom simple or cheap. The greatest effectiveness is typically achieved when people talk face to face. This one-to-one communication is, of course, much more expensive (far less efficient) than an instruction sheet, online guide, or owner's manual. But if the message is crucial to the customer's satisfaction with the product, it can be well worth the extra cost. The Acura dealer described earlier apparently believed in investing in personalized, face-to-face communication when he taught his customer about the features of his new car.

We can attribute much misunderstanding to overemphasizing efficiency when we should focus on effectiveness. Sometimes it doesn't pay to be efficient. The cheap, easy way to transfer information (e.g., the email from the e-merchant who identified products only by SKU numbers) doesn't do the job.

> When conveying important information, sometimes it doesn't pay to be efficient.

Creative companies surprise their customers by breaking away from the usual and by using a variety of media for various messages. Chevrolet, for example, went beyond the owner's manual years ago when it provided an audiotape to teach customers how to use the features of their car or truck. Some companies provide DVDs to teach customers how to assemble or use a product. Online help and telephone hotlines (if well designed and responsive) have saved many a frustrated consumer.

Be Open and Trustworthy

Companies build goodwill with customers by being open and honest. Face it. Customers can get almost any information about your products or services online. Transparency is a fact of modern life and, by contrast, keeping secrets is more difficult than ever. Relationship building calls for trust and openness.

Provide Timely Answers

In addition to being efficient and effective, messages should also be timely. This means that the information is readily available when the customer needs it.

Many organizations now have online help services with **frequently asked questions (FAQs)** that can give quick answers. The best ones use several levels of FAQs. Some questions address the basic needs of prospects and newer customers. Other FAQs are for experienced customers who know their way around the company's products and services.

Companies can no longer make customers work hard for needed information. In the early days of personal computers, documentation (the instruction manual) was notoriously bad. It was hard to read and often grammatically clumsy. Today's technology buyer wouldn't stand

A Case in Point
Chipolte Restaurants

A recent article in *Fast Company* highlighted Chipolte restaurant chain's chief marketing officer, telling how he believes in openness with information not common in the industry. Says CMO Mark Crumpacker, "Typically, fast-food marketing is a game of trying to obscure the truth.... [T]he more people know about fast-food companies, the less likely they'd want to be a customer."[4] Chipolte's approach is to tell customers exactly what is in its burritos and other products. In doing so it also communicates its "Food with Integrity"

mantra, stressing the use of meat from free-range chickens, naturally raised pigs, and dairy from cows that are hormone free. The company's openness with information projects transparency and, at the same time, promotes a stance against industrial–farming practices that they see as unhealthy and unethical. The next steps are to develop healthy-eating stories that can appear on company packaging. All this is connected to a strategic goal of changing the food culture toward more natural, less processed options.

for that for a minute. The informational bar has been raised considerably. What passed for the norm in the 1980s or 1990s would be totally unacceptable in today's plug-and-play world. For that matter, what has passed for "plug-and-play" a few years ago is no longer acceptable. One reason Apple has cultivated loyalty and captured large market share is because i-Phones, i-Pads, and i-Pods are so easy to use. Even the least technologically sophisticated consumer seems to be able to figure out how to use these products without fear of getting it wrong.

An interesting recent example of timely, well-placed information is a smart shopping cart. This is for people who don't want to take the time while they're in the middle of shopping to check their phone or read lists for information on what foods are best. A new device puts that information front and center and helps nudge consumers toward better buying decisions.

"The Lambent Shopping Trolley Handle is a 16-LED multicolor display that clips onto any shopping cart and signals product information via pattern changes. One color pattern might indicate that a product is organic, and another might tell you if it's local (low, medium, or high food miles)."[5]

Better Information for Internal Customers

Let's look at internal customers for a moment. Employee communication also poses opportunities for exceeding expectations with information. The best companies to work for typically use active, multifaceted employee communication and training efforts. Great companies provide extensive training and information that creates high levels of employee engagement.

Progressive companies are constantly looking for media options that allow them to A-plus their internal customers. Internal networks, blog sites, as well as organizational rituals like regular bull sessions, informal chats, opportunities to work with different departments, or even the office layout can stimulate open communication and idea sharing.

The best companies typically use active, multiple media employee interaction and training, thus exceeding their employees' expectations.

USE TECHNIQUES THAT ENHANCE MESSAGE CLARITY

Regardless of the media used, information must be clear and understandable. Intelligent companies seek clarity by presenting their messages with short, clear sentences, a logical sequence of information, and enough repetition to effectively teach the message receiver. They also test messages with similar readers, getting their feedback, before publishing final versions.

Audit of Your Company's Writing

How clear are the messages you are sending customers? Many organizations assume they are doing just fine but, in reality, could benefit from having a professional business communication expert do an audit of their written documents, telephone scripts, and presentations. Communication consultant Dr. Sherron Bienvenu[6] has completed projects for companies who recognized that their written documents were not of the quality they wanted. (By the way, we often have blind spots. The message may make perfect sense to us because we understand the lingo and the products while the same messages leave less informed customers scratching their heads.)

Her auditing approach was straightforward. She analyzed a sample of the letters and memos sent to the client's customers and quickly recognized communication tactics that could be improved upon. Among the problems she found are some you too may be experiencing in your documents:

1. *Abrupt tone.* While most readers appreciate business writers getting directly to the point, many of these letters were too abrupt.
2. Use of *clichés or jargon.* Clichés are overused, stale phrases; **jargon** is specialized language the company may well understand but the customer may not. If you are not sure the customer will know the meaning of a term, use a simpler, clearer description.

3. Use of *stock numbers or abbreviations*. In many cases the reader may not understand or recognize these.

4. *Failure to express appreciation*. The most powerful phrase in any relationship is probably *thank you*. Instead of telling a reader that her order cannot be shipped as planned, start the message with a thank you for ordering or thank you for her patience.

5. *Failure to offer an alternative* to solve a problem. Don't just tell readers what you cannot do; tell them what you can do. Take the initiative to solve the customer's problem if at all possible.

6. *Failure to provide a reasonable explanation*. Don't say "it's against our policy" and think that that does it. Take a moment to explain why the policy is as it is—in terms the reader can understand (even if he or she may be disappointed).

As any author would testify, we can constantly improve the wording of almost anything we write or say. Wise companies periodically look at their messages to edit and re-edit messages. This is critical to ongoing improvement and the opportunity to create A-plus information.

Frequently review your company's written materials to be certain they communicate clearly and with appropriate tone.

Use Some Redundancy

People don't always get your messages immediately. For example, you get better results by presenting information verbally (with words) and graphically (with pictures or diagrams). Likewise, an owner's manual with a supplemental DVD, reference chart, online help program, or telephone hot line will improve the likelihood of customer satisfaction with your product. Such redundant media are keys to understanding.

Make Key Information Easily Accessible with Graphics and Icons

Sometime you can create A-plus information by simply providing clear signs. I consulted with a hospital that had a rather unusual floor plan. What appeared to be the main entrance opened onto a large foyer area with a reception desk. But, because the local folks knew that just about everyone came in through the emergency room entry, this reception area was not staffed. People unfamiliar with the hospital would come in this front door and have no idea where to go—and with no one to help them. When the hospital learned of this confusion, they improved the signs and added some color-coded strips on the floor to lead to various departments.

Sometimes something as simple as better signs or color-coded lines can surprise the customer with A-plus information.

Signs can have marketing and employee benefits as well. One example comes from the pharmacy department in a large retail store. Pharmacy employees faced the large burden of stocking all those little bottles, jars, and boxes in perfectly straight rows in aisle after aisle. Every time a customer picked something up to read the label, the display needed to be straightened or the products turned to faces front. It was a lot of work. So, the store began replacing traditional shelves with a system of bins. Instead of facing a shelf of aspirin bottles, say, the shopper saw a blowup of the aspirin bottle's label. Under that blowup was the bin, into which the aspirin bottles had been dumped.

The enlarged sign provided A-plus information and solved the problem of stocking—a clerk could just roll a trolley of merchandise to the aisle, open the bin, dump in the goods, and move on. No more straight lines.

Shoppers liked it better, too. Instead of facing a row of bottles with tiny print, they saw a large, easy-to-read version of the label. It was much easier on the eyes, especially for elderly shoppers.

CREATE AND SUPPORT CUSTOMER USER GROUPS AND CLASSES

Organizations that bring groups of customers together for user's groups are also offering A-plus information. Such groups are naturals for craft shops, computer stores, financial institutions, and so on and may also work in other arenas. Examples are food stores that offer cooking classes, credit unions that sponsor free classes on investments, budgeting, and personal finance, or auto repair shops that offer classes on auto maintenance. Learning with other people provides social support and makes the process more effective.

One of my clients was a medium-sized tire shop and auto repair business. While brainstorming ideas for giving A-plus information, the employees decided to offer auto maintenance classes, specifically aimed at their female customers. Through some creative advertising and frequent mention of the classes to customers, they got a pretty good turnout. The classes covered tips for tire care, guided tours of a car's exhaust system (with a mechanic showing the parts on a car on a lift), even a session on maintaining auto paint and upholstery. The groups were small at first but grew as customers became aware that the classes ran every other Tuesday evening at 7. And you can bet those who attended the classes were loyal customers.

Motorcycle manufacturer Harley Davidson brings A-plus service to its customers via its Harley Owners Group (HOG). Started in 1983 in an attempt to stem slipping sales, HOG grew from 33,000 members to about 700,000 today.

Harley found that people were giving up riding because they didn't have anyone to ride with. HOG brings Harley riders together for rides or to swap tips. "It gives a person a way into a subculture," says Mike Keefe, HOG's director. In a recent *Investor's Business Daily* story, Keefe describes spending eight days riding and camping out with other Harley owners. "In the mornings, I'm standing in line with six other naked men waiting to use a cold shower. You can't get much closer to a customer than that."[7]

Incidentally, Harley buyers get a one-year HOG membership free with bike purchase. After that, it costs $40 a year. It's common for Harley executives and administrative workers to take part in HOG activities, thus fostering open communication with customers. This is an excellent example of A-plus information sharing.

Utah Community Credit Union (UCCU) recently launched an excellent Web site aimed at teaching young people how to better manage money. The site, *www.BeMoneySmart.org*, has friendly talking characters that show youth how to handle money and win awards for saving and for good grades. Although UCCU gets no direct income from the site, it creates much goodwill, exceeds its members' expectations, and supports its vision of people helping people with financial matters. (By way of disclosure—your author served on the Board of Directors for UCCU, although he had little to do with their innovative BeMoneySmart program.)

Internal customers—employees—can also gain great benefit from user groups. Repair technicians, for example, can be encouraged to create "**communities of practice**" where they can share tips and ideas. Cross-departmental cooperation can be enhanced by getting to know each other and each other's functions in the company. Often such groups meet informally over lunch or a few beers after work. Enlightened companies encourage and promote such information-sharing activities.

> Wise companies support information sharing among employees with such things as communities of practice.

Businesses should try to increase the level of interaction with their customers and employees using any available media. If a business values its customer relationships, it will want to interact with those customers at every conceivable opportunity. Such interactivity can occur in a wide variety of ways.

PAY SPECIAL ATTENTION TO A-PLUS INFORMATION IN E-COMMERCE

As discussed earlier, e-commerce faces some special challenges and opportunities in providing A-plus information. Two critical actions are to make customer support easily accessible and to honor the customer feedback loop.

Make Customer Support Accessible

One of the greatest challenges of business today is providing timely, effective support to customers who have questions. E-commerce is especially vulnerable to complaints of lack of support. Electronic commerce relies heavily on email for communicating with customers—sometimes too heavily.

Web site developers often describe a commonly heard complaint about e-commerce: that companies by design are leaving their phone numbers off because they don't want to spend money to have someone stand by and answer the phone. Their feeling seems to be that companies ought to be able to answer questions on the Web. Indeed, a substantial number of companies don't provide an email address and or phone numbers for customers to ask questions. In many cases, this is shortsighted. Offering customers the option of talking live to a company representative can create the opportunity for "high touch" service to supplement the high tech. One Web site that sells a fairly mundane product (floor mats) is StopDirt.com. Erika Wilde, the business owner, encourages phone calls and even initiates some calls to follow up on customer satisfaction. Because Erika is pleasant and fun to talk with, she solidifies her customer's loyalty with such personal touch communication. This relationship building has, over the years, created strong repeat business and more than a few friendships.

Honor the Customer Feedback Loop

A related and all-too-common complaint of e-commerce customers is the lack of responsiveness when they do contact the company with a problem. Have you experienced this? Too often, our requests seem to drop into a black hole somewhere and we get no response at all.

A survey by e-tailer trade group Shop.org showed that about a quarter of shoppers never received a response to an email request for assistance. "It's retailing 101: Don't ignore your customers," says Mary Helen Gillespie, president of E-BuyersGuide.com. "Plus, it's not just bad business, it's extremely rude even by today's standards."[8] Answer your email!

Making your company more accessible to your customers is an excellent way to exceed customer expectations and surprise with service that's better than anticipated. But if you offer help lines, be sure they are adequately staffed with knowledgeable people.

EVALUATE YOUR A-PLUS INFORMATION EFFORTS

Measuring the effectiveness of information you give to customers can assess whether or not a company is delivering A-plus service. Two key measures are logging common questions and auditing communication effectiveness.

Logging Common Questions (FAQs)

Maintaining a current FAQ page can be challenging, but can provide your customers with A-plus information.

Develop a system for keeping track of common customer questions. If several people are asking the same questions or experiencing similar confusion, you have an information problem.

This advice applies to all companies, not just the technologically sophisticated. The smallest shop can make notes of recurring customer concerns and encourage all employees to share their experiences. However this information is gathered, managers need to make it worthwhile for employees to record and pass on the customer's feedback. Offer employees incentives for listing and reporting customer comments. Teach your employees to make notes of customer responses (and teach employees to do so if you are a manager), preferably in front of customers so that they know they are being heard.

Audit Your Company's Communication

A **communication audit** is a process for determining the quantity and quality of information flowing through the company as well as that coming into the organization from outside stakeholders. Often done with the help of a communication consultant, an audit uses multiple approaches to objectively pinpoint communication roadblocks, identify overload problems, and assess the effectiveness of the company's formal and informal communication networks.

Consider auditing your company's communication with customers.

Such audits can range from considering relatively informal observation to gathering information with interviews, to **content analysis** of the documents you give customers. Content analysis looks systematically at messages to check for consistency, clarity, and tone. To be effective, such analysis usually uses a third party—a professional outside the organization—to identify message problems, especially information that may confuse customers such as in our earlier example of shipping information using only SKU numbers, not descriptions of the merchandise.

When checking messages, put yourself in the mind-set of your customer and ask, "Does this information exceed my expectations?" As we discussed earlier, consider using a communication specialist to analyze the content and clarity of messages your company sends customers and employees.

For internal customers, remember that internal communication effectiveness reveal a great deal about the status of employee relations. Employees who feel free to communicate and who see that their input is being considered are far more likely to be loyal to the company than are those who feel outside the communication loop. A primary variable in employee engagement is the feeling that their input is being heard. The same principle holds all customers, of course. Open multiple communication channels and regularly look for opportunities to exceed expectations in information handling.

A FINAL THOUGHT

Overall, giving customers and employees clear, appropriate, easy-to-use A-plus information is a powerful way to build loyalty. Look carefully at the quality, quantity, and usability of the messages conveyed in all company interactions. Then find ways to pleasantly surprise people with even better, clearer, more timely, and more interesting information. Put on your creativity hat. Listen for unmet information needs and encourage customers and employees to suggest ways to provide A-plus information. The payoff can be substantial in building customer and employee loyalty.

Summary of Key Ideas

- Ignoring communications from customers (external and internal) will damage goodwill. Take the time necessary to answer calls, emails, text messages, and letters. Honor the feedback loop by responding to input.
- Ineffective instructions and poor information quality can damage business relationships. Clear, useful, and effective messages exceed customer expectations.
- The impact or various informational media varies. Companies make the most of messages by considering both communication efficiency and effectiveness. Effectiveness is often more costly but to exceed expectations companies should be willing to pay the necessary price to enhance communication quality.

- A-plus opportunities arise when we break away from the "normal" and use a variety of media for various messages. Companies can enhance communication by creating and supporting customer user groups (such as the HOGs), communities of practice, classes, or online advice (such as BeMoneySmart.net).
- Companies build goodwill with information transparency—by being open and honest about, for example, product ingredients.
- Good companies provide responsive and easy-to-use support, and answer inquiries from all customers. Tracking FAQs and auditing routine information your company shares with customers can reveal opportunities for improving message content and tone.

Key Concepts

A-plus information
communication audit
communication
    effectiveness
communication efficiency

communities of practice
content analysis
frequently asked questions
    (FAQs)

information
    accessibility
informational
    hand-holding

jargon
media selection
message clarity
user groups

Reviewing the Facts

1. Why is it potentially important for organizations to provide better-than-expected information to customers?
2. Consider various ways to exceed expectations with A-plus information. Why are these likely to strengthen customer relationships?
3. What do we mean by communication *media*? Which media do companies you deal with use to communicate with their customers? What are some alternatives that could be seen as A-plus service?
4. Explain the difference between communication efficiency and communication effectiveness. Give an example that depicts each.
5. The Internet and e-commerce provide several challenges to providing A-plus information. What are some of these challenges?
6. How can e-commerce be used to supplement other forms of information and potentially build greater customer loyalty?
7. What is a communication audit and how could it help a company provide A-plus information?

Applying the Ideas

1. The author states that virtually all products have "an informational component?" To what extent do you agree or disagree with this statement? Has it always been this way? What products do you buy that have more information today than they had in the past? Give specific examples.
2. Select five consumer products you use and examine the information that is provided with them. Write a paragraph for each product describing the product and all associated information. (For example, as mentioned early in the chapter, a can of soup has certain information provided on its label—preparation instructions, nutritional information, perhaps recipes, etc.) Then brainstorm other possibilities that could be associated with that product. How could the company provide other information that would enhance the buyer's experience? Let your imagination go and be creative.
3. Identify a product you are familiar with that goes beyond what a customer might expect with regard to information. If similar products use only written materials, look for one that supplements its written materials with some other media. Describe the relative effectiveness of this approach. How could the company take the idea of A-plus information even further? Be creative.
4. Assume that you feel a communication audit would be helpful to your company (or a company you are familiar with). Identify five questions you would like that audit to answer.
5. Use your favorite search engine to find information about what companies are doing to exceed customer expectations in information. Select an industry you are interested in (such as automobiles, video games, sporting goods, hospitality, motorcycles, collectables). Visit three sites and describe what they offer. Evaluate the relative creativity and effectiveness of these sites. To what extent do they exceed your expectations?

Consider this Case

Bumble and Bumble Exceed Expectations with School for Stylists

Hair care companies everywhere spend a bundle on ads in trendy fashion magazines and in television advertising campaigns. But one niche player, Bumble and bumble (B&b), has a different strategy—they provide their customers (salon owners) with in-salon workshops. As an added service, they offer hair care lessons and business education to salon owners and stylists through Bumble and bumble University, its self-styled center for the craft, culture, and commerce of hairdressing.

Eli Halliwell, senior operating officer for Bumble, prefers taking the company's message to salons and stylists, empowering them with knowledge. His goal is to make them knowledgeable, passionate, raving fans of their brand. Foregoing a large advertising budget, B&b seeks to work with only the narrow band of the best salons in the industry to create a very deep, integrated relationship.

Bumble & bumble University (Bb.U.) delivers a curriculum that is "extremely exciting, challenging, and inspiring," according to Jack Ray, a Raleigh salon owner. "It's a real honor to be working with the same people that are behind the scenes of the fashion shows in Milan, Paris, and New York."[9]

"We contrast that to everyone else in the industry, which we see as 'inch-deep and mile-wide'; they have very little relationship because they use distributors and they have a very broad set of clients," says Mr. Halliwell.

Probes

1. How does Bumble and bumble illustrate the principle of A-plus information?

2. How can this approach be a win–win for customers and company alike?

3. What possible applications can you think of for similar businesses?

Consider this Case

The Nontechy Solution

Monika specifically timed her visit to the Sociology Department for a quiet day before winter classes began. As a 19-year-old student at a well-regarded private university, Monika was gathering information about various majors and sociology sounded interesting. She had completed most of her general education courses and had a 3.8 grade point average.

It was 10 a.m. when she respectfully entered the department office. A middle-aged woman was typing something into a computer and did not look up. After about 30 seconds of standing at the receptionist's desk, Monika cleared her throat and asked, "Can I get some information about majoring in sociology?"

The woman never looked up. Instead, she pointed to a bulletin board and resumed typing. Feeling chastened, Monika apologized for interrupting her, and went to the bulletin board, feeling awkward and a bit embarrassed. On the board, she found pages that had been clipped from the University catalogue (which she

had already read) and a few pictures of professors in the department, but little additional information. After her rude reception, she decided to not even ask for an appointment with an academic adviser. "I guess they aren't really interested in attracting students into their program," she said to herself. She left and never again returned to that office.

Probes

1. In what ways did this department miss an opportunity to create a positive relationship with a potential customer?

2. If you were the department chair and had observed this situation, what would you do? (Assume that the success of the department depends on attracting good students.)

3. How could the department move toward exceeding student expectations regarding the information it provides? Come up with some creative ideas.

Building a Customer Service Strategy: Your Ongoing Case

Let's go back to the ongoing case you selected. This will be either your current employer, a specific organization you want to work in, or one of the two hypothetical organizations described in Chapter 1: Independent Auto Sales and Service (IAS) or Network Nutrition Distributors (NND). Now consider the following questions as you develop a customer service strategy:

Strategy Planning Questions

1. Assume you are in a leadership position in the organization. How could you impress upon employees the importance of answering customer messages in a timely manner? How could you make this easier for employees?

2. Develop a plan to audit the communication effectiveness of your company. How would you go about this?

- What kinds of messages should be analyzed?
- How could you assess how understandable the messages are for your customers?
- What are some ways you could make the messages even clearer?
- What are some other media not being fully used that could exceed customer expectations? (Remember: Media are not all electronic. Some very old-fashioned media such as personal visits, conversations, or letters can have significant impact.)

3. Explore ways other companies handle communications. Identify five ideas used by others that could be useful to your company's goal of A-plus information. Remember that companies in different industries may have good ideas you could adapt.

Notes

1. Bruce Horovitz, "Where's Your Domino's Pizza? Track It Online, *USA Today*, January 30, 2008.

2. Christopher Muller, restaurant expert at the University of Central Florida, who's less than enthusiastic about pizza-tracking tech.

3. Sean Michael Kerner, "Insurance Companies Score Online Customer Respect," March 28, 2005, *http://www.clickz .com/stats/sectors/professional/article.php/3493201*

4. Danielle Sacks, "For Exploding All the Rules of Fast-Food," *Fast Company*, March 2012, p. 125.

5. "A Shopping Cart That Guides You to Good Food Decisions." Downloaded June 24, 2012, *http://www .fastcoexist.com/1679704/a-shopping-cart-that-guides-you-to-good-food-decisions.*

6. See Dr. Bienvenu's Web site: *www.ChinUp.net.*

7. Mike Angell, "By Focusing on Customers, Firms Can Boost Shareholder Value," *Investor's Business Daily*, October 11, 2002, p. A-4.

8. Quoted in Frank Barnako, *Internet Daily* (sponsored by CBS MarketWatch), September 10, 1999.

9. Quoted from news release by Samuel Cole Salon, "New York State of Mind: Jack Ray to Provide Bumble and Bumble Training in His Raleigh Salons," *http://www.pr .com/press-release/48671*, August 15, 2007.

CHAPTER 12

Exceed Customer Expectation with Convenience and Timing
Make Things Easier for Customers

The Way It Is...A Little Extra Convenience

Marcia was a regular customer at the Perimeter Center Publix Supermarket in Atlanta. During the busy Christmas holiday season, she discovered a delicious low-fat eggnog. But after trying it, she came back for more only to discover the store was out.

A chat with the dairy section employee brought promises that more would be coming in soon. But when she returned to the store a day later the product was again out of stock. This time the employee said, "More is coming in tomorrow and I'll set some aside for you." When she returned the next day the delivery truck had been late and again, and she got no eggnog.

This time the employee offered her A-plus convenience. He apologized and told her that as soon as the delivery comes in, he will set some aside for her and *deliver it to her home* on his way home from work! And he did.

Home delivery! What a concept. A generation ago, home delivery of milk and other products was commonplace. In the twenty-first century it may be making a comeback. Online grocery delivery services, at-home auto oil changes and glass replacement, and a number of other services are reintroducing consumers to a level of convenience not often found in today's business world. Companies are recognizing the opportunities to exceed expectations with greater convenience.

Enhancing speed and convenience for customers is a critical tactic. E-commerce sites live and die by their speed and responsiveness. Traditional businesses build great loyalty among customers who value the ways they respect their time and try to provide easy, timely transactions.

UNDERSTAND A-PLUS CONVENIENCE AND TIMING

Customer convenience arises from speed of service and ease of doing business. Organizations that strive for efficient, easy-to-use services capture customer loyalty.

Let's look first at the first component, speed. Surpassing what the customer anticipates about speed may be one of the simplest yet most powerful ways of building customer loyalty. The ubiquitous convenience store personifies key elements that can be applied to other businesses. C-stores allow parking at the door, reasonable selection, quick, out-the-door-in-a-minute service. Some now offer credit card scanning machines that allow the customer to pay almost instantly with a tap of their card. Pay at the pump gas dispensing is now everywhere and makes things quick and easy for customers and store employees alike. Likewise, quick delivery of products ordered online has made the old line in many commercials "please allow 4 to 6 weeks for delivery" to sound like something from the dark ages. We want it NOW!

The reason people like businesses that offer quick service is simple: People today value time, perhaps more than ever before. Unfortunately, aside from convenience stores, many companies are far too casual about wasting customers' time. They often don't even recognize when they are taking longer than the customer expects. They are so wrapped up in their own internal systems—the ways they do things—that they don't even consider the possibility that they are eating up a lot of the customer's time and patience.

We live in a world of commerce where we expect nearly instant gratification. We see things on the Web, order them, and fully expect that they will arrive on our doorstep in a day or two. When they do, we are likely to reorder; if they fail to make the anticipated deadline, we are likely to be disappointed and will quit shopping with that company in favor of one that hustles a bit more.

Despite this, many companies still fall into the trap of overpromising and underdelivering. They make vague or unfulfilled commitments involving their customers' time. Here are a few examples:

Companies that overpromise and underdeliver when it comes to speed of service soon drive customers to more efficient competitors.

- A major computer distributor in Europe tells the customer that their mainframe will be restored to service "soon." The customer thought that "soon" meant 20 minutes or so; to the technician, who better understood the complexity of the problem, "soon" meant about eight hours.
- Some phone or cable companies routinely tell customers that they will be at their home to install service "between 7:30 a.m. and 5 p.m." on a given date. Is the customer expected to sit around all day waiting for the installation?
- A medical clinic's most common complaint was that patients had to wait too long for the doctor. Customers felt that doctors had little regard for the value of their time. The result was a negative spiral where patients showed up later than the appointment time figuring that the doctor will be running late. The clinic then scheduled even more slack into the system and the situation got worse.
- A customer has a negative experience with an online business that makes a big deal of offering products overnight so the customer will have them the next day (at no extra charge, according to company promotions). But when a customer's merchandise doesn't show up for five days, the opportunity to give A-plus convenience is long gone. So is that customer's loyalty.

On a more positive note, a number of businesses are built on the simple premise of giving A-plus speed and convenience. Federal Express promises package delivery "by 10:30 a.m." while it knows it can have the package there by 9:30 or 9:45. Customers are routinely surprised because most businesses fail to meet their own deadlines, thus showing disrespect for the customer's time. Likewise an office equipment repair company used a similar practice. When customers called for a technician to fix their copy machine, it promised that someone would be at their office by 2 o'clock when the company knew the rep would be there by 1:30 or so. This pleasantly surprised clients.

Consistently beating a time deadline provides customers with A-plus speed and convenience.

The Disney amusement parks create A-plus speed by having signs showing how long it will take to get on the "Space Mountain" ride from a given point in a cue. They have actually scheduled in a little fat. The "eight minutes wait from this point" was really five and a half minutes. The customers are pleasantly surprised. Restaurants that tell patrons a table will be available in 15 minutes and then seat them in 10 minutes will be far more popular than one promising 15 minutes and delivering it in 18 or 20 minutes.

HOW TO PRODUCE A-PLUS CONVENIENCE

We can exceed customer expectations and provide A-plus convenience and speed by applying or adjusting actions that convey to customers that the company seriously values the customers' time and wants to do business in an expeditious way that makes the customer's life easier.

Customers are constantly demanding to enhance convenience.

As with any A-plus tactic, companies need to be ever-vigilant to ways of improving systems and behaviors that can enhance convenience. If you don't offer better and better convenience, your competition will. Customers want it, and you need to provide it. So, let's look at some key actions we can consider.

GIVE SERIOUS REGARD TO CUSTOMER TIME AND CONVENIENCE

Time is a valuable commodity. When we disregard it or fail to share our customer's sense of urgency, we discount our customer. Few things are more frustrating than waiting for something that seems to take longer than necessary. In fact, of all the pet peeves identified in my research and described by seminar participants, slow service is at or near the top of everyone's list.

Speed is easier to work with than convenience. In fact, the nice thing about creating A-plus speed is that you have a lot of control. You can clearly create the expectation by giving customers an estimate of how long something will take. Once the customer anticipates a particular time period, you can simply beat it.

Customers often don't know how long things take. You need to advise them and, in so doing, set the expectation.

Give customers an honest and realistic perception of how long something will take to complete. A nurse in a hospital told me of a situation where a patient was sent to the blood lab for a blood test. The phlebotomist drew the blood sample and took it behind a curtain to be sent off for analysis. Upon returning to the patient, he asked what the results of the test were. The lab technician laughed and explained that the test was to be done at another facility and results would not be ready until the next day. The point is that customers don't always know how long things take. You need to tell them.

Too many businesses fall for the temptation to promise quicker service and hope for the best. They hate to deliver unpleasant news, so, instead, offer a time that sounds good even when it cannot be realistically delivered. In doing so, they miss a significant opportunity to under-promise and overdeliver. It is better to give a realistic time you can beat rather than a pie-in-the-sky estimate you cannot meet.

In addition to having regard for customers' time, companies need to think about time's cousin: customer convenience. Offering A-plus convenience is one of the most powerful ways to build loyalty. This is illustrated by two kinds of businesses, pizza and auto lubrication.

The most popular restaurant food in America is pizza. In the late 1950s, when pizza was gaining widespread popularity across the country, it was served just like any other restaurant entree. People ordered their pizza, waited 15 or 20 minutes for it to be baked, and ate it at the restaurant. Then came the convenience pioneers like Domino's. Early in the life of this pizza chain, it made the strategic decision to not have eat-in restaurants, to focus exclusively on take-out (what Europeans call "take away") and on delivery service.

ANOTHER LOOK
Managing Queues

An increasing number of organizations are using **queue management systems (QMS)** to manage queues (or lines, as we say in the United States). What may have once been limited to a bakery or butcher shop where customers took a number has now expanded to electronic versions applied in businesses from banks to bus stations to auto parts stores.

Modern queue management systems can allow a service center to manage long lines without the customers physically standing in a line. A customer wanting for a particular service presses a switch and receives a receipt with a "queue number." The customer can then sit in the seating area or continue to shop while waiting for his or her turn without having to stay in a physical line. After serving the previous customer, the service employee presses a switch and notifies the QMS that it is free. The QMS display then calls the next number on the queue.

A simple system like this makes waiting more comfortable and fair. Customers know they are being served in the order they arrived and can occupy themselves with other things while waiting, if they wish.

The strategy was a hit. People came to associate Domino's with the 30-minute delivery guarantee and in turn Domino's and its competitors taught America a new way of buying restaurant food. Since then, countless pizza chains and other independent restaurants have followed that model. Today, meals prepared outside the home account for nearly half the U.S. food dollar spending. The Food Marketing Institute says that "Americans want to spend no more than 15 minutes preparing a meal…Today's shoppers want their food and they want it now." Seven out of ten households buy "home meal replacements" (otherwise known as take-out) at least once a month.[1]

Of course, the choices now go far beyond pizza or restaurant meals alone. Supermarkets and delis provide a wide range of prepared meals that need nothing more than heating and eating. Food producers are packaging ingredients together to prepare complete meals without having to buy each ingredient separately. Shredded potatoes, chopped peppers, onions, and diced ham are provided in separate plastic bags within a box describing the meal. Pizza crusts are sold with packets of topping, while prepared sandwiches are packaged with chips and cookie to make an instant box lunch. All these efforts are attempts to meet customer needs for convenience.

Another classic convenience breakthrough is the stand-alone automobile oil change business which emerged in the late 1970s and 1980s. Before companies like Jiffy Lube, Q-Lube, and Minute Man, auto owners needing an oil change typically took their car to a dealership or service station. They dropped it off, caught a ride to work, returned after work, and picked up their car. It could easily be an all-day deal and was pretty inconvenient. Then came the quick lube shop.

Today, auto owners go to a Jiffy Lube or similar shop, have a cup of coffee in a customer lounge while a team of technicians pounces on their car, changes the oil, checks the tires and all fluids, vacuums the inside, and so on. The whole process takes 10 or 15 minutes. This is A-plus convenience.

Products packaged together allow the convenience of not having to shop for separate ingredients.

Recent years have seen an expansion of mobile restaurants (think taco trucks and much more) and other goods that come to the customer. One funky truck in Portland, Oregon, is a clothing boutique on wheels. Vanessa Lurie drives a clothing-laden 1969 Cardinal Deluxe-converted motor home. She jokes that people don't know what to think of the brightly colored vehicle. "People thought I was a bakery," she says, adding that they would come in expecting cupcakes, not plaid bow ties and vintage dresses.[2]

Entrepreneurship consultants often encourage such mobile businesses saying that a truck is a cheaper and faster way of doing business, one backed by the power of social media and the freedom to go to your customers, rather than waiting for them to come to you.[3] From the perspective of customer service such businesses also add enhanced convenience.

Mobile businesses ranging from food trucks to clothing boutiques add unexpected convenience for customers.

ANOTHER LOOK

Convenience and the Older Customer

The fastest-growing age group on earth, according to United Nations research, is people above 60. In the United States alone, people over 65 will soon rise to 20 percent of the population. That's a lot of people.

Older customers have special needs which can provide special opportunities to exceed expectations with added convenience. Researchers at prestigious universities are actively studying the effects of aging and changes in people's abilities as they get older. Some very simple changes businesses are making to provide convenience to these customers is to make packages easier to open and provide instructions in print easy to read. Some restaurants offer special parking spaces for "senior citizens" and easier physical access including ramps for wheelchairs.

New products also serve the special needs of seniors. A Teaneck, New Jersey, shoe manufacturer has created a shoe that uses GPS technology that records where the wearer walks—and can send alerts to caregivers if someone suffering from Alzheimer's disease of dementia wanders away and gets lost.[4]

While service providers may not be necessarily involved in designing products, the empathy for older customers can lead to positive ways of surprising them with thoughtful touches that add convenience to their shopping experience.

CONSIDER THE USE OF VIRTUAL WAITING TECHNIQUES

Waiting can cause customer dissatisfaction that impacts the intent to be a repeat buyer. Although waiting can be an expected part of some services such as elegant dining, it is, for most customers, an annoyance to be minimized or avoided. So, what can companies do to reduce waiting time for customers? And if waiting times cannot be avoided, what can companies do to minimize their unpleasantness? A breakthrough article published by the Cornell University Hotel and Restaurant School[5] summarizes some creative and effective ways to apply **"virtual waiting."**

Hospitality management scholars Duncan Dickson, Robert C. Ford, and Bruce Laval suggest three possible strategies for mitigating the dissatisfying nature of waiting:

1. Manage the *reality of the actual wait* through the use of techniques that better match capacity with customer demand.
2. Manage the *perception* of the wait by distracting customers so that wait times don't seem so long.
3. *Make the wait invisible* through developing virtual queues, which allow customers to participate in other activities while they wait for an appointed time at their desired activity.[6]

Match Capacity to Demand

Organizations can easily determine their busiest times and slower times. The first step to reduce undue waiting is to plan for peak-time loads with adequate staffing. Supermarkets that open additional checkout lines in the early evening when customers are shopping after work are doing such capacity management. Likewise, organizations that hire additional employees to handle holiday or seasonal demand and tax services who gear up for longer hours during tax season are adjusting to meet customer demand.

On the other side of the coin, companies can beef up low demand periods by enticing customers to come in when business is slow. Restaurants that offer "early bird" dinner specials, bars that have special happy hour prices, and resorts that offer off-season rates are examples of ways companies try to even out the demand and thus minimize customer inconvenience and waiting times.

Respond to How Customers Perceive the Wait

A good way to make waiting less unpleasant is to be distracted. Think about what we all do to break boredom. We listen to a headset while jogging. We read a book or magazine when stuck in a doctor's office or at the bus station. Some folks are contented to simply "people watch" while at an airport or in busy mall.

Companies can help provide for customer distraction. While waiting in a line at an amusement park, we are likely to see cartoon characters or a marching band go by. While in line at my local post office, I can view stamp collections or watch the Discovery channel playing on a mounted TV set. I've seen office waiting rooms with elaborate fish tanks or soothing fountains. All such things can help reduce the annoyance of waiting times.

Make the Wait Invisible

Restaurants located in shopping malls give customers a pager that flashes when their table is available. In many cases, when the wait is expected to be long, they are encouraged to go shopping or walk through the mall—the range on the pager is sufficient.

MAKE THINGS EASIER FOR CUSTOMERS

Another way businesses can provide A-plus convenience and timing is by taking the hassle out of cumbersome systems. Unnecessary paperwork is an area where many companies can improve. Smart companies regularly look at the forms or applications customers need to complete and determine if these are all really necessary. They check for **redundancy** or requests for unnecessary information that may be making the paperwork process more difficult than it needs to be. Some of the better mortgage or consumer loan companies make the application process streamlined by precompleting parts of the paperwork. For example, a credit union mortgage department I recently worked with downloaded all relevant credit and account information from my account before giving me forms to complete. I needed to fill out only a few lines.

Continuously check for unnecessary redundancy. Don't require customers to do anything repetitive or unneeded.

Likewise a used auto dealership I bought from had all the information about the car preprinted on the sales documents. The sales rep slipped a few forms into his computer printer and the otherwise-complicated paperwork was reduced to a matter of a few signatures. This provided a surprising convenience for the buyer and moved the sales process along more efficiently.

By contrast, I recently had the unpleasant experience of filling out some forms for a health care provider. Too often a new patient at a doctor's office is required to fill out a stack of forms, each time re-entering his or her name, address, phone number, social security number, and such. Page after page of forms, all requiring the same information! It gets annoying. Input the data one time and cut the repetition.

Repetitious or unnecessary paperwork is annoying. Make life easier for your customer by simplifying forms, applications, and so on.

Look at your organization to determine if you are requiring **repetitive busywork** from your customers, then A-plus them by eliminating it. Contact management systems and computerized records can easily gather and store a great deal of customer information, making it unnecessary for repetitive work. Check into the use of these.

CREATE ONCE-AND-DONE SERVICE

"That's not my department," may be one of the least-favorite phrases for customers. Having to repeatedly tell a story to person after person while seeking a solution drives people nuts. Strive for **once-and-done** service. Make it easy for customers to get everything they need and any problem solved at a single place or through one person authorized to take "ownership" of the customer's issue.

Try to solve customer transaction problems in one easy step—not by passing the customer off to others.

The Ritz-Carlton Hotels are well known for their simple employee position that they are "ladies and gentlemen serving ladies and gentlemen." When a hotel guest asks any employee for something, that employee "owns" that request or problem until it is fulfilled or solved. If a guest asks a maid where he can get a copy of a foreign language newspaper, the maid will either get the paper for him or find out where the guest can get it. The maid is empowered to take the time to run to a news stand if that will get the guest what he wants. It's once-and-done service. And it blows customers away. Employees are given a substantial annual budget they can spend on their customers with no questions asked. The chain won the prestigious Malcolm Baldrige Quality Award in part because of such an exceptional service philosophy.

At the heart of once-and-done service is employee willingness and ability to take responsibility for meeting needs and reducing customer inconvenience. Strong companies hire people with initiative and empower them to do whatever the customer needs.

MAKE DOING BUSINESS EASY

A major business publication announced a "secret weapon" used by discount retailers to "once again trounce traditional department stores." "Was it sophisticated pricing, the latest in-store design, or cutting-edge inventory management? Actually, after twenty years of growing discounter dominance, a simpler explanation rolls into view: the shopping cart."

Simple things like shopping carts and convenient store location can enhance customer loyalty.

The article goes on to say that the impact of something as simple as a shopping cart is significant. A marketing research firm found that "the average shopper with a cart buys 7.2 items, while the customer without a cart buys 6.1."

Shopping malls are beginning to recognize the importance of making shopping easier. Worried about competition from point-and-click e-commerce, developers are working to cluster similar stores together so customers can comparison-shop.

The traditional mall was designed to be difficult to navigate. Retailers wanted people to wander through the mall to increase exposure to other stores. The more the customer walks, the greater the chance he or she will find something else to buy. But e-commerce is changing this too. People want to compare prices and selection at similar stores and they don't want to have to walk far to do it. (After all, they can do it very easily online.) Many frustrated, time-pressed shoppers have already defected from malls to big-box discounters (Walmart, K-Mart, Target, Home Depot) where they can get everything they need in one place.

More commonly, customers are using online retailers whose Web sites make it easy to compare products and pricing. This kind of service has allowed Amazon.com (and countless lesser-known sites) to become marketing powerhouses. The A-plus convenience offered online has created a whole generation of active online shoppers.

OFFER ANCILLARY SERVICES

Loblaw's Supermarkets, Canada's largest chain, offers an ever-growing range of **ancillary services** to its shoppers. A recent innovation at a new Toronto store is a complete women-only fitness club equipped with saunas, tanning beds, and a day care center, offering everything from treadmills to Tae-Bo classes, just steps from the cauliflower. Such ancillary services create A-plus convenience for the chain's customers while providing one-stop shopping for almost every need.

One of the wildly popular ancillary services offered by Starbucks (and competing) coffee shops is wireless Internet connections. Many a student and businessperson spends hours (and dollars) at such shops while working via a Wi-Fi connection.

SIMPLIFY THE PRODUCT

The running joke about people being unable to program a DVD player indicates the constant need to simplify products for exceptional **ease of use**—and convenience. The computer industry has made quantum leaps with plug-and-play technology. Tech giants Apple and others have made a dramatic impact on smart phone and personal entertainment products with their products' exceptional ease of use. One illustration of a simplified product is the Jitter Bug phone™ marketed to people who want a cell phone that simply makes phone calls. It has no built-in camera or music player, no video games, no hi-tech gizmos. It is a simple phone with easy-to-read large keys and a simple, straightforward billing plan. And it is selling very well, especially among seniors. The product advertises widely, especially in publications for retired persons, and fills a significant need. Sometimes less is more in the eyes of the customer.

Simplification of products sold can improve customer convenience and win loyalty.

On a more mundane level, product packaging is responding to the customer's desire for convenience. A Kellogg cereal, Special-K plus, was packaged in a re-sealable box that looks like a half-gallon milk carton. It contains the same amount of cereal as larger, more cumbersome boxes but stores in less space and is easy to pour. Premeasured products and portion-size packages are additional examples of achieving additional convenience through packaging.

MEASURE YOUR A-PLUS CONVENIENCE EFFORTS

Ongoing evaluations of customer convenience can reduce the risk of turnoffs. As with any measurement, the critical element is to get into the customer's frame of reference. Try using mystery shoppers to go through what your customers must. This will help you evaluate the speed and convenience they experience.

Mystery shopping, which we discussed in Chapter 8, is a process whereby companies send researchers who act like customers to gather information about the customer experience. After visiting a business, "shoppers" should be able to tell you answers to these kinds of questions:

1. *How long do customer contacts take?* Use a stopwatch to calculate average times for a variety of types of transactions. Chart these times after any changes are made in procedures or policies.

   Keep in mind, however, that it may not be the absolute amount of time but rather the customer's perception of time that is important. You can better measure this if you ask a customer how long he or she had to wait for a service, and compare this time with the actual time observed. Customers will often report a longer time than it really took. A wait of one minute may seem like two or three to the customer.

   By contrast, sometime customers do not want fast service. Be careful to not rush a customer when more leisurely, personalized service may be the standard you seek. A gourmet restaurant does not push its customer to chow down and get moving. Likewise, some stores seem to savor their customer contact time.

   For example, Kiehl's is a little 148-year-old New York company that makes and sells hair- and skin-care products for men and women. While competitors push product out the door, Kiehl's philosophy of business is different. They intentionally keep their business small to preserve their brand of customer service. (Their customers include actresses Winona Ryder and Sarah Jessica Parker.) At the Kiehl's store, the staff is famous for spending a half-hour with one customer. While a long line waits, the employee grills customer after customer about skin- and hair-care characteristics and then disgorges detailed information about the products.[7]

   Remember, too, our discussion about Zappos.com in Chapter 1. The company's call center personnel are encouraged to talk with customers as long as the customer wants. Building a relationship through extended conversation is seen as more important than fast service—*for some buyers*. Know your customers!

2. *How easy is your telephone system?* A persistent pet peeve is the clumsy telephone system. Call your own company to hear for yourself how well or poorly your phone menus are. Check, especially, the following questions:

   - Can you get to a live person at any time? Does the caller know how to do that?
   - Are you requesting too much information from customers before they get to speak with someone? (Do you really need their account number, for example?)
   - Do you offer too many choices (more than four, typically, would be too many) for customers to remember?

SERVICE SNAPSHOT

Mickey D's Speed Measurement

In a recent visit to my friendly neighborhood McDonald's, I noticed a small digital readout on the cash register—facing the customer. It displayed the "average service time" in seconds. On that day, it told me that the average customer order was filled in 72 seconds. I was impressed.

3. *Do you currently offer delivery, immediate online chat, instantaneous email responses, or the like?* If not, would such options be possibilities your company could consider?

4. *Do you know what kinds of conveniences your competitors are offering?* If not, send an explorer group to visit them and see what they are doing. Then adopt the good ideas.

A FINAL THOUGHT

Customers are easily surprised by efficient service that goes beyond what they anticipate. Likewise they appreciate anything that can make life more convenient for them. This need has spun off some pretty innovative time-savers such as drive-in mortuaries, quickie-wedding chapels, and the like. While those examples may carry the principle further than most of us want to go, they do reflect the almost universal desire for efficient, timely service (except when customers prefer slow service) with a minimum of inconvenience.

Apply the "little things" principle. The little things can make big differences. I saw an example of this during the busy Christmas season when a package shipping store sent a greeting card to all its customers and included with it shipping forms so the customer could fill it out in advance when bringing in a package to ship. Another little thing that is a pet peeve of mine is when restaurant servers make customers wait for their check or for beverage refills instead of just providing them. My favorite servers anticipate my needs and meet them promptly.

Beverage refills without having to ask provide a convenience that is easy to give and is much appreciated by customers.

Summary of Key Ideas

1. Providing customers with service that exceeds their expectations with regard to timing and convenience can build loyalty. The first step in this process is to be aware of customer time.

2. Some companies (such as overnight air delivery services, for example) set the time expectation they know they can beat. A promised 10 a.m. deliver arrives at 9:45, thus exceeding customer expectations.

3. Convenience innovations have come from such diverse industries as pizza restaurants, auto lube centers, and mobile shops. More companies are exploring additional convenience options undreamed of in years past.

4. Waiting is a source of annoyance to customers and can be mitigated by reducing the actual wait (with appropriate staffing, etc.), by distracting or entertaining the waiting customer, or by using virtual waiting such as restaurant pagers. Queuing systems are important to maximize operational efficiency and provide fairness in service to customers.

5. Providing product simplicity and ancillary services can create A-plus convenience for customers. Overcomplex

products may be appropriate for some customers, but annoyingly complicated for others. Nearby services (such as dry cleaning or banking associated with a grocery store) can enhance convenience.

6. Online shopping's popularity arises from its ability to do easy, quick, comparison shopping.

7. Companies can get a clearer picture of their convenience and timing situation by using mystery shopping (timing activities) and explorer groups who check out what other organizations are doing.

8. A-plus convenience does not always mean quick service. Some situations such as personalized skin-care consultations or luxurious dining may be intentionally slow. But even within these more lengthy transactions, prompt responses to customer needs, such as the diner's beverage refills, should be handled promptly.

9. Call centers should balance efficiency with the need to deliver a human touch. Some customers want to chat—and that provides an opportunity for relationship building.

Key Concepts

ancillary services	once-and-done	redundancy	virtual waiting
ease of use	queue management systems (QMS)	repetitive busywork	

Reviewing the Facts

1. This chapter makes the case for providing efficient service, assuming that customers today are increasingly concerned about time. What evidence do you have that people are more concerned about time than in the past? How have expectations been shaped by modern business practices?
2. What companies and industries have done a good job of providing increasingly timely and/or convenient service? Describe five such businesses—preferably ones that have innovated in recent years.
3. How does the idea of A-plus convenience overlap with A-plus information? Value?

4. What are some downsides to quick service? Describe situations under which speed of service is not important to a customer. Are there, however, aspects within slow-serve situations that still require timely service? Describe some.
5. Explain in your own words key strategies for exceeding customer expectations with regard to speed and convenience.
6. What is "virtual waiting"? Describe several ways this could be applied to a business you are familiar with.

Applying the Ideas

1. Suppose you are considering starting an appliance repair business. What are some convenience services you could possibly apply to exceed customer expectations? Be creative. Brainstorm as many ideas as possible.
2. Of all the businesses you deal with, which ones do the best job of giving A-plus convenience/speed? Which do the worst job? How could the poor performers do better?

3. Select a business you are familiar with that does not currently use virtual waiting techniques. Explain how it could do so.
4. Write a report describing how the increase in online shopping has affected customer demand for efficient, convenient service. How could a "brick-and-mortar" store selling similar products compete?

Consider this Case

"Service" at the Donut Shop

Early one morning Harry found himself hungry, alone, and lost in the land of no customer service as he stumbled into a donut shop. It was a rainy, gray morning and he was tired. Cars were parked at odd angles because the lines on the lot had long ago faded. The parking lot was dirty and the trashcans overflowed.

Inside were disorganized lines of people, most wearing parkas, waiting to buy donuts. There appeared to be no systematic way of serving customers. The bold ones stepped up and demanded service while the more timid (or courteous) hoped for attention from the clerk. Harry waited for about seven minutes as the two clerks repeatedly took orders, disappeared into the back room, reappeared, and took peoples' money. All along Harry observed the uncleared, coffee-stained counter where he soon would sit to eat his donut. It hadn't been cleared recently, and it apparently wasn't going to be cleared now. Customers groaned, as the advertised two-for-one sale didn't apply when they ordered donuts of different prices, and the clerks explained with bored, unsmiling expressions.

Harry noticed a middle-aged woman (could she be the manager?) sitting on a crate just outside the back door smoking a cigarette and reading a tabloid newspaper. She seemed oblivious to the dismal scene in the shop.

Harry finally reached the head of the line and came face to face with a 17-year-old girl who had been condemned to serve him. Something in her teenage face told him that all was not well in the service economy. Harry asked her how she liked her job.

She looked him straight in the eye and said, "It sucks!"

Probes

1. Assume you are the owner of this donut shop. What would you do? What specific behaviors would you seek to change?
2. Focus on the problems of slow service. What could be done, specifically, to improve this?
3. To what extent might the slow service be a source of employee irritation and dissatisfaction? Explain.

Consider this Case

Waiting for the Doctor

As a young and ambitious physician, Rebecca Stacie was constantly looking for ways to improve office efficiency. She had recently decided to work as a sole practitioner in her own medical clinic specializing in internal medicine. Within a few months, word had gotten around about how helpful and thorough she was—she seemed to be more caring and more willing to take time with patients.

But her popularity had a downside. As her patient load increased, she began to hear grumbling from her patients about the long wait times. One rather outspoken elderly patient had told her point blank that she was fed up with all the waiting. "You schedule me for 9 a.m. and I get here a few minutes early. Then I sit in the waiting room for 20 minutes or more. Then your nurse calls me into an exam room and I get to sit there for another half hour. I show you the courtesy of being here on time and I'd appreciate it if you'd show similar respect for my time, doctor."

Dr. Stacie apologized and said she would work on being more punctual, although it was very difficult to judge how long each patient visit would take. When she asked her office staff if they were hearing more complaints they said they were. "And the problem is taking on a new look," said her office nurse. "Patients are showing up later and later. They don't even apologize. They typically say they know they'll be waiting and the doc will be late, so why should they try to get to their appointment on time." Of course, the tardy patients tie up everyone else and the problem gets worse for everyone.

Probes

1. If you were managing Dr. Stacie's office, what actions would you take to try to A-plus patients with timely services? Be specific.
2. How might you manage the patient's expectations more effectively?
3. Could Dr. Stacie use any other techniques discussed in this chapter? How?

Building a Customer Service Strategy: Your Ongoing Case

Let's go back to the ongoing case you selected. This will be either your current employer, a specific organization you want to work in, or one of the two hypothetical organizations described in Chapter 1: Independent Auto Sales and Service (IAS) or Network Nutrition Distributors (NND). Now consider the following questions as you develop a customer service strategy:

Strategy Planning Activities

1. This chapter talks about three strategies to dealing with customer wait times. These are (1) manage the reality, (2) manage the perception, and (3) make the wait invisible. Assume that you are a manager for the company or organization you selected

for your cases. Write a recommendation report describing how it could apply each of these three strategies to create A-plus timing and convenience. Be specific about exactly what you would recommend.

2. How, specifically, would you conduct an A-plus idea-gathering session focusing on convenience issues? Before brainstorming possible ideas, what information would you want to gather? How would you get that information?
3. Of all the ideas on convenience and timing discussed in this chapter, which one or two would be likely to give your company the greatest immediate benefit? How could you implement it?

Notes

1. Jane Bennett Clarke, "Washed, Cooked and Priced to Go," *Kiplinger's Personal Finance*, January 2000, p. 135.
2. Hadley Malcolm, "Entrepreneurs Keep on Truckin'," *USA Today*, June 27, 2012, p. 3B.
3. Ibid.
4. "GPS Shoe Lets Families Keep Track of Elderly," *The Tampa Tribune*, February 6, 2012, p. 3.
5. Duncan Dickson, Robert C. Ford, and Bruce Laval, "Managing Real and Virtual Waits in Hospital and Service Organizations," *Cornell Hotel and Restaurant Administration Quarterly*, February 2005, pp. 52–68.
6. Dickson, *et al.*, p. 52.
7. Hilary Stout, "The Ad Budget: Zero. The Buzz: Deafening," *Wall Street Journal European Edition*, December 30, 1999, p. 4.

PART **5**

Living Life and Leading Others

This book has been structured around the acronym *LIFE.* We discussed the importance of "little things"—attention to details to give better service. We also explored some of the "insights" necessary to tune in to possible customer turnoffs and the ever-changing service environment. The concept of "feedback" is the F in our acronym and we talked about its usefulness in providing controls and improvement ideas. "Expectations" is the E in LIFE and we spent several chapters elaborating on ways we can exceed customer expectations to strengthen relationships and loyalty.

In this final part we focus on ways to influence others to apply the LIFE principles for exceptional customer service. You need not be a formal leader in an organization, although having managerial authority gives you a broader array of tools you can use. You can influence your peers and even your bosses through your example. You can expand your career success by applying the ideas developed with the *LIFE* acronym.

In Chapter 13 we address the challenges faced when we attempt to influence change—when we try to get others to cooperate in new ways for the betterment of the ways we serve customers. Also, in this wrap-up chapter, we discuss the significant challenges of getting people involved—fully engaged—in the kinds of activities needed to create and implement an ongoing strategy for providing exceptional customer service.

CHAPTER 13

Influencing Others to Give Great Service
Roles of the Mentor, Supervisor, Manager, or Leader

After reading this chapter, you should be able to

1. Acknowledge the need for constant change and recognize that such change is difficult.

2. Articulate a clear vision for customer service in your organization.

3. Organize processes, people, and resources to achieve the vision.

4. Lead and motivate employees.

5. Create and sustain an effective work culture.

6. Acknowledge that customer service work can be stressful and that we pay a price for performing "emotional labor."

7. Identify and use six sources of influence in bringing about change and service improvement.

8. Continuously harvest A-plus ideas.

9. Empower and engage employees in important activities and decisions.

10. Tie the reward system to appropriate actions.

The Way It Is... Britany Moves to Management

Britany Howard had been with her company for almost two years and was, by all measures, an excellent employee. She had joined CostSavers* shortly after graduating from the local university where she had been a history major. Britany had excellent people skills and a strong work ethic—she was, in fact, outstanding. And so it seemed a logical move for her to take on management responsibilities. CostSavers' regional executives needed a person to take the lead role at its newest location, soon to be opened in Rosemont.

When Britany was asked to accept the new position, she was shocked. That evening she told her father, "I'm only 23 and they want to give me all that responsibility?" "I wonder if I can do that?" Her dad, an experienced manager himself, told her that "management isn't for everyone, Brit. I've seen companies routinely move their best workers into management positions and then have this 'promotion' turn out badly. I know you can do it, but remember that it's different from what you have been doing."

During her first few weeks as the new manager, Britany read several management books. What struck her most was the realization that some very effective service employees succeed because of their personality, sensitivity, or some other skills that they really can't "manage" others into doing. "Wow, that sounds like me," she said to herself. "I've been good at what I do with customers, but I don't even realize what makes me successful. I guess I just go on my instinct or intuition. I doubt that I can teach others

*A fictitious company

to be like me." The books called this **tacit knowledge**—knowledge within them that people have inside them but that they can't really explain or share.

In talking further with her father, Britany came to realize that the critical element in managing is to accomplish work through the efforts of others. She realized that she needed to shift her perception of what work is important. She needed to multiply her efforts by getting others to be productive. She could no longer go it alone, despite her great service skills. She had to focus on different key skills to direct and motivate the actions of her subordinates.

"That's why managers make the big bucks," her father said wryly.

"Yeah—that is a little trickier than what I've been doing," Britany mused.

This chapter is about managing others in a very broad sense. The ideas we'll discuss are appropriate for supervisors and managers but are also useful to others who seek to influence colleagues and associates to up their game. Customer service excellence calls for the cooperation of others as organizations seek to accomplish goals. Let's look at some of the basic management functions that Britany is concerned about and also some skills people in nonmanagement positions can use to influence service excellence.

ARTICULATE A VISION: WHAT MANAGERS SHOULD DO FIRST

Many experts advocate that the first step in developing a customer-driven strategy is to articulate a theme. This theme should be succinct, clear, and descriptive of the organization's uniqueness. Managers should gather ideas from customers and potential customers by asking them a few key questions, such as: "What five things do you want when doing business with us?" and look carefully at the language they use.

Similarly, managers should ask employees, "If you were our customer, what five things would you like to get from a company like ours?" "What do you think our customers want?" and jot down their responses. If your department or company has not done this effectively, consider raising these questions in staff meetings.

As you gather perceptions from customers and employees, managers will be likely to notice some terms coming up over and over again. Perhaps people will mention speedy service, cleanliness, friendliness, or personalized attention. These are good words to articulate in a customer service theme.

When drafting a theme for the organization, managers should remember to do the following:

- Using participation of and input from customers and employees is very important. The customers can best tell you what they're looking for in an organization like yours, and the employees' participation will ensure that they will accept and, hopefully, live by the intention of the theme.
- Write several rough drafts of the theme; avoid being too quick to come up with the finished version. Phrase the final version in 10 words or fewer.
- If possible, try to make the theme into an acronym, where the first letters of each word form a word in themselves.

The organization's theme should describe its uniqueness—its unique **service proposition**. This proposition should answer this question: "What distinctive service does this organization offer customers?" When the company has identified this, everyone in the organization should choose roughly the same words to describe this distinctiveness. A simple way to verify this is to ask employees to describe the organization's theme. Especially invite an employee who's been with the organization for 10 days or less to identify the theme. If the theme has been prominently displayed and is easily remembered, it will always be at top-of-mind for employees. That is the hallmark of a successful theme.

LOOK INSIDE

What's Your Organization's Vision?

If you are currently working in an organization, try this: Interview at least five managers and employees (more if you can reasonably get to them) asking them to finish this statement in 15 words or less:

- The vision of this organization can best be stated as _____

(If you are not currently employed, try this with your school. Ask students, faculty, and administrators if they can state the vision of the school in 15 words.) Then answer the following questions:

1. To what extent do you get general agreement?
2. Does the degree of agreement seem to be higher among higher-ranking managers/administrators?
3. If you were a top executive in this company, what would you do about this?

Note: Typically agreement on the company's **vision statement** rarely exceeds 40 percent, even among top executives!

What good does it do just to be able to repeat such a phrase? The answer is that it's a start. Repeating some words may seem meaningless at first, but most organizations fall far short even of that level of agreement. Focusing people on a common theme can be well worth the effort. A theme, however, is not necessarily forever. As an organization changes directions, as markets or economic conditions change, a theme may be modified. Some organizations may want to use a theme statement for a limited period of time much the way advertisers use a slogan for only a few years. Here is an important note: By having employees participate in clarifying a theme, they will feel more committed to it. This has been shown time and again since the earliest studies in human relations: Participation enhances buy-in. Besides, frontline people know the customers best and can give great ideas on how to better serve them. Never overlook the ideas of this group of experts. The employees on the firing line have the best ideas. Use them.

Managers, first and foremost, must set—and sell others on—the vision for great customer service.

A clear vision of the importance of customer loyalty should be at the core of every manager's beliefs. Increasingly, more companies are recognizing the value of customer loyalty as a predictor of future success against their competitors. The rationale is simple. The more loyal customers you have, the harder it is for your competitor to pick away your business. The first task of effective managers is to express the importance and vision. This vision must describe what the organization means for customers. Avoid "to be the best *wigit* producer in the world," unless you can phrase that in terms of customer needs: Perhaps, "To produce and distribute the highest quality *wigits* that best meet our customer needs."

PLAN A STRATEGY FOR CUSTOMER LOYALTY

Planning a strategy involves looking ahead to what must be done to maintain and improve performance, to solve problems, and to develop employee competence. To plan, a manager sets objectives in each area that are to be pursued each week, each month, and each year. Having articulated a clear vision, the manager then thinks through such questions as the following:

Planning a strategy is a key leadership function that requires thinking through many questions.

- What specific actions have to be done to reach our objectives and how can the company get employees to do them?
- How will these activities be carried out? What tools or technology will be needed?
- Who (which individuals, departments, or teams) will do the work? When will these activities take place?
- What resources will the company need to provide?

Such planning involves getting lots of input from customers and employees, and acting on the input received. Managers need to have an open mind, realizing that they do not have all the

LOOK INSIDE

Ask Some Potentially Disquieting Questions

A starting point for determining how strongly managers (and employees) accept the vision of customer importance may be to answer questions like the ones given below. A positive response to one or more of these may not be devastating, but if a manager answers yes to most of them, the organization is likely to face an uphill battle to substantially improve customer service. Companies need to walk the talk, not just have good intentions.

Answer yes or no if your company, organization, or department does the following:

1. Pays frontline, customer contact people a low, flat wage.
2. Rarely if ever tries accessing your own company via call centers, Web sites, or help desks to assess the friendliness of such technology.
3. Offers customer contact people little or no training in the fundamental behaviors associated with customer service.
4. Offers no special incentives to employees for taking exceptional care of the customer.
5. Punishes or reprimands employees for giving poor customer service but takes good service for granted.
6. Places greater emphasis on winning new customers than retaining the ones it already has.

7. Offers no awards or recognition for noncustomer contact people's efforts to serve customers.
8. Initiates special customer service programs or campaigns that last for a few weeks or months but are soon forgotten.
9. Rarely, if ever, devotes time to listening to customers and helping them solve problems.
10. Makes no consistent effort to measure service quality as perceived by customers.
11. Makes no attempt to gather employee ideas for better service.
12. Fails to hold employees at all levels accountable for generating ongoing service improvement.
13. Fails to give employees the authority to act on behalf of the customer, instead holding them to careful application of company rules without exception.
14. Creates opportunities for employees at all levels to support and influence the behaviors of colleagues as they seek to improve customer service.

Most managers would have to answer "yes" to several of the above questions indicating missed opportunities. That is not necessarily an indicator of poor service policies, but it could point to some potential problem areas. The process of asking lots of penetrating questions is a valuable management activity.

answers; much can be learned from others. Nonmanagers need to freely give their thoughts and participate with a sincere interest in company success.

Many organizations use practices that are counterproductive to good service. They may not realize that they have drifted away from supporting their good intentions, but they often have.

Most managers would have to admit to some failures to "walk the talk" of good service-producing leadership.

ORGANIZING PROCESSES, PEOPLE, AND RESOURCES TO ACHIEVE THE VISION

The management function of organizing involves arranging the work sequence and assigning areas of responsibility and authority. Having decided the objectives and activities of each individual or work unit, the manager must do the following:

- Assign specific responsibilities to employees.
- Give employees the supporting authority to fulfill their responsibilities.
- Work to reduce potential problems caused by systems (staffing, training, work layout, etc.). Remember that systems involve anything having to do with the delivery of products or services to the customer. Constantly organizing and improving systems is a major service leadership responsibility.

As a manager assigns work, he or she must also grant authority to carry out that work. In the best service organizations, employees at all levels have considerable latitude to creatively serve customers and solve their problems or concerns.

Assigning work must be accompanied by granting authority to carry out that work.

Granting authority is difficult for some managers. Employees will not always use it well—they'll make mistakes, perhaps that cost much. But to err on the side of giving the customer too much is often a golden opportunity to provide A-plus service. Managers must learn to let go of hard-and-fast rules and instead allow people to take initiative to serve customers exceptionally well.

Many companies with exceptional reputations for customer loyalty give their employees unusually broad authority. A service-leading hotel, for example, tells its employees they can make an adjustment for a customer without getting management approval so long as the decision does not cost more than $2,000. That is a substantial authority. At the opposite extreme is the all-too-common company that requires supervisory approval for almost any service-related expense. Trust people to use discretion wisely and you will seldom be disappointed.

LEAD AND MOTIVATE EMPLOYEES

The management functions of motivating, commanding, and coordinating are often summed up in the term *leading*. The manager leads by enabling the organization to achieve its objectives. To do this, he or she does the following:

- Shows the direction employees must go
- Generates the energy (motivation) that stimulates subordinates to action
- Provides the needed resources (tools, technology, training, budgets, etc.)

Modern management emphasizes the **motivation** aspects of this function. An organization's leaders set the tone for motivation throughout. Motivation can be simply defined as "providing motives for action." Leaders provide motives or reasons why people should act in particular ways by setting an example, encouraging appropriate behaviors, and using rewards and disincentives (punishments) appropriately. (Note that rewards are not all tangible. Positive recognition and thanking are powerful rewards.)

ANOTHER LOOK

Hire People with Emotional Intelligence

═══

Employees can learn a company's product lines or services, but their abilities to interact well with others are innate and enduring. Stated another way, companies can teach some skills but not others.

In the mid-1990s, the term **"emotional intelligence"** emerged to describe characteristics that we tend to call people skills. The essential elements in EQ* are given:

- Self-awareness (the understanding of one's own motives and actions)
- Self-management (the ability to control impulses)
- Self-motivation (the ability to stimulate action toward desired outcomes)
- Empathy (the ability to see a situation from another person's perspective)
- Social skills (the ability to adapt communication to situational needs)

Customer service can obviously benefit from these characteristics. But are these teachable? Many people would argue that the answer is probably not. Traits as fundamental as "warmth" and "friendliness" cannot be trained. If this is true, a company can avoid the futility of trying to train someone to be empathetic or to use a "natural smile" by hiring the right type of person in the first place—by hiring people who have high emotional intelligence?

But simply hiring people with good EQ scores isn't enough. Companies must also trust their employees to use their EQ skills appropriately to meet customer needs.

Probes

1. To what extent do you agree with the idea that personality traits such as those defining emotional intelligence cannot be trained?
2. What kinds of steps should managers take to assure that they are hiring people with good EQ?
3. How can managers best display trust in their employees allowing them to use their good EQ on behalf of customers?

*The term EQ is used to contrast with the more commonly understood IQ or Intelligence Quotient.

ACKNOWLEDGE THAT CUSTOMER SERVICE WORK CAN BE STRESSFUL

"**Emotional labor**" is the term researchers use to describe labor that involves managing emotions so that they are consistent with organizational or occupational display rules, regardless of whether they are discrepant with internal feelings.[1] In the context of customer service, this means that it can be hard work to project upbeat, positive emotions at all times as is often required in customer contact jobs.

The term "emotional labor" was first defined by the sociologist Arlie Hochschild as the "management of feeling to create a publicly observable facial and bodily display."[2] This "display" takes the form of verbal and nonverbal communication. Jobs involving emotional labor are described as those that

- require frequent face-to-face or voice-to-voice contact with the public
- require the worker to produce an emotional state in another person (e.g., make them happy, comfortable, relaxed, reassured)
- allow the employees to exercise a degree of control over their emotional activities

Clearly, these functions are typical of customer service jobs. We have contact, we try to create positive emotions in our customers, and we almost always have discretion in how we project our emotions to others.

Giving great customer service can be stressful and demanding, especially when our personal emotional state is out of sync with customers. Everyone has bad days or gets into emotional funks now and then. To make things tougher, we may find ourselves dealing with people who are upset, unhappy, and even irrational at times. We may find ourselves pressured by too much work and too little time. We may feel stressed by the boredom of repetitive tasks and unappreciative bosses.

But then again, all jobs have their stress-producing characteristics. In fact, the less control we have over our daily activities, the greater the stress levels. Studies have shown that low-control positions such as receptionists, toll takers, and so on are quite stressful. Stress isn't just for air traffic controllers or police officers. We all face it.

Working Conditions That May Lead to Stress

The following conditions are often causes of undue stress for employees. If you are a manager or supervisor, you should be aware of these and seek ways to minimize their detrimental effects. If you are a nonmanagement employee, you should give feedback to management just as customers must give feedback to companies. If you are experiencing unproductive stress because of these kinds of conditions, communicate your concern to your supervisor. Don't convey it as whining or complaining, but rather explain how current work conditions are counterproductive to the organization.

It is very difficult to give great service if you do not receive appropriate support from your organization. Good working conditions are truly a win-win-win for the company, you, and the customers. Open the communication channels and explore ideas for improving work conditions to reduce the burden of emotional labor.

NONSTOP ACTION   Stress arises from heavy workload, infrequent rest breaks, long work hours, and shift work. It also stems from hectic and routine tasks that have little inherent meaning, do not utilize workers' skills, and provide little sense of control. No one can continuously give good customer service without taking breaks. For example, dealers at the gaming tables in Las Vegas get breaks as often as every 20 minutes. To stay sharp and remain responsive to customer emotions, service people need to stay fresh. Effective managers are aware of the psychological pressures placed on customer contact people.

MANAGEMENT STYLE   Employees feel increased stress from managers who fail to allow participation of workers in decision making, from ineffective communication in the organization, or from lack of family-friendly policies. People in customer service positions should be encouraged to participate in generating ideas for improving customer experiences, for example. Such participation supports the feeling of engagement in their jobs and pays off with good ideas, as well.

INTERPERSONAL RELATIONSHIPS   A poor social environment and lack of support or help from coworkers and supervisors can create unproductive stress for service employees. Poor social environment may arise when people distrust each other, argue frequently, engage in inappropriate humor or harassment, or treat each other with disrespect. One measure of a good place to work—and of high employee engagement—is work conditions where people can become friends.[3] Organizational leaders can facilitate good relationships by providing safe ways for employees to get together, for example, in sports, social activities, or with job rotation systems that allow people to meet and work with others.

UNCLEAR WORK ROLES   Conflicting or uncertain job expectations, too much responsibility, or too many "hats to wear" can generate stress. Service employees should have clear instructions on how to handle most problems they may encounter—and the authority to improvise when a new situation comes up. This can be tricky. Companies need an appropriate number of rules or standard procedures, but must also allow some leeway for individual discretion. Some successful companies allow extensive employee leeway.

CAREER CONCERNS   In times of economic downturn, stress arises from job insecurity—people worry about cutbacks or layoffs. But even for people in secure positions, a lack of opportunity for growth, advancement, or promotion can cause stress. Employees never want to feel that their jobs are dead ends or that they are at the whims of uncontrollable forces. Also, uncertainty associated with frequent and rapid change (fairly common condition in today's workplace) can likewise create undue stress.

POOR WORK ENVIRONMENT   Stress can arise from unpleasant or dangerous physical conditions such as crowding, noise, and air pollution or from ergonomic problems such as awkward placement of equipment. A workplace needs to feel fundamentally safe. No worker should be exposed to danger or repetitive movement problems like carpel tunnel from excessive keyboarding. Ergonomically friendly equipment and a generally pleasant work atmosphere can minimize these kinds of problems.

Companies lacking in a good work environment can suffer from "tired company syndrome." A tired company is marked by a dated look and feel, excessive caution and hesitance to change, a propensity to look to the past, being behind the technology curve, and a tendency to smother new ideas. These are stifling places to work. Employee stress is a natural outgrowth of such an environment.

ANOTHER LOOK
Nordstrom Kept It Simple

Striking an appropriate balance between a sufficient number of rules and allowing employee's discretion has long been a challenge for companies. For many years, new employees at famed retailer Nordstrom were given a copy of the famous "**Nordstrom's Employee Handbook,**" which was not a book at all. It was a single 5 × 8-inch gray card containing 75 words:[4] **Welcome to Nordstrom**

We're glad to have you with our company. Our number one goal is to provide outstanding customer service.

Set both your personal and professional goals high. We have great confidence in your ability to achieve them.

Nordstrom Rules: Rule #1: Use good judgment in all situations. There will be no additional rules.

Please feel free to ask your department manager, store manager, or division general manager any question at any time.

However, new hire orientations now provide this card along with a full handbook of other more specific rules and legal regulations, as the way Nordstrom operates has evolved.

In summary, job stress is a reality of modern working life. Customer service suffers when people feel an inordinate number of stressors. Emotional labor requires managing stress. Employees with high EQ tend to handle emotional labor better than those who score low in EQ. That said, organizational leaders can take many actions to alleviate negative stress; being aware of its impact is a good starting point.

CREATE AND SUSTAIN AN EFFECTIVE ORGANIZATIONAL CULTURE

A company's culture is shaped by its shared sense of vision, values, heroes, rites, and rituals. When a company's **organizational culture** is clear and unambiguous, it serves as unspoken guidelines for employee behavior.

Organizational culture is the firm's self-identity or shared mind-set. It identifies the company in the mind of its customers. Think, for example, what comes to mind when you consider brands such as Google, Harley Davidson, Ben and Jerry's, Chick Fil-A, Apple, Facebook, or Zappos. Organizations like these project a shared mind-set that is appealing to their customers.

Culture arises from the stories employees tell, the ways people dress and behave, the little rituals that make employees feel a part of the company—and the way they treat their customers. Internal customers (employees) see the culture reinforced with things like birthday celebrations, Friday afternoon popcorn, or informal gatherings around the coffee pot. Likewise the things people discuss and admire—the stories people repeat—become part of the folklore of the company and reinforce its culture. If your people enjoy talking about that crazy time Harry drove all the way to a customer's house on a stormy Friday night, they are reinforcing cultural values. If your people talk about the time Bess diffused that really upset customer and made him her best friend, they are reinforcing cultural values. One oft-repeated story is about the Nordstrom manager who accepted a return of some tires the customer was unhappy with—even though Nordstrom never sold tires! That rather odd decision by a manager many years ago set the shared vision for customers: Nordstrom will always take back unsatisfactory merchandise. This has been a pillar underlying Nordstom's vision: It shouts that customers can trust Nordstrom.

Management can impact the culture by consistently looking for things to celebrate or actions to instantly reward. Some sales-oriented companies use rather silly sales "skits"—dressing up in ridiculous costumes and acting out "sales successes" to get the service reps fired up about selling. At the end of a successful initiative, they celebrate with food, entertainment, and prizes. These kinds of things make an organization's culture vibrant and lively. In short, they can make a company a fun place to work.

By contrast, I recall going to a fast-food restaurant at lunch time. I stood in the line and, upon reaching the clerk, smiled and said hello asking how he was doing. He totally ignored my

---

ANOTHER LOOK

How Can Managers Reinforce a Service Culture?

"Culture" stems from the agreed-upon values of an organization. These values are learned and reinforced with such things as shared language (e.g., "A-plus service" "Think different"), material symbols (uniforms, office layout, furnishings), rituals (Friday afternoon popcorn, celebrations), and stories (repeated narrative that illustrates behaviors supporting the culture).

Managers cannot "create" a culture but they can influence it. Actions such as an undeviating focus on the corporate vision and frequent reference to heroes (recognition of people who have done outstanding things) strengthen the culture. Rites and rituals such as open-door policies, parties, picnics, Friday dress-down days, employees decorating their own workspace, after-work socializing, and so on can all sustain a positive culture.

When a culture is built around customer-centered values, the company is well on its way to creating loyalty. As employees internalize the shared values—make them their own—managers find the need to supervise is greatly reduced. Employees will act in ways that support the organization's vision.

An organization's culture can have a dramatic impact on employee behavior and managers do much to shape the culture.

smile and my greeting and, instead, deadpanned: "For here or to go?" I ordered and looked around. Virtually none of the young people in the restaurant were smiling. And I soon saw why: Their adult manager had no trace of a smile on her face either. She was grimly *working*. No time for frivolity. The whole atmosphere of that restaurant was poisoned by its shear absence of joy.

CONTINUOUSLY HARVEST A-PLUS IDEAS

Building customer loyalty is a team sport. No one person can anticipate all customer needs or come up with every possible idea for exceeding expectations. Employees at every level should feel a part of the team, having their input valued. For A-plus to work it must have a constant flow of new ideas. Employees at all levels in an organization can and will come up with good ideas. Managers should get their people to meet regularly to discuss creative ways for handling customer needs and surprising them with an unanticipated plus. Two ways to harvest creative ideas are through the use of brainstorming and nominal group processes (NGP).

Managers can harvest A-plus ideas using brainstorming and the nominal group process.

Use Brainstorming When You Need Creative Ideas

The term **brainstorming** has become synonymous with any kind of creative thinking, but originally the term referred to a specific technique using explicit rules for idea-generation and development. This approach requires a communication climate in which free expression of all kinds of ideas is valued and encouraged—no matter how offbeat or bizarre they may seem. This climate should be loosely structured, friendly, and highly tolerant of humor. Strict application of four basic rules makes brainstorming a powerful process for creative idea-generation:

- *Don't criticize any ideas.* No comments; no grunts or groans; no thumbs down gestures. Just let it come out and be recorded. This is harder than it sounds.
- *No idea is too wild.* What sounds bizarre or offbeat may contain a germ of an idea that could work. This can also liberate the creative juices.
- *Quantity of ideas generated is important.* Push to get as many ideas without regard to whether or not they make any sense at this point. More is better.
- Seize opportunities to *hitchhike*—add to or amplify on ideas suggested by others. One technique for this is to require that people repeat the other person's idea and then add to it or take it in another direction.

The rules of brainstorming are easier to state than to obey—especially the second one. Unless great care is taken, nonverbal cues can be interpreted as evaluations of ideas, and that can discourage additional "wild ideas." When using brainstorming, the participants should prominently post the rules as a constant reminder.

The climate of a brainstorming session set by the meeting leader can promote or hamper the use of brainstorming. A climate that encourages humor, irreverence, and informality will work best.

After brainstorming, a team should process the information generated in a systematic manner to see which ideas could be applied. Here is one process that can be useful:

Use Nominal Group Process to Sort and Prioritize Ideas

After generating possible ideas with brainstorming, consider processing these ideas—weeding through them—with a technique called the **nominal group process**.

The nominal group process provides a systematic way for processing creative ideas such as those generated with brainstorming.

NGP is an idea-processing technique that is particularly useful when dealing with potentially emotional or controversial ideas (as highly creative suggestions can be). Rather than having group members immediately speak up with their point of view (a process that may *commit* them to that view since they've voiced it publicly), the NGP has participants write their ideas, privately. Following a clear description or restatement of what the group is trying to accomplish, group members spend 10–20 minutes writing promising ideas about possible solutions. These may be ideas triggered by brainstorming or from other sources.

ANOTHER LOOK

Community Credit Union Creates a "Prime Member" Program

Community Credit Union (CCU)* is the third largest credit union in the state and has a good reputation for customer service. They regularly survey their "members" and receive excellent ratings including high Net Promoter Scores. In short, they do a lot of things right.

The Board of Directors appreciates the good work of the management team but also knows that member loyalty requires constant attention. In board discussions the idea of creating some form of recognition or special benefits for their very best customers has come up several times. The executive team agreed that a "Prime Member" program could be useful. One of the board members was a marketing professor who recommended a series of idea-generating meetings to gather ideas for such a program.

A group of 12 mid-level branch managers were called together with three top executives and given an agenda that identified two major questions:

- How can we best determine who would qualify as a "prime member"?
- What kinds of incentives would these people appreciate?

The first question is a bit more complicated than it might be for another type of business. A retailer, for example, might simply identify people who buy the most from the company. A credit union, however, is a financial cooperative owned by its members. As such, its main goal is not pure profit but the degree to which it serves "underserved" people. To further complicate the question, members who frequently bounce checks and incur late-fee penalties generate a lot of profit to CCU. The idea of the Prime Member program is not intended to encourage such behavior.

The second question also generated a lot of ideas utilizing brainstorming in a fun atmosphere where creativity was encouraged.

CCU invited an independent consultant to run the meetings. This was done to reduce the likelihood that participants may feel uncomfortable or creatively restrained working with their bosses.

The consultant instructed each participant to list his or her best ideas as each topic was discussed. The participants then independently ranked their best ideas on a written form provided by the consultant. The notes were given to the vice-president of marketing, who had all notes compiled.

The outcome of this initial meeting was a foundation for a new program aimed at customer loyalty. Twenty-one criteria were listed for "who should qualify" ranging from how much money on deposit, loan balances, loan payment history, frequency of branch visits to "how good-looking they are." The top three criteria emerged as "tenure" (how long they have been customers), high use of checking or debit cards, and NPS enthusiasm (did they recommend CUU to friends).

The question of what incentives CUU should give these prime members generated 33 ideas ranging from "personal banker" service to a prestige credit card, invitations to be on an advisory council to meet with the Board of Directors (engagement), annual recognition banquet, special communications to keep them more fully informed of CUU activities, and, my personal favorite, pony rides.

Probes

1. How effectively did CCU apply principles discussed in this chapter? What could they have done better?
2. Critique the process used. Could your company or organization apply these same processes to create special customer recognition? What are the advantages and disadvantages of doing so?

*Although a true story, the organization's name has been changed: Credit unions were created in the 1930s at a time when banks rarely loaned to lower-income consumers. As cooperatives, CUs receive tax advantages that for-profit banks do not in exchange for accepting the mandate of providing financial services to people of all income levels.

When the group gets back together, each participant describes one idea from his or her list, which is written on a flip chart in full view of the group. Ideas are recorded but not discussed at this point. This round-robin listing of ideas continues until the members have no further ideas. People may then clarify or amplify on an idea, as necessary. Then a silent vote is taken where participants rank-order the ideas. The steps of the process, once again, are given:

1. Silently generate solution ideas in writing (or, listing of ideas from brainstorming sessions).
2. Record (usually on large flip charts or a white board) the ideas in round-robin fashion— get one idea from person A, then one from person B, and so forth until all have given their first idea. Then repeat the process.

3. Discuss the merits of each idea. Get clarification if necessary.
4. Vote on the ideas by ranking them. (Several votes may be needed before the group accepts a final solution or priority list of actions to take.)

The ongoing use of groups or teams to generate A-plus ideas can be one of the most powerful rituals a company can engage in. Managers serious about maximizing customer loyalty should be doing this.

INFLUENCING OTHERS TO CHANGE

Improving customer service requires a willingness to change and improve. As a manager you are often called upon to bring about behavior changes. If you are not a manager or other formal leader, you can still change your own behaviors and impact others if you understand the process of influencing change.

First, we acknowledge that people resist change until they understand how such change can benefit them. (This is the "what's-in-it-for-me" principle that underlies any form of persuasion.) We also resist change for reasons such as fear of the unknown, comfort with current habits, concerns about the ability to do the new behavior, and many others.

Distinguish Between Behaviors and Outcomes or Attitudes

To overcome resistance to change, you must first be specific about what new behavior you want to achieve (or get others to do). Using broad terms like "give better service" describes a desired outcome but fails to describe explicit behaviors. "Better service" will look different to different people. To influence change, you need to identify *specific behaviors* needed to constitute "better service." Behaviors, as contrasted with outcomes or attitudes, are visible, measurable actions. A first (and critical) step in influencing change is to identify explicit behaviors that you can objectively measure.

Behaviors we could objectively observe and measure include such things as

- Greeting the customer
- Making eye contact
- Offering to help
- Answering the phone within 10 seconds
- Giving the customer instructions on how to use the product/service
- Offering to answer customer questions
- Wearing a company uniform
- Responding to customer email within a certain time
- Providing a written estimate
- Giving the customer your cell phone number and inviting him to call if he has any problems
- Explaining the warrantee

Vital behaviors in customer service are those specific actions likely to have the greatest impact on customer loyalty.

These are only a partial list and your company may focus on others. To enhance your organization's service you need to identify, hopefully working as a team, **"vital" behaviors**—those actions that are likely to have the most impact on customers. This, of course, is an ongoing process that involves careful analysis of feedback.

Apply the Influencer Model

When we try to get people to do something, two questions will come to their mind: (1) Why should I want to? ("what's in it for me?") and (2) can I do it? These reveal motivation and ability. You influence people to change by answering these two questions.[5]

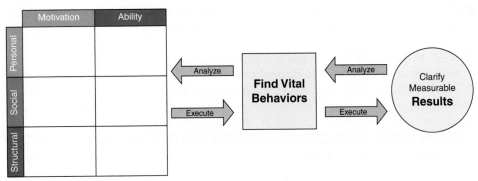

EXHIBIT 13.1 The *Influencer* Model of behavior change.

The best-selling book by behavioral scientists and business consultants Kerry Patterson and his associates is called *Influencer: The Power to Change Anything*. In it, the authors present an exceptionally effective model. In short, this model explains how successful influencing arises from understanding six **sources of influence** which, when used in concert, greatly improve the likelihood of successfully changing behaviors. The model is summarized in Exhibit 13.1:

The authors' research finds that you are dramatically more likely to bring about successful change if you use all six sources of influence versus using just one or two. Let's look at each source briefly (Exhibit 13.2).

SOURCE 1—PERSONAL MOTIVATION   The key to using personal motivation as an influencer is to make the undesirable, desirable. The problem is that many new, desired behaviors are boring, frightening, scary, or uncomfortable. Help people overcome this anxiety by trying the vital behavior and recognizing how it ties in with their values. For example, an employee may hate to make follow-up calls to customers although management thinks that is a vital behavior necessary for customer service. How can you help that employee? Perhaps by walking him

	Motivation	Ability
Personal	1 Make the Undesirable Desirable	2 Over Invest in Skill Building
Social	3 Harness Peer Pressure	4 Find Strength in Numbers
Structural	5 Design Rewards and Demand Accountability	6 Change the Environment

EXHIBIT 13.2 Six Sources of Influence.

through the process, making calls together. Help him recognize how follow-up calls tie in with personal values such as enjoying personal relationships with customers.

SOURCE 2—PERSONAL ABILITY   Invest in skill-building. Golfer Arnold Palmer once said, "It's a funny thing, the more I practice the luckier I get." We use personable ability as an influencer when we apply deliberate practice to improve our personal skills. If, for example, explaining a warrantee to a customer is a desired vital behavior, employees need to know all about the warrantee and about how to explain it to customers. People can build this skill by practicing in role plays with other employees, or by critiquing or learning from other successful employees. This becomes a source of influence that can result in lasting change that enhances customer service.

SOURCES 3 AND 4—SOCIAL MOTIVATION AND ABILITY   Harness peer pressure and find strength in numbers to influence people. Long-standing bad habits are almost always influenced by other humans who either encourage and enable the wrong behaviors or discourage and disable the right ones. The key is to use the power of social pressure by finding strength in numbers.

Enlist the power of those who motivate. Look for potential motivators in opinion leaders, formal leaders, and your colleagues. Provide opportunities for employees to work together to learn from each other and provide mutual support.

SOURCES 5–6—STRUCTURAL MOTIVATION AND ABILITY   Design effective rewards, demand accountability, and change the environment are structural sources of influence. These are influencers that are things, not people. What kinds of things support change? Among these are rewards and incentives. The key is to ensure that incentives support desired behaviors.

Managers often jump the gun with structural motivators—they think that offering a tangible reward will automatically produce the desired behaviors. They may think that giving a cash bonus will always boost sales, for example. But studies show that this is not consistently true. At some point "carrots" and "sticks" lose their ability to motivate for a variety of reasons. The *Influencer* approach recommends that rewards be used only after personal and social sources have been applied. It's more important that people are doing the right things from personal and social motivation than external rewards.

When you do use rewards, be sure that the incentive is linked to vital behaviors. Reward doing the right things, independent of the results. For example, reward quick responses to customer emails even if you cannot show a direct impact on profitability. Inevitably, rewarding the right vital behaviors will produce the right results—eventually.

Structural ability can include such things as classes and formal instruction but it can also refer to use of space and equipment. If a vital behavior is to have personal meetings with clients, structural ability might include providing conference rooms for these meetings. If following up and providing handwritten notes are a vital behavior, providing the materials, time, and place to do these is structural support. If you want employees to spend more time doing X, provide ways for them to spend less time doing Y. For example, look to see if paperwork can be reduced or eliminated. Change the environment to make bad behaviors harder and good behaviors easier.

Offering tangible rewards for certain behaviors should not be the leader's first option. Personal and social support will bring better results.

CONTROL THE PROCESSES

The management function called **controlling** involves comparing actual results to expected or planned-for results so as to identify any deviation from plan. Typically, any deviation from the plan calls for adjusting actions designed to motivate or engage employees, reviewing the reward systems, reconsidering activities to close the gap, or changing the objectives to be more realistic.

The key to effective controlling is to measure, specifically, what you want to achieve and what you are currently achieving. If, for example, quick access to your call center is a key feature of your service efforts, measure customer waiting times. If Web page ease-of-use is essential, poll customers about their experiences in navigating your site. If attractive merchandise display is important, check it often. If restaurant and restroom cleanliness are priorities, clean them early and often.

Of course, getting the input from customers does little good if you don't follow through on implementing ideas for improvement. We often see managers who get their employees to say they are going to do something, only to have that action drop through the cracks when people get busy with other tasks. Management consultant David Ulrich says, "the importance of feedback is not in the data—it's in the follow-up." He explains that typically 10 percent of people will actually make changes based on feedback (including correction from their manager). But this number jumps to between 40 and 60 percent who will change how they do things if the feedback is followed up. Simply a brief call from the manager asking how the change is going can dramatically increase the likelihood that employees will improve.[6]

For controlling to be effective, managers should focus on the kinds of "measurables" that make a difference. If, for example, you want to encourage your frontline employees to always ask customers if they would like to try a new product, measure how often the employees actually do that. If you calculate a positive relationship between employee appearance and customer loyalty, measure the degree to which employees meet agreed-upon appearance criteria. Measure specific behaviors not idealized outcomes or attitudes. "Giving good service" is a rather vague outcome—it means different things to different people. "Ask the customer if there is anything else they need" is a behavior—you can observe it. Focus on vital behaviors—those specific actions that can be observed and that make a difference.

Help Employees Set Contributing Goals

What managers focus on tends to improve. **Goal setting** is a powerful tool for focusing effort, especially when the targeted improvements are measurable. Managers need to be fully involved in the process of setting measurable goals. They set the goals for their department, store, company, or workgroup. They should also help individual employees set goals for themselves. During performance reviews, managers should ask employees about their job-related intentions and suggest ways to make individual goals compatible with group objectives.

Goal setting helps establish priorities, as well as determine the sequence and timing of strategy steps. Managers can't fix everything at once, so they should look for the kinds of results that can give the most impact relative to the effort involved—the most bang for the buck. They should first pick the low hanging fruit—so long as that fruit is important to organizational success. Accomplishing good results with the easier challenges—getting early wins—can motivate the troops to tackle the more difficult problems later.

Managers typically need to budget for improvements. Many changes, especially those designed to solve systems or value turnoffs, require the expenditure of money or other resources. You may need to hire more people, provide more training, change the location or layout of the business, purchase additional technology, and so on. All these should be done with an eye to determine how the change can help employees to better meet the organization's service goals. If expenditures don't help employees and customers, they have no justification and should not be implemented.

EMPOWER EMPLOYEES

Managers cannot and should not run the whole organization alone. Ultimately, employee empowerment is the key to corporate excellence. **Empowerment** happens when employees are given the authority and latitude to take initiative on behalf of customers. Everyone wins with effective empowerment. First, customers benefit because the employee can cut through traditional procedures and give them what they need without having to forever get approval of higher management. Second, the employee wins because he or she feels satisfaction in helping customers by asserting creativity and initiative. Third, the company wins because its employees and customers are better satisfied.

Getting good ideas from customers or others does little good if you don't implement them.

The importance of feedback is not in the data but in the follow-up.

Empowerment gives employees the authority to work on behalf of the customer.

Empowering employees can be scary for managers. Many managers are hesitant about letting go of authority. They fear that employees will make mistakes or fail to use good business sense, thus "giving away the store." But employees rarely do and the benefits of empowering far outweigh the potential risk of an occasional mistake.

Empowerment should be accompanied by training. Teach people about the impact of their decisions—the potential downside in failing to follow through with a customer request, for example. The employee should understand how that action can impact customer loyalty, company profitability, and, ultimately, job security for employees.

TIE THE REWARD SYSTEM TO APPROPRIATE ACTIONS

One of the characteristics of many companies described as great places to work has been the casual, fun-loving, creative workplace with far less attention to decorum or organizational hierarchy. Scenes of high-tech workers on scooters, working in casual dress in a collegial environment, have changed the face of businesses worldwide. Companies routinely rated as the best to work for often have such comfortable cultures. But not all organizations are quite so fun-loving. Many maintain a more formal atmosphere but still provide high employee satisfaction, especially when the reward systems are creative and, well, rewarding.

A note of caution, however, is warranted. As the *Influencer* model reminds us, rewards are a form of structural support and, as such, should not be the first thing used to try to motivate behavior. First look to personal and social forms of support for change. Is the action you want from people consistent with their personal desires or values? Is the organization providing social support for the actions? Are others helpfully encouraging the desired behaviors? If those two factors are reasonably present, then looking to structural support (i.e., the reward system) is an appropriate step. Don't assume that offering a particular reward automatically gets you the kinds of behavior you want to motivate.

This is, in part, because of an oversimplification notion of how rewards work. In fact, a common problem in some companies is that people are rewarded for the wrong things and may even be punished for doing good things! Traditional compensation that, for example, pays people a flat hourly rate rewards people for *using up time.* The more time you use, the more money you make. Likewise, people who try something innovative or unusual (often a desired action in today's rapidly changing workplace) are sometimes punished when the idea fails, thus extinguishing the likelihood that they will ever try to innovate again. Failures of well-intentioned ideas should be *rewarded* if companies are to grow. Managers should be very careful to ensure that their people are rewarded for the right things, and not punished for honest attempts to innovate.

Employees should be rewarded for the right things. Beware of unintended consequences of reward systems.

A small western hospital initiated an A-plus Patient Loyalty program they called Excel! As part of their efforts, they trained every employee in the hospital in A-plus strategy building, got every department involved in idea-generating sessions, and rewarded their people very effectively. Employees earned reward points from a variety of desired actions, including the following:

- Receiving a positive comment card from a patient or guest
- Receiving an "atta-boy" or "atta-girl" recognition coupon from a supervisor anywhere in the hospital
- Contributing a helpful suggestion
- Participating in team brainstorming to generate new A-plus ideas
- Reading the monthly newsletter and completing a short quiz
- Attending optional follow-up training sessions after work hours

Employees from each department who received the most points attended a special "Excel-abration" luncheon with games and prizes. At the end of the year, the monthly winners from each department were invited to a lavish "Excel-abration" dinner with substantial prizes such as TVs, mountain bikes, cruise tickets, and cash. Overall, this hospital did it right. The result was long-term, ongoing service excellence and very motivated employees.

The reward process is not mysterious. Managers need to determine exactly what kinds of actions are worthy of reinforcing and then develop a mechanism for rewarding those actions. As with most things, getting employee involvement in the development of the reward program makes a sense. People will gladly tell you what they think they should be rewarded for and they will also tell you what rewards will best turn them on. You just have to ask.

A FINAL THOUGHT

You need not be an official manager or executive in a company in order to influence the quality of customer service. Your example to colleagues can be contagious. You can be a force for good in utilizing the kinds of vital behaviors needed to give exceptional service.

If you are in a managerial or supervisory position, your ability to influence usually expands. You are likely to have access to resources and flexibility to do a broader range of things, to provide incentives, and to get the tools and facilities your people need.

It is ironic that in many sales organizations, salespeople who demonstrate world-class performance and build the strongest customer relationships are often "rewarded" by being promoted out of the jobs they do best. All too often, great sales reps become managers or corporate marketers, regardless of whether they have the right talents for those roles. Similarly, outstanding customer service reps become supervisors, then department managers, because that's the only way to earn more money or prestige. A study of one call center showed that it had 11 layers of management—a system that evolved in part to let them frequently promote people as a way to reward outstanding performance. Ironically, reps who were the best at working with customers could be literally 10 times removed from ever speaking with a customer again. This may be a good place to repeat a key point made early in the chapter: Not all employees will or should be advanced into management positions. In fact, managing requires special skills not everyone has. Consider creating ways that great employees can still be "promoted" without necessarily becoming managers. Develop incentive opportunities that can afford true engagement by all employees. Ideally a great sales rep or service provider should earn more than his or her manager!

That said, good managers play a huge role in any organization's success in developing customer loyalty. Indeed, the first and most important use of a manager's time should be to guide the customer service process. Managers who follow through with the kinds of actions discussed in this chapter will make a positive difference in their organizations—and can be well on the way to creating and sustaining exceptional customer loyalty.

Summary of Key Ideas

- Managing is the process of getting work accomplished with and through the efforts of other people.
- A clear vision of the importance of customer loyalty should be at the core of every manager's beliefs. He or she must articulate that vision.
- An effective manager must think about a service strategy looking ahead to what must be done to maintain and improve performance, to solve problems, and to develop employee competence.
- Getting people to change and improve their service ability can be challenging. Using the *Influencer* model shows how the application of six sources of influence greatly improve the likelihood that change efforts will succeed.
- A manager must organize his or her team by assigning responsibilities, giving employees the supporting authority to fulfill their responsibilities, and reducing potential problems caused by systems (staffing, training, work layout, etc.).
- Managers lead by enabling the organization to achieve its objectives. To do this, he or she shows the direction employees must go, generates the energy (motivation) that stimulates subordinates to action, and provides the needed resources.
- Managerial behaviors go a long way toward creating conditions under which employees can feel empowered in the organization. Managers play an important role in shaping an organizational culture. Culture is shaped by a shared sense of vision and values.
- When people's jobs require dealing with emotions of customers and others, they are engaged in "emotional

labor." Projecting appropriate emotions which may be different from what the person is actually feeling can become stressful. Leaders need to be aware of the potential toll of such stress on employees.

- Organizational culture is learned and reinforced by language, stories, material symbols, and rituals.
- Managers should harvest creative, A-plus ideas through the use of brainstorming and nominal group processes.
- The management function called *controlling* involves comparing actual results to expected or planned-for results so as to identify any deviation from plan.
- Managers should measure specific behaviors (actions) rather than vague outcomes or attitudes whenever possible. Identifying which behaviors are "vital" to success helps focus on actions that get the best results.
- Managers need to be fully involved in the process of setting measurable goals for their workgroup. They should also help individual employees set goals for themselves.
- Ultimately, employee empowerment is the key to A-plus service. When employees have the latitude to take initiative on behalf of customers, everyone wins.
- Good managers use hoopla and fun to create an environment where people like to work. They also check to be sure they are rewarding the right behaviors.

Key Concepts

brainstorming	empowerment	Motivation	sources of influence
controlling	goal setting (group and	nominal group	tacit knowledge
emotional intelligence	individual)	process	vision statement
emotional labor	harvesting A-plus ideas	service proposition	vital behaviors

Reviewing the Facts

1. What are the key distinguishing factors that make management work different from nonmanagement work?
2. How can a manager best set a strategy for improving customer loyalty? What steps make sense?
3. Explain the concept of vital behaviors. How do behaviors differ from outcomes or attitudes?
4. Explain the steps in applying the *Influencer* model to a specific customer service behavior change.
5. How important is organizational culture? What kinds of things create and sustain a culture?

6. Describe brainstorming in your own words. What are the critical elements that must be present for this to work?
7. How can nominal group process be useful in processing new ideas?
8. Why is employee empowerment important? What causes some managers to resist empowering employees? Should all employees be equally empowered? Defend your answer.

Applying the Ideas

1. Ask three of your classmates, friends, or coworkers to describe the actions of the best and worst manager they have worked for. To what extent do these descriptions reflect the ideas in this chapter? To what extent do these managers fulfill the roles discussed here?
2. Read the most recent copy of *Fortune* magazine's annual feature issue on the "100 Best Companies to Work for in America." (See *www.Fortune.com*.) Pick one company you are interested in and compare it against the descriptions of key management challenges described in this chapter. For example, what does the article say about the company culture, the training provided to employees, and opportunities for employees to maximize their talents.
3. Select a company or organization you are familiar with (perhaps somewhere where you now work or have worked) and articulate what you think its vision statement should be. If it already

has a publicized vision/mission statement, how does this compare with what you would express? To what extent does the company seem true to this mission? What contradictions do the company exhibit? Describe your reasoning.

4. Select a company or organization you are familiar with (perhaps somewhere where you now work or have worked) and get a group together to brainstorm some possible A-plus ideas for boosting customer loyalty. Apply the principles of brainstorming described in this chapter and have fun with the process. Write a brief report of your group's ideas with comments about which ideas the company might realistically try. If you are not currently employed or you lack familiarity with the company, use your class as the organization. Brainstorm ways the class could exceed your expectations. Be creative and have some fun with this. Remember that only a few ideas arising from brainstorming can actually be implemented.

Consider this Case

Am I a Manager or Not?

The following request for advice appeared on the company's internal blog. This blog was set up so that employees (internal customers) could freely express concerns and ideas.

> I'm in a situation where I manage three different groups; however, I am not really the manager but actually in the same job category as the people I "supposedly" manage. The problem is my boss has given me the responsibility of all of these jobs; however, I do not have the authority to delegate to any of the people I manage. They all go crying to my boss. My tendency then is to try to "do it all." I've spoken to my boss about the way I feel, "responsibility but no authority" and he does not know what I mean. He says just give it to him and he'll find someone to do it. I feel disrespected, overworked and my self-respect is rapidly diminishing. What approach would be most effective for me to take?

Probes

1. Suppose you knew who this writer is and that you were the manager of her boss. What would you say to the manager to help resolve this problem?
2. What fundamental violations of good management principles are apparently being revealed by this employee?

Consider this Case

We Can't Go on Meeting Like This

Frieda came out of the meeting shaking her head. She told Terry, "If I have to sit through another one of these meetings, I'm going to put a gun to my head. Such a waste of time!"

"What happened, Frieda?" Terry asked.

"Okay—I'll tell you what happened. Nothing! That's what happens in all these freakin' meetings. Georgette says she wants new and creative ideas for exceeding our customers' expectations. She says 'be creative,' and then when anyone comes up with even a slightly 'out there' idea, she gets into an immediate debate about why that won't work or she says 'we tried that before,' and that kills that. Then we all sit there and look at each other until Georgette pipes up with her latest lame idea."

"This whole 'let's get creative' emphasis is so bogus. Everybody in that room has good ideas, but she can't seem to let go of control or open her mind enough to try something new. So, our meetings spend hours justifying what she thinks we should do instead of generating new ideas. The woman drives me nuts."

Probes

1. What advice would you give Georgette for better use of meetings?
2. How typical is Frieda's response? Describe similar experiences you have had with meetings.
3. What could Frieda and the other employees do to improve this situation? How can they be assertive in recommending changes to Georgette?

Building a Customer Service Strategy: Your Ongoing Case

Let's go back to the ongoing case you selected. This will be either your current employer, a specific organization you want to work in, or one of the two hypothetical organizations described in Chapter 1: Independent Auto Sales and Service (IAS) or Network Nutrition Distributors (NND). Now consider the following questions as you develop a customer service strategy:

Strategy Planning Activities

1. Review the discussion of the process used by Community Credit Union to establish a "prime member" program. Outline the pro- and con- arguments for your organization creating such a program. If the advantages outweigh any disadvantages, what could your organization do to provide special benefits to its best customers? Map out a process for creating such a "prime customer" program.

Be sure to identify

- who would be involved in developing the program,
- which customers would be eligible for the special benefits, and
- a description of what such benefits might initially look like.

2. How could your organization better empower employees at all levels to participate in customer loyalty efforts? What could you do to create a feeling of ownership in the processes? Be specific and detailed.

3. We discussed "vital behaviors" in this chapter. Name three to five specific behaviors you see as vital to service excellence. (Be sure these are actually behaviors, not outcomes or goals. They should be explicit, visible, and measurable.)

4. Based on your list of vital behaviors described in (3) above, how could you apply the six sources of influence to get people to do these? Present your best ideas in the form of the chart below:

Subject of Influence Attempt: To Get [Who?] to Do [What?]

Source of Influence	Motivation: Is It Worth It?	Ability: Can I Do It?
PERSONAL	(Make undesirable desirable)	(Surpass your limits; master details)
SOCIAL	(Harness peer pressure)	(Find strength in numbers)
STRUCTURAL	(Design rewards; demand accountability)	(Change the environment)

Notes

1. As sited in Wikipedia, *en.wikipedia.org/wiki/Emotional_labor*. Downloaded March 27, 2009.
2. Arlie R. Hochschild, The Managed Heart: Commercialization of Human Feeling (Berkeley, CA: University of California Press, 1983).
3. A widely used measure of employment engagement called the Q12 was developed by the Gallup polling organization. It found that a positive response to the statement, "I have a best friend at work" relates very strongly to high worker engagement. Friends are important.
4. *Lessons of the Nordstrom* Way, *eCustomerServiceWorld.com*.
5. See Kerry Patterson, Joseph Grenny, David Maxfield, Ron McMillan, and Al Switzler, *Influencer: The Power to Change Anything* (New York: McGraw-Hill, 2008).
6. David Ulrich, consultant and professor at the University of Michigan, in a lecture delivered upon receiving an award from the Dyer Institute for Leading Organizational Change, Marriott School of Management, Brigham Young University, March 10, 2006. See also *www.daveulrich.com*.

APPENDIX

How to Lead or Participate in an A-Plus Idea-Generating Meeting
Use the Group Process to Boost Customer Satisfaction and Loyalty

In this appendix, we will focus on 12 specific tips that will enable you to conduct or participate in meetings designed to generate A-plus ideas. When focused on improved service, such meetings can tap the ideas of the group to provide a gold mine of profitable customer service ideas. These 12 action tips help run an effective A-plus meeting.

ACTION TIP 1. MAKE THE MEETING'S PURPOSE ABSOLUTELY CLEAR

Meetings are of two general types: informational and problem solving. Don't confuse them. The most legitimate use of the group process is to bring a variety of inputs on a specific problem or decision. A-plus idea generation requires good group skills. Don't waste time at the meeting just giving out information.

Clarify the specific topic up front so that people come to the meeting with the right mind-set. Tell participants that the meeting will seek to generate A-plus ideas from each of the three categories of ways to exceed expectations: value, information, and convenience and timing.

ACTION TIP 2. INVITE THE RIGHT PEOPLE

People invited to a meeting should:

1. Have some expertise. However, don't discriminate against people in lower organizational positions. Typically customer contact people have the most experience with A-plus opportunities, but others may also have ideas.
2. Have a vested interest in the outcome of the discussion—they have shown a desire to participate in efforts to improve customer loyalty.
3. Have some skills in group decision making and they should be able to express themselves reasonably well. Avoid narrow-minded, inflexible people or those who may dominate the group.
4. Share the overall values of the organization. If participants are antagonistic or in disagreement with the company's goals or vision, it makes no sense to have them participate in decisions affecting the company's direction.

In addition, be sure, to invite the right *number* of people. Have enough to represent a variety of opinions but not so many that the process bogs down. A-plus meetings work best with 4 to 12 participants. Five to seven is usually optimal.

ACTION TIP 3. ASSIGN ADVANCE PREPARATION

Participants should know what the meeting is about and what kinds of information and/or ideas they may need to gather and bring with them. If the central focus of the meeting will be on generating A-plus ideas to enhance customer *convenience*, telling people in advance will let them think about competitors' tactics, creative ideas being used by other companies, and perhaps needed data such as sales results others have experienced. If the focus will be on A-plus information, encourage participants to carefully observe ways companies share information with customers. Get people thinking on the right wavelength even before the meeting.

ACTION TIP 4. START ON TIME AND USE A REALISTIC SCHEDULE

A major concern of meeting attendees is the meeting's failure to start and end on time. Don't wait "a few minutes until the rest of the folks get here" or you'll find yourself doing so every time. Get a reputation for prompt starts and people will get there on time. Likewise, don't run over time. If you've scheduled 90 minutes, stop at or before that deadline. If you really want to shock people, end the meeting early! When the work is done, quit.

Schedule breaks. Have refreshments. Encourage people to walk around the room, draw on flip charts, and sit where they like. Do whatever is necessary to make the experience pleasant and satisfying.

ACTION TIP 5. CREATE A POSITIVE CLIMATE

If you are the leader, thank people for coming to the meeting. Let people know that they were selected because they can contribute valuable insights and ideas. Set a good psychological climate by your example. Let people know that the discussion can be casual and that they are encouraged to be creative.

Also set up the meeting room appropriately so that participants:

1. Can see each other face to face (do not sit in rows, auditorium style)
2. Are provided with table(s) and writing materials
3. Use a whiteboard, newsprint flip charts, or transparencies to capture ideas
4. Are encouraged to move around the room freely to relieve tension or fatigue
5. Are provided with refreshments if the meeting will run more than a few hours

ACTION TIP 6. BE AWARE OF A "HIDDEN AGENDA"

Although we may agree on the discussion topic, people in meetings often have unspoken objectives called "hidden agenda." These may include such things as:

- Getting some "exposure" (i.e., to favorably impress others)
- Providing a "status arena" where they can assert power or show off their ability
- Providing a chance to socialize with others (This can be okay so long as the socializing doesn't get too far off topic.)
- Diffusing decision responsibility so that one person won't have to take all the heat if a decision fails
- Getting away from unpleasant work duties

If achieving one's hidden objectives doesn't take away from the effectiveness of the group, don't worry about it. If the ulterior motives of the hidden agenda deter the group from accomplishing its work, talk with participants candidly (in private) and solicit their cooperation in putting the group's needs above their own.

ACTION TIP 7. REWARD GROUP MEMBER INPUT

Never let a group member's input be met with prolonged silence. To do so will quickly extinguish further input from that person—and from others. Bear in mind that stating an opinion or idea can be somewhat risky for people. They risk being perceived as wrong, naive, unimaginative, or any of dozens other possibilities. When their comments are met with dead air, it may be seen as punishing— causing them to be embarrassed.

By acknowledging contributions, we create a climate where more will be offered. A simple "good thought" or "you might be on to something there" can go a long way toward drawing out further input. Even if the idea doesn't make much sense to you, you can come up with a neutral response like "okay" or simply "thanks."

ACTION TIP 8. MONITOR PRESSURES TO CENSOR

The problem of pressure to censor information is a bit more complex. Two common forms of such pressure are:

- Individual dominance
- Groupthink

Individual dominance happens when certain individuals dominate a discussion by force of their personality, organizational position, or personal status. These people may be particularly charming (and thus disproportionately influential because everybody likes them!) or highly autocratic or hard-headed. Reduce this dominance by drawing other people into the discussion.

Groupthink describes a condition of like-mindedness which can arise in groups that are particularly cohesive. While cohesiveness is normally a good condition in groups, it can be carried too far. This can happen when the group members' desire for consensus or harmony becomes stronger than their desire for the best possible decision. Here are seven symptoms of groupthink:

1. An overemphasis on team play and getting along harmoniously.
2. A "shared stereotype" view that competitors or those in opposition to us are inept, incompetent, and incapable of doing anything well.
3. Self-censorship of group member; personal doubts are suppressed to avoid rocking the group's boat.
4. Rationalization to comfort one another and reduce any doubts regarding the group's agreed-upon plan.
5. Self-appointed "mindguards" (who are sort of like bodyguards who protect us from "bad" thoughts) that function to prevent anyone from undermining the group's apparent unanimity and "protect" the group from information that differs from their beliefs.
6. Direct pressure on those who express disagreement.
7. An expression of self-righteousness that leads members to believe their actions are moral or ethical, thus letting them disregard objections to their behavior.

Each of these symptoms of groupthink damages creative or original thinking and effective decisions or idea generation.

ACTION TIP 9. DON'T ALLOW CONFLICT TO BECOME DESTRUCTIVE

Traditionally, it has been assumed that conflict should be avoided in meetings. The term "conflict" conjures up images of fistfights or people screaming at each other. In reality, conflict is simply a state of incompatibility. It is neither good nor bad. What creates conflict problems are the participants' reactions to it.

We typically respond to conflict in one of several ways:

1. We can attempt to *avoid* conflict by not expressing opposing views and by withholding any disagreement. Here we keep from rocking the boat and minimize the possibility of being subjected to rejection or reprisals from others. (Groupthinkers respond this way.) The drawback here is that some good ideas—ideas that can best impact the group's effectiveness—may be withheld in the interest of avoiding conflict.
2. We get into a win-lose orientation, leading to a no-holds-barred, open warfare among participants.

3. We *manage conflict* to regulate it but not eliminate confrontation. Recognizing that the abrasive actions of opposing views—like sandpaper on wood—polish the final product, the skillful leaders seek free exchange of information but without the win-lose destructiveness of unregulated conflict. Accomplishing this calls for communication skills that encourage the generation of information without inhibiting or turning off participants.

This third response, managing conflict, is by far the most useful. Incidentally, a sense of humor helps. Laughter can be the most potent, constructive force for diffusing business tension. Humor is what brings back perspective.

ACTION TIP 10. AVOID OVERCENTRALIZED LEADERSHIP

Effective meeting managers work to move the group away from the traditional leader toward group-centered leadership or self-managed teams. The leadership process of guiding and directing the group's activity should move from person to person within the group rather than be centered in one individual. Having each group member take some part of the leadership role can overcome dominance and conflict problems. The result is what is called "group-centered leadership." This is contrasted with traditional leadership in the following list.

Traditional Leadership	Group-Centered Leadership
1. The leader directs, controls, polices the members, and leads them to the proper decision. Basically it is his or her group, and the leader's authority is acknowledged by members.	1. The group, or meeting, is *owned* by the members, including the leader. All members, with the leader's assistance, contribute to its effectiveness.
2. The leader focuses attention on the task to be accomplished, brings the group back from any diverse wandering, and performs all the functions needed to arrive at the proper decision.	2. The group is responsible, with occasional and appropriate help from the leader, for reaching a decision that includes the participation of all and is the product of all. The leader is a servant and helper to the group.
3. The leader sets limits and uses rules of order to keep the discussion within strict limits set by the agenda. He or she controls the time spent on each item lest the group wander fruitlessly.	3. Members of the group take responsibility for its task productivity, its methods of working, its assignments of tasks, and its plans for the use of the time available.
4. The leader believes that emotions are disruptive to objective, logical thinking, and should be discouraged or suppressed.	4. Feelings, emotions, and conflict are recognized by the members and the leader as legitimate factors in the discussion process.
5. The leader believes that a member's disruptive behavior should be handled by talking to the offender away from the group; it is the leader's task to do so.	5. The leader believes that any problem in the group must be faced and solved within the group and by the group.
6. Because the need to arrive at a task decision is all-important in the eyes of the leader, needs of individual members are considered less important.	6. With help and encouragement from the leader, the members come to realize that the needs, feelings, and purposes of all members should be met so that an awareness of being a group forms.

ACTION TIP 11. USE BRAINSTORMING TO GENERATE CREATIVE IDEAS

Remember that the term "brainstorming" is not just some generic way of creative thinking. Brainstorming is a specific technique using explicit rules for idea generation and development. This approach requires a communication climate in which free expression of all kinds of ideas is valued and encouraged—no matter how offbeat or bizarre they may seem. The approach works well for generating A-plus ideas. Brainstorming uses four underlying beliefs:

1. *No idea may be criticized.* No comments; no grunts or groans; no thumbs down gestures. Just let it come out and be recorded.
2. *No idea is too wild.*
3. *Quantity* of ideas generated is important. Push to get as many ideas without regard to whether or not they make any sense at this point.
4. *Hitchhiking is important.* Participants should add to or amplify ideas suggested by others.

The climate set by the meeting's leader can promote or hamper the use of brainstorming. A climate that encourages humor and informality will work best.

ACTION TIP 12. ASSIGN SPECIFIC FOLLOW-UP ACTIONS

Be sure that group members have their "marching orders." A brilliant A-plus idea will be of no value if it isn't implemented. The people who made the decision are the best ones to direct implementation.

Follow-up assignments typically include informing people of the new action, training people in how to implement it, and communicating to key people about the action and its timing. Don't end the meeting without giving people specific assignments.

A FINAL THOUGHT

Meetings hold the potential for generating good ideas if they are handled well. A meeting aimed at generating A-plus ideas will be more successful if you apply the tips presented in this appendix. Now, let's try on the behaviors and see what great ideas we can generate.

Applying the Ideas: Plan and Run a Brainstorming (A-plus) Meeting

Select one of the seven organizations that follow and run an A-plus meeting. Come up with at least two below ideas for each of the A-plus categories (i.e., value, information, and convenience and timing).

1. The company you are currently working in (After the meeting, prepare a memo describing your ideas and present it to your boss.)
2. Your university bookstore
3. A restaurant you frequently patronize
4. Your favorite supermarket
5. An electronics or appliance store
6. An upscale clothing shop (boutique)
7. Your class imagined as a "company" interested in developing A-plus ideas for making the students (customers) more satisfied with the course

Try your skills at setting a climate, articulating the topic, running the meeting, capturing ideas, and planning the follow-up necessary to implement the ideas your group produces. Prepare an oral report of your findings—both ideas generated and observations about the group process—to your class.

INDEX